BBC

DOCTOR WHO

THE COMPLETE VISUAL COLLECTION

SONTARAN

OOD

DALEK

DAVROS

CYBERMAN

HATH

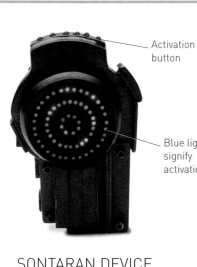

Activation button

Blue lights signify activation

SONTARAN DEVICE

SONIC SCREWDRIVER

Casing frazzled from using too much power to attract the Atraxi

WARP STAR

Carbonized shell

Crystal contains power to explode a space station

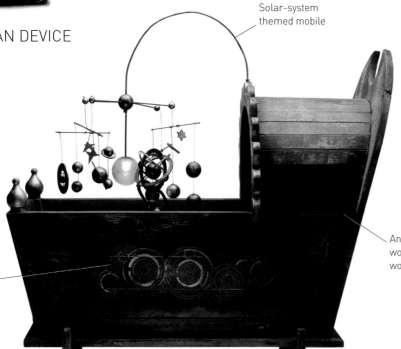

Solar-system themed mobile

Gallifreyan writing possibly spells the Doctor's name

Ancient wooden crib worn with age

THE DOCTOR'S GALLIFREYAN CRADLE

Clear fluid reduces risk of dehydration

Saturnyne blood transforms cellular structure from human to Saturnyne

Blood for transfusion flows through fine tubes

Cuff restrains victim during transfusion

Shackle binds victim's ankle

SATURNYNE CHAIR

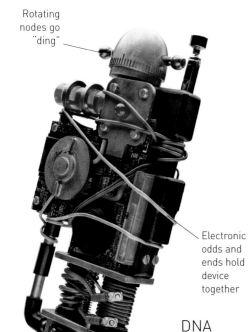

Rotating nodes go "ding"

Electronic odds and ends hold device together

DNA SCANNER

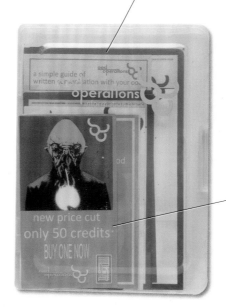

Map of the company's complex

a simple guide of written communication with your ood

operations

new price cut only 50 credits BUY ONE NOW

Vouchers for the office canteen

OOD OPERATIONS PRESS PACK

Enhanced targeting gear

Stun ray muzzle

FREEDOM FIGHTER GUN

Device is used to send and receive voice messages

WRIST COMMUNICATION UNIT

BBC
DOCTOR WHO
THE VISUAL DICTIONARY
UPDATED AND EXPANDED

Written by JASON LOBORIK, NEIL CORRY, JACQUELINE RAYNER, ANDREW DARLING, KERRIE DOUGHERTY, DAVID JOHN, and SIMON BEECROFT

Living figure grown from Androzani trees

WOODEN QUEEN

Antigravity device allows robot to hover in midair

Coils capable of incinerating victims

ROBOTIC ANTIBODY

Visor reflects landscape of Utah desert

American flag

Interior of suit contains alien intelligence technology and built-in communication faculties

ABZORBALOFF CANE

Shape of the Ood Operations company logo

Stolen 1960s Apollo astronaut suit

Casings trap River inside suit

RIVER SONG'S SPACESUIT

OOD OPERATIONS SCULPTURE

DK

CONTENTS

MYSTERIOUS VISITOR

TIME AND TIME AGAIN, fate seems to thrust a mysterious time traveler, known as the Doctor, into the right place at the right time. However, because the Doctor always arrives at times of catastrophe, some legends have evolved to suggest that he is the cause of these events. In fact, he is usually instrumental in the resolution of crises, but like a storm, he can also leave damage in his wake. The Doctor was a crucial figure in the Last Great Time War between the Daleks and the Time Lords in which, for the sake of the universe, he was driven to bring about the destruction of the Daleks in order to save the Time Lords and his home planet, Gallifrey. The Doctor continues to appear where he is needed to alleviate the chaos created in both time and space.

THE DOCTOR

Target: Earth

Many alien races have sought to invade Earth, to enslave humanity, rob it of its mineral wealth, or simply destroy the planet. Displaced beings, such as the Nestene Consciousness, Gelth, and the Zygons, have sought refuge on Earth, while the Daleks have made it the focus of many attacks, once even towing it to another galaxy. A megalomaniac Time Lord, known as the Master, has twice tried to conquer Earth and make it a launch pad to wage war on the universe. Fortunately for humanity, the Doctor has often defeated these plans and saved the world.

England, and London in particular, have seen more than a few attempts at alien invasion. However, few citizens of the 20th or 21st centuries would be aware of them, thanks to the efforts of UNIT and the Torchwood Institute. These are Earth-based organizations that defeat and cover up alien threats.

The Super Highway

The Doctor travels in a TARDIS—an advanced piece of Time Lord technology that can time travel. His Type 40 ship looks like a 1950s police box. TARDISes move from one moment or place to another by passing through the time vortex: a swirling mass of energy that links all points in time and space.

Earth eventually dies in the year 5.5/Apple/26. It is destroyed naturally by the expanding Sun, not by an enemy.

As humankind spreads out into galaxies farther afield, they have cause to be grateful for the presence of the Doctor there too. On the planet Trenzalore, which the Doctor defended for centuries, the children drew pictures of the Doctor's greatest adventures as a gift to thank him for saving them.

RENEGADE TIME LORD

THE DOCTOR believes himself to be the last surviving Time Lord—a long-lived and incredibly technologically advanced race that possesses the secret of time travel. The Time Lords preferred to observe the universe and rarely interfered in the affairs of other worlds, whereas the Doctor has a strong sense of right and wrong, and a firm conviction that he should intervene to prevent injustice. Unable to agree with a policy of non-intervention, the Doctor became a renegade, stealing a TARDIS and using it to explore time and space.

POLICE PUBLIC CALL BOX

POLICE TELEPHONE
FREE
FOR USE OF
PUBLIC
ADVICE & ASSISTANCE
OBTAINABLE IMMEDIATELY
OFFICERS & CARS
RESPOND TO ALL CALLS
PULL TO OPEN

There is Only One Doctor

When Time Lords come to the end of their lives, they have the ability to regenerate their bodies and carry on living. Although each regeneration brings out different facets of a Time Lord's personality, the Doctor's essential character has remained unchanged for centuries.

The Doctor's playful, occasionally child-like traits conceal an extensive knowledge of the universe and deep wisdom born of experience. In his newest regenerative form, he prefers to listen and think before acting—to learn the measure of the many aliens he encounters around the universe.

Mythical Hero

The Doctor's appearances on Earth and services to humanity have gone down in legend and references to him are scattered throughout folklore. The "Man in the Blue Box" takes on an almost religious significance in this stained glass window from a London church.

The TARDIS

The Doctor has a gift for appearing at critical moments in time when catastrophe is about to strike, including the launch of the *Titanic* and at the eruption of Krakatoa in Indonesia.

Traveling Through Time

The gift of time travel also brings responsibility. The rules of time are fluid and complicated. Actions have consequences, and not all time is in flux—some tragedies cannot be reversed.

Maintaining Time

The Doctor has prevented catastrophe from rewriting the future of Earth many times. He sees his relationship with humans as a strength, but his enemies regard it as a weakness that is easy to exploit. By threatening Earth during World War II, the Daleks know that Winston Churchill will call his good friend the Doctor, who walks straight into the trap.

Missed Opportunities

Some moments are temporal tipping points, where decisive action could create a new timeline. When the future pivots around human-Silurian negotiations for a cohabitation deal, the Doctor is hopeful for a new era on Earth. Sadly, talks break down, the Silurians return to hibernation and life on Earth continues as before.

Fixed Points

Some events are fixed and cannot be changed. The Doctor can only mourn and carry on. On Bowie Base One, the Doctor refuses to follow the rules of time and rescues the crew. But base leader, Adelaide Brooke, was destined to die. She insists on maintaining the fixed order of things and so kills herself.

Man's Best Friend

The Doctor feels a special affinity for the human race. Even though he has witnessed the very worst of human behavior, he is still awed by their potential for goodness. He cannot bear to stand by and watch humanity suffer—especially if children are crying.

The Doctor believes that the moment you pick up a weapon, you have lost the argument. He always looks for a peaceful solution first, trying to negotiate or give aliens a choice. For example, when confronted with the Saturnynes' plan to sink Venice, he tries to reason with Rosanna Calvierri. However, he often finds himself in situations where violent action is necessary. He destroys the Saturnynes because they won't abandon their plan and they show such little respect for the human beings in their care.

Despite his vibrant personality, the Doctor is sometimes overwhelmed by his belief that he is the last surviving Time Lord. He has developed strong relationships with many humans, but they are limited because of his extraordinary longevity and the fact that his life is fraught with danger. He leads a solitary life, punctuated by the company of people who travel with him, but who must always return to their own lives.

THE DOCTOR FACTS

- The Doctor's body temperature is a cool 59-61 degrees Fahrenheit (15–16 Celsius), lower than the typical human body temperature of 98.6 degrees Fahrenheit (37 Celsius).

- This Time Lord is qualified in "practically everything," but has never actually received a medical degree.

- He was a member of a Time Lord clan called the Prydonian Chapter. This was said to be the most powerful and devious of all the chapters.

- At the Prydonian Academy, the young Doctor just scraped through with a 51 percent pass, and it was on his second attempt.

- River Song may be the only non-Gallifreyan to know the Doctor's real name, although the Doctor claims that it is unpronounceable for humans. His nickname at the Prydonian Academy was "Theta Sigma."

ANATOMY OF THE DOCTOR

ALTHOUGH HE LOOKS LIKE a human being (and once claimed human ancestry on his mother's side), the Doctor is an alien being and his Time Lord physiology has many differences from our own. Physically, the Doctor is stronger, has sharper senses, and greater powers of endurance than a human being, and can cope with heat, cold, radiation and powerful forces better than humans can. There are also some differences to his internal anatomy that have confused many Earthly doctors.

Two Hearts

Time Lords have two hearts and a binary vascular system, which enables them to survive major accidents and many physical and temporal shocks that would kill a human being. They also have a respiratory bypass system that enables them to survive without breathing for some time.

Time Lord life-energy is tremendously vibrant and powerful. When the TARDIS's power supply is almost totally destroyed, save for one cell, the Tenth Doctor recharges it by breathing his own life energy into the remaining power cell, giving up 10 years of his life in the process.

Nutrient fluid preserves severed hand

The Doctor's Hand

When the Doctor's right hand is severed by a Sycorax warrior, residual regeneration energy allows him to grow another. His friend Captain Jack acquires the original, and the liquid surrounding it bubbles whenever the Doctor or a product of his DNA is near. Later, after a run-in with a Dalek triggers the Doctor's regeneration process, he blasts his regeneration energy into his severed hand, healing himself without having to change appearance—but effectively using up one whole regeneration.

Body can absorb Roentgen radiation, endure massive gamma radiation strikes, and survive cyanide poisoning

The Doctor's clothes help him appear non-threatening to humans

Gray hair, not red as the Doctor might prefer

Thick eyebrows appear, according to the Doctor, to look angry of their own accord

Eye color can change with regeneration

Heightened senses can pinpoint historical eras by smell

Enhanced sense of taste can identify different blood groups

Two hearts are supported by a binary vascular system

Body temperature is lower than a human's

Highly developed Time Lord brain has huge memory capacity and telepathic ability

New face chosen by the Doctor, although he cannot initially remember why

Respiratory bypass system allows short-term survival in airless environments

Two Doctors

A new version of the Doctor is created after a biological metacrisis combines genetic information from the Doctor's severed hand and from the human Donna Noble, with energy from an abortive regeneration. Although he looks like the Tenth Doctor, this half-Time Lord and half-human creation has only one heart and is unable to regenerate.

THE DREAM LORD

Physically, the Doctor is stronger than any human, but psychologically, he is just as vulnerable. Owing to his long and dramatic life, he's seen many dark things. When psychic pollen gets into the TARDIS machinery, it induces a dream state for the Doctor, Amy, and Rory. It feeds on the Doctor's fears and insecurities. This malign manifestation calls itself the Dream Lord, and revels in taunting the Doctor and playing games of life and death.

The Dream Lord wears a smarter version of the Eleventh Doctor's clothes

The Doctor's capacity to regenerate is limited. It can be increased or halted – as shown when his Time Lord nemesis, the Master, temporarily suspends the Doctor's ability to change. Without his regenerative abilities, the Doctor's body would be more than 900 years old, so he becomes a tiny wizened creature as he reaches his true age.

Clothes shrunk to fit miniature Tenth Doctor

WIZENED TENTH DOCTOR

As a Time Lord, the Doctor relies on different bacteria from humans to keep him alive. Not knowing this, the Silurians begin a decontamination process on him to neutralize what they diagnose as harmful germs and viruses in his system—leaving him screaming in agony.

A Minimalist Approach

Every time the Doctor regenerates, he selects an outfit to suit his new personality. Now more than 2,000 years old, the Twelfth Doctor sought a more sedate look than his previous incarnations. He was aiming for minimalist, but worries he looks more like a magician instead. This is a newer, fresher Doctor, who has turned away from the younger, more quirky styles of his previous incarnations.

Comfortable, thick-soled shoes suitable for running—useful when making a quick escape

REGENERATION

IN CASES OF ADVANCED age, mortal illness, or fatal injury, Time Lords have the ability to regenerate their bodies to create a new physical form. There is a notable shift in personality too, due to chemical changes in the brain. The regeneration process takes many hours. It is hugely traumatic and can cause mental and psychological instability until it is completed.

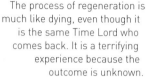

As cellular restructure begins, the Doctor's body starts to glow with regeneration energy. The process might begin with the hands morphing first, for example, followed by the rest of the body.

The process of regeneration is much like dying, even though it is the same Time Lord who comes back. It is a terrifying experience because the outcome is unknown.

REGENERATION FACTS

- ◗ **Most regenerations are triggered when a Time Lord is too badly injured to survive. But some Time Lords can control the process.**

- ◗ **Time Lords supposedly have limited regeneration cycles—they can only regenerate 12 times, allowing for 13 bodies. However, the High Council can bend the rules.**

- ◗ **The regenerative process can be very painful and disorienting.**

- ◗ **The Doctor's arch enemy, the Master has regenerated numerous times in order to cheat death.**

- ◗ **It might be possible for a Time Lord to choose the form he or she regenerates into.**

Youthful demeanor

Unlike previous regenerations inside the TARDIS, when the Tenth Doctor regenerates it creates havoc in the spacecraft. Possibly because of the incredible amount of radiation he's absorbed, the Doctor's regeneration energy shoots out from his body with such force that it causes the console to explode. The appearance of the TARDIS's interior can also change as the Doctor gets a new physical form.

THE TENTH DOCTOR

The Tenth Doctor finally meets his end, not at the hand of a great enemy, but when he chooses to save his companion Donna's grandfather, Wilfred Mott, from a radiation chamber. Selflessly stepping into his place, he absorbs a fatal dose of radiation—which begins the regeneration process. Although he accepts the inevitability of regeneration, the Tenth Doctor does not yet feel ready to go. This time there is no cheating the process, unlike a previous time—when he stopped his regeneration before he changed, stating that he liked his current self too much.

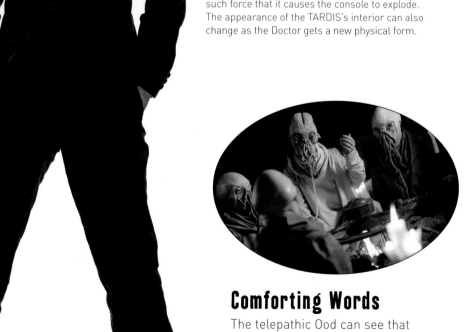

Comforting Words

The telepathic Ood can see that the Tenth Doctor's death is coming. In gratitude for his rescuing them in the past, they sing to the Doctor to soothe his transition and give him strength for the agonizing process.

It is faithful companion Clara who appeals to the Time Lords to save the dying, aged Eleventh Doctor. They give him another lifecycle and he uses the excess regeneration energy to destroy the Daleks invading Trenzalore.

Having moments before believed he was facing certain death, and being willing to die for the people of Trenzalore, the Doctor welcomes this unexpected gift from the remaining Time Lords.

It's not just Time Lords that can regenerate. In certain obscure circumstances, such as exposure to energies from the TARDIS, others can absorb Time Lord abilities. The Doctor is delighted to discover that River Song, conceived in the TARDIS, can regenerate just like a Time Lord.

Growing Old

Despite their regenerative powers, Time Lords cannot fight old age forever. After spending hundreds of years defending the planet Trenzalore from alien armies, the Eleventh Doctor becomes wrinkled and gray. He knows that he has used up all his available regenerations and that, this time, death will be final—or so he thinks.

The Eleventh Doctor retains his love of human fashions, particularly bow ties, to the end

THE TWELFTH DOCTOR

A New Face

A new body requires a period of readjustment. Confusion, erratic behaviour and memory loss are common. The Doctor has been known to demand apples, or fish fingers dipped in custard soon after regenerating. The Twelfth Doctor just needs a suitable outfit to wear in cold Victorian London, where he finds himself after crash-landing the TARDIS.

A Good Man?

Although there's a new face in the TARDIS, the latest version of the Doctor is still the bravest man in the universe. He uses brain over brawn, proudly defends Earth, lives life with a passion, and never hides his anger when he sees the suffering of others. The Twelfth Doctor is still the man monsters have nightmares about. Perhaps more tinged by war and sadness than before, this new incarnation is particularly concerned with whether his reputation is as a good man or a bad one.

THE ELEVENTH DOCTOR ON TRENZALORE

Raggedy clothes borrowed from man found on streets

MANY FACES: ONE TIME LORD

TIME LORDS ORDINARILY HAVE 13 lives before their bodies are unable to regenerate any more. In this time a Time Lord can adopt many faces, be forced to change, or choose to do so. In response to extraordinary circumstances, extra lives can be bestowed.

The Eighth Doctor

With the Time War raging between his people and the Daleks, the Eighth Doctor refuses to join the fight—until the fateful day he crash-lands on Karn. The immortal Sisterhood of Karn pleads with him to help save the universe. The Doctor eventually realizes that he has to play his part, deciding to cast off the mantle of "Doctor" and become a warrior, or the War Doctor, instead.

Ceremonial robes favored by the Sisterhood

Disheveled clothes from life spent running

The Other Doctor

After ordinary human Jackson Lake's wife is killed by the Cybermen, he wants to forget. He finds an infostamp—a steel object for storing compressed data—but it backfires and streams facts about the Doctor into his head, causing him to believe that he is the Doctor. He may not be a Time Lord, but Lake's courage and ingenuity are genuine and gain him a companion. Brave and resourceful servant Rosita Farisi throws in her lot with him when he saves her life.

Rosita becomes nursemaid to Jackson Lake's motherless son.

Victorian gentleman's outfit

Not only does Jackson Lake believe he is the Doctor, he also calls his screwdriver a "sonic" screwdriver and builds a TARDIS—a hot air balloon he names a "Tethered Aerial Release Developed In Style".

JACKSON LAKE

ROSITA FARISI

PRIESTESS OHILA

The prophetic Sisterhood of Karn once saved the Fourth Doctor's life, and many years later, they bring his eighth incarnation back from the dead. Their leader, Ohila, believes the Doctor is the only one who can save the universe.

Priestess Ohila prepares several versions of the Elixir of Life for the Doctor. Each potion would trigger a regeneration into a different body and personality. This process makes the transformation much more painful than on previous occasions.

The First Doctor becomes worn out and changes after defeating a fierce Cyberman invasion.

The Time Lords transform the Second Doctor's appearance and exile him to Earth.

The Third Doctor dies from radiation poisoning while fighting the arachnid Great One.

The Fourth Doctor gives his life and falls to his death in order to stop the evil Master.

The Fifth Doctor's worries that he won't regenerate after being poisoned are not founded.

The Sixth Doctor regenerates after being badly injured when the TARDIS is attacked.

Tardy

The Doctor has a close relationship with his TARDIS and affectionately calls her "Tardy". He doesn't like people interfering with how he flies her, but he lets River Song show him how to open her doors with a click of his fingers, not needing the key!

Walking on Air

An air shell extended from the TARDIS enables Amy Pond to experience the full effect of the cosmos, floating freely and safely in open space.

More Powerful than a Black Hole

The Time Lords artificially created a black hole called the Eye of Harmony. The captured energy of this black hole is the source of the TARDIS's power and is so strong that the TARDIS can escape from the gravitational pull of another black hole. The Doctor uses this tremendous power to tow Earth back to its rightful position, after it is moved to the Medusa Cascade by the Daleks.

Spare TARDIS key concealed behind "P"

POLICE

Phone concealed behind panel has only recently become functional

POLICE TELEPHONE
FREE
FOR USE OF
PUBLIC
ADVICE & ASSISTANCE
OBTAINABLE IMMEDIATELY
OFFICERS & CARS
RESPOND TO ALL CALLS
PULL TO OPEN

The Doctor's TARDIS is stuck in the shape of a 1950s London Police Box because its chameleon circuit has been damaged

TARDIS exterior is virtually indestructible

INSIDE THE TARDIS

TIME LORD TIME-SPACE engineering allows the TARDIS to be significantly larger on the inside than on the outside. Because the TARDIS is dimensionally transcendental, its interior and exterior exist in different dimensions, and are connected by a space-time bridge at the TARDIS's entrance. The interior can be configured in almost any way as per the TARDIS pilot's wishes.

The Eye of Harmony

The TARDIS's space-time travel is fueled by a temporal energy called Artron energy, generated both by the Eye of Harmony (an artificial black hole on Gallifrey) and by Time Lords' minds. Artron energy from the Eye was transferred to a miniature copy of the Eye and stored in the TARDIS console. In one sequence of events, to prevent the TARDIS from exploding, the Eleventh Doctor travels to the heart of the TARDIS, where the Eye of Harmony resembles a volatile star.

On the sentient planet House, the Doctor is able to build a new TARDIS out of spare parts from old, wrecked TARDISes. Consisting of a rudimentary console and powered by the female embodiment of the TARDIS matrix—Idris—the makeshift junk TARDIS was unstable, but successful, in flight.

Famous Visitors

The usual response from astonished visitors to the TARDIS is, "It's bigger on the inside than the outside." But artist Vincent van Gogh sees things differently from most people. His first comment is about the color scheme—he likes it.

Inside the maze-like TARDIS are many customized rooms including a library lined with books, an immense wardrobe full of clothes for the Doctor's companions, a cinema, a swimming pool, a garage, and, of vital importance, an engine room.

Freezing Cold

When psychic pollen gets into the time rotor, a manifestation of the Doctor's psyche—the Dream Lord—appears to set the TARDIS on course for a cold sun that could freeze everything to death.

Rival Pilot

River Song seems to understand the TARDIS better than the Doctor does. Not only does she fly and land it all by herself, but she also does so more smoothly than him. She's good, but then she's had a good teacher—a future version of the Doctor.

All Hands on Deck

Although the TARDIS's hexagonal console was designed to have six pilots, the Doctor has been flying solo for years. But after the defeat of Davros and the Reality Bomb, the Doctor is joined by all the old faces, who help as the TARDIS tows Earth back to its rightful position.

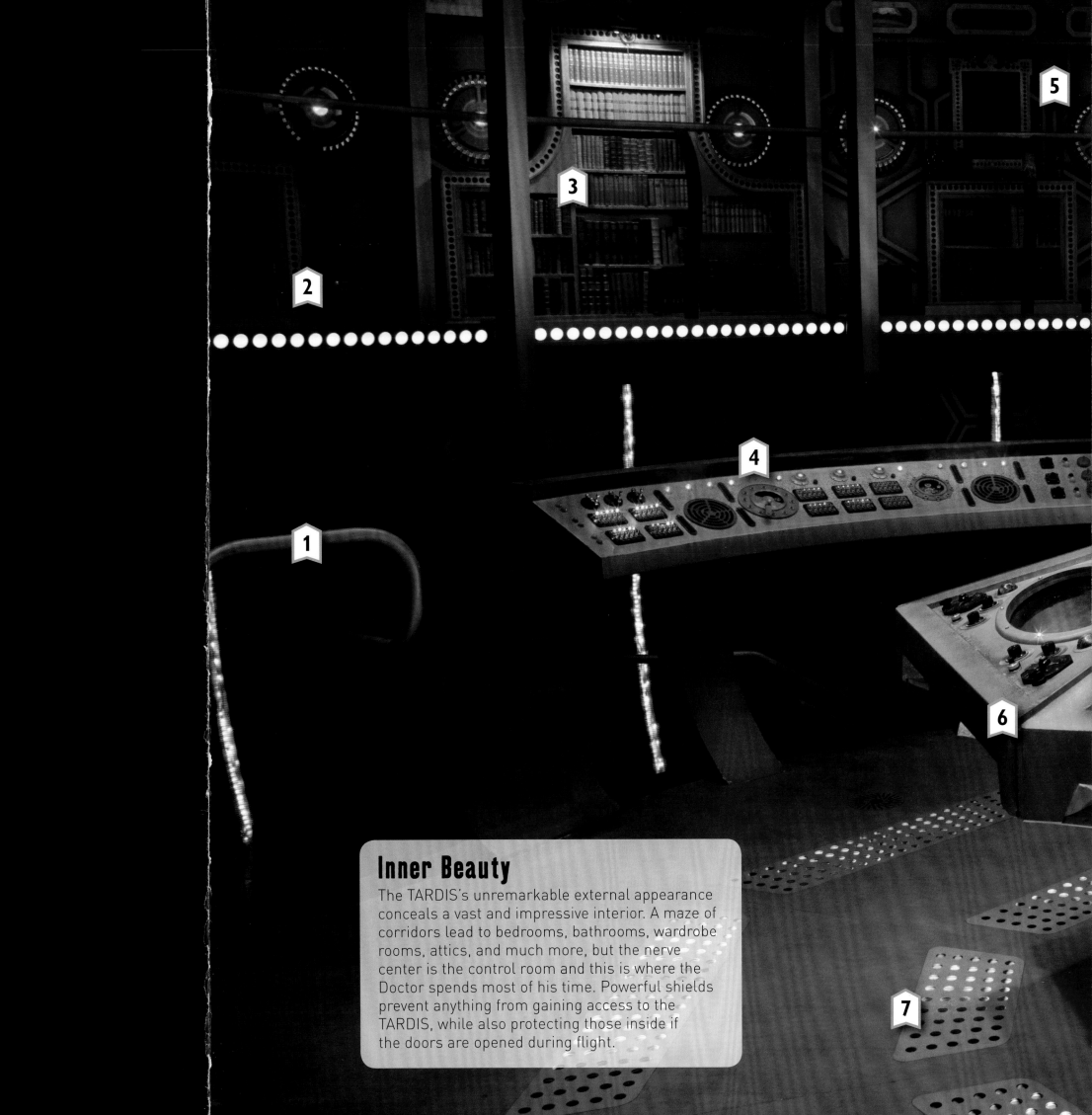

Inner Beauty

The TARDIS's unremarkable external appearance conceals a vast and impressive interior. A maze of corridors lead to bedrooms, bathrooms, wardrobe rooms, attics, and much more, but the nerve center is the control room and this is where the Doctor spends most of his time. Powerful shields prevent anything from gaining access to the TARDIS, while also protecting those inside if the doors are opened during flight.

Jacket dirtied by battle in the Time War

Three versions of the Doctor encountering himself in the same timeline in order to stop the Time War causes a paradox anomoly. The TARDIS tries to compensate for this by refreshing its desktop and changing its interior.

The War Doctor

Having chosen to fight as a warrior in the Time War, this tougher, battle-weary incarnation believes he has lost the right to call himself "the Doctor". He decides the only way to end the fighting is to destroy both Daleks and Time Lords, but in events that rewrite time, he instead teams up with his other selves to save his people, to their great gratification.

During the Last Day of the Time War, the War Doctor flies the TARDIS through a solid wall, crushing the Dalek army that has come searching for him.

Having stolen the galaxy-obliterating weapon the Moment, the War Doctor agonizes over his decision to use it—an act which would destroy billions of lives but would end the war.

Face and mannerisms bear striking resemblance to the Fourth Doctor

Practical, protective leather gaiters

THE CURATOR

An enigmatic old man, the Curator is possibly a future Doctor who has decided to revisit the form of a previous incarnation.

The Twelfth Doctor

A contrast to his boyish predecessor, the older-looking Twelfth Doctor is a fearsome character with a burning passion for knowledge and adventure. It takes his friends some time to get used to him, but it's not long before his youthful energy and personality shine through.

The Seventh Doctor is killed accidentally when a surgical probe punctures his second heart.

The dying Eighth Doctor takes the life-giving Elixir of Life to become the War Doctor.

The War Doctor realizes that his old body is wearing thin and that he must change once again.

Saving Rose from vortex energy causes the Ninth Doctor's regeneration.

Rescuing Wilfred Mott causes the Tenth Doctor to be fatally poisoned by radiation.

Having spent centuries on the planet Trenzalore, the Eleventh Doctor regenerates after reaching old age.

SONIC SCREWDRIVERS

THE STANDARD TOOLKIT in a TARDIS contains equipment needed to tune and repair the ship. One of the most useful tools, the sonic screwdriver, uses variously focused soundwaves to make repairs where human hands cannot reach. As well as turning screws, it can open locks, operate and repair ship systems remotely and take many kinds of readings and scans.

Time Technology

Sonic screwdrivers are a common Time Lord device. In fact, the Doctor has a number of them onboard the TARDIS, though he usually favors one particular unit. To a Time Lord, their technology is simple: if need be, the Doctor could build himself a new one from scratch in almost no time.

Although the sonic screwdriver is made from the most advanced Time Lord materials and technology, it still can't break deadlock seals or override the protocols on the *Byzantium* ship, which are being controlled by the Weeping Angels.

High-kinetic sonic waves can open almost all kinds of mechanical or electronic locks.

A reversed mode can also seal locks—useful when trying to keep an alien werewolf at bay.

The screwdriver's range of functions is almost limitless, including the interception of signals, medical diagnostics, repairing organic parts, operating machinery, and scanning new threats—like the Weeping Angels.

Sonic screwdriver's voice activation setting can cause problems when the Doctor regenerates and has a new accent

---

THE WAR DOCTOR'S SONIC SCREWDRIVER

Extendable diode

A simpler design in comparison with later models, the War Doctor's sonic was built first and foremost to be portable and functional. The outer casing might look different, but the internal sonic mechanism is the same as inside the Eleventh Doctor's casing hundreds of years later. In that amount of time, the War Doctor can start a calculation to break a material previously untouchable by sonic: wood!

In the mysterious Library, the Doctor meets River Song. Although she knows him well, for him this is their first meeting. The fact that she has an advanced sonic screwdriver, given to her in the future by the Doctor, is a sign of their strong friendship.

TARDIS Controls

The central console contains all the controls needed to fly the TARDIS. It is here that the Doctor sets the coordinates that determine the time and place of the TARDIS's materialization.

This multi-purpose monitor is a window to the outside world. Its live feed shows what's going on beyond the TARDIS and displays statistical data.

After damage from regeneration energy, the TARDIS reconfigures itself to a different template. The functions—like this atom accelerator—are the same, but they have all-new controls.

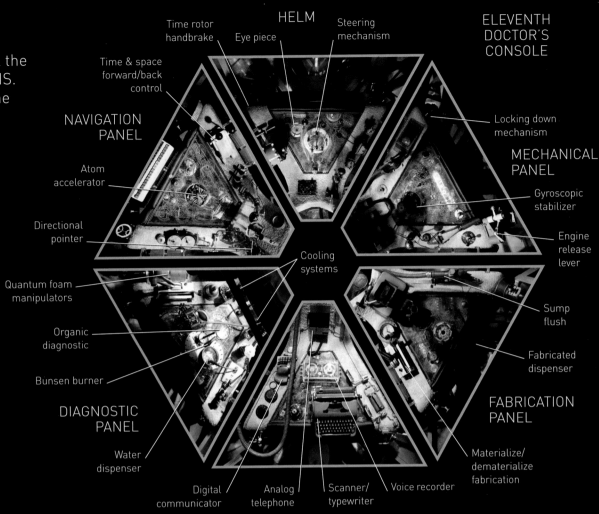

HELM
- Time rotor handbrake
- Eye piece
- Steering mechanism
- Time & space forward/back control

ELEVENTH DOCTOR'S CONSOLE
- Locking down mechanism

NAVIGATION PANEL
- Atom accelerator
- Directional pointer

MECHANICAL PANEL
- Gyroscopic stabilizer
- Engine release lever
- Sump flush

- Cooling systems

- Quantum foam manipulators
- Organic diagnostic
- Bunsen burner

DIAGNOSTIC PANEL
- Water dispenser

- Fabricated dispenser

FABRICATION PANEL
- Materialize/dematerialize fabrication

- Digital communicator
- Analog telephone
- Scanner/typewriter
- Voice recorder

COMMUNICATIONS PANEL

Cloister Bell

The cloister bell rings if the TARDIS, or the universe itself, is in dire peril. It begins to sound when Rose gives the Doctor her "Bad Wolf" message—code for "the end of the universe" and when the exploding time energy is wiping out the existence of time.

KEY FOR THE TWELFTH DOCTOR'S TARDIS

1 **Guard rail provides something safe to hold onto during bumpy flights.**

2 **Away from Gallifrey, the Doctor furnishes his TARDIS with oddments picked up on his travels.**

3 **Book-lined shelves and armchairs lend a cozy feel to the TARDIS's console room.**

4 **Secondary navigation panel.**

5 **The Doctor's professed love of "round things" may have influenced the newest design.**

6 **Hexagonal console shape is Gallifreyan. When "refreshed," previous versions of the "desktop" are archived in the TARDIS.**

7 **Access beneath the flooring allows the Doctor to make repairs to the underpanels of the console.**

8 **TARDIS coordinates can be fixed by entering them here.**

9 **The time rotor on the central column rises and falls when the TARDIS is in flight.**

10 **The TARIDS's telepathic cicuits extend the Doctor's Time Lord gift of languages to those in its vicinity, as long as the Doctor's brain is functioning fully.**

11 **One of two monitors for surveying the exterior of the TARDIS.**

12 **Stairs lead up to the upper level of the console room.**

13 **Pathways lead deeper into the TARDIS, and also back to the blue police box doors.**

Materialization beacon indicates when TARDIS is arriving or departing

BLIC ALL **BOX**

THE TARDIS

THE DOCTOR IS able to travel through time and space using a machine called the TARDIS. A triumph of Time Lord temporal engineering, TARDISes are "dimensionally transcendental" which means that the interior and exterior exist in different dimensions and they can change both their external appearance and internal layout. When the Doctor decided to flee Gallifrey and roam the universe, he stole a TARDIS awaiting servicing for a variety of malfunctions and faults. He has never been able to fully repair it, making his travels often erratic and uncontrolled.

A St. John Ambulance badge reflects the use of old police boxes as a point of first aid

The TARDIS can be unlocked by a key, by remote systems and even with the snap of the Doctor's fingers

TARDIS FACTS

TARDIS CORAL

TARDISes are organic vessels, grown on the Doctor's home planet of Gallifrey. A new TARDIS can be grown from a piece of coral, but this process takes many centuries.

- The name TARDIS is an acronym of "Time And Relative Dimension In Space."

- The Doctor's TARDIS is a Type 40TT Capsule, considered obsolete by the Time Lords. There were originally 305 registered Type 40 TARDISes.

- The TARDIS has a "chameleon circuit," which is supposed to change its external appearance to blend in with its surroundings, wherever it lands.

- The TARDIS is able to use its telepathic circuits to translate almost any language for the benefit of its occupants.

- The exterior shell of the TARDIS seems to weigh no more than an ordinary police box: it can be picked up and moved with suitable machinery.

When the War Doctor meets future incarnations of himelf wielding sonic screwdrivers like weapons, he is most alarmed. The key to the purpose of the Doctor's handiest gadget is in its name: it's a screwdriver, designed to fix things, not attack people.

Sonic screwdrivers can remotely detonate explosives, such as bombs, and activate missiles. At a certain power setting, it can even blast a door clean off its hinges.

The beam from a sonic screwdriver can interact at a molecular level with another object, for example to "cut" a rope by unraveling the individual fibers at a particular point. It can also produce a high-energy beam capable of generating heat in order to burn or slice through many kinds of material.

Screwdriver Operation

Sonic screwdrivers contain Gallifreyan circuitry, allowing their operator to switch between different functions using slight adjustments to the exterior casing. However, the device must be directed toward its object for maximum effectiveness. The Doctor keeps the tool on him for as long as its power cells allow between recharges.

THE ELEVENTH AND TWELFTH DOCTORS' SONIC SCREWDRIVER

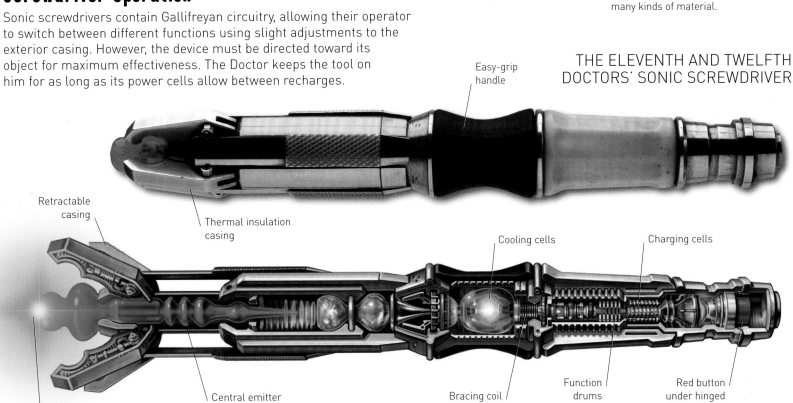

Easy-grip handle

Retractable casing

Thermal insulation casing

Cooling cells

Charging cells

Primary emitter cluster

Central emitter cluster

Bracing coil

Function drums

Red button under hinged casing

Earlier Sonic

This previous version of the sonic proved itself invaluable, getting the Doctor and his friends out of danger time after time. It was finally destroyed when the Eleventh Doctor used it to activate everything around him, hoping the Atraxi would notice the alien technology as they hunted for Prisoner Zero. As a result the outer casing burned to a crisp.

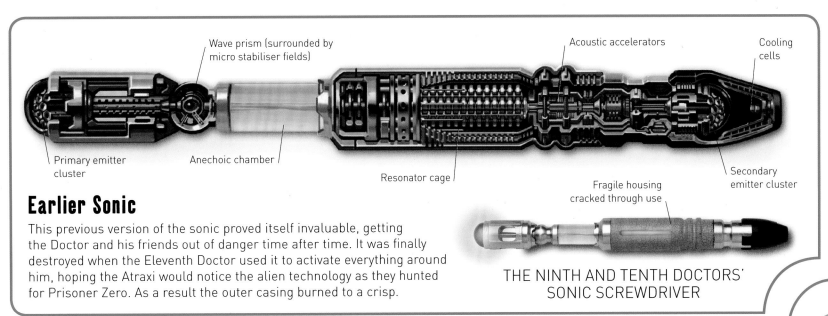

Wave prism (surrounded by micro stabiliser fields)

Acoustic accelerators

Cooling cells

Primary emitter cluster

Anechoic chamber

Resonator cage

Fragile housing cracked through use

Secondary emitter cluster

THE NINTH AND TENTH DOCTORS' SONIC SCREWDRIVER

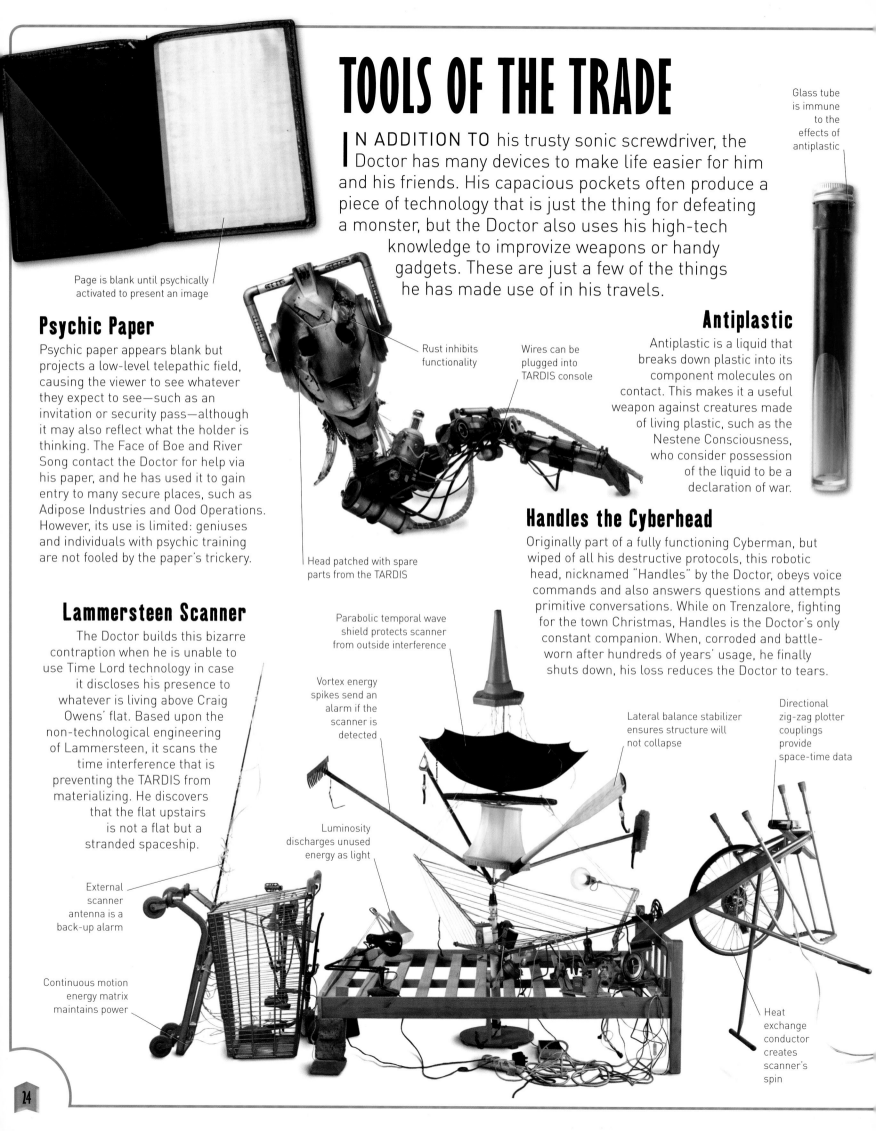

TOOLS OF THE TRADE

IN ADDITION TO his trusty sonic screwdriver, the Doctor has many devices to make life easier for him and his friends. His capacious pockets often produce a piece of technology that is just the thing for defeating a monster, but the Doctor also uses his high-tech knowledge to improvize weapons or handy gadgets. These are just a few of the things he has made use of in his travels.

Page is blank until psychically activated to present an image

Psychic Paper

Psychic paper appears blank but projects a low-level telepathic field, causing the viewer to see whatever they expect to see—such as an invitation or security pass—although it may also reflect what the holder is thinking. The Face of Boe and River Song contact the Doctor for help via his paper, and he has used it to gain entry to many secure places, such as Adipose Industries and Ood Operations. However, its use is limited: geniuses and individuals with psychic training are not fooled by the paper's trickery.

Rust inhibits functionality

Wires can be plugged into TARDIS console

Head patched with spare parts from the TARDIS

Glass tube is immune to the effects of antiplastic

Antiplastic

Antiplastic is a liquid that breaks down plastic into its component molecules on contact. This makes it a useful weapon against creatures made of living plastic, such as the Nestene Consciousness, who consider possession of the liquid to be a declaration of war.

Handles the Cyberhead

Originally part of a fully functioning Cyberman, but wiped of all his destructive protocols, this robotic head, nicknamed "Handles" by the Doctor, obeys voice commands and also answers questions and attempts primitive conversations. While on Trenzalore, fighting for the town Christmas, Handles is the Doctor's only constant companion. When, corroded and battle-worn after hundreds of years' usage, he finally shuts down, his loss reduces the Doctor to tears.

Lammersteen Scanner

The Doctor builds this bizarre contraption when he is unable to use Time Lord technology in case it discloses his presence to whatever is living above Craig Owens' flat. Based upon the non-technological engineering of Lammersteen, it scans the time interference that is preventing the TARDIS from materializing. He discovers that the flat upstairs is not a flat but a stranded spaceship.

Parabolic temporal wave shield protects scanner from outside interference

Vortex energy spikes send an alarm if the scanner is detected

Luminosity discharges unused energy as light

Lateral balance stabilizer ensures structure will not collapse

Directional zig-zag plotter couplings provide space-time data

External scanner antenna is a back-up alarm

Continuous motion energy matrix maintains power

Heat exchange conductor creates scanner's spin

Visual Recognition Device

Like much Time Lord technology, this complex gadget looks simple. When a person or creature is placed before it, the mirror displays the name of its species and planet of origin. The Doctor uses it to find out more about the mysterious Krafayis creatures that are picked up on the machine's screen, even though they are normally invisible to the human eye.

Handle for sturdy grip

Activation switch makes clamp stick to surface

Base attaches to any kind of object

Mirror

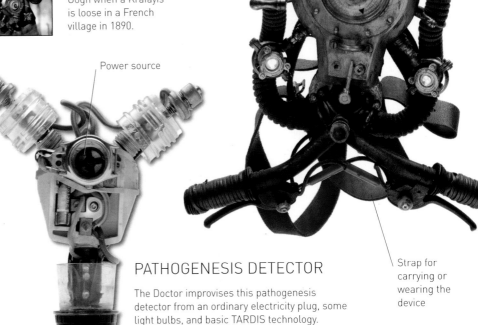

Internal power supply

A present to the Doctor from one of his godmothers, the visual recognition device helps the Doctor, Amy, and the artist Vincent van Gogh when a Krafayis is loose in a French village in 1890.

Strap for carrying or wearing the device

Magna-Clamp

Alien magna-clamps, discovered on Earth by Torchwood operatives, cancel the mass of any object they are attached to, rendering anything up to the weight of two tons virtually weightless. They form an unbreakable bond with any surface, which the Doctor and Rose find useful when they want to avoid being pulled into the Void, while every Dalek and Cyberman is sucked in.

Power source

Gravity Globe

Wide beams of light are easily supplied by these portable gravity globes. Defying gravity, they float high in the air and are, as such, very useful in large enclosed spaces. The Doctor uses one to explore the dark Weeping Angel-infested caves of Aplan Mortarium.

PATHOGENESIS DETECTOR

The Doctor improvises this pathogenesis detector from an ordinary electricity plug, some light bulbs, and basic TARDIS technology. It tracks creatures and flashes red whenever alien life forms, such as Adipose, are nearby.

ELECTROMAGNETIC POWER SOURCE

This power source is a core component of cyborgs (part-robotic, part-biological creatures). It can also be used to create a strong electromagnetic pulse that will scramble the circuits of any robot in the vicinity.

Power-level display

Coral from the organic body of the TARDIS

Rotating probes

Bulb glows red in presence of suspicious findings

Bell makes satisfying "ding" sound

Antenna for scouring landscape for alien DNA

DNA Device

Known by the Doctor as the "machine that goes ding," this homemade device supposedly lights up in the presence of aliens who are not in their natural form. Intended to detect shape-shifting Zygon DNA, it is instead distracted by innocent rabbits and horses. The Doctor claims it can also microwave frozen dinners and download comics from the future.

Tribophysical Waveform Macro-kinetic Extrapolator

This extrapolator can be used as a form of transport, as it acts as a pan-dimensional surfboard, shielding its user in a force field and then riding energy waves to a preset destination. It can be misused to lock onto another's energy source and take their power. Integrated into the TARDIS, it emits a force field that helps the ship resist external forces exerted upon it, and it also speeds up the TARDIS refueling process.

TIME LORDS

LONG AGO, THE DOCTOR'S people, the Time Lords, were a great civilization. They built an advanced society on their planet, Gallifrey, where they thrived for millions of years. However, they were corrupted by the fighting of the Great Time War and their values became twisted—so much so that they posed a threat to the entire universe, and even to time itself.

Steely gaze

Space where White Point Star once sat

Staff of office

Two hearts, as with all Time Lords

High Council Lord President

As the legendary founder of Time Lord society, Rassilon was a revered hero to many of his people. However, by the end of the Time War, the power he exercises as Lord President has corrupted him and he has become obsessed with avoiding death at all costs. Having made a link with rogue Time Lord the Master, Rassilon removes a White Point Star from his staff and sends it to Earth, creating a psychic link that will allow Gallifrey to escape the Time War.

RASSILON

The Ultimate Sanction

After the Daleks discovered that the Time Lords had tried to tamper with history to prevent their creation, they declared war and the conflict called the last Great Time War began. Driven to ensure their survival at any cost, the High Council planned the Ultimate Sanction: to destroy the universe and all of time. They would then evolve into a higher consciousness to exist outside of time.

The Great Time War is time-locked, so the events cannot by changed with time travel. On what will be the last day of the war, the trapped High Council are aware of their imminent destruction. They seek approval for use of the Ultimate Sanction to escape their demise.

Gloved hand shoots electricity bolts

Interior pockets contain Time Lord devices

Before all versions of the Doctors come together to save Gallifrey, the Time Lords plan to use Earth as the key to their escape. Despite his loneliness, the Doctor is unable to rejoice in the return of his people. He knows he must destroy them all over again. It's a heart-breaking decision, but they are still set on the Ultimate Sanction, which he cannot allow. The Doctor shoots the White Point Star, severing the link between Gallifrey and Earth, and returning the Time Lords, led by Rassilon, to the last days of the Time War.

Gallifrey

The Time Lords come from Gallifrey, a planet located in the constellation of Kasterborous, some 29,000 light years from Earth. Until its destruction in the Great Time War, Gallifrey is a divided world. The Time Lords dwell in vast citadels enclosed in mighty glass domes, while the Outsiders, the outcasts of Gallifreyan society, lead tribal lives in the wilderness beyond the cities.

Gallifrey's Capitol is the seat of Time Lord power. It houses the Academies of Learning, the time-monitoring facilities, the controls for the impenetrable forcefield that protects the planet and the Eye of Harmony—the artificial black hole that provided the energy needed for time travel.

Gallifrey's second city, Arcadia, is supposedly the safest place on the planet—protected by 400 sky trenches. However, on the last day of the Time War, the Daleks blast their way through Arcadia's defenses and the city's destruction is captured forever in a 3D painting.

The Doctor remembers Gallifrey as a beautiful planet. Underneath its burnt orange sky was a world of endless snow-capped mountains, with silver-leafed trees and plains of red grass. However, by the end of the Time War, the planet has been ravaged by the Daleks.

The War Council

Led by the military General, the Time Lord War Council was established to deal directly with the Dalek assault on Gallifrey. From their meetings within Gallifrey's Capitol War Room, the War Council rejects the authority of the High Council and President Rassilon in a last-ditch attempt to save Gallifrey.

Rich red and purple colourings of Council

COUNCIL MEMBER

The Seal of Rassilon

Lightweight protective armor

Different ceremonial robes and collar from the High Council

ANDROGAR

THE GENERAL

THE MOMENT

Otherwise known as the "Galaxy Eater," the Moment is the most destructive weapon in all of creation and feared even by the Time Lords themselves. Classed as a forbidden weapon, it is kept securely in Gallifrey's time vaults—until it is stolen by the War Doctor, who intends to use it to destroy the Time Lords and the Daleks, and so end the war.

Gallifreyan markings

Intricately carved cogs and wheels

Big red button in the shape of a glowing jewel

The Moment's basic form is a wooden box full of whirring gears, but when the War Doctor complains about the lack of an activating button, it morphs into a shape that matches his expectations.

Expanded metal form

Surface can become red hot when activated

Gallifrey Stands

With the Dalek firepower increasing, the General commands the Doctor to carry out his alternative plan to save Gallifrey, realizing that they have no other options. All thirteen of the Doctor's incarnations come together to freeze Gallifrey in a single moment in time, preserving it in a parallel pocket universe.

The Moment's Conscience

The Moment is such a sophisticated device that it actually became sentient and developed a conscience. When the War Doctor tries to use it, the Moment's interface activates in the form of Bad Wolf Rose Tyler and attempts to convince him not to commit genocide.

RIVER SONG

ARCHEOLOGIST-FOR-HIRE River Song is a formidable woman. Exceptionally brave and fiercely loyal, she is a good ally to have, although the Doctor finds her reckless at times. The Doctor and River have always met at different points in their time streams, which makes for a complicated relationship. The Doctor is wary of her because of this, but he accepts that their lives are inextricably linked.

Muddled time streams

River and the Doctor are always meeting in the wrong order because her past is his future. Her last meeting with the Doctor is his first. On the Library world, she courageously sacrifices herself to save the Doctor, because she knows how important he is to the future.

Scanner and communicator for locating life forms and assessing terrain

Leather holster and spare pockets

Serial number

Energy bolt firer

RIVER'S PISTOL

Unsentimental River has no qualms about using weapons— once even shooting dead a Dalek in the National Museum.

Light-weight material

Extraordinary Explorer

River Song is no ordinary professor of archeology. She is highly experienced in her field and has led many treacherous expeditions. Her outfits always hide an array of gadgets, such as hallucinogenic lipstick and disarming weapons disguised as earrings, and she has proved herself to be a skilled gun-fighter, especially against the Daleks and the Silents. She has a particular fascination for the Weeping Angels—beings she has investigated and fought several times.

Strap secures holster for gun

HOME BOX

A Home Box records data onboard a spacecraft, similar to the black box on a plane. The one River uses to reach the Doctor is from the starliner *Byzantium*. When the Doctor finds it, it is 12,000 years old and kept as a museum exhibit.

Message reads, "Hello, sweetie!"

Old High Gallifreyan writing

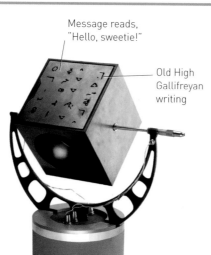

River uses the *Byzantium*'s Home Box to send a message to the Doctor when she is in urgent need of his help. She carves her coordinates into the metal and then jumps out of the ship into space, confident that the TARDIS will appear in time. River has such faith in the Doctor that she's prepared to stake her life on it.

SQUARENESS GUN

This gun could be the same one used by Captain Jack Harkness. River has a habit of borrowing what appear to be his belongings—including a vortex manipulator.

Handle contains short-life dark matter battery

Switch sets function: Sonic Cannon, Blaster, or Disruptor

Sonic waves form pulsing squares of blue light that can cut through walls

SONIC SCREWDRIVER

Wave amplifiers

Master function key houses neural relay

Setting dials

Enhanced emitter lens is superior to the Tenth Doctor's screwdriver

TARDIS remote return

User recognition ring

The Doctor giving River one of his sonic screwdrivers is a sign of his great respect for her.

DIARY OF SPOILERS

River refuses to reveal any "spoilers" about the Doctor's future, and uses her diary to keep track of their time streams. He has a matching diary monitoring events from his own point of view. To allow her to recognize the Doctor, her diary contains pictures of all his different faces.

Cover resembles the TARDIS

Confident and used to getting her own way, River treats the Doctor with a familiarity that no one else would presume to have. She enjoys showing off, and revels in the fact that she can fly the TARDIS better than he can. He isn't used to finding himself in such a position, but they still make a good team.

Trained Killer

As an adult, River Song is again captured by the Silence. She is forced into an automated Apollo spacesuit and placed under Lake Silencio in Utah to wait for the Doctor. Although the Doctor's death is meant to be a fixed point in time, River's affection for the man she loves gets in the way. She refuses to shoot him and time itself begins to unravel.

Melody Pond

River is actually Amy and Rory's daughter, born Melody Pond, and, thanks to the influence of the time vortex, with the Time Lord ability to regenerate. She discovers this power for the first time in 1970s New York after escaping from her kidnappers the Silence – who intended to raise her to become the Doctor's assassin.

Concealed pistol

MELS

After traveling to England, Melody eventually grows up alongside her parents, who nickname her "Mels," although they have no idea who she really is. Her identity is fully revealed when she regenerates into the familiar form of River Song in front of her astonished parents.

Frail body hides inhuman strength

Although she didn't kill the Doctor at Lake Silencio, River still serves a prison sentence at the Stormcage Containment Facility in order to convince the Silence that their target is finally dead. She is eventually released after the Doctor erases records of himself from every database in the universe.

CLARA OSWALD

FOR A LONG TIME, Clara is an inexplicable mystery to the Doctor, since he can't fathom how the same person can possibly exist at different points in time and space. He initially meets Oswin Oswald on the Daleks' asylum planet before an encounter with Clara Oswald—a barmaid-and-governess from Victorian times. By the time he meets the original modern-day Clara, he becomes obsessed with solving the mystery of his "impossible girl" once and for all.

Comfortable clothes suitable for teaching at school or a sudden, unplanned adventure

Stylish leather skirt

Adapting to Change

Having developed a special bond with the Eleventh Doctor, Clara is shocked when he regenerates into a brand new body. She finds it difficult relating to a version of her friend who not only looks radically different, but who also seems more alien and distant. Over time, however, she learns to get to know the Doctor all over again and warms to his new persona.

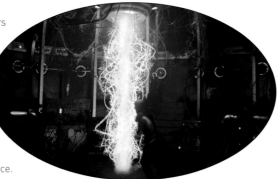

When the Great Intelligence enters the Doctor's time stream in an attempt to rewrite his life, Clara realzes that it's her destiny to reverse its baleful influence. She bravely enters the time tunnel herself and is scattered into a million different fragments, each aspect of herself determined to save the Doctor at different points in time and space.

CLARA OSWALD FACTS

- At some point, each version of Clara says the same enigmatic phrase to the Doctor: "Run, you clever boy, and remember me."

- Adventurous Clara has become used to thrills with the Doctor and so enjoys riding her motorcycle to work every day.

- One of Clara's splintered selves ends up on Gallifrey where she persuades the First Doctor to take a different TARDIS from the one that he intended to steal.

- Clara is determined to one day make the perfect soufflé, although most of her attempts seem to go badly wrong.

A Loyal Friend

Clara is smart, witty, and headstrong—admirable qualities shared by the many different versions of herself. The perfect companion to the Doctor, she is brave and resourceful and willing to take the lead, even in the most terrifying of situations. For all her strength of character, though, she is never afraid to allow her caring side to shine through. She brings hope to the Doctor when he is scared that there might be none left for him, and sees the goodness in him that he cannot.

CLARA'S COPY OF *101 PLACES TO SEE*

Embossed cover worn with age and use

Clara's handwriting records her age

The modern-day version of Clara longs to travel the world, and one of her most treasured childhood possessions is a book full of wonderful places to visit. Each birthday, Clara crosses out her previous age and writes in the new one on the inside page.

Dalek Oswald

A fast and funny junior entertainment officer aboard the starship *Alaska*, Oswin Oswald believes she has survived alone on the Daleks' asylum world for a whole year. In reality, she has subconsciously created a dream-world for herself in order to block out the appalling truth—that she's actually been turned from a human into a Dalek.

Victorian Clara

The Victorian version of Clara is a feisty and fearless girl who leads a secret double life, alternating between jobs as a posh governess and down-to-earth barmaid. She's curious about the Doctor and his time machine, but, tragically, her time with him is cut short when she is killed by the Great Intelligence's sentient ice governess.

Clara's book of places to see originally belonged to her mom, Ellie, who tragically died when Clara was only a teenager. Clara regards the book as a precious object as a result.

Following the death of Victorian Clara, an obsessed Doctor withdraws to a place of solitude and paints a striking portrait of her. He hopes it will inspire him to unravel the perplexing mystery of her existence.

Some time after quitting her job as a nanny, Clara becomes an English teacher at Coal Hill—the same school that the Doctor's granddaughter Susan once studied at. Alongside the Doctor, "Miss Oswald" ends up defending Coal Hill against a rampaging alien war machine.

The Maitland Family

Expression displays cheerful demeanor

When the Doctor first meets modern-day Clara, she's working as a nanny for the Maitland family. She intended to stay with them for just a week, but when Artie and Angie's mother died, their grief strikes a chord with her and she decides to stay on and look after the family.

Arms crossed in stubborn teenager pose

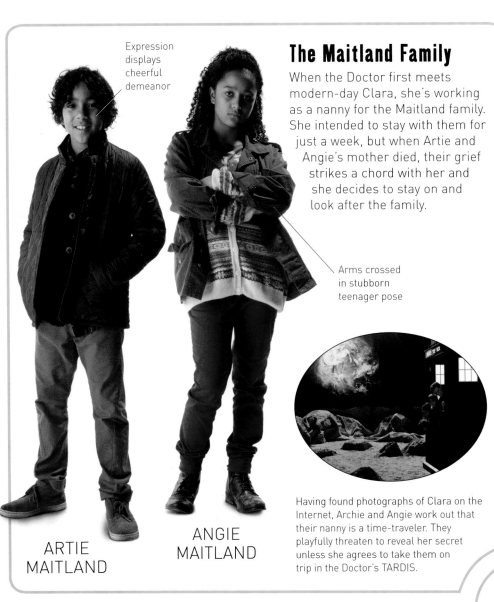

ARTIE MAITLAND

ANGIE MAITLAND

Having found photographs of Clara on the Internet, Archie and Angie work out that their nanny is a time-traveler. They playfully threaten to reveal her secret unless she agrees to take them on a trip in the Doctor's TARDIS.

DANNY PINK

A MATH TEACHER at Coal Hill School, Danny Pink is a man haunted by his military past, despite all the good work he did during his time as a soldier. While he is brave, loyal, and principled, Danny can also be shy and nervous around others, and it takes him time to overcome his awkwardness with colleague Clara. When he, at last, becomes close to her, he can't help getting caught up in her incredible adventures with the Doctor, and soon discovers that his life has changed forever.

Short military haircut

Habitual standing-to-attention stance

Sensitive Subject

Danny's outwardly tough persona belies his true feelings. He finds it difficult to talk about his army days, particularly when questioned about the lives he took during active service. He believes that people often misunderstand the life of a soldier, and jump to wrong conclusions about the kind of man they think he is.

Pajamas provided by care home

RUPERT PINK

Danny grew up in a children's home in Gloucester in the 1990s. Even as a little boy, he hated his real name, Rupert, and decided he wanted to change it when he got older. When the Doctor connects Clara to the TARDIS's telepathic circuits, she is subconsciously thinking about Danny's past and accidentally takes the time machine back to Rupert's time zone, where the pair of them help the lonely young boy deal with an unseen alien terror lurking in his bedroom.

Formal clothes adhere to dress code for teaching at Coal Hill

The Trials of Teaching

As a new teacher at Coal Hill School, Danny finds it a challenge getting along with some of his pupils, especially when they start probing him for details of his life as a soldier. However, he feels on surer ground when he's back in military mode, barking out orders as the head of the Coal Hill Cadet Squad.

Colonel Orson Pink

Hailing from a hundred years in Earth's future, Colonel Orson Pink was the first man on the planet to travel in time, after being inspired by the incredible stories of one of his great grandparents. Orson's pioneering exploits went disastrously wrong, however. He was meant to travel forward only a few days, but somehow overshot and ended up stranded on a wilderness world—becoming the last man standing at the very end of the universe.

Sanctuary Base 6 logo

Airtight helmet

Protective orange spacesuit from the Doctor's TARDIS wardrobe

Socket for attaching oxygen tube

Danny has an uneasy relationship with the Doctor to begin with, since the Time Lord reminds him of some of the hardened officers he served under in the army. Danny is wary of how the Doctor keeps pushing Clara to do things that put her life in danger, and he can't help but feel protective toward her.

When Coal Hill School is threatened by a deadly Skovox Blitzer, Danny is lucky to escape the ensuing battle with his life. First, he is shot at by the Blitzer's laser cannon, then almost dragged into a whirling time vortex opened up by the Doctor as means of disposing of the alien war machine.

Blossoming Romance

Although they're attracted to one another, Danny and Clara have something of a tempestuous relationship. Danny is sensitive to Clara's spiky humor and the pair seem to misunderstand each other at almost every turn. Her strange and regular disappearances with the Doctor don't help him to trust her. However, when Clara learns more about Danny's past and possible future, she warms to him much more and the pair gradually form a close relationship.

AMY POND

Amy's clothes reveal her great sense of style

BRAVE, BOLD, AND DECISIVE, Amy is a good traveling companion for the Doctor. She is not afraid of dangerous situations, speaking her mind or even challenging her Time Lord best friend. Her whole life changed when she first met the Doctor when she was seven years old. Although a TARDIS malfunction meant that she had to wait 12 years before seeing him again, she's never looked back since!

Gutsy Pond!

Confident and fearless, Amy is ready to deal with anything that comes her way. But a small part of her is still the vulnerable child who was abandoned, first by her parents and then by the Doctor. When he finally returns, she is all grown up, but it takes her a while to forgive him. After the Doctor resets the universe, time is rewritten, meaning Amy's parents never went away.

Wedding ring worn with pride

Amy and her Boys

Amy has had the Doctor on a pedestal since she was a child, but has pragmatically settled with Rory. When the Doctor returns and she travels in the TARDIS, it turns her head and she starts doubting her relationship with Rory. However, adventures eventually reveal the Doctor's fallibility and Rory's strength. She comes to happily take Rory as her husband. But far from settling down, they leave their wedding party to return to the TARDIS with the Doctor.

Amy is not daunted by the famous or powerful people she meets as a result of traveling with the Doctor. She doesn't hesitate to take charge of formidable prime minister Winston Churchill when the Daleks threaten Earth. He is impressed with her bravery and leadership, and wishes he had more people like her in his war effort against the Nazis.

AMY POND FACTS

- Amelia Jessica Pond changes her name to Amy after the Doctor says that Amelia sounds like something from a fairy tale.

- Amy's parents are Tabetha and Augustus, but she is raised by her Aunt Sharon when her parents are swallowed by a crack in time.

- Amy moved to Leadworth, England from Inverness, Scotland when she was young, but never lost her Scottish accent.

- In a break from traveling with the Doctor, Amy becomes a model, but quits when she realizes it is damaging her relationship with Rory. She then turns to travel writing.

Artist Vincent van Gogh is an unusual character. An outcast in his village, people find him very difficult. Amy isn't intimidated and uses her charms to diffuse a tense situation and win him over. He loves her frankness and passion for life.

Amy and the Doctor settle into a comfortable friendship. Her insight brings new perspectives to the Doctor, and he helps her to be brave in the face of many fearsome aliens and enemies. In quiet moments, they bicker about the most ordinary things—such as his habit of reading books backwards and his dislike of her reading glasses.

The Doctor is distraught when Amy and Rory become stuck back in time by the Weeping Angels. He learns to travel without them, but at his moment of regeneration, he imagines both a young Amelia and grown-up Amy returning to him, comforting him by calling him "Raggedy Man" once again.

Newborn Melody Pond, wrapped in a blanket

Mother of Melody

Amy's darkest hour comes when the Order of the Silence steals her and Rory's baby to brainwash and use as a weapon against the Doctor. Motherhood is a big change for independent Amy Pond, and losing her newborn is a difficult loss to deal with.

Sterile hospital clothes

Amy and Rory are astonished when they discover the woman they have traveled with on several occasions, River Song, is in fact their daughter Melody Pond! Having absorbed energies from the TARDIS, she was born with the ability to regenerate like a Time Lord—meaning their child was not lost to them, as they feared, after all.

PAPIER-MÂCHÉ DOLLS

Blue shirt resembles the one worn by the Doctor when he appeared in Amy's garden

To while away her loneliness and convince herself that she wasn't imagining everything, Amy made puppets of the Doctor and put on shows.

Smiley face carved by Amelia, like her mother used to do

SMILEY APPLE

When the Doctor returns, he convinces Amy he has been gone only for a few minutes because the carved apple she gave him is still fresh.

AMELIA'S DRAWINGS

The crashed TARDIS in Amy's garden

Woolly hat for autumn

Amelia Pond

Little Amy, called by her full name Amelia, is the girl who waits a long time for the Doctor. He needs to stabilize the TARDIS and promises he'll be back in five minutes. But the engines phase and he doesn't come back for 12 years. Amelia grows up unable to convince anyone that the Doctor is real, including four psychiatrists. She grows up feeling abandoned and set apart from anyone else, but she never gives up her dream of time travel.

Warm clothes, ready for adventures with the Doctor

Very little scares Amelia, not even an alien man in a box falling from the sky in the middle of the night.

Eager to join the Doctor in the TARDIS, determined Amelia packs her suitcase for traveling the stars.

RORY WILLIAMS

RORY WILLIAMS is a straightforward guy, content with his life in sleepy Leadworth, England, so long as he is with Amy Pond, the love of his life. They have known each other since childhood, but he has always felt second-best to Amy's spaceman Doctor. Rory is astounded to discover that the Doctor is real, and he is initially worried: a flesh-and-blood rival is a more serious threat than an imaginary friend.

Life with the Doctor is dazzling and can blind people to the things that are important. The Doctor senses that Amy has drifted too far from Rory. So he brings Rory along for a trip in the TARDIS so the couple can reconnect. Rory is surprised how distant Amy seems when he'd seen her only a few hours earlier. For her, she's not even sure how long it's been since she saw him.

Nurse Rory

Compassionate Rory makes a good nurse, but he would have preferred to have been a doctor. He isn't very forceful and struggles to stand up to people who intimidate him, like hospital consultants or even self-assured Amy. But when it really matters, Rory proves that he is brave and has the strength to stand up to anything to protect those he loves.

Amy feels torn between the exciting Doctor and ordinary Rory. However, events in a dream sequence help her realize that Rory is the one for her. In the dream, he is killed by alien Eknodines and she kills herself by crashing an RV because she'd rather die than live without him.

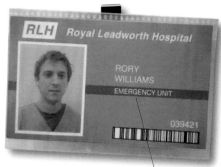

RORY'S HOSPITAL PASS

Rory's work pass gives him and Amy access to Leadworth Hospital when they are tracking Prisoner Zero to stop the Atraxi from destroying Earth.

Pass shows that Rory works in the ER

Pointy nose subject of teasing by the Doctor

Tougher stance result of confidence developed from adventures in TARDIS

Rory and the Doctor

Rory and the Doctor do not hit it off when they first meet. However, when Rory travels in the TARDIS, he witnesses first hand the appeal of the Doctor. The Doctor shows him things he could never have imagined before, and gives him renewed faith in the universe.

Rory's Dad

Brian Williams never truly bonded with his son Rory until they adventure together aboard the TARDIS. Father and son discover their shared piloting skills when they command a Silurian Ark and fight off dinosaurs together.

Rory has always known that he was meant to be with Amy forever. When he is sent back in time by a Weeping Angel, he thinks he will never see his beloved wife again. But Amy has grown to realize that her love for Rory is forever too. Even knowing she will never be able to see the Doctor again, Amy chooses to join Rory in the past, where they live the rest of their lives together.

IN LOVING MEMORY
RORY ARTHUR WILLIAMS
AGED 82

AND HIS LOVING WIFE
AMELIA WILLIAMS
AGED 87

RORY AND AMY'S GRAVESTONE

Rory and Amy's humble gravestone sits in a New York cemetery. It is initially engraved with just Rory's name, but when Amy goes back in time to be with her husband, her name appears on the gravestone too. Its simple wording reveals that they lived on into their eighties together.

Unassuming granite gravestone

Nestene Rory

In an alternative timeline, Rory is consumed by energy from the cracks in the universe and ceases to exist. However, in 102ce, he appears as a Roman centurion. He looks like Rory and believes he is Rory, but he is in fact an Auton: a Nestene duplicate retrieved from Amy's memories. He doesn't age and can live indefinitely, but he is not immortal. His plastic body cannot heal, so he must keep away from heat and radio signals.

Skin looks human but has slight plastic sheen

Armor of a Roman Centurion

Amy and Rory have only just rekindled their relationship when Rory succumbs to Nestene control. He is desperate to be human, but he cannot stop himself from shooting Amy. In order to keep her alive, the Doctor encloses Amy in the stasis-locked Pandorica until he can revive her.

Rory displays his dedication to Amy by guarding her in the Pandorica Box for 2,000 years. He becomes part of the Pandorica legend as the mystery figure "the Lone Centurion." He is written about by Emperor Hadrian, and Isaac Newton and Samuel Pepys call him a friend. The story of the Lone Centurion ends with him carrying the Box from a burning warehouse during the Blitz. However, Rory's story continues: he is by the Pandorica to be reunited with Amy when she is revived in 2010, and is ready to use his Auton weapon to protect her and the Doctor.

LEADWORTH

THE QUAINT ENGLISH village of Leadworth in rural Gloucestershire, England, is home to Amy Pond and Rory Williams. With little more than a church, a pub, a post office, a fire station, and a duck pond, the village is not vibrant, but it does have a strong sense of neighborliness. Leadworth is the last place you would expect anything out of the ordinary to happen.

Life in the village might seem idyllic, but it is actually the focus of a terrifying alien threat. A dangerous alien, called Prisoner Zero, has escaped imprisonment by the Atraxi and is hiding in Leadworth and causing local people to fall into comas. In an attempt to recapture the alien, the Atraxi threaten to incinerate Earth.

Amy's House

Strange disturbances around a crack in space and time bring the TARDIS to this house, where Amy Pond lives with her aunt. The Doctor discovers that Amy is no ordinary girl: her house has too many rooms and the crack in her wall has been pouring the power of the universe through her dreams.

Memorial to those from the Leadworth area who died in the two World Wars

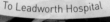

To Leadworth Hospital

Amy doesn't remember ever seeing any ducks on the duck pond

Pub is the heart of village life and where Rory's bachelor party is interrupted by the Doctor

Leadworth Hospital

Royal Leadworth Hospital, on the outskirts of town, is where Rory works as a nurse. The hospital is also the focus of the alien Prisoner Zero, when it is on the run from the Atraxi. The multi-form creates psychic links with coma patients and takes on their appearances to disguise itself as human.

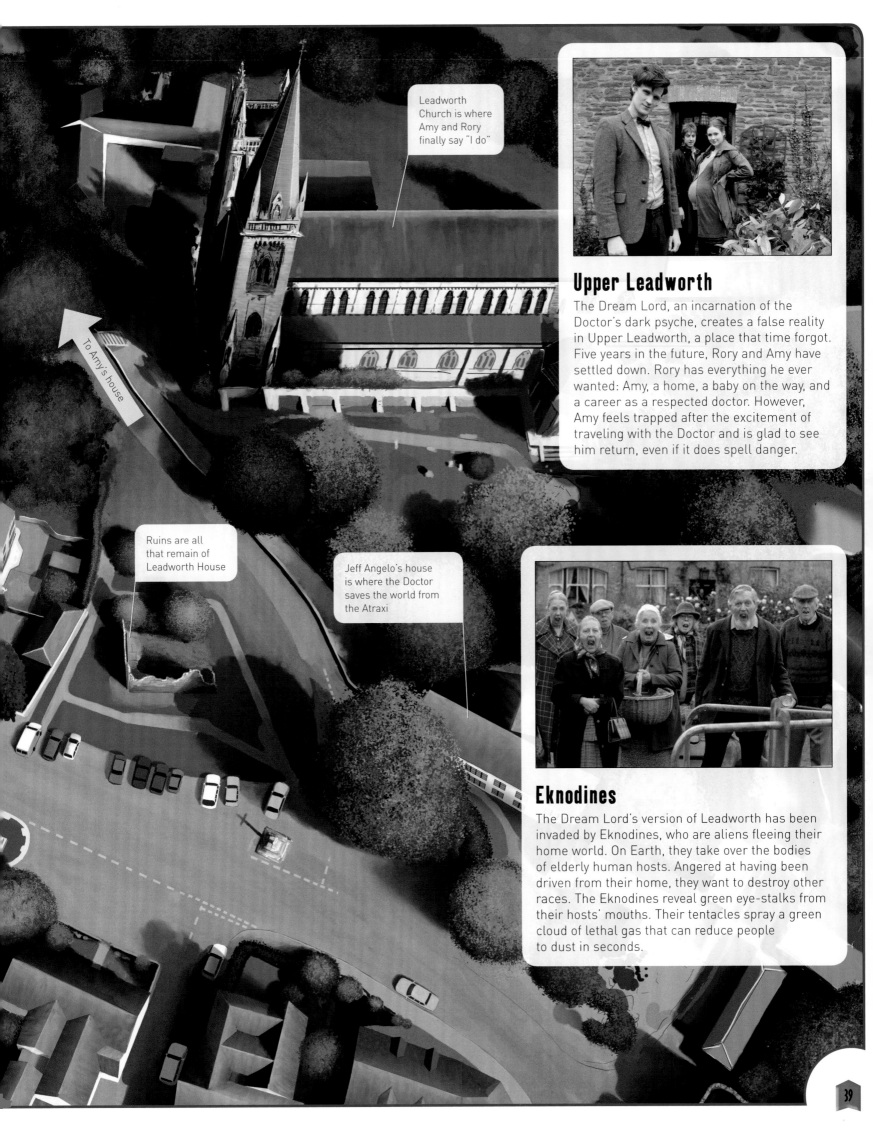

Leadworth Church is where Amy and Rory finally say "I do"

To Amy's house

Ruins are all that remain of Leadworth House

Jeff Angelo's house is where the Doctor saves the world from the Atraxi

Upper Leadworth

The Dream Lord, an incarnation of the Doctor's dark psyche, creates a false reality in Upper Leadworth, a place that time forgot. Five years in the future, Rory and Amy have settled down. Rory has everything he ever wanted: Amy, a home, a baby on the way, and a career as a respected doctor. However, Amy feels trapped after the excitement of traveling with the Doctor and is glad to see him return, even if it does spell danger.

Eknodines

The Dream Lord's version of Leadworth has been invaded by Eknodines, who are aliens fleeing their home world. On Earth, they take over the bodies of elderly human hosts. Angered at having been driven from their home, they want to destroy other races. The Eknodines reveal green eye-stalks from their hosts' mouths. Their tentacles spray a green cloud of lethal gas that can reduce people to dust in seconds.

CAPTAIN JACK HARKNESS

BORN IN THE BOESHANE PENINSULA, "Jack" was recruited to the Time Agency, a mysterious espionage organization, but left after it stole two years of his memory. Used to the free and easy ways of the 51st century, and blessed with natural good looks and winning ways, he put his enormous charm to work as a con man, taking the identity of a Captain Jack Harkness. He has never revealed his true name.

Stripes for rank of Captain

Stranded on Earth in 1869 after leaving Satellite 5, Jack moves to the site of Cardiff's Rift to wait for the Doctor. He is recruited by Torchwood Three. In 2000, he becomes leader and builds a team including Ianto Jones and Gwen Cooper.

A Hidden Hero

Captain Jack surprises himself by discovering that he can be courageous and selfless. After meeting the Doctor, he leaves his criminal ways and the two become good friends. During Jack's ensuing adventures, he proves himself as a hero—one who is willing to risk his life for a noble cause.

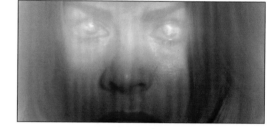

Jack owes his immortality to Rose Tyler, who brings him back to life after he is exterminated by Daleks on Satellite 5. Rose opens the heart of the TARDIS and absorbs the Time Vortex. She gains its tremendous powers, but is unable to fully control them, causing Jack to be returned, not for one lifetime, but forever, a mistake which he proceeds to put to good use.

World War II overcoat

Microphone

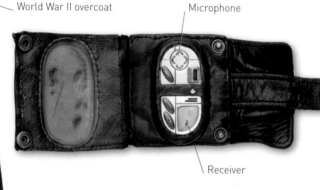

Receiver

VORTEX MANIPULATOR

Jack wears a vortex manipulator on his wrist. He uses the device to travel through time. Jack discovered this most useful of gadgets at the Time Agency. In addition to time travel, it can scan for alien technology, project simple holographics, and perform basic medical examinations.

The Face of Boe sacrifices himself to free the people of New Earth, and imparts his dying secret to the Doctor: "You Are Not Alone." This hint that the Master is living as Professor Yana at the end of the universe gives a clue to the fact that the Face of Boe has been to the far future as Captain Jack.

The Face of Boe

What happens to an immortal who keeps aging? Jack had been a poster boy in his homeland, the Boeshane Peninsula, earning the nickname "the Face of Boe." The Doctor has met another Face of Boe—a giant alien head. Is this who Captain Jack will become after billions of years?

DONNA NOBLE

Confident face hides self-doubt

Fiery red hair matches her fiery temper

S HE WAS A LOUDMOUTH who hated Christmas, could not point to Germany on a map, and deep down, thought she was worthless. But being with the Doctor allows long-term temp Donna to see herself in a new way. She shows she has compassion and sense, and when she saves the cosmos from Davros's Reality Bomb, Donna is the most important woman in the whole universe.

Donna missed the Sycorax invasion (hungover) and the Cybermen (scuba-diving in Spain), but she has front row seats for the Racnoss.

Unlikely Friends

Thanks to Donna's quick temper and sharp tongue, she and the Doctor do not hit it off at first. As their relationship develops, however, Donna learns that not only is she intelligent and compassionate, but she can also do some real good in the world. Eventually, the Doctor considers Donna his best friend.

Being with Donna changes the Doctor and it turns out that without her, there would be no Doctor at all. A beetle belonging to a being known as the Trickster reveals an alternative timeline in which Donna never met the Doctor and he was killed by the Racnoss.

TRICKSTER'S BEETLE

This giant stag beetle attaches itself firmly to a victim's back, changing her timeline and causing chaos. It can be seen only by those with psychic abilities.

Giant insectoid form

Smart suit for office work

Donna's compassion influences the Doctor. When they visit Pompeii she convinces him to save Caecilius's family, and she shares responsibility for destroying the city so that he doesn't have to bear the weight alone.

Wilfred Mott

An amateur astronomer with an interest in aliens, Wilf adores Donna, his only grandchild, and thinks she should go with the Doctor as it is a once-in-a-lifetime opportunity to explore the stars. He has his own role to play in saving the world from the Time Lords, and the Doctor sacrifices his tenth incarnation to save him.

Sylvia Noble

Donna's mother cannot forgive the Doctor for helping to ruin Donna's first wedding. She does not want her daughter to go away with him. Deep down, Sylvia is proud of Donna, but is not very good at showing it.

The Doctor-Donna

Donna becomes the only person who can save the universe from Davros when she fuses with the Doctor's severed hand. This creates a human Doctor and also gives Donna the knowledge of a Time Lord—becoming the "Doctor-Donna." But a Time Lord brain is so powerful that a human host cannot survive. The Doctor must say goodbye: if Donna ever remembers him, she will die.

ROSE TYLER

LONDON TEENAGER Rose Tyler's world is transformed the night she is attacked by possessed mannequins. A mysterious stranger called the Doctor saves her life and offers her a way out of her dull life as a shop assistant—a chance to travel across the universe. But this amazing adventure comes at a cost. Rose must leave behind her mom, Jackie, who is also her best friend, her boyfriend, Mickey, and the life she knows on Earth.

Traveling Companion

Rose is quick witted, intelligent, and determined—assets that make her the ideal traveling companion. Overawed by life with the Doctor at first, she soon takes to time travel with gusto. Best of all, Rose has a wicked sense of humor that makes their adventures together fun.

Parallel Rose

Rose is thrilled by her exciting life with the Doctor, whom she begins to realize she loves. But her time with him comes to a sudden end when she is sucked into a parallel world. She returns to reality in times of great need, but must always return to her parallel existence.

When she looks into the heart of the TARDIS, Rose absorbs the energy of the time vortex. It gives her great power over time and space, but starts to destroy her. The Doctor sacrifices his ninth incarnation to save her.

Discount clothes from Hendrik's department store

Mickey Smith

Rose's boyfriend Mickey is jealous when Rose leaves with the Doctor, but he soon gets his chance at adventure too. When forced to rely on himself, and after facing many deadly aliens, Mickey becomes a brave freedom fighter.

A Doctor for Rose

Rose's forays into this reality often save the day, but she must still return to her parallel life. Despite their love, the Doctor cannot join her. However, his human clone version—created from his hand—can. He is just like the Doctor, except that he is Rose's own kind.

Jackie Tyler

After Pete Tyler's death, Jackie was left to raise their daughter on her own. Jackie is funny and popular, although often brash. She loves Rose and resents the Doctor for taking her away, but feels affection for him too.

MARTHA JONES

CAPABLE AND INDEPENDENT, medical student Martha Jones impresses the Doctor right from the start. When the Royal Hope Hospital is transported to the moon by the rhino-headed Judoon, Martha remains calm, while all around her panic. Within hours of meeting the Doctor, she not only saves his life, but manages to save Earth too.

Standard issue white medical coat

Comfortable clothes are perfect for the hectic schedule of a doctor

Medical Student

Martha is less in awe of the Doctor than his previous companion Rose was. As a medical student, she is comfortable in the world of science, and quickly grasps the complex concepts his world revolves around. She spends much of her time feeling second best to Rose, but her actions show that she is just what the Doctor ordered.

Martha is compassionate and positive. When the warmongering Sontarans create a clone of her for their army, her clone self looks into her mind, sees all her hopes and dreams, and changes allegiance as it dies.

When the Master ravages life on Earth, Martha becomes a legend by spreading hope and telling stories of the Doctor around the world. But her success wipes out her celebrity: she is forgotten when the Master is defeated and time is reversed.

The Jones Family

Martha learns that families and the Doctor do not mix when her family is used as pawns by the Master. She feels responsible for their suffering, and gives up time-travelling to keep mom, Francine, dad, Clive, and sister, Tish, safe from future danger.

A United Front

With Martha's record of saving the world, it is no surprise that the Unified Intelligence Taskforce (UNIT)—the organization tasked with defending Earth—want her on their medical staff. It might look like she has become a soldier, but principled Martha is working from the inside to stop the fighting. The Doctor taught her well.

HUMAN ALLIES

AS WELL AS HIS regular traveling companions, the Doctor has always relied on others to help him overcome the many alien threats to planet Earth. More often than not, his human allies are innocent bystanders caught up in the fight, while others are willing adventurers—as brave and selfless as the Doctor himself.

CRAIG OWENS

SOPHIE

Craig and his girlfriend, Sophie, have the Doctor to thank for bringing them together as a couple. They are now the mostly happy parents to a son—Alfie.

The FBI Agent

A hard-bitten ex-Bureau agent from 1969, Canton is, at first, somewhat bemused by the Doctor and his incredible time-ship. However, he quickly grows to respect the alien Time Lord and his companions, and remains loyal to them until old age.

CANTON EVERETT DELAWARE III

Mr. Sofa Man

An unashamed couch potato, Craig's life is turned upside down when he takes the Doctor in as a lodger. He has twice been drawn into the Doctor's investigations, and despite his desire to be left alone, now counts the Doctor as his friend.

JOHN RIDDELL

The Arwell Family

Bereft mom Madge and curious children Cyril and Lily were facing a gloomy evacuation in the countryside during World War II. An encounter with the Doctor brings them closer together, and enables them to free an endangered race of tree creatures.

MADGE

CYRIL

LILY

Madge's World War II pilot husband, Reg, was believed lost at sea, but thanks to Madge and the Doctor's heroics, the Arwell family is happily reunited in time for Christmas.

The Big Game Hunter

Self-professed thrill-seeker John Riddell has seen much excitement alongside the Doctor. His highlight was hunting dinosaurs on a Silurian Ark in space, an adventure that made him feel more alive than ever before.

Ghost Hunters

In the 1970s, psychology professor Alec Palmer and his psychic assistant, Emma, are looking for a ghost called Hila Tacorian, a pioneer time traveler trapped in a pocket universe. The Doctor uses Emma's psychic powers to free the lost human.

MAJOR ALEC PALMER

EMMA GRAYLING

- Security firm HC Clements acted as one of London Torchwood's many fronts for 23 years.
- Torchwood Three was charged by Queen Victoria with policing the Rift in Cardiff, Wales.
- There is a Torchwood Four, but nobody, not even Captain Jack, knows its location.
- Torchwood is a top-secret organisation – very few are supposed to know of its existence. Drugs are used to erase the memories of those who find out about it.

TORCHWOOD

IN 1879, QUEEN VICTORIA VISITED Torchwood House in Scotland, where she met the Doctor and discovered the existence of aliens. Determined that the British Empire would be ready for its next extraterrestrial visitors, she founded the Torchwood Institute to protect Britain and its territories from aliens—with the Doctor listed as enemy number one. Bases were established in London, England (Torchwood One), Glasgow, Scotland (Torchwood Two), and Cardiff, Wales (Torchwood Three).

Window was originally a marine outlet pump

JACK HARKNESS

Torchwood Tower (London) was built to reach a spatial breach 600 feet above sea level.

Yvonne Hartman

Over the years, the Torchwood Institute moved from battling aliens to exploiting their technology, its motto being: "If it is alien, it is ours." Under Yvonne Hartman, this attitude led to a battle between Daleks and Cybermen at Canary Wharf in London, and the destruction of the Torchwood Institute.

Powerful and mysterious Rift Manipulator

A New Torchwood

After the Battle of Canary Wharf, Captain Jack returned Torchwood to its original ethos of defending the Earth. Torchwood Three's HQ, the "Hub," lies under the Oval Basin in Cardiff's Bute Docks. It has many levels reaching deep underground and may be entered via an invisible lift in Roald Dahl Plass, or a disused tourist information center.

Jack in Charge

Captain Jack has been at Torchwood for over a century. He recruited a new team to run Torchwood Three: Suzie Costello, Dr. Owen Harper, Toshiko Sato, and Ianto Jones. Suzie was later replaced by police officer Gwen Cooper. Jack is fiercely loyal to his team, even to the point of turning down an opportunity to rejoin the Doctor to stay with them. He inspires loyalty in return, although his refusal to explain his elusive past can cause resentment.

Torchwood Team

Ianto Jones and Gwen Cooper use the Rift to provide the power to tow the Earth back home after the planet is abducted by Daleks.

45

UNIT

THE UNIFIED INTELLIGENCE TASKFORCE (UNIT) was set up in the late twentieth century to deal with the alien menaces facing humankind. Although its remit is similar to Torchwood's, UNIT is a predominantly military organization. The Doctor once spent several years as UNIT's scientific advisor after he was exiled to Earth by the Time Lords for meddling in the affairs of other planets.

Dark clothes to match black uniforms worn by UNIT troops

Civilian clothing with a slight military tone

Located beneath the Tower of London is UNIT's HQ, which also houses a vast store of alien artifacts known as the Black Archive. The collection is considered so dangerous that the security protocols surrounding it are the most stringent on Earth. People's minds are automatically erased each time they leave so that they forget what they saw, and in the event of an alien incursion, a nuclear warhead can be exploded to destroy its contents.

When three versions of the Doctor become imprisoned in the Tower of London in 1562, the Eleventh Doctor scrawls a numerical sequence on the wall, hoping that modern-day UNIT will find it and realize that it's the activation code for a vortex manipulator stored in the Black Archive!

Kate Stewart

Intelligent and strong-minded, Kate Stewart is UNIT's Chief Scientific Officer and the daughter of Brigadier Lethbridge-Stewart, the Doctor's old friend and colleague. Thanks to Kate, UNIT is now led by science rather than military might, and her leadership and investigative skills are proven to be resilient under pressure.

Striped scarf reminiscent of the Fourth Doctor's

Spare pens and inhaler for asthma kept in pocket

Osgood

With her quirky and excitable personality, Kate Stewart's scientific assistant, Osgood, is an unconventional member of UNIT. But despite her nervous nature, she bravely helps defend UNIT HQ during the Zygons' infiltration attempt.

The Doctor has always had something of an uneasy relationship with UNIT, often disapproving of its blunt, militaristic ways. He's particularly annoyed when a UNIT helicopter airlifts his TARDIS to the National Gallery to get his attention, instead of simply asking for his help!

Pulling both cords operates teleport

PROJECT INDIGO TELEPORT

UNIT's experimental teleport, Project Indigo, uses technology salvaged from the Sontarans. Untested, unstabilized, and with no coordinates, it is a possible death trap. But Martha uses it anyway because she is UNIT's only hope of finding the Doctor when Davros threatens the whole universe.

The *Valiant*

UNIT's flagship, *Valiant*, is an aircraft carrier with a difference—it floats in the air, not on the sea. It was designed by evil Time Lord the Master, while he was masquerading as Mr. Saxon and working for the Ministry of Defense, and he later made it his base of operations on Earth. After the Master's defeat, UNIT readopted the ship—but not before checking it thoroughly for any Time Lord tricks. Colonel Mace uses its strong engines to disperse the Sontarans' poisonous gas.

OSTERHAGEN KEY

25 nuclear warheads have been placed under the Earth's crust, so that if the suffering of the human race reaches crisis point, they can be detonated by the holders of the Osterhagen Key. When Earth faces destruction from Davros, Martha is sent by UNIT to prepare the Key for detonation. Three Osterhagen stations must be online to use the Key.

Central panel conceals teleport base code

UNIT is based in Geneva but has branches worldwide. The British section was initially headed up by Brigadier Lethbridge-Stewart, and he remained its leader for many years before retiring. He was later succeeded by the likes of Colonel Mace and, eventually, Kate Stewart. The US forces in New York were commanded by General Sanchez until his tragic death during a Dalek invasion.

Reinforced helmet

UNIT Armory

After years of fighting alien menaces, UNIT has amassed a stock of unusual weapons, each with a very specific purpose. Silver bullets are kept in case of a werewolf attack, while anti-Dalek shells are troops' best hope of defeating Daleks. Gold-tipped bullets are reserved for Cybermen, and following recent intelligence, rad-steel coated bullets have been added to the arsenal to overcome Sontaran defenses.

A UNIT soldier is always battle-ready, although many never encounter an alien.

UNIT "wings" cap badge, adopted in the 1990s

Identification badge

In especially hazardous conditions, UNIT may also mobilize specially trained, heavily armored soldiers.

UNIT FACTS

- Martha Jones gets a job as a UNIT medical officer following the Doctor's recommendation.

- The Doctor is still officially a member of UNIT, never having resigned. However, he has never considered himself bound by the organization's rules and regulations.

- UNIT and Torchwood reluctantly share intelligence and resources, and staff are occasionally seconded between organizations.

Armoured gear to protect against alien attack

UNIT
PRIVATE

UNIT
SOLDIER

SARAH JANE SMITH

FEARLESS REPORTER Sarah Jane Smith traveled with the Third and Fourth Doctors, but when the Fourth Doctor was suddenly recalled to Gallifrey, he left her behind on Earth, without even saying goodbye. When the Doctor didn't return, Sarah Jane assumed he was dead. Many years later, they are reunited and they continue to meet when danger threatens. He has turned up in both his tenth and eleventh incarnations to help her battle alien threats.

Thirty years after he left without saying goodbye, the Doctor meets Sarah Jane when they happen to be investigating strange events at a school. However, she doesn't recognize his tenth incarnation.

Curious Companion

Sarah Jane's natural curiosity, intelligence, and compassion make her a perfect partner for the Doctor on his adventures. Even after the Doctor leaves her, Sarah Jane devotes her career to investigating occurrences that are too strange or dangerous for other journalists to explore.

Mr. Smith

Aiding Sarah Jane in her adventures is supercomputer, Mr. Smith. He was created through a union between her laptop and a Xylok crystal, which scans for alien threats from its attic hideaway. Among other talents, Mr. Smith can link up with all the telephone exchanges in the world.

A Courageous Captive

Sarah Jane proves her courage when she allows herself to be taken captive by the Daleks. The Daleks transport her to Davros's Command Ship in the Medusa Cascade, where the Doctor and a group of his other companions are also being held. Sarah Jane joins forces with Jack Harkness, using her warp star to create a weapon capable of destroying the ship.

After Davros's plan is thwarted, Sarah Jane helps to pilot the TARDIS and tow Earth back to its position in the solar system.

Motherhood

Sarah Jane adopts a young boy as her son. He was created from DNA samples by an alien race called Bane, in a quest to find the archetypal human. Sarah Jane rescues the boy and names him Luke.

Smart suit for carrying out investigations in school

K-9

LOYAL AND FEARLESS, boasting vast memory banks and highly sophisticated sensors, robotic dog K-9 became indispensable to the Doctor during his fourth incarnation. He traveled everywhere with the Doctor and would defend him at all costs. When the Doctor's companion Leela decided to remain on Gallifrey, K-9 stayed with her. The Doctor then built a replacement, K-9 Mk II, and a third model was sent to Sarah Jane Smith. After K-9 Mk III is blown up defeating the Krillitane, the Doctor presents Sarah Jane with K-9 Mk IV.

Thirty years after the Doctor gave him to Sarah Jane, K-9 is not in a good shape. The British climate and salted roads have taken their toll, but fortunately the Doctor is on hand to repair his old friend.

Old Friend

A brilliant doctor named Professor Marius created the original K-9 in the year 5000, using a mobile computer and laboratory to assist him. Even K-9's most recent incarnation, Mk IV, looks similar to the original—styled after Marius's beloved pet dog.

K-9 FACTS

- **After the first K-9 helped the Doctor defeat a sentient virus, the robot's maker, Professor Marius, gave his creation to the Time Lord so he could assist him on his travels.**

- **According to the Doctor, K-9's design is the height of fashion in the year 5000.**

DATA-COM PROBE (EXTENDED)

K-9's telescopic data-com probe extends and retracts from in front of his "eyes"

Tracking sensors

Multi-wavelength optical spectrum sensor

Gravitronic brain enables K-9's artificial intelligence

Signal booster antenna

Operator's manual console

Data-com probe (retracted)

Sensor can analyze all known substances

Photon blaster

Each K-9 model is equipped with a photon blaster in the snout. This weapon demonstrates Professor Marius's awareness of potential space threats.

Housing for fully buffered deutronic battery

Name tag contains tracking beacon

Removable cover to primary drives

All-terrain protective alignment buffer

K-9 MK IV

JOHN SMITH

JOHN SMITH—THE MOST ordinary of names—has often been the Doctor's alias of choice when wanting to blend in. But, when the Tenth Doctor needs somewhere to hide from the deadly Family of Blood, he not only adopts the name, but actually becomes John Smith. The Family is able to track a Time Lord anywhere in time or space, so the TARDIS rewrites the Doctor's DNA to make him truly human.

JOURNAL OF IMPOSSIBLE THINGS

The Doctor's real life seeps through into John Smith's dreams, which he records as fiction in what he calls his "journal of impossible things." The TARDIS, the Doctor's old companion Rose, and many monsters feature, as well as memories of the Earth's future such as World War I (1914–1918).

Arch sends electrical charges through the body to rewrite its cellular structure

Mortarboard is symbol of authority

Human body takes the appearance of the Tenth Doctor

Human senses are dull in comparison to a Time Lord's

Cane used for corporal punishment

Books provide Smith with historical informaton

From Doctor to Teacher

The TARDIS places John Smith in Herefordshire, England in 1913 as a history teacher at Farringham School for Boys. The disguise is so complete that Smith believes that he has always been human and is the Nottingham-born son of watchmaker Sydney and nurse Verity. He is an ordinary man of narrow experiences who knows nothing of the Doctor.

Teacher disguise built on Doctor's love of knowledge

Nurse Joan Redfern, a young war widow, is the Matron of Farringham School. Joan's unassuming but caring personality appeals to shy and insecure Smith. As an ordinary man, he can see the beauty in an ordinary woman. However, falling in love is something the Doctor never allowed for in his plan. Eventually he realizes that he must sacrifice his happiness for the greater good and return to his Time Lord existence.

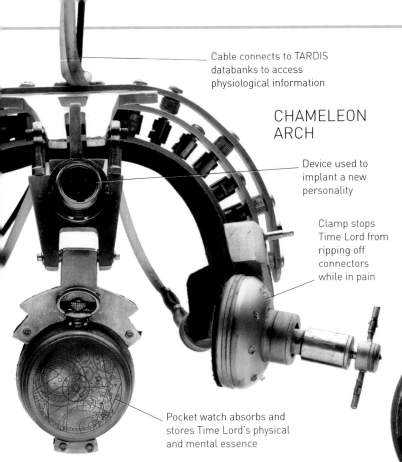

Cable connects to TARDIS databanks to access physiological information

CHAMELEON ARCH

Device used to implant a new personality

Clamp stops Time Lord from ripping off connectors while in pain

Pocket watch absorbs and stores Time Lord's physical and mental essence

The TARDIS's chameleon arch can alter a Time Lord's physiology to any compatible species without affecting his outer appearance. Once transformation is complete, a Gallifreyan fob watch – a symbol of the Time Lords' mastery over time – stores the original memories, personality and biological data, which are restored the moment the watch is opened.

Rewriting Cells

The process of transforming every cell from Time Lord to human is agonizing. Two hearts compress into one, the body temperature rises, and the respiratory bypass system vanishes. However, because the natural physiology is eager to reassert itself, the cells return to their original shapes painlessly.

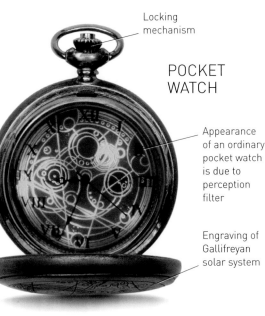

Locking mechanism

POCKET WATCH

Appearance of an ordinary pocket watch is due to perception filter

Engraving of Gallifreyan solar system

Martha is the only one who knows the truth about John Smith. The Doctor has trusted her with his life, but in the meantime, she has to endure the racism, sexism, and classism of the early 1910s, even from John Smith himself.

Smith the Caretaker

The Doctor has used his alias as John Smith many times in order to investigate aliens on Earth without arousing human suspicion. With a Skovox Blitzer skulking in the vicinity of Coal Hill School, the Time Lord goes undercover as the school's new caretaker, intending to corner the deadly war machine.

Winding button turns wearer invisible

INVISIBILITY WATCH

To avoid being detected by the Skovox Blitzer, the Doctor uses an invisibility watch—an ingenious device that works by reversing light waves. The Doctor is worried that if the Skovox Blitzer detects his superior intelligence, it may self-destruct and blow up planet Earth in the process.

Caretaker's coat

SKOVOX BLITZER

Scanner detects human body heat

Battle-scarred outer shell

Powerful laser weapon

Spider-like appendages allow movement across all terrains

The Skovox Blitzer is one of the deadliest killing machines ever invented. When the warring Skovox and Overite races were wiped out, their self-replicating drones carried on fighting, and somehow one such Skovox war machine fell to Earth through a time fissure.

DALEKS

XTERMINATE! EXTERMINATE!
The battle cry of the Daleks, and the
mindset it represents, has made them
feared throughout the universe. Concealed
inside armored life-support casings, the
Daleks are ruthless conquerors, who believe
in the superiority of their own race and hold
all other beings in contempt, suitable only for
extermination. Across time, Dalek aggression
has led to interstellar wars and encouraged
alliances against them. Of all the Doctor's
enemies, the Daleks are the oldest and
deadliest. He has defeated them time
and time again, but Daleks are
resilient and driven to
survive at any cost.

Eye-stalk is a Dalek's
weakest point

Batch recognition code
of individual Dalek

Dome rotates
to provide 360°
field of vision

Upper casing
opens to
expose Dalek
being

Solar-energy
absorbing
slats

Tactical
environment
scanner grid

Telescopic
manipulator arm

Death ray
gun

Sensor
globe

Inside a Dalek

Daleks originated as Kaleds on the planet Skaro.
A thousand-year war led to environmental
contamination, causing the Kaleds to mutate and
degenerate into weak, tentacled creatures.

Genetically Modified

The Kaled scientist, Davros, built
armored life-support systems to
support the now tentacled Kaleds. He
genetically engineered them, instilling
an overwhelming drive for survival
and a hatred of all other species,
while magnifying their intellect and
stripping them of all "unnecessary"
emotions. He named the perfect
"killing machine" he had
created... the Dalek.

Hoverpad base conceals
motive power system

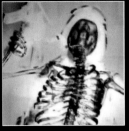

A Dalek's arm is strong enough to crush a human skull, but it can also kill by extracting all brain waves.

A Dalek's death ray gun uses a ray beam to destroy every cell in a human body.

Extermination Tools

Each warrior Dalek is equipped with a manipulator arm and a ray gun. The arm can interface with computer systems or mimic hand movements with its "sucker" made of morphic material. The "death ray" is a directed energy weapon that can stun or kill.

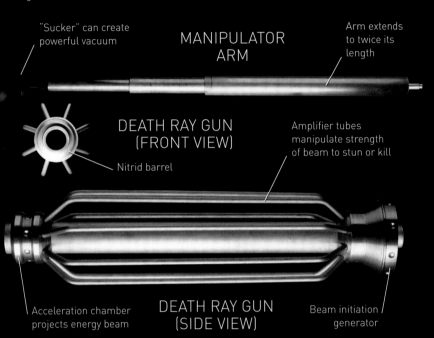

"Sucker" can create powerful vacuum

Arm extends to twice its length

MANIPULATOR ARM

DEATH RAY GUN (FRONT VIEW)

Nitrid barrel

Amplifier tubes manipulate strength of beam to stun or kill

Acceleration chamber projects energy beam

DEATH RAY GUN (SIDE VIEW)

Beam initiation generator

The brilliant and psychotic Davros created the Daleks.

Key Dalek Battles

The Daleks have waged war across time and space since their creation, but the complexities of time travel, and the Time Lords' attempts to change Dalek history, make a comprehensive timeline of their battles and invasions difficult. Here are some of their attempts at conquest:

◼ Generations after their creation, Daleks were still battling their neighbors, the **Thals**, when they were first encountered by the Doctor in his first incarnation.

◼ While chasing the **First Doctor** through time, a Dalek execution squad fought, and was defeated by, the robot **Mechanoids** in the 23rd century. This was the beginning of a long war between the two races.

◼ The Daleks fought another long war, over many centuries, with the android **Movellans** from star system 4-X-Alpha-4, as both tried to expand their stellar empires. When that war became stalemated, the Daleks traveled through time to seek help from their ancient creator, Davros.

◼ **Reviving Davros** led to factions within the Dalek hierarchy and a series of **civil wars** between different groups supporting and opposing Davros.

◼ In the 22nd century, the Daleks twice invaded **Earth**, the first time after the destruction of **World War III** and later, around Earth year **2164**, intending to turn it into a giant battleship to aid their wars of conquest.

◼ By the year **4000**, the Daleks planned a master strike to **conquer the galaxy** with the aid of similarly power-hungry allies. When the Doctor defeated their plans, the alliance self-destructed and embroiled the Daleks in new conflicts.

◼ Learning of the **Time Lords'** attempts to thwart their creation, the Daleks attacked Gallifrey and the **last Great Time War** began.

◼ **Gallifrey** was seemingly destroyed in the attempt to wipe out the Daleks, but the **Cult of Skaro** and the **Emperor** survived. By the year 200,100, the Emperor had rebuilt the Dalek race, then largely destroyed by **Rose Tyler**.

Dalek Point of View

The eye-stalk of the Dalek battle armor provides enhanced vision in the natural colors of Dalek sight. Inbuilt multi-spectral sensors also allow the Dalek to see in infra-red, x-ray, and ultra-violet modes. The single eye-stalk is a Dalek's weakest point as it has no back-up system.

To avoid capture or to atone for failing a mission, a Dalek is fitted with a self-destruct system for complete obliteration. The components of this system are mounted in the Dalek's sensor globes.

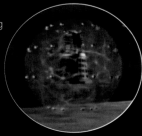

The Daleks' casing is made from Dalekanium—an extremely robust bonded polycarbide material. It can be penetrated by bastic-tipped bullets, so the Daleks created an energy shield for additional protection.

Dalek battle armor is designed to open up, so that repairs, system enhancements, and medical treatments can be carried out. Even without its weaponry, the Dalek is a dangerous creature and has been known to kill.

Equipped with anti-gravity generators and gyroscopic stabilization systems, Daleks can glide across any terrain or hover over any obstacle—even a steep staircase is no hindrance.

DALEK FLAGSHIP

EMERGING FROM HIDING above Earth, the Dalek fleet is armed, dangerous, and all-powerfully gigantic. The massive flagship that commands the fleet transports the Dalek Emperor, who is worshipped as a god by the rest of the Daleks. The Emperor is wired into the ship's systems—allowing him total control. From there he can operate the entire fleet using his mind alone.

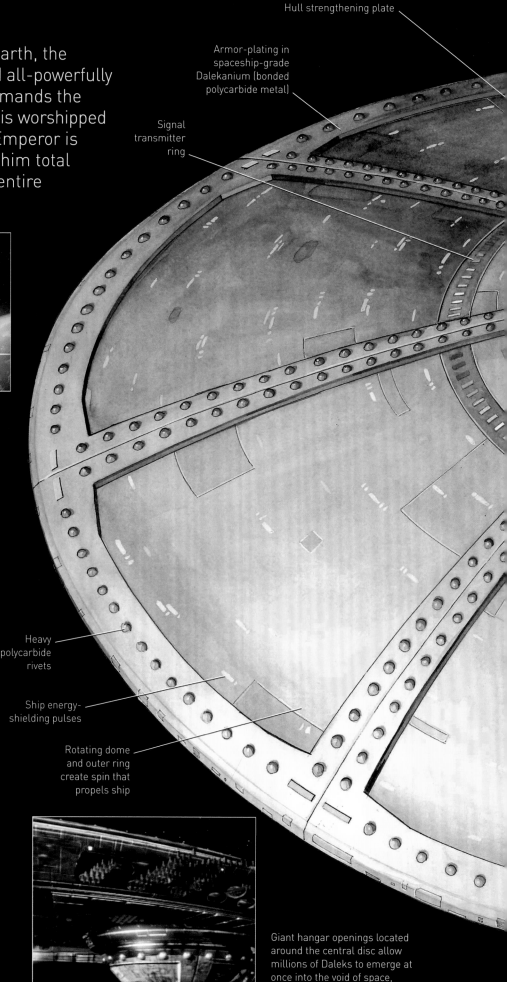

Hull strengthening plate

Armor-plating in spaceship-grade Dalekanium (bonded polycarbide metal)

Signal transmitter ring

Heavy polycarbide rivets

Ship energy-shielding pulses

Rotating dome and outer ring create spin that propels ship

Giant hangar openings located around the central disc allow millions of Daleks to emerge at once into the void of space, heading toward Earth.

Hidden Army

Long ago, this ship escaped from the Great Time War, slipping away into "the dark space." It had one lone, badly injured Dalek onboard, who became the Emperor. Over the centuries, the Emperor hatched a plan to harvest humans from Earth to supply the genetic material for a host of new Daleks. For this end, the flagship is teeming with a Dalek army, poised to attack Earth.

FLAGSHIP FACTS

- The flagship was used during the Great Time War between Daleks and Time Lords.

- The Dalek Emperor intends to create "Heaven on Earth" by bombing the planet until it is radioactive rubble.

- Rose destroys the Dalek fleet, including the flagship, when she gains enormous powers from looking into the time-space vortex at the heart of the TARDIS.

DALEK EMPEROR'S LIFE-TANK

Power/communication spikes

Dalek Emperor at center of control room

Hull damage from the Great Time War

Supercomputer housing connected to all systems aboard the ship

TARDIS

Acceleration compensator

Armored shielding

Computer power feed assembly

Storage vats for molten polycarbide used in Dalek manufacture

Housing for humans awaiting "processing"

Science labs where Daleks extract from human captives the one cell in a billion considered fit to be nurtured into a Dalek

The Dalek Emperor masterminds operations from a fortified chamber at the center of the ship. A breathable atmosphere in the room allows human captives to be brought before him for inspection. Their fate is sealed when the Emperor selects one of two grappling hooks situated below his life-tank, deciding whether or not they are eligible for DNA harvesting.

Shield generator array

Computer core

Reactor/power generator

Computer systems matrix

Ventilation/cooling vanes

Dalek training hangar

Vertical transport shaft

Overseer observation platforms

Torpedo ports arrayed around central axis

Hangar doors

Daleks arranged in formation, ready for battle

Cell array around which electromagnetic pulses travel to create rotation for forward movement

Dalek manufacturing hangars

DAVROS

DAVROS IS RESPONSIBLE for creating the Daleks. The scientist foresaw a day when the chemical warfare that raged on his home planet would cause his people, the Kaleds, to mutate. Obsessed with the survival of his race, he experimented with their mutations and invented an armored machine to carry them. Ambitious Davros then went further, making chromosomal changes to Dalek embryos to remove their consciences and emotions. But his plan backfired when his creations declared him unnecessary to their plans and attempted to kill him.

Insane Leader

The Doctor regards Davros as one of the most dangerous, and certainly the most insane, of his enemies. While the Time Lord has a grudging respect for some of his adversaries, Davros is not one of them. The Doctor is unsurprised to discover that the events of the Time War have inspired bitter Davros to want to destroy all living things.

Davros enjoys taunting the Tenth Doctor. He claims that the Doctor is responsible for innocent deaths, despite his abhorrence of violence, as he takes ordinary people and turns them into weapons to die in his name.

Like many children with their parents, the Daleks' relationship with Davros is a combination of reverence and contempt. They look to him to solve their problems, but still believe that they are better off without him.

Microphone and amplifier enable speech

Single lens replaces sightless eyes

Face scarred by his accident

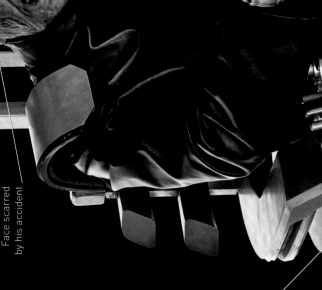

Wheelchair generates its own power

Heart and lung machine keeps Davros alive

Mechanical fingertips shoot energy bolts

Davros's Accident

Davros's pride will not let him speak of the accident that maimed him. Yet a lesser creature would have died from the injuries that left him with only a head, torso, and one withered arm and hand (later shot off and replaced with a mechanical copy). A single blue lens gives him sight since his eyes are withered. His hearing and voice are also artificially aided. Davros's technical genius has prolonged his life far beyond its natural span.

Every Dalek creature has been grown from a cell taken from Davros's body. The Daleks' proud creator revels in the idea that all his "children" are literally his own flesh and blood.

Chair inspired the design of the Dalek shell

Chair can adopt hover mode

WEELCHAIR CONTROL PANEL

Davros's customized wheelchair helps him get around—and it also keeps him alive. Without the chair's life-support system, Davros would not survive for even 30 seconds. Davros has turned this weakness into a tool, building devices into the chair that can help him further his evil plans of total destruction.

Operates suspended-animation field

Signal to summon Daleks

Connection point for external electrical devices

Remote control to regulate the environment

Frictionless base allows silent movement

Controls life-support functions

Motor and directional controls

Daleks remote control

THE GENESIS ARK

WHEN THE SECRETIVE Torchwood Institute attempts to harness energy from a spatial disturbance over London, it unwittingly breaks through a wall between dimensions. A sinister metal sphere emerges through the breach, which the Doctor instantly recognizes as a Void Ship—containing the Genesis Ark. Sensing that nothing good can be inside it, the Doctor urges Torchwood to send it back through the Rift.

THE VOID SHIP

This hypothetical craft was designed to exist outside space and time, traveling between dimensions. The sphere fills all who go near it with foreboding. In theory it does not exist because it lacks both radiation and atomic mass.

When the Void Ship activates, Torchwood's lab screens go wild with readings that show that the object suddenly has height, mass, and an electromagnetic field. The Sphere Chamber doors immediately seal shut to put the area in automatic quarantine.

Dalek Transporter

A sinister casket is concealed inside the Void Ship. Known as the Genesis Ark, it has dimensionally transcendental Time Lord technology similar to the TARDIS, and was used during the Great Time War for the sole purpose of imprisoning the armies of the Time Lords' deadliest enemy—the Daleks.

The Ark's Purpose

As the Ark is activated in the sky above London, the Doctor finally understands what the Daleks meant by "Time Lord science." Like the TARDIS, the Ark is much larger on the inside than on the outside. It was used as a prison ship for the millions of the Daleks captured during the Great Time War.

Dalek Sec elevates the Ark the 48 square kilometers needed for activation.

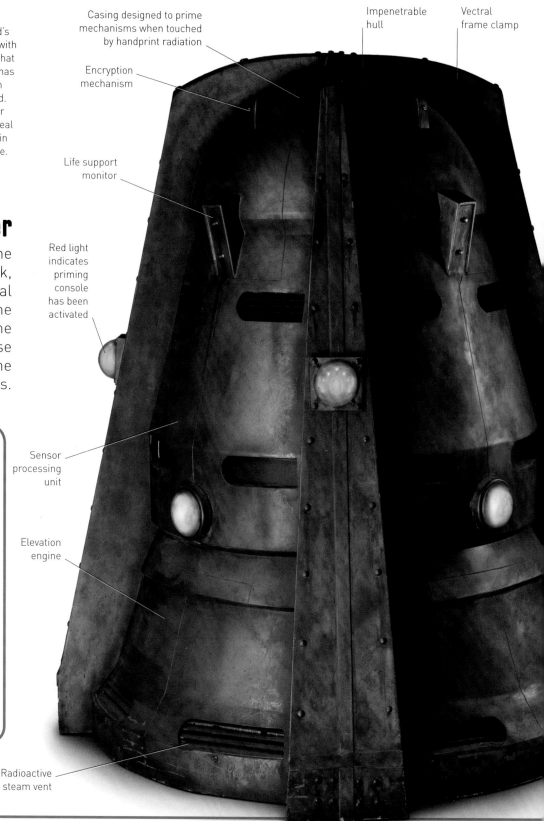

Casing designed to prime mechanisms when touched by handprint radiation

Encryption mechanism

Impenetrable hull

Vectral frame clamp

Life support monitor

Red light indicates priming console has been activated

Sensor processing unit

Elevation engine

Radioactive steam vent

The Key to the Ark

Rose and Mickey witness the Genesis Ark and four Daleks—the Cult of Skaro—emerging from the Void Ship. The Daleks must keep Rose and Mickey alive because a time-traveler's touch is the key that opens the Ark. As humanoid time-travelers, Rose and Mickey soak up the universe's background radiation—the power source for the Ark. When fighting rages between Daleks and Cybermen in the sphere chamber, Mickey is shoved against the Ark and touches it, causing it to activate.

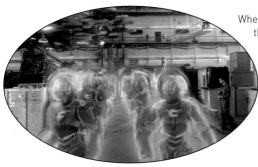

When the Void Ship bursts through the breach in time and space, it is followed by a small army of humanoid, ghostly figures. The "ghosts" are soon revealed to be Cybermen, entering from a parallel world, intent on invading.

The Battle of Canary Wharf, London

As soon as the Void Ship opens, Daleks and Cybermen detect each other's presence. A historic exchange begins as the two rival races, who have never encountered each other before, refuse to identify themselves to the other. Talking leads to fighting: airborne Dalek legions from the Genesis Ark begin a spectacular battle with the parallel-world Cybermen. Leader Dalek Sec orders his airborne forces to exterminate all life forms below in Canary Wharf, but the Dalek supremacy is short-lived. The Doctor opens the breach once more, sucking almost every Dalek and Cyberman back into the Void.

CYBER EAR-PIECE

The Cybermen use cyber ear-pieces to control some of the members of Torchwood. The only way for the link to be destroyed is to disrupt the signal—which proves fatal to the wearers of the ear-pieces.

Neck strap

Transporter disc

Charged metal alloy

The Parallel World Transporter is worn around the neck and can transport only one person at a time safely. It is used by a group of humans from a parallel Earth, who materialize into Torchwood to help in the fight against the emerging Cybermen.

PARALLEL WORLD TRANSPORTER

The Ark releases millions of Daleks over London. The Battle Daleks organize themselves into flying squadrons of 12 or 16.

DALEK SEC

AS LEADER OF THE Cult of Skaro, Dalek Sec is tasked by the Dalek Emperor with finding new ways for Daleks to breed and prosper. Following a failed plan to grow Dalek embryos, the ambitious Sec comes up with a radical idea: purity has led to near extinction for the Daleks, so he decides their biological destiny lies with humans, in what he calls the Final Experiment.

Fanatical Leader

The utterly ruthless Dalek Sec is the Black Dalek leader of the Cult of Skaro, guiding the research of his colleagues. These select Daleks have a strong bond of loyalty to each other, and are driven by the need to extend the Dalek Empire throughout space and time. Under the leadership of Sec, the Cult dedicates its existence to finding new ways to exterminate the Daleks' adversaries, by creatively thinking in "non-Dalek" ways. Like their leader, each Dalek is assigned its own name and personality, in the belief that understanding and mimicking the individuality of many of their enemies will allow them to discover new and more terrifying ways to overcome them.

Dalek is equipped with automatic distress call if casing is breached

Swiveling eye-stalk and rotating dome provide almost spherical field of vision

Forcefield broadcast antennae

Rotating mid-section gives Dalek 360° range of fire

Death ray beam emitter sends out an immense electrical discharge

Sensor globes capable of free flight provide remote battlefield intelligence

Luminosity discharge valve dissipates excess energy from Dalek's cells, through light and sound emission

Sensor grid louvers allow waste heat exhaust

Manipulator arm's telescopic tube and swivel mount provide tremendous reach

"Sucker" tool, made of morphic material, can assume various useful shapes

Dalekanium outer casing is lightweight, yet incredibly strong

CULT OF SKARO FACTS

- The Cult of Skaro consists of four members, led by Dalek Sec. This small number can be strategically useful, but they are too few to be a military threat on their own.

- The Cult is named after the Dalek homeworld Skaro, which was devastated by a supernova generated by the Seventh Doctor. The planet was finally obliterated during the Great Time War.

- In order to "think like the enemy," the Cult Daleks are encouraged to develop their imaginations.

- Unlike ordinary Daleks, Cult members do have some emotions, which mimic those of other life forms. They also have a sense of self-preservation that is not found in Dalek warriors.

- The Cult's existence was kept so secret by the Daleks that even the Doctor thought they were a legend.

Hoverpad base with anti-gravity generators enables Dalek to hover and fly

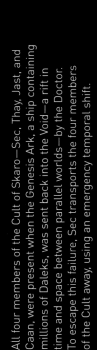

The Cult members escaped the destruction of the Dalek race at the end of the Great Time War by fleeing in a Void Ship with the captured Genesis Ark. Their ship used a spatial disturbance to break through to Earth.

DALEK CAAN

All four members of the Cult of Skaro—Sec, Thay, Jast, and Caan, were present when the Genesis Ark, a ship containing millions of Daleks, was sent back into the Void—a rift in time and space between parallel worlds—by the Doctor. To escape this failure, Sec transports the four members of the Cult away, using an emergency temporal shift.

DALEK JAST

DALEK THAY

CULT OF SKARO

A SECRET ORDER OF Daleks, the Cult of Skaro, consists of four members. Their role is to think like the enemies of the Daleks in order to find new ways of exterminating them. They exist outside the normal Dalek hierarchy, above even the chief Dalek, the Emperor. To emphasize their special status, they even have individual names—Sec, Thay, Jast, and Caan.

In 1930, New York City is in the grip of an economic depression, with mass unemployment and thousands destitute. The Doctor and his companion Martha turn up here soon after the Daleks arrive.

Becoming Human

Dalek Sec is so dedicated that he is willing to experiment upon himself. He becomes the first ever Dalek-human hybrid. The other three members of the Cult of Skaro—Daleks Thay, Jast, and Caan—believe that Daleks should remain pure, but Sec disagrees. He is convinced that a genetic merger with humans will herald the beginning of a new era of Dalek rule.

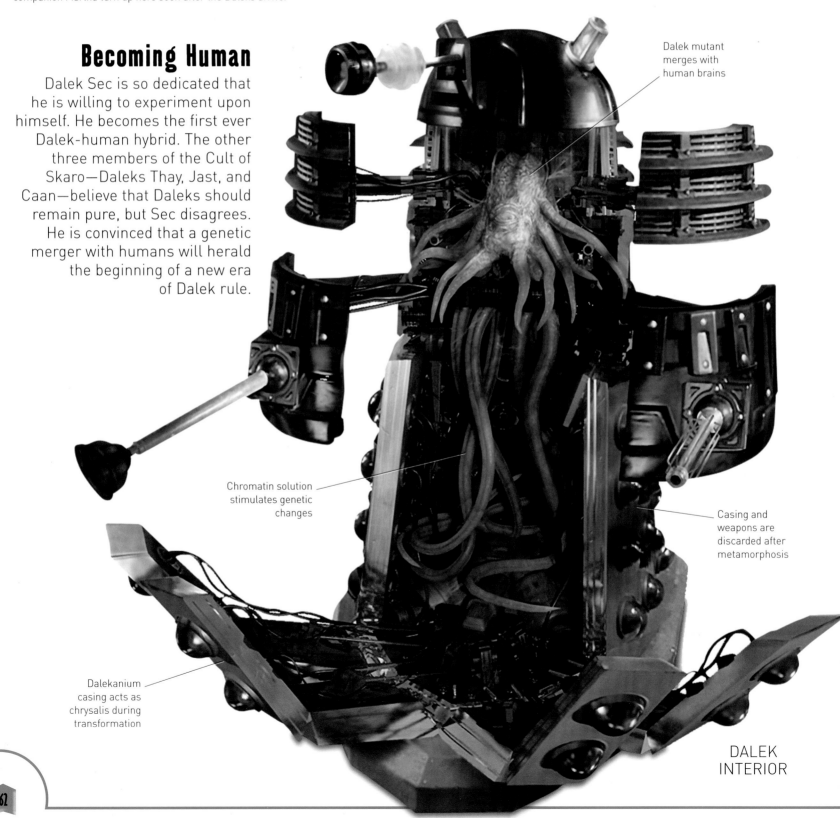

Dalek mutant merges with human brains

Chromatin solution stimulates genetic changes

Casing and weapons are discarded after metamorphosis

Dalekanium casing acts as chrysalis during transformation

DALEK INTERIOR

Energy Converter

Dalek Sec's plan to forge a new Dalek-human race requires a powerful energy source. A huge solar flare is due to pass by Earth, and will provide the necessary Gamma radiation. The Daleks must attract the flare and conduct its energy, so they engineer and build the tallest point in New York—the Empire State Building.

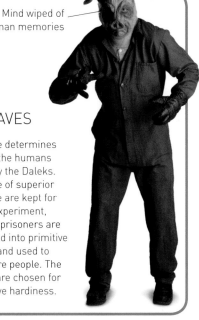

Mind wiped of human memories

PIG SLAVES

Intelligence determines the fate of the humans captured by the Daleks. While those of superior intelligence are kept for the Final Experiment, less clever prisoners are transformed into primitive pig slaves and used to abduct more people. The pig genes are chosen for their relative hardiness.

Dalek-Human Hybrid

Ambition, hatred, aggression, and a genius for war—that is what Dalek Sec thinks being human is all about. When he combines with the ruthless and ambitious Mr. Diagoras, he believes he is getting more of the same. But Sec discovers something unexpected—positive emotions. He decides that Daleks must return to emotions—both positive and negative ones.

Human brain creates emotions

Tentacles from Dalek mutant

Exposed flesh makes hybrid vulnerable

Mr Diagoras's suit is a remnant of a former identity

Hybrid gains dextrous fingers

DALEK SEC– MR. DIAGORAS HYBRID

Hooverville

Solomon, the leader of New York shanty town Hooverville, cares for his fellow outcasts, but when he tries to extend the hand of friendship to the Daleks, he is exterminated. However, his courage inspires Dalek Sec, who feels compassion for the first time.

The purpose of Daleks is to be supreme! Sec's fellow Daleks disagree that their race should renounce their purpose by embracing emotions and becoming humanized. They declare their one-time leader to be an enemy of the Daleks, and he is exterminated while compassionately trying to save the Doctor's life.

Dalek Humans

Human DNA is spliced with Dalek Sec's genetic code, creating a new race. But some Time Lord gets in the mix, and the humanoid Daleks turn from unblinking servitude and begin to question orders. This leads to their extermination, but not before they kill Daleks Thay and Jast.

Dalek Caan

With Daleks Sec, Thay, and Jast all dead, Dalek Caan is the only surviving member of the Cult of Skaro—the last Dalek in the universe. Caan rejects the Doctor's offer of help, operates his emergency temporal shift, and vanishes.

DAVROS'S EMPIRE

MEGALOMANIAC EMPEROR DAVROS has only one ambition—to see a universe ruled by Daleks. Rescued from the Time War, his warped mind believes that co-operation between species is impossible and that ultimately only one race can survive; he is determined that race will be the Daleks. His plans are based on the Daleks annihilating every other being in the universe. This apocalyptic short-cut will make Davros Emperor of an empty infinity.

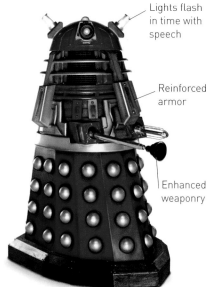

Lights flash in time with speech

Reinforced armor

Enhanced weaponry

The Supreme Dalek

Although Daleks were engineered to have no emotions, the Supreme Dalek is guilty of pride when it believes that the Daleks have finally triumphed over the Doctor. Charged with activating the Reality Bomb, its strength and determination see it retain control as other Daleks falter, but it meets its end thanks to Captain Jack Harkness.

Arm raised in glee at destruction

DAVROS

Bomb Maker

In order to build his empire and destroy all life forms other than the Daleks, crazed Davros creates the Reality Bomb. This fearsome technology cancels out the electrical fields that hold together atoms, obliterating the fabric of reality itself. Davros wants to see the Daleks exterminate their way to victory.

Dalek Caan

The only surviving member of the Cult of Skaro, Dalek Caan went insane when he jumped into the Time War to save Davros. This mind-altering experience brought him the gift of prophecy.

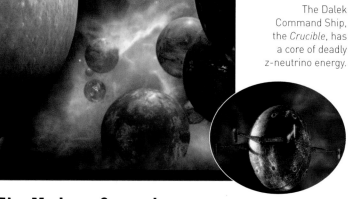

The Dalek Command Ship, the *Crucible*, has a core of deadly z-neutrino energy.

The Medusa Cascade

27 celestial bodies, including Earth, Adipose 3, Pyrovillia, Callufrax Minor, Jahoo, Shallacatop, Woman Wept, Clom, and the Lost Moon of Poosh, vanish from their normal orbits and appear together in the Medusa Cascade. This is not chance, but careful design by Davros. In their new formation, with the Dalek *Crucible* at their center, they function as a transmitter designed to focus the wavelength of the Reality Bomb.

Masters of Earth

Once again, Daleks terrorize the citizens of Earth. This time, however, they set their sights higher than the destruction of the human race: Earth has a role to play as part of the machinery of the Reality Bomb.

The Subwave Network

The Subwave Network is a piece of undetectable sentient software used to seek out and communicate with anyone who can help to contact the Doctor. Sarah Jane Smith uses her computer, Mr. Smith, to connect them all from different places in time and space.

Ex-Prime Minister Harriet Jones feels responsible for Earth's citizens, and sacrifices her life to help contact the Doctor.

The Secret Army

The Subwave Network enables the Doctor to communicate with Captain Jack Harkness, Sarah Jane Smith, and Martha Jones—previous companions of the Doctor, collectively called "the Children of Time" by Davros. Together, they help the Doctor fight the Daleks.

The Mr. Copper Foundation developed the Subwave Network used by Harriet Jones.

Distinctive albino appearance

The Shadow Proclamation

Nearly all species recognize the authority of the Shadow Proclamation, an imposing galactic regulatory body and police force that both sets and enforces laws. Its directives proscribe alien interference with planets and their populations, and govern the rules of parlay between species.

THE ARCHITECT

An elegant, pale humanoid figure, known as the Architect, speaks on behalf of the Shadow Proclamation.

The Judoon are hired as enforcers and bodyguards for doing the Shadow Proclamation's work. The muscle-bound creatures are perfect for situations that require a show of force.

The End of the Daleks

The Doctor is reluctant to take a life, but his half-human, half-Time Lord incarnation has no qualms about destroying the whole Dalek race. This version of the Doctor blasts the Dalekanium power feeds, annihilating the Daleks and their ship, and bringing an end to Davros and his evil plans.

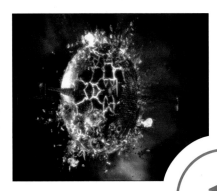

DALEK ASYLUM

IMPRISONED ON A SNOW-CAPPED PLANET deep in space are the most dangerously insane Daleks the universe has never seen—feared even by their own kind. This asylum planet is protected by a forcefield, somehow damaged when a spaceship crash-lands there. Fearing that the abandoned, unhinged Daleks will escape and wreak havoc on their jailers, the Daleks' governing body—the Parliament—resorts to desperate measures and turns to the Doctor for help.

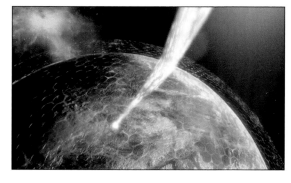

The Parliament ship is equipped with a gravity beam, which is powerful enough to penetrate the asylum planet's forcefield. The Doctor, Amy, and Rory are catapulted by it toward the planet at incredible speed. The beam also cushions their landing to prevent serious injury.

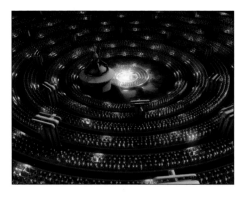

The Dalek Parliament is a huge spaceship protected by a fleet of saucers. Inside the heavily armed vessel are countless ranks of bronze Daleks who are presided over by the Dalek Prime Minister. When they're first brought aboard the ship, the Doctor and his friends are kept in a holding cell directly below the vast hall.

Battle-damaged outer shell

Deranged Daleks

The asylum extends to the core of the planet and is filled with millions of battle-scarred Daleks, surviving in a dormant state. One particular area—the Dalek equivalent of "intensive care"—contains the crazed survivors of wars on planets such as Spiridon, Kembel, Aridius, Vulcan, and Exxilon. In other words, these are the Daleks that survived an encounter with the Doctor himself, and so, are unlikely to look kindly on him.

Unlike its inferiors, the Dalek Prime Minister is housed in a glass casing which allows the Kaled mutant within to be fully visible.

Dalek inside rests in a dormant state

Casing covered in dirt and rust from asylum

OSWIN OSWALD

A young junior entertainment officer named Oswin Oswald is apparently the sole survivor of the spaceship *Alaska* after it crashes into the asylum world. She intrigues the Doctor with her ability to hack into the Dalek's advanced systems. The truth is that Oswin has been fully converted into a Dalek within the asylum, but subconsciously chose to deny it.

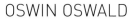

Belt full of high-tech gadgets

In order to capture the Doctor and his friends, the Dalek Parliament uses humanoid slaves who have been conditioned to serve their masters without question. When one of these puppets is activated, a Dalek eyestalk extends from its head, while a powerful gunstick protrudes from the palm of its hand.

Primitive Dalek casing

IRONSIDES

IN WORLD WAR II, the constant bombing of the Blitz pushes Britain to the brink of despair. But Professor Bracewell offers hope: he has invented robots with greater firepower than any other human-made weapon—the Ironsides. Destructive but obedient, they appear to be both the perfect soldier and the perfect servant. However, the Ironsides are truly Daleks plotting an elaborate scheme to ensnare the Doctor.

Positronic brain

PROFESSOR EDWIN BRACEWELL

Scottish scientist Professor Bracewell is extremely proud of his fearsome and loyal Ironsides, whom he believes will stop the war. He is stunned to discover that he didn't make them, and, in fact, they made him. He is simply an android, implanted with false memories of another human's life. The Daleks were using him as part of their plan.

Bracewell is powered by an Oblivion Continuum— a captured wormhole, that, if detonated, would destroy the Earth.

Union flag shows apparent allegiance to Great Britain

Ironsides have kit bags, just like soldiers

Suction cup for fetching files and carrying tea trays

Painted khaki, like soldiers' fatigues

The Perfect Warrior

Everyone except the Doctor thinks that the Ironsides are subservient robots, invented by Professor Bracewell. The deadly fighting machines offer assistance in any way they can to fool the humans— even serving cups of tea—and their deadly firepower is capable of blowing enemy aircraft out of the sky.

Famous "V" for Victory sign

1940s tailoring

Winston Churchill

Although suspicious at first that the Ironsides are too good to be true, Prime Minister Winston Churchill quickly sees the potential of these killing machines, and is eager to harness their power. He uses the Ironsides to exterminate Nazi aircraft, and refuses to listen to the Doctor. Churchill cannot see a downside to Bracewell's obedient robots.

The subservience of the Ironsides doesn't fool the Doctor for a moment. In frustration, he attacks one of them, and repeats his name and their true identity. Finally, the Ironsides reveal the truth: they are Daleks and they have been waiting for this testimony from the Doctor to unleash the next part of their plan.

PARADIGM DALEKS

MILLENNIA AGO, the Daleks seeded the universe with Progenitors, devices carrying Davros's pure Dalek DNA. Their creators lost track of them and the Progenitors became a legend. But in a crippled ship, three Daleks lived on with one of these mythical devices. When the Doctor is tricked into activating it, the resurrection of a shiny new breed of so-called Paradigm Daleks begins.

Restoration of the Daleks

Larger and more powerful than previous Daleks, the new super race of Daleks plans to breed a new army—vaster, deadlier and more cunning than ever. The first five to emerge represent familiar Dalek ranks, but redesigned: the white Supreme Dalek leader, the orange Scientist, the blue battle-planning Strategist, the yellow Eternal, and the red fighter Drone.

Impenetrable casing

THE PROGENITOR

Designed to store pure Dalek DNA, the Progenitor is the key to rebuilding the Dalek race and can be operated only by Daleks. Because the Progenitor does not recognize the impure Daleks, they cannot activate it. Instead, they concoct a plan to use the Doctor's testimony that they are Daleks to unlock the machine and begin the resurrection process.

MAIN CENTRAL CONTROL PANEL

The buttons on the control panel of the Dalek ship carrying the Progenitors are shaped to be operated by Dalek sucker tools.

Larger, reinforced Dalekanium casing houses superior organic creature

Sucker tool is ideally suited to Dalek machinery, but can morph for other needs

A New Race

In order to survive over the millennia, the three Daleks protecting the Progenitors have become contaminated with other DNA and are no longer recognized as pure Dalek. Once they have engineered the new, clean race of Paradigm Daleks, they willingly submit to their extermination—nothing impure is tolerated by this terrible race.

THE SUPREME

THE SCIENTIST

Unlike the eye-stalk of the impure Daleks, behind the eye-stalk of the new true breed is a living, blood-shot organic eye.

Stone Progenitor Dalek

The Paradigm Daleks failed in their attempt to destroy Earth. However, some, including the Supreme, escaped and returned to help trap the Doctor in the Pandorica when all believed the Time Lord was responsible for bringing about the end of time. All-consuming energy leaking through the crack in time and space leaves a stone imprint residue of the Dalek as it ceases to exist. When the Doctor successfully resets the universe, these Daleks are erased from all history, past, and present.

A blast of Alpha Mezon through the eye-stalk is fatal

Weapons still functional as dormant stone Dalek can come alive again

THE STRATEGIST

Improved scanner

Bonded polycarbide in Dalekanium now in bright colors

Red color of Drone commander

THE ETERNAL

THE DRONE

INSIDE A DALEK

ONBOARD THE SPACESHIP *Aristotle* in the Ryzak solar system, a damaged Dalek has been taken prisoner after it was found floating and abandoned in space. The mutant inside has been badly injured—to the extent that it has apparently turned good—and the Doctor agrees to be miniaturized so he can enter the Dalek's casing and give it the urgent medical attention it needs. But while a face-to-face encounter with a Dalek is perilous enough, being inside one is even more dangerous.

Damaged Dalek

Nicknamed Rusty by the Doctor, the injured Dalek has been poisoned by leaking radiation from one of its damaged power cells. The radiation has had the extraordinary effect of expanding the mutant's consciousness, causing it to develop a new sense of morality. However, after the Doctor repairs the damage, he's horrified to discover that the Dalek immediately reverts back to its normal, murderous self, exterminating any perceived enemy in its way— including the soldiers onboard the *Aristotle*.

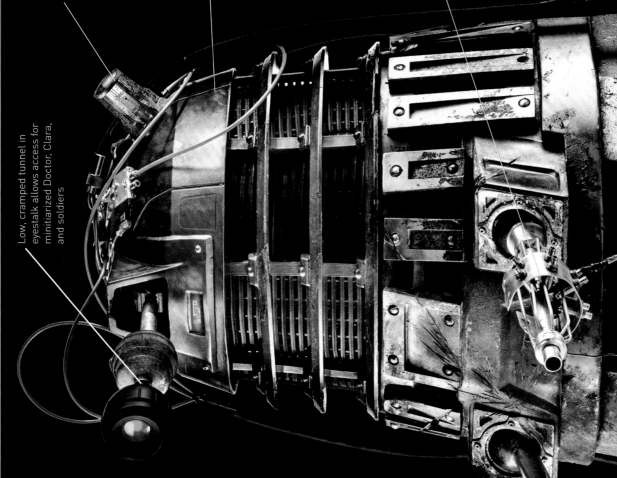

Broken lights lead soldiers to believe Dalek is deactivated and therefore safe to disassemble

Supplementary cortex vault brain keeps Dalek pure and full of hatred

Weapons non functional due to fractured fuel cell

Low, cramped tunnel in eyestalk allows access for miniaturized Doctor, Clara, and soldiers

Damage caused by explosion

RUSTY – FRONT VIEW

Wires put in place to monitor any activity

RUSTY – BACK VIEW

COLONEL MORGAN BLUE

As brave and fiercely determined as his niece, Colonel Morgan Blue is the man in charge of the spaceship *Aristotle* and its Dalek prisoner. When the Dalek goes on its killing spree, the Colonel makes a hard decision and commands Journey to destroy the creature at all costs—even if it means sacrificing his beloved niece in the process.

Insignia of the *Aristotle* spaceship

Flecks of white in beard from many years spent fighting Daleks

Powerful sidearm does not inspire the Doctor's trust

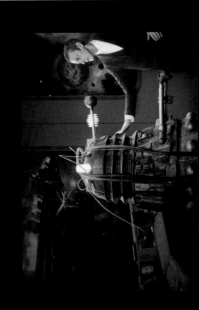

Comms unit functions even when miniaturized

Nano-controller can either maintain or reverse the state of compression

Grenades

LIEUTENANT JOURNEY BLUE

A member of the Combined Galactic Resistance, Journey Blue is a tough young soldier who leads the mission to enter the Dalek casing. Her orders are to help heal the creature's injuries, but when it suddenly starts exterminating every human in sight, Journey changes the objective of the mission, and instead, decides to try to destroy the Dalek from within.

Heavy-duty combat clothing

The Doctor and the Dalek

The Doctor plugs his own mind into the mutant's in a bid to show it the wonder of creation, but the creature instead becomes fascinated by the Doctor's hatred of its species and transforms into a Dalek-killer. The Doctor is left troubled by the fact that there is good in the Daleks—but is there any in himself?

71

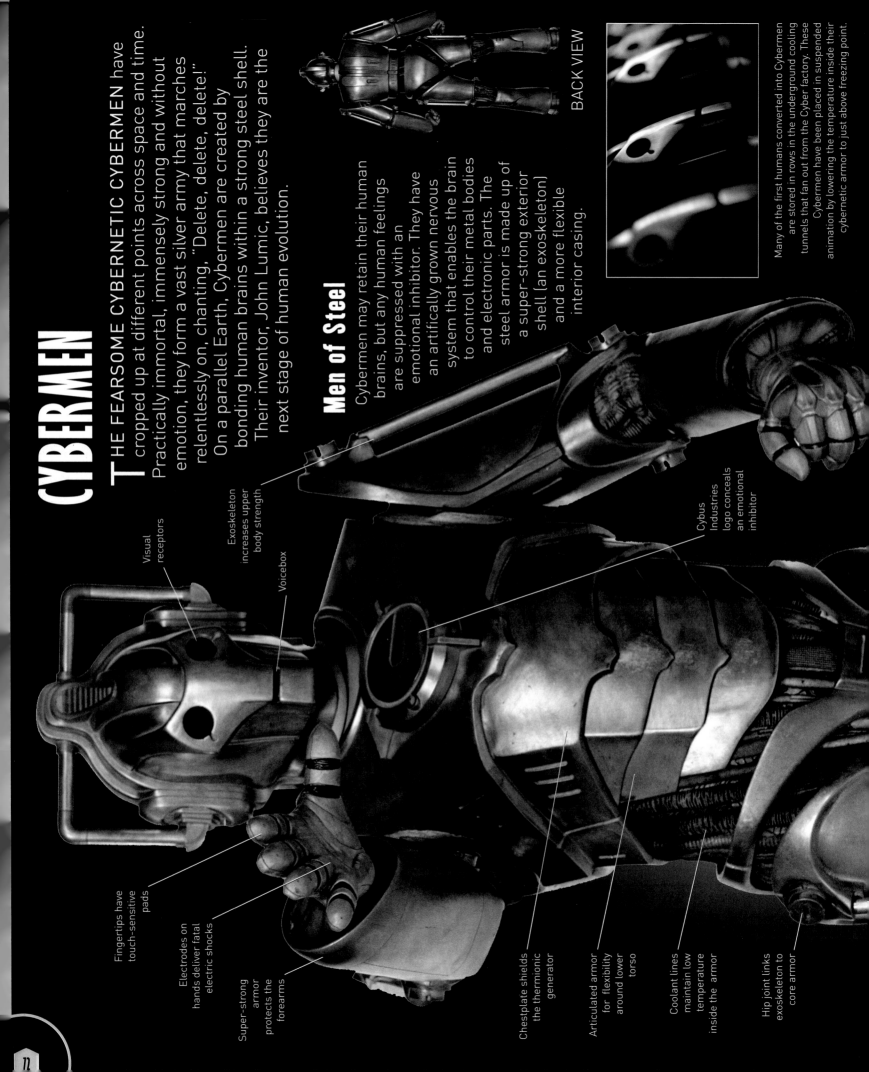

CYBERMEN

THE FEARSOME CYBERNETIC CYBERMEN have
cropped up at different points across space and time.
Practically immortal, immensely strong and without
emotion, they form a vast silver army that marches
relentlessly on, chanting, "Delete, delete, delete!"
On a parallel Earth, Cybermen are created by
bonding human brains within a strong steel shell.
Their inventor, John Lumic, believes they are the
next stage of human evolution.

Men of Steel

Cybermen may retain their human
brains, but any human feelings
are suppressed with an
emotional inhibitor. They have
an artifically grown nervous
system that enables the brain
to control their metal bodies
and electronic parts. The
steel armor is made up of
a super-strong exterior
shell (an exoskeleton)
and a more flexible
interior casing.

BACK VIEW

Many of the first humans converted into Cybermen
are stored in rows in the underground cooling
tunnels that fan out from the Cyber factory. These
Cybermen have been placed in suspended
animation by lowering the temperature inside their
cybernetic armor to just above freezing point.

Visual
receptors

Exoskeleton
increases upper
body strength

Voicebox

Cybus
Industries
logo conceals
an emotional
inhibitor

Fingertips have
touch-sensitive
pads

Electrodes on
hands deliver fatal
electric shocks

Super-strong
armor
protects the
forearms

Chestplate shields
the thermionic
generator

Articulated armor
for flexibility
around lower
torso

Coolant lines
maintain low
temperature
inside the armor

Hip joint links
exoskeleton to
core armor

CYBERMEN FACTS

- A Cyberman's armor is made from an extremely strong manganese-steel alloy.

- All Cybermen's brains are linked to form a single collective consciousness.

- The human brain inside the Cyber-armor is stored at 42.8 degrees Fahrenheit in a patented solution.

- Each individual Cyberman is powered by a thermionic generator.

Weaponry

John Lumic's company, Cybus Industries, has a weapons division that dominates the global arms market. The Cybermen's energy weapons are created in Lumic's Blue Skies laboratory, which specializes in experimental technology. This particle beam gun is capable of delivering a pulse that is deadly to humans.

Each Cyberman's particle beam gun is powered by hydrogen gas and fires beams of deadly electrons. It has an outsized grip to fit a Cyberman's large hands but can also be fitted onto the body at the arm.

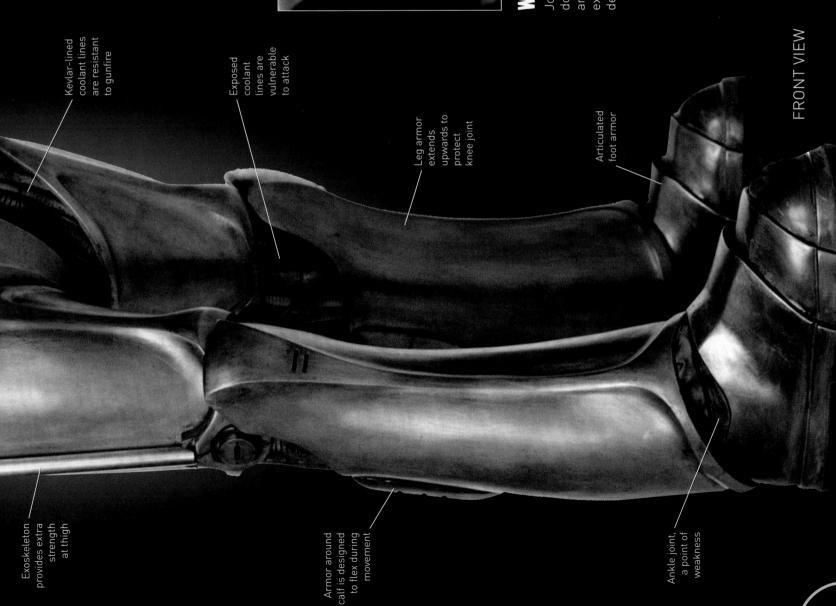

Exoskeleton provides extra strength at thigh

Kevlar-lined coolant lines are resistant to gunfire

Exposed coolant lines are vulnerable to attack

Armor around calf is designed to flex during movement

Leg armor extends upwards to protect knee joint

Articulated foot armor

Ankle joint, a point of weakness

FRONT VIEW

CYBUS INDUSTRIES

A MASSIVE BUSINESS empire called Cybus Industries controls the global media, finance, communications, property, and technology on a parallel Earth. When the TARDIS crashes on this planet, the Doctor and his companions are curious about the huge organization. Its mega-rich but dying leader, John Lumic, has secretly spent years and millions of dollars researching human immortality. His plan is to "upgrade" humanity into a race of immortal Cybermen.

John Lumic

The founder of Cybus Industries is a scientific genius whose inventions have made him the most powerful man on Earth. But he suffers from a terrible wasting disease that has confined him to a wheelchair and will ultimately kill him. Power and the fear of death have turned him into an insane megalomaniac who sees mortality as the ultimate enemy. To him, humanity and individuality are expendable in his narrow-minded search for an end to death.

Air Ship

With crime rampant on the streets of parallel Britain and a night-time curfew in place, Britain's wealthy elite has taken to living in giant air ships floating above London. These zeppelins are manufactured by Cybus Industries, whose leader, John Lumic, has his own luxury model. His ship has a transmitter from which he can send instructions and signals to people's EarPods.

Bow is reinforced to withstand headwinds

EarPod transmitter

Satellite transmitter

Rigid hull, made from a light aluminium alloy

Horizontal fin for stability

Spotlights, used when landing airship in darkness

Bridge at front of gondola

Gondola with accommodation and facilities for passengers and crew

Starboard propeller

Ventral fin

Port propeller for forward thrust

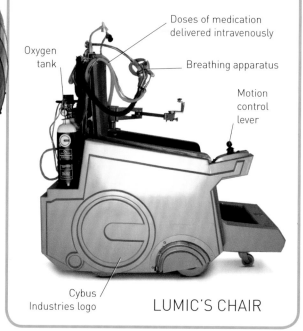

Doses of medication delivered intravenously

Oxygen tank

Breathing apparatus

Motion control lever

Cybus Industries logo

LUMIC'S CHAIR

On this parallel Earth, everyone wears an EarPod. Developed by Cybus Industries, these sophisticated communications devices download news and entertainment directly into the user's brain and exert a form of mind control.

Earpiece shaped like Cybus Industries logo

Microwave antenna

Durable plastic polymer coating

EARPOD

The Cybus Factory

Lumic secretly converts the disused buildings at Battersea Power Station in London into a factory for creating Cybermen. This is just one of many similar factories around the world. As Lumic attempts to perfect his cyber-conversion techniques, many of London's homeless people are abducted and experimented on. Inside the factory, there are hundreds of cylindrical conversion chambers. Each chamber is designed to transform a human into a Cyberman in less than a minute. The factory is capable of converting thousands of people a day into emotionless Cybermen.

The brain is the only part of a human that survives inside a Cyberman. Lumic has to find a way to remove the human brain without killing it. He realizes that speed is vital. With pain receptors in the brain deactivated by EarPods, the powerful cutting gear cuts open the human skull, carves out the brain, and transfers it into its new metal home in seconds. The remaining body is simply incinerated.

A Cyberman's human brain is housed in its steel helmet. Once in place, the brain is flooded with a chilled protein solution that preserves and nurtures it, eliminating cellular decay.

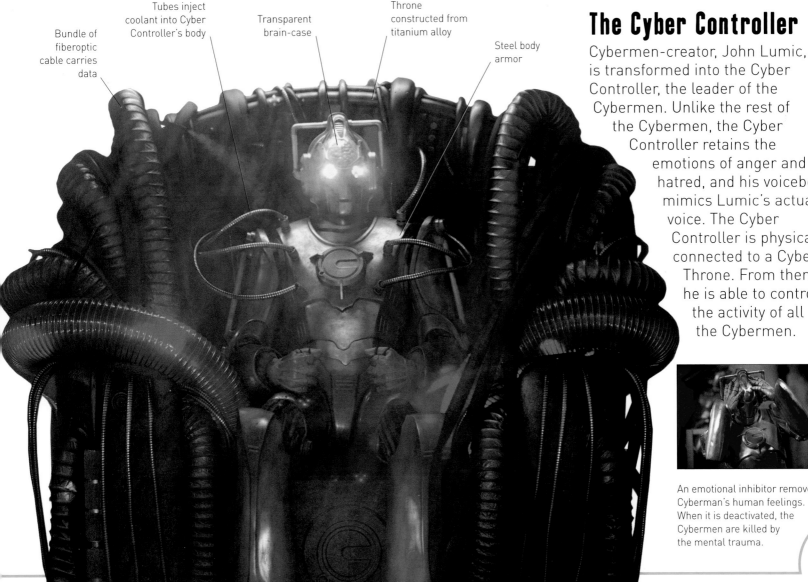

Bundle of fiberoptic cable carries data

Tubes inject coolant into Cyber Controller's body

Transparent brain-case

Throne constructed from titanium alloy

Steel body armor

The Cyber Controller

Cybermen-creator, John Lumic, is transformed into the Cyber Controller, the leader of the Cybermen. Unlike the rest of the Cybermen, the Cyber Controller retains the emotions of anger and hatred, and his voicebox mimics Lumic's actual voice. The Cyber Controller is physically connected to a Cyber Throne. From there, he is able to control the activity of all the Cybermen.

An emotional inhibitor removes a Cyberman's human feelings. When it is deactivated, the Cybermen are killed by the mental trauma.

THE CYBERKING

W**HEN THE CYBERMEN** were sucked into the Void during the Battle of Canary Wharf, the Doctor thought he had seen the end of them. But a few survived and broke back into the world, using a time-traveling Dimension Vault stolen from the Daleks. They arrived in London in December 1851 and set about creating the CyberKing—a giant battleship to lead their invasion of Earth and the conversion of the human population into Cybermen.

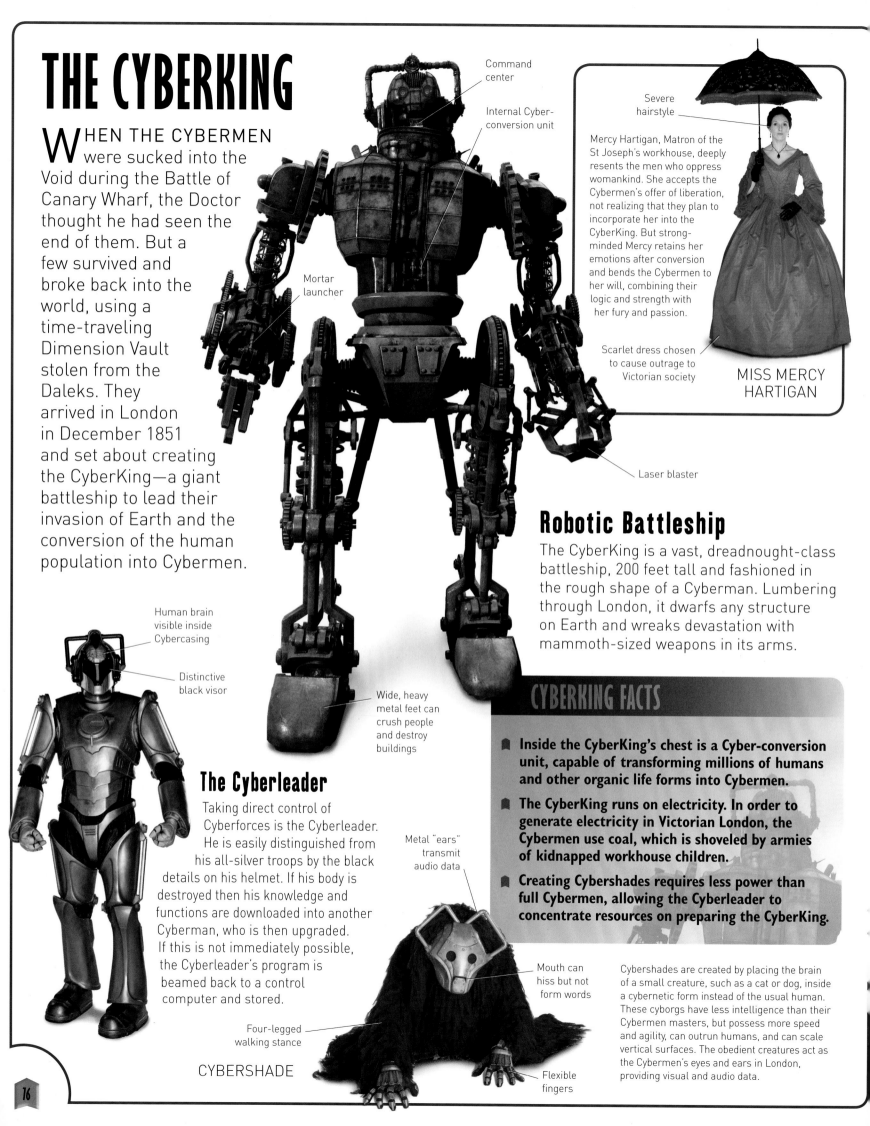

Command center

Internal Cyber-conversion unit

Mortar launcher

Laser blaster

Severe hairstyle

Mercy Hartigan, Matron of the St Joseph's workhouse, deeply resents the men who oppress womankind. She accepts the Cybermen's offer of liberation, not realizing that they plan to incorporate her into the CyberKing. But strong-minded Mercy retains her emotions after conversion and bends the Cybermen to her will, combining their logic and strength with her fury and passion.

Scarlet dress chosen to cause outrage to Victorian society

MISS MERCY HARTIGAN

Robotic Battleship

The CyberKing is a vast, dreadnought-class battleship, 200 feet tall and fashioned in the rough shape of a Cyberman. Lumbering through London, it dwarfs any structure on Earth and wreaks devastation with mammoth-sized weapons in its arms.

Human brain visible inside Cybercasing

Distinctive black visor

Wide, heavy metal feet can crush people and destroy buildings

CYBERKING FACTS

■ Inside the CyberKing's chest is a Cyber-conversion unit, capable of transforming millions of humans and other organic life forms into Cybermen.

■ The CyberKing runs on electricity. In order to generate electricity in Victorian London, the Cybermen use coal, which is shoveled by armies of kidnapped workhouse children.

■ Creating Cybershades requires less power than full Cybermen, allowing the Cyberleader to concentrate resources on preparing the CyberKing.

The Cyberleader

Taking direct control of Cyberforces is the Cyberleader. He is easily distinguished from his all-silver troops by the black details on his helmet. If his body is destroyed then his knowledge and functions are downloaded into another Cyberman, who is then upgraded. If this is not immediately possible, the Cyberleader's program is beamed back to a control computer and stored.

Metal "ears" transmit audio data

Mouth can hiss but not form words

Cybershades are created by placing the brain of a small creature, such as a cat or dog, inside a cybernetic form instead of the usual human. These cyborgs have less intelligence than their Cybermen masters, but possess more speed and agility, can outrun humans, and can scale vertical surfaces. The obedient creatures act as the Cybermen's eyes and ears in London, providing visual and audio data.

Four-legged walking stance

CYBERSHADE

Flexible fingers

HEDGEWICK'S WORLD

ONCE THE BIGGEST amusement park in the universe, Hedgewick's World has become an abandoned ruin. However, an army of Cybermen are entombed there, awaiting the arrival of a suitable life form to convert into a new Cyber-Planner. When the Doctor visits the planet, the cyborgs believe he will help make the next version of the Cybermen completely unbeatable.

Head swivels 360°

Blaster built into arm

Hand can detach to mount its own attack

The Cyberiad

This new breed of Cybermen is controlled by a Cyberiad: a collective consciousness that allows their Cyber-Planners to control any individual Cyberman. This hive mind also enables all of the Cybermen to pool their processing power to solve a problem, and can distribute software patches to upgrade individual cyber units—to be resistant to electrocution, for example.

During the Cyber-Wars between humanity and the Cyberiad, the Cybermen built a bunker on Hedgewick's World. They then repaired critically damaged units there, using the visitors to the amusement park as spare parts.

Cybernetic parts grow to cover face

Eccentrically patterned waistcoat

Webley is the eccentric owner of Webley's World of Wonders—a collection of strange alien artifacts, including many alien waxworks. Having become trapped on Hedgewick's World, he is keen to leave, but ends up being partially converted into a Cyberman.

WEBLEY

The Cybermites attempt to convert the Doctor into a Cyber-Planner, but the process ends up giving him a split personality. Both the Doctor and his ruthless alter-ego, Mr. Clever, decide to play a game of chess, agreeing that the winner will gain total control of the Doctor's mind.

Combat clothing disguises true identity

Emperor Ludens Nimrod Kendrick, also called Longstaff 41st, escapes to Hedgewick's World to hide from the pressure he faces as the defender of humanity. Known simply as Porridge, his real identity is eventually revealed, and he must face the responsibilities that come with his august positon—including deciding to activate a bomb to destroy the three million Cybermen, along with the entire planet of Hedgewick's World.

CYBERMITE

The Cybermen once programmed miniature metallic Cybermats to carry out certain tasks, such as spreading plague or draining enemies' energy supplies. On Hedgewick's World, however, they use swarms of much smaller cybernetic insects called Cybermites which can partially convert people into Cybermen and also upgrade themselves.

CYBERMAT

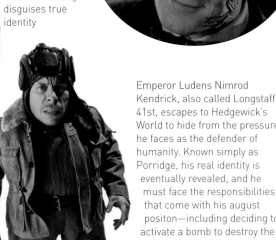

PORRIDGE

WEEPING ANGELS

WEEPING ANGELS ARE ALMOST as old as the universe itself. They feed off potential energy by sending people into the past. Confined to history, their victims live out their lives. In the present their victims are dead, and the Angels feast on the days they might have had there. The deadly Angels are quantum-locked— they are free to move when no one can see them—and, so, they can easily go by entirely unnoticed.

A touch from an Angel's hand is perilous

Placid pose, with eyes, fangs, and teeth hidden

Angelic appearance frequently found in graveyards

Alien Assassins

The moment a Weeping Angel is seen, it turns into harmless stone. In this observed state, the Angels are harmless, but if their victim so much as blinks, the Angels are set free to attack. The Angels move incredibly fast—they can cross a room in the blink of an eye, and that's only about 250 milliseconds!

Sally Sparrow

When photographer Sally Sparrow breaks into the creepy old house Wester Drumlins to take some atmospheric pictures, she discovers the Weeping Angels. Many people have disappeared near the house, having fallen prey to the Angels. One of their victims is the Doctor, stranded in 1969 with his companion Martha Jones.

Sally peels back the wallpaper in the house to reveal a message from the Doctor—addressed to her! She's alarmed, but it takes more messages before she is ready to believe that someone is speaking to her from the past.

KATHY'S LETTER

Sally Sparrow

When the Angels zap Sally's best friend, Kathy, back to 1920, she finds a new life in Hull. But before Kathy dies in 1987, she makes her grandson Malcolm promise to deliver a letter to Sally in 2007, explaining her disappearance.

With the help of Kathy's brother Larry, Sally compiles a folder of information for the Doctor. This completes the link so that, in his future, he will be able to communicate with her from the past.

Parts scavenged from 1960s machines

IMPROVISED TIMEY-WIMEY DETECTOR

The Doctor's homemade Detector can find the Angels' victims by tracking disturbances in time. Designed to go "ding" when it detects anomalies, it also unintentionally boils any egg within 30 paces.

Tricking the Angels

The potential energy of the TARDIS could feed the Angels forever, but the power released would be enough to destroy the sun. As the creatures from Wester Drumlins surround the TARDIS, hoping to access this energy, it dematerializes, leaving them staring at each other. Constantly observed, this group of Angels will remain stone forever.

Cherub Angels

The Weeping Angels are constantly adapting. A collection of seemingly innocent Cherub Angels in Julius Grayle's basement are actually baby Weeping Angels—as malicious and hungry as their older, fully-fledged relatives.

In Winter Quay in 1930s New York, some Weeping Angels manage to source enough power to take over the biggest statue around—the Statue of Liberty. Snarling and hungry for time energy, this super army of Angels can be defeated only by creating a paradox in time that wipes them all from existence.

Angel Collector Grayle

Crime boss Grayle is a serial collector of unusual artifacts that he keeps locked up in the museum in his house in Manhattan. Primary amongst his curiosities are the moving statues he has discovered and deems to be most valuable. He even hires a private investigator to find more of them and source further information.

Grayle summons Angel-expert River Song to provide more insight into his captured creature. Despite its being shackled, it is still not safe for River to get too close. The Angel reaches out a hand and grasps her arm so tight that River must break her wrist in order to escape.

Greedy expression

1930s gangster-style pinstripe suit

JULIUS GRAYLE

Arm was bound by manacles in Grayle's house

Mouth open wide in silent scream of pain and terror

MUSEUM ANGEL

The prize of Grayle's collection is a Weeping Angel that he keeps chained and hidden behind a curtain in his house. To learn more about these creatures that appear everywhere without anybody noticing, Grayle has the Angel tortured to discover whether it can feel pain. Upon looking at its face, River Song diagnoses that it is calling out in distress to its fellow Angels in New York City.

Body bears scars as lasting sign of torture

ARMY OF ANGELS

The *Byzantium*, a Galaxy-class starship, can travel for years without stopping to refuel. When a lone Weeping Angel, pulled from the ruins of Razbahan, is transported in the ship's hold, it induces a phase shift in the warp engines. The ship crashes into a site full of hundreds of Angels, all waiting to feast on the ship's massive fuel reserves.

WEEPING ANGELS are the most malevolent and deadly life form ever produced by evolution. These quantum-locked, stone killers feed off the potential life-energy of any being that crosses their path. When the *Byzantium* spacecraft crashes in the 51st century, the Doctor meets a powerful new breed, reenergized by feasting on temporal energy and the radiation escaping from the damaged ship's drives. They have been patiently waiting in hiding to form themselves into a formidable army.

Amy and the Doctor are summoned to the wreck of the *Byzantium* to help Second Class Bishop Father Octavian and his army of Clerics defeat the newly empowered Angels.

New Super Breed

At the site of the crashed *Byzantium*, there is a crack in the universe, just like the one in Amy Pond's bedroom. It is spilling out temporal energy that the revitalizing Angels there plan to feed on. They think consuming it will give them dominion over all time and space. They do not realise that the power is so strong, it will destroy them and wipe them from from having ever existed.

Serene face masks violent intentions

Angel can control the *Byzantium's* systems telepathically

Aplan Mortarium

The crash site of the *Byzantium* is actually an Aplan Mortarium or "Maze of the Dead"—a network of catacombs. It stands on Alfava Metraxis, the home planet of the Aplan race, who were wiped out by the Angels in the 47th century. Under the high-vaulted ceilings are broken statues that are actually starving Angels, desperate to be fed.

51st Century Church

Three thousand years in the future, the Church has become a military unit. Under Father Octavian, twenty armed Clerics are assigned to protect the Doctor and fight the Angels. They are all killed by Angels or by temporal energy spilling out of the crack in the Aplan Mortarium.

The Angels take over the *Byzantium's* systems, trapping those inside. The Doctor's sonic screwdriver cannot override the Angels' signals, and the Clerics' guns are no use.

Camouflage worn instead of Bishop's robes

FATHER OCTAVIAN

Blank page without pictures, because an Angel's image is just as deadly as an Angel itself

Scrawled handwriting, as if written in a frantic hurry

Text carries stark warnings

THE BOOK OF ANGELS

This ancient book is the definitive work and only known book on the Angels, written by a man called Rastan Jovanich. How he knew so much about the Angels is unknown, but possession of that knowledge drove him mad. The book is handed to the Doctor at the *Byzantium* crash site. He keeps it and later stores it in the TARDIS.

Eyes are covered to prevent Angel from immobilizing itself by looking at another Angel

Worn-down stone and dull coloring shows Angel has not eaten for centuries

ERODED ANGEL

When weakened by hunger, Angels wear away, so that they look just as an ancient statue would. This starving Angel has lost most of its original form, including its wings.

When a person looks at something, it creates a mental image in their brain. In this way, an Angel enters through Amy's eyes and establishes itself inside her mind.

Fatal Footage

As anything that holds the image of an Angel will become an Angel itself, the three-second loop of security footage of the Angel in the hold is deadly. Amy freezes the recording on a blip at the end of the loop to render the Angel powerless.

The cruel and mischievous Angels enjoy taunting the Doctor, playing with his guilt over Cleric Bob, a member of the Church that they remorselessly killed. The Angels revel in telling the Doctor that Bob died in fear, after the Doctor had promised Bob that he would be safe.

APLAN MORTARIUM ANGEL FACTS

- **Weeping Angels can be very patient for centuries. It doesn't mean that they are dormant.**

- **Rather than just displacing people in time like some Angels, the breed at the *Byzantium* crash site is more violent. They break humans' necks.**

- **Angels can strip the cerebral cortex from a person and reanimate a version of his or her consciousness, in order to communicate with their voice.**

- **As well as killing for the fun of it, Angels enjoy playing with people's emotions, inciting extra fear, anger, or guilt.**

THE GREAT INTELLIGENCE

THE GREAT INTELLIGENCE is an evil entity with no physical form. In its endless quest to find a physical existence for itself, it attempts to possess the bodies of other beings. During one such attempt, the Intelligence takes over carnivorous alien snow that can mimic and mirror whatever it finds. When the snow succeeds in creating an ice replica of a human being, the Intelligence believes it now has the blueprint for an army that will wipe out humanity.

Victorian top hat

Face devoid of emotion

Walking stick wielded as status symbol

Snow Globe

Awaiting the chance to find a physical form, the Great Intelligence inhabits a large glass globe. It is filled with samples of parasitic snow, through which the Intelligence gathers information about humanity.

Doctor Simeon

As a solitary young boy who preferred his own company to that of other children, Walter Simeon met a talking snowman, unaware that it was made of parasitic snow that fed on his fear and loneliness. Many years later, Simeon has become a cold-hearted doctor and a servant of the Great Intelligence. He sets up a company called the GI Institute as a front for the entity's plan to conquer humanity.

After scanning the DNA of a governess who died in a tragic accident, the Great Intelligence's alien snow produces a perfect ice version of her body. The ice governess then comes to life and goes on the rampage.

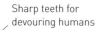

Sharp teeth for devouring humans

CARNIVOROUS SNOWMAN

The Great Intelligence creates flesh-eating snowmen from living snow. These savage foot soldiers will help it take over the world. Living snow is not frozen water, but is formed from multinucleate, crystalline organisms, which can assume the shape of a snowman within seconds. It also retains a reflection of the thoughts and memories of the people it consumes.

Memory worms are fat alien insects that can wipe a person's memories by touch or biting. When one bites Simeon, his head is rendered empty, leaving it fully vulnerable to possession by the Great Intelligence.

Brooch with bold design

MISS KIZLET

Enslaved by the Great Intelligence at a young age, Miss Kizlet has served her master throughout adulthood. Under its command, she is head of a company that is using wi-fi to upload people's souls to the Internet. The Intelligence then feasts on their minds, growing more powerful in the process.

Professional 20th-century office clothes

Spoonheads

More formally known as Servers, the Spoonheads are robotic wi-fi base stations. A beam that can absorb the minds and souls of humans shoots out from the back of each robot's spoon-shaped head.

Although a Spoonhead's true appearance is crude and basic, it can disguise itself as a human being by using an image from the subconscious mind of the person it is about to attack. The Doctor is able to hack into this system and create a Spoonhead version of himself, which he then uses to infiltrate Miss Kizlet's computer.

Featureless face

Mouth opens wide to utter Great Intelligence's messages

On the 65th floor of the Shard building in London, Miss Kizlet has a wall of screens showing all the people who have been captured and uploaded to the Internet. Each terrified victim repeats the same words over and over: "I don't know where I am."

Miss Kizlet's sophisticated tablet can control the minds of her employees. By moving a slider on the screen, she can make someone more paranoid or more obedient. She can even alter the level of their IQ. In the form of Walter Simeon, the Great Intelligence also uses this technology to communicate with and give instructions to Miss Kizlet.

The Great Intelligence can inhabit any of its Whisper Men at will. When it takes over one of these faceless slaves, the Whisper Man's features quickly morph into those of Doctor Simeon once more—whose form the Great Intelligence continues to use to communicate with others.

Funeral clothing echoes outfit worn by Doctor Simeon

Whisper Men

The Whisper Men are the snarling, blank-faced servants of the Great Intelligence. They get their name from the ominous whispered messages of doom that they bring. Lacking a truly physical form, they are almost ghost-like—their bodies can easily reform when attacked and they can pass their limbs through living beings.

On the planet Trenzalore, the Great Intelligence enters the Doctor's time stream, intending to turn all his victories into defeats in order to kill him. However, its plan is foiled when Clara jumps into the time stream, repairing the damage to history and saving the Doctor.

THE OOD

A HUMANOID HERD SPECIES with squid-like tentacles, the Ood live in telepathic harmony on their snowy planet, the Ood-Sphere. Contrary to popular belief, their kind is not naturally subservient. However, their peaceful existence and their connection to a central hive mind has left them vulnerable to enslavement—under the possession of the Beast on Krop Tor and even at the hands of humans.

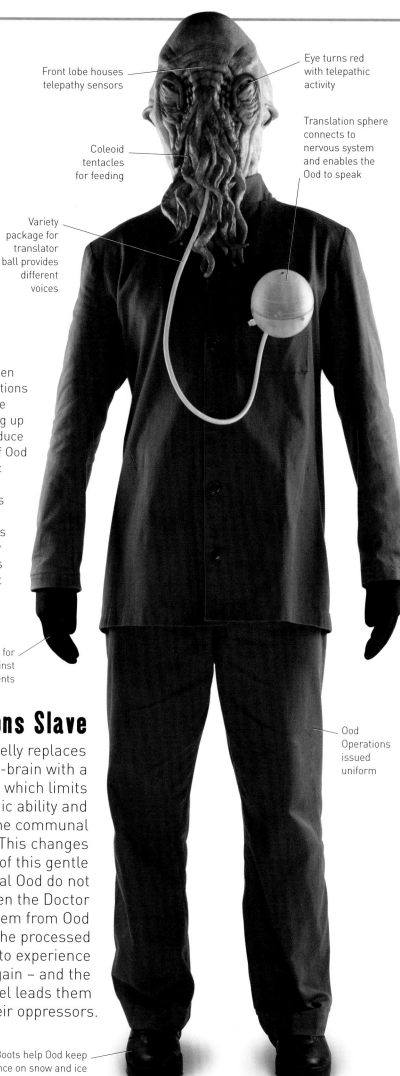

Front lobe houses telepathy sensors

Eye turns red with telepathic activity

Coleoid tentacles for feeding

Translation sphere connects to nervous system and enables the Ood to speak

Variety package for translator ball provides different voices

Gloves worn for protection against machine solvents

Ood Operations issued uniform

Boots help Ood keep balance on snow and ice

Ood Operations

The entrepreneurial Halpen family creates Ood Operations to sell Ood throughout the Human Empire. By setting up breeding farms, they produce hundreds of thousands of Ood servants for the domestic and military markets. The company lobotomizes the Ood into servitude. By the 42nd century, it has convinced all of humanity that the Ood's only goal is to receive orders and that they would die without tasks to perform.

NATURAL OOD

In their natural state, Ood have two brains. They mainly use the brain in their head, but memory and emotions are processed by the hind-brain, which is held in the peaceful Ood's hands.

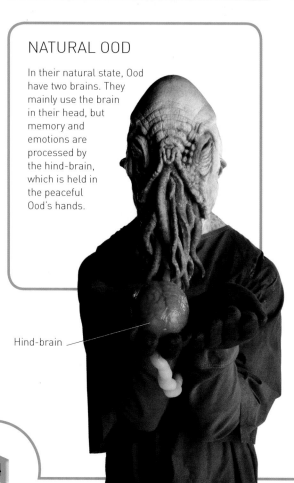

Hind-brain

Ood Operations Slave

Ood Operations cruelly replaces the Ood hind-brain with a translation sphere, which limits the Ood's telepathic ability and cuts it off from the communal Center Brain. This changes the very nature of this gentle species. Natural Ood do not kill. But when the Doctor helps to free them from Ood Operations, the processed Ood begin to experience emotions again – and the anger they feel leads them to destroy their oppressors.

Mr. Halpen

Ruthless Ood Operations CEO Mr. Halpen is prepared to go to any lengths in order to protect his reputation. When things start to go wrong, he is ready to wipe out every captive Ood in the Ood Operations' factory complex.

The Center Brain

The telepathic Center Brain connected the Ood in beautiful song for millennia, until Halpen's ancestors discover it beneath the Ood-Sphere's Northern Glacier. Ood Operations keeps it locked up in captivity for 200 years.

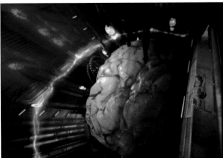

Single-dose cup for "tonic"

OOD SIGMA'S OOD OPERATIONS BELT

Ood Sigma is Halpen's personal servant. The belt is symbolic of a trusted executive slave status.

Supply of Ood-graft hair "tonic" administered to balding CEO Halpen

OOD FACTS

- There appear to be no male or female Ood, which suggests the species may be hermaphrodite.

- The Ood have no personal names, but are given designations according to their functions, such as "Server Gamma 10."

- The Ood communicate through a low telepathic field rated as Basic 5. Basic 30 is the equivalent of screaming, and Basic 100 would result in brain death.

- The Ood sing an endless song. When they are freed, the song goes out through the galaxies, calling all of Oodkind home.

- The Eleventh Doctor rescues a lone Ood and intends to return him to the Ood-sphere. He temporarily leaves him with Amy and Rory, where he acts as their Ood butler.

Patchwork People

A motley crew of humanoids, including a lost Ood, live on the malevolent, sentient asteroid House—all existing off of the energy it provides. The asteroid itself is a junkyard for old TARDISes that have fallen through a rift in time and space. The so-called "Patchwork People" are servants to House. To prolong their servitude, their body parts are renewed with bits of dead Time Lords.

IDRIS

Idris is a reluctant inhabitant of House, and she is the only Patchwork Person to not be renewed with foreign body parts. She becomes consumed with the matrix of the Doctor's TARDIS when he is lured to House, and she helps him to escape.

UNCLE

The darkly sarcastic humanoid named Uncle helps lure more Time Lords to House. His borrowed eyes are thirty years younger than the rest of him.

Loose fabric hides alien right ear

Original body parts

AUNTIE

Uncle and Auntie work as a pair. Both dependent on House for their existence, they die when he dies. Auntie goes first, followed swiftly by Uncle.

Arm originally belonged to a famous Time Lord

NEPHEW

The Ood known as Nephew becomes enslaved by House and develops the ability to drain minds and souls. The Doctor is unable to return him to his natural Ood state.

Translation sphere linked to House

PLATFORM ONE

THE LUXURY SPACE STATION *Platform One* cruises through space between stars. When Rose chooses the future for her first trip in the TARDIS, the Doctor shows off his time-traveling skills by taking her to the year 5.5/Apple/26, five billion years in the future. They arrive on *Platform One* half an hour before the Sun is due to engulf the Earth. They join the galaxy's rich and elite, who have assembled to witness the planet's demise.

Guest list

Guests' names

Touch-sensitive screen

SPACE PANEL

This electronic device is used by the Steward to check the guest list for the Earth event. It connects with *Platform One's* mainframe computer system, authenticating the guests' identification details.

Luxury Viewing Platform

Guests can be assured that they will be able to watch the natural phenonemon of the Earth dying in safety and comfort. A force field and solar filters protect *Platform One* from the extreme heat of the Sun, while air conditioning on the space station regulates the temperature inside. All the systems are automatic, run by a huge fan-cooled computer mainframe.

Solar filters prevent the Sun from burning up everyone inside

Maintenance girders

Exo-glass in the viewscreens is capable of self-repair.

Disk-shaped hub houses the marble-lined Greeting Hall and other formal rooms

Communications sensors

The Sun had been threatening to swallow the Earth for years, but the planet was saved by the UK's National Trust. It used gravity satellites to stop the Sun's expansion and restored the planet to its former glory. But when the Trust's money ran out, the Earth was evacuated and left to die. From *Platform One*, Rose's first view of Earth from space is of a dying world.

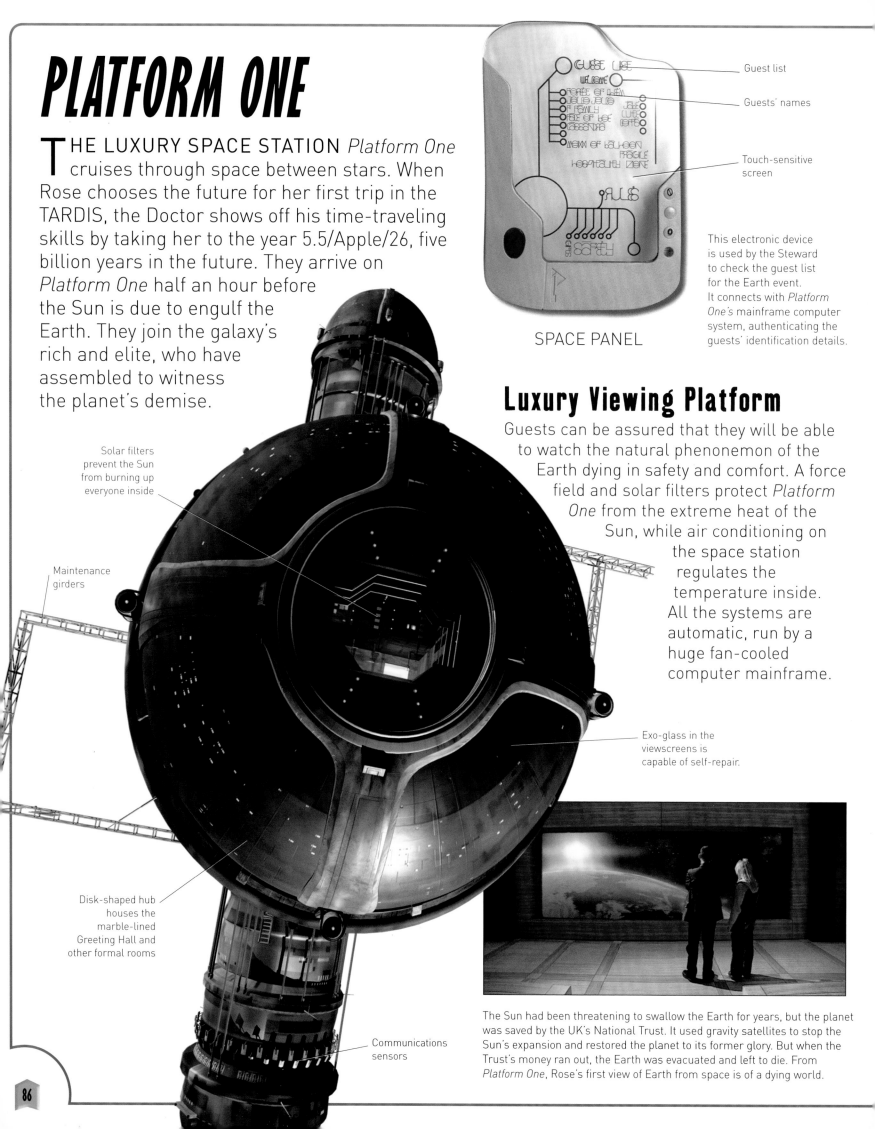

Blue skin

Formal robe of welcome

Swept up "bird's nest hairstyle" is adorned with leaves

Luxurious robe with a jewel-encrusted collar is sign of Jabe's high status

Ceremonial armor of lacquered paper

The Trees from the Forest of Cheem are an arboreal species descended from the tropical rainforests on Earth. They are highly intelligent and have deep respect for all life forms. As the owners of vast amounts of land and forests on many planets, they have great wealth and influence.

Official robes, made of woven paper and gold thread

JABE

A seven-foot-tall alien, Jabe is the leader of the Trees, visitors from the Forest of Cheem. This noble, woody creature has a scanning device that reveals the Doctor's true identity, and she sympathizes with his plight as the last Time Lord.

COFFA AND LUTE, JABE'S COMPANIONS

Elaborate, flowing dress hides lianas—retractable, vine-like appendages

Helmet and visor for protection

Guard's uniform

THE STEWARD

As the manager of *Platform One*, the Steward, a blue-skinned humanoid, has many duties, including acting as host, greeting, and announcing visitors. At first, he thinks that the Doctor and Rose are intruders, but the Doctor uses his psychic paper to convince him that he has an invitation. Obedient to the rules, and very dedicated to his job, the Steward fastidiously orders that the TARDIS be towed away for illegal teleportation and issues the Doctor with a ticket to reclaim it later.

PLATFORM ONE FACTS

- *Platform One* is owned by a vast intergalactic corporation, and the galaxy's elite pay to watch artistic events on the luxury space station.

- Teleportation, religion and all forms of weapons are forbidden on *Platform One*.

During Earth's final moments, *Platform One*'s shields are damaged and the guests are too concerned about saving their own skins to watch the event they came to see.

Thousands of blue-skinned humanoid aliens work as guards on *Platform One*. One of them, a plumber called Raffalo, tells Rose that she is from Crespallion, which is part of the Jaggit Brocade, affiliated to the Scarlet Junction, in the Convex 56. This makes Rose realize how far away from home she is.

PLATFORM GUARD

GUESTS OF *PLATFORM ONE*

WATCHING THE DESTRUCTION of Earth from the *Platform One* observation station is a strictly invitation-only event, reserved for the galaxy's wealthy elite. The honored guests, from many worlds and a variety of races and species, have all come to pay their final respects to Earth—and to network with the universe's most influential beings.

Chain of rank

THE ADHERENTS OF THE REPEATED MEME

The faceless, black-robed Adherents are greeted as guests on *Platform One*. But they are really remotely operated droids controlled by Lady Cassandra. Their gifts of metal spheres contain sabotaging robot spiders.

Vision sensor

Tough metal exoskeleton

ROBOT SPIDER

The "spiders" are programmed to sabotage the *Platform One* computer, lift the sun filters, and destroy the space station. They come scuttling out of metal spheres passing as gifts from the Adherents.

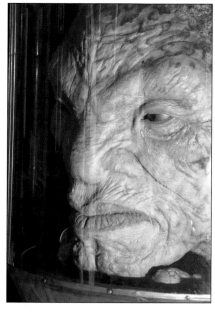

THE FACE OF BOE

The sponsor of the *Platform One* event is a huge humanoid head called the Face of Boe. He is the last of Boekind and, at millions of years old, the oldest being in the Isop galaxy. Boe's head is kept in a huge jar, and instead of hair, he has tendrils that end in small pods. This influential alien is one of the few survivors when *Platform One* is almost destroyed as planet Earth explodes.

Thick, leathery reptile skin

Heavy fur cloaks

Large four-fingered hands with sharp nails

THE BROTHERS HOP PYLEEN

These two wealthy lizard brothers are from the clifftops of Rex Vox. The pair made their fortune by inventing Hyposlip Travel Systems. They favour fur clothes, which keep their cold-blooded bodies warm.

THE AMBASSADORS OF THE CITY-STATE OF BINDING LIGHT

Oxygen levels must be monitored strictly at all times in these Ambassadors' presence, due to their race's sensitivity to the gas.

CAL "SPARKPLUG" AND GUEST

The cybernetic superstar Cal "Sparkplug" MacNannovich arrives with his "plus-one."

Face mask provides a special mix of air

Huge feathered head

MR. AND MRS. PAKOO

These bird-like creatures may be husband and wife, but it is impossible to tell who is who. The pair have huge eyes and vicious-looking beaks. Their feathered heads give away their avian origins, although they walk like humans.

Anti-gravity chair powered by servo-motor

THE MOXX OF BALHOON

This goblin-like creature's legs are crippled by disease. He travels around on a speedy anti-gravity chair. This device replaces his bodily fluids every 20 minutes because otherwise he sweats dangerous glaxic acid. The Moxx greets visitors with formal spitting.

LADY CASSANDRA

THE LAST "PURE" HUMAN, Lady Cassandra O'Brien Dot Delta Seventeen, is the only human that hasn't interbred with other species. Being incredibly beautiful in the past, Cassandra was adored by everyone. Now, her desire to keep thin and wrinkle-free means that she is prepared to murder the guests on *Platform One* and cash in on the insurance money to pay for more plastic surgery.

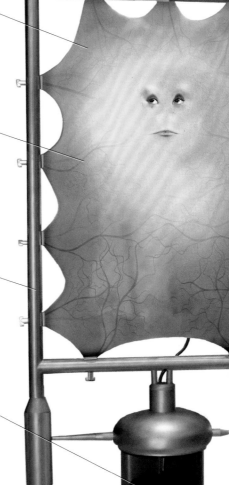

Lipstick and skin are all that are left of Cassandra's body

Skin would disintegrate without constant moisturization

Metal frame connects nerve fibers to Cassandra's brain

Brain kept in a jar of preserving solution

Cassandra gives this rare ostrich egg to the Steward. It actually contains a teleportation field that Cassandra uses to escape from *Platform One* as her plan to blow up the satellite is put into action.

Egg of extinct fire-breathing ostrich

CASSANDRA'S "GIFT"

Skin Deep

After 708 plastic surgery operations, Cassandra is finally as thin as she always wanted to be. Reduced to a translucent piece of skin with eyes and a mouth, stretched across a frame, she is still obsessed with her looks. Rose is repulsed by her shallowness.

Lady Cassandra was thought to have died on *Platform One*, but her faithful servant, a forced-growth clone named Chip, hides her brain in a hospital on New Earth. With access to medicine and supplies, he cares for her while spider robots search for a new body.

In the heat of the near explosion of *Platform One*, Lady Cassandra's skin dries out and explodes. She appears to have died, but her brain survives.

PERSONAL ASSISTANTS

Magnification goggles for seeing the tiniest wrinkle

Cassandra's personal assistants are always close by, ready to spray her with a scientifically patented moisturizing formula.

Gloves and masks protect Cassandra from germs

Moisturization formula canister

Canister can be filled with acid and used as weapons

CASSANDRA FACTS

- Cassandra's "pure" human parents were the last to be buried in Earth's soil.
- She was born an American male but was surgically transformed into an English woman.
- She has been married several times.

THE SLITHEEN

THE LUSH, ABUNDANT planet of Raxacoricofallapatorius, on the edge of the Milky Way, is home to a species of green-skinned, calcium-based bipeds. While most Raxacoricofallapatorians are peaceful and law-abiding, one particular family's criminality has given the entire species a bad reputation: the Slitheen clan. Banished from their own star system, the Slitheen now terrorize other worlds—including Earth.

Second Skins

As wanted criminals on many worlds, the Slitheen are often forced to work in disguise. Earth-based Slitheen use compression field-generating neck collars to squeeze their huge bulks into the empty skin vessels of their human victims. However, gas exchange during compression causes painful flatulence and they find human skins cramped, preferring their "naked" form.

The Slitheen family thinks nothing of profiting from planetary war. On Earth, family members stage the crash-landing of a spaceship in order to kick-start a nuclear war and turn the planet into radioactive slag, which can then be sold in other galaxies as spaceship fuel.

Well-adapted Lifeforms

Raxacoricofallapatorians are well suited to life on their own planet. They use their powerful arms to swim from island to island in the great burgundy oceans, and their large eyes pierce through blizzards at the four poles. Forced to abandon this world, one clan poses as influential humans in the British government, seeking war for their own ends.

The Slitheen fitted their human costumes with zips, hidden under hairlines or hats. Unzipping produces a burst of contained compression energy.

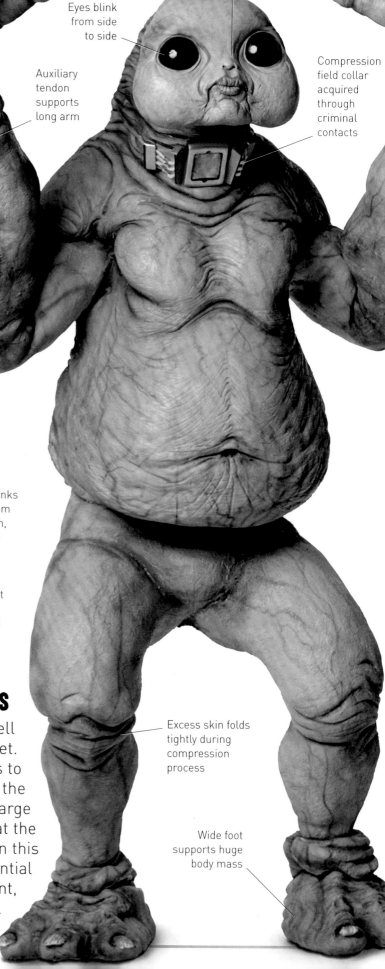

Poisonous fingertips

Extraordinary sense of smell can locate fellow Slitheen across vast distances and even detect deaths of loved ones

Eyes blink from side to side

Auxiliary tendon supports long arm

Compression field collar acquired through criminal contacts

Excess skin folds tightly during compression process

Wide foot supports huge body mass

RAXACORICOFALLAPATORIAN FACTS

- Raxacoricofallapatorian society is organized entirely around its large, powerful families.

- Family names are a complex affair, with any number of hyphenations expressing the exact branch and sub-branch of complicated family trees.

- The Slitheen is one of the planet's oldest families, tracing its line back to the legendary Huspick Degenerate scion, who controlled an illegal spice-smuggling organization.

Fatal Weakness

Raxacoricofallapatorians' living calcium structure is highly vulnerable to certain substances, most dangerously acetic acid, which almost always causes a fatal explosive reaction. On their home planet, the most heinous criminals were executed by being lowered into vats of acetic acid, ensuring a slow, painful, melting death.

Slitheen Lifecycle

The Slitheen, like all Raxacoricofallapatorians, hatch from eggs, using their powerful claws to break through the shell. The TARDIS reverts the Slitheen criminal Blon back into an egg in order to return her to her home planet and give her a second chance to live a better life.

Attack on Parliament

The closeness of the Slitheen clan is its undoing when all the Earth-based members hold a triumphant family gathering in 10 Downing Street in their natural form. Given a single, reasonably contained target, the Doctor decides to risk launching a Harpoon missile.

The Abzorbaloff

Originating on Raxacoricofallapatorius's sister planet Clom, the creature known as the Abzorbaloff can absorb other creatures in order to steal their knowledge and consciousnesses. The process is highly unstable and requires a limitation field device to avoid the remnants of the most recently absorbed victims, pulling him apart from the inside.

Faces of absorbed victims remain visible in flesh

Cane contains limitation field that stops Abzorbaloff from being absorbed himself by trapped consciousnesses

The Slitheen named Blon Fel Fotch Pasameer-Day Slitheen impersonating Margaret Blaine of MI5 broke rank with the family and teleported away from the Downing Street blast using a teleporter device hidden in her earrings. She vowed revenge on the miserable human race.

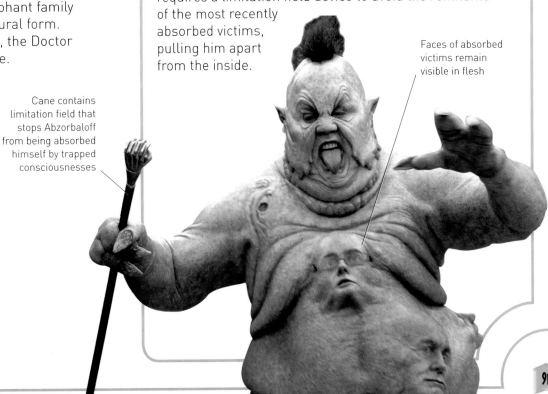

SATELLITE 5

ORBITING EARTH in the year 200,000, the Satellite 5 space station is the planet's largest media hub. Replacing all earlier broadcast satellites, it transmits news and entertainment throughout the Fourth Great and Bountiful Human Empire. The space station is also home to thousands of human employees, including journalists, who collect the news remotely via neural implants, and the Editor, who oversees them. Also onboard is the Jagrafess, a gigantic slug-like alien, who secretly manipulates the news in order to turn humans into slaves.

In a media centre on Satellite 5, journalists use the chips in their heads to gather news stories from across the Empire. They send the news via data hand plates to Cathica, a journalist implanted with an infospike in her forehead. She lies on an infochair and processes the news before transmitting it to the Empire. However, unknown to the journalists, the news is really going to the Jagrafess for editing before transmission.

The Editor

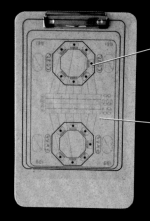

The mysterious, softly spoken, and ruthless Editor manages the space station from Floor 500. Unseen and unknown, the Editor monitors the journalists' thoughts via the chips in their heads. He was appointed by a consortium of interstellar banks, who installed the Jagrafess to profit from humanity's enslavement.

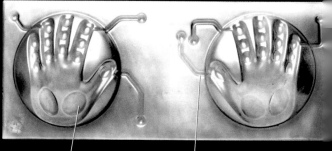

Biogenetic analyzer

Data defragmenter breaks down news for transmission

DATA HAND PLATES

CLIPBOARD

Media center seating system

Clipboard's infopaper displays data

CURRENCY STICK

A currency stick is used like a credit card aboard Satelllite 5. It can be topped up with currency at onboard credit terminals.

Chip inside interfaces with pay stations

An infospike is a portal installed in the forehead that connects the brain to Satellite 5's computers. The infospike opens with a click of the fingers and connects to the computers via spheres of energy in the media centers.

The Freedom Foundation

The Freedom Foundation is a group of 15 humans who discover Satellite 5's manipulation of humanity and are determined to stop it.

Eva Saint Julienne, using the alias Suki Macrae Cantrell, is the last surviving member of the the Freedom Foundation. Her comrades have all been eliminated. On Floor 500, she pulls a gun on the Editor, but she is killed by the Jagrafess.

Safety catch

Standard P9 phasic barrel

Secondary barrel fires XJ7 microplosives

Semi-organic polymer grip molds itself to user's hand

FREEDOM FOUNDATION P9 5 PISTOL

Freedom Foundation Manifesto

- **Closure of Satellite 5**
- **Full investigation into Satellite 5's activities**
- **No individual to own more than three media outlets**
- **Freezing of the assets of Satellite 5's backers**

Space Station

Satellite 5 functions as a regular working media hub—except for one section, which has been secretly modified to accommodate a highly unusual occupant: the Jagrafess. This gigantic creature lives on Floor 500, the topmost floor of the orbital platform. Since the Jagrafess's fast metabolism produces massive amounts of heat, a secondary ventilation system and auxiliary heat sinks were introduced to vent heat away from Floor 500. This has resulted in the top floor icing up like an Arctic winter, while the floors below are unbearably hot.

Excess heat vent

Medium range antenna

Fusion generators

Floor 500 media center is occupied by the Jagrafess and the Editor

Floor 247 specialises in lifestyle programming

TARDIS lands on Floor 139 next to a fast food joint

Main residential floors

Docking ring

Floor 16, the non-emergency medical center

Main transmitter broadcasts 600 channels across the Empire

Array of signal receivers

The Jagrafess

The Jagrafess's full name is the Mighty Jagrafess of the Holy Hadrojassic Maxarodenfoe. The Editor calls him Max for short. This monstrous, slimy alien with razor-sharp teeth is the true ruler of the Empire.

Holographic screens monitor Satellite 5 activity

Keyboard for manual entry

Chairs for the drones who operate the terminals

Floor 500 media center

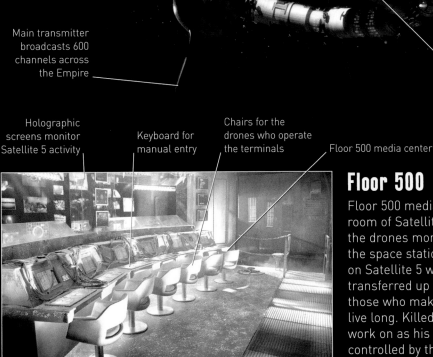

Floor 500

Floor 500 media center is the control room of Satellite 5, where the Editor and the drones monitor all human activity on the space station. Everyone who works on Satellite 5 wants to be promoted and transferred up to Floor 500. However, those who make it to the top floor don't live long. Killed by the Jagrafess, they work on as his drones—puppets controlled by the chip in their heads—until their bodies wear out.

THE SYCORAX

THESE SKINLESS HUMANOIDS orginated on a barren asteroid named the Fire Trap in the JX82 system. Consisting of many warlike tribes, the Sycorax fight with swords, whips, and their own school of magic spells and curses. To survive, these interstellar scavengers ransack other planets. One tribe, the Halvinor, crash through Earth's atmosphere, planning to steal its land and minerals, but don't anticipate encountering the regenerating Doctor when he takes Rose home for Christmas.

SYCORAX FACTS

- Sycorax can live for over 400 years.

- There are many Sycorax tribes, including the Halvinor tribe that invades Earth. Each claims one of the many asteroid ships as their own.

Sycorax Great Hall

This enormous hall was hollowed out of the Fire Trap's core many centuries ago. Its primitive structure is combined with space-age technology, such as a teleporter to travel on and off the asteroid. The hall is used for tribal meetings and the hole in the roof lets in solar and lunar light for ancient Sycorax rituals.

The Halvinor Sycorax ship is an asteroid fitted with powerful engines taken from an alien ship that collided with them. It is used by the Sycorax to raid other planets for food and resources. As the ship moves to attack Earth, it is powered by an All Speed Inter-System Type K engine.

The devastating effect of the Sycorax whip is seen on the prime minister's aide, scientist Daniel Llewellyn.

Sycorax Leader

It took two and half centuries for the Halvinor Leader to become head of his tribe. He rose through the ranks by various trials of strength and combat, and leads the blood-controlled invasion of Earth.

Thong conducts huge energies

Handle contains micro-fusion generator

Trophy from previous battle

SYCORAX WHIP

The Sycorax whip, when used on a human body, instantly destroys all the atoms of human flesh, so that only a pile of charred bones remains.

Fierce Warriors

The Sycorax adhere to traditions of honorable combat and will never turn down a challenge. They are naturally well-equipped for battle: part of the Sycorax skeleton lies outside the skin, covering the top and sides of the head and leaving the lower part of the face exposed to the elements. This exoskeleton, which can be smooth or jagged in texture, resembles a fearsome helmet.

Claw of pet Razorback

Fearsome bone helmet

Blood mane from leader's first kill

Trophies of conquered species

The Sycorax use ancient technology in order to take over worlds. When an Earth probe containing A+ human blood crashes into their ship, they feed it into a control matrix and enslave everyone on Earth who has A+ blood.

Forearm guard

Judoon-skin belt

Lanyard of the order of Prokraxis

Red robe signifies high rank

Protective Baltaric spats

Plumage of Courage

Pommel embedded with precious stones

SYCORAX SWORD

Barbed handle

Weapons like this sword, along with primitive-looking knives and spears, are adorned with trophies from battles won. They look simplistic, but are nonetheless effective in battle.

The Doctor challenges the Sycorax Leader to single combat for the fate of Earth. Honor-bound to accept, he is defeated by the Time Lord and the Sycorax agree to leave humanity alone.

NEW EARTH

Fluted cap worn by all Sisters

Cat-like features

TWENTY YEARS AFTER the Doctor and his companion Rose watched the Sun expand and obliterate Earth, revivalists were inspired to seek a similar world. The ideal place was found and named New Earth 50,000 light-years away in galaxy M87. The Doctor takes Rose there in the year 5,000,000,023, and visits again with his companion Martha 30 years later to see how, if at all, humanity has advanced.

Sisters of Plenitude

New New York's hospital is run by the humanoid feline Sisters of Plenitude and their controlling leader, Matron Casp. They specialize in treating incurable diseases, and their reputation for almost-miraculous cures is well-known. The sisterhood is as single-minded about its mission to cure patients as it is fiercely secretive about its treatment methods.

Dazzling New New York—the fifteenth since the United States' original—is New Earth's major city. It is ruled by the Senate, who live in the gleaming Overcity, while the poorer citizens live in the grim Undercity below.

MEDICAL SCANNER

Display of patient lifesigns

Menu navigation

Position adjustment control

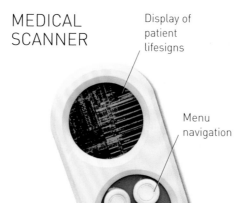

NEW NEW YORK'S HOSPITAL

In the year 5,000,000,023, a hospital commands an imposing coastal position on New Earth. Its gleaming, sterile wards are sealed from the outside air to prevent contamination. Visitors are disinfected when they enter the building's elevators.

Universal symbol for hospital

Ambulance landing bay

Landing area for non-emergency vehicles

Human Farm

Deep in the basement of the hospital is the secret of the Sisters' healing powers. Human clones are infected with every known disease and experimented on to find new cures. When the Doctor and Rose discover the clones are sentient, they free them, and a new human species is born.

The Undercity Motorway

By the time the Doctor returns in 5,000,000,053, life in New New York has drastically changed. Many denizens of the Undercity have set off on the Motorway, dreaming of a better life higher up. This highway is 20 lanes across and 50 lanes deep. Its traffic moves five miles every 12 years, but is going nowhere because the exit has been sealed to protect it from danger above.

Holographic presenter Sally Calypso's fabricated broadcasts convince the Motorway residents that all is normal in New New York.

Communicators, self-replicating fuel, muscle stimulants for exercise, and waste products recycled as food mean no one has to leave their car. Even babies are born onboard. Valerie and Thomas Kincade Brannigan's litter of kittens are Children of the Motorway, and have never known any other way of life.

Fur turning gray with age

Gun carried in case of Motorway pirates

Decorative design adds color to plain gray uniform

Functional buttons

NOVICE HAME'S BRACELET

Novice Hame's bracelet is actually a teleportation device, and also controls external lights.

Macra

The giant, crab-like Macra were once the scourge of galaxy M87. They forced humans to mine the poisonous gas they fed on. Over billions of years they devolved into simple beasts and were kept in the New New York Zoo. Escaped specimens have bred and now thrive beneath the smog-shrouded Motorway, hunting its travelers.

Novice Hame

Catperson Novice Hame nurses the Face of Boe as penance for the Sisters of Plenitudes' clone experiments. She is there when a virus kills everyone in the Overcity, and the Face of Boe hastily seals the Undercity, using his life-force to protect them and keep it running for 24 lonely years. She is also there at his death, but first, they happily see the Doctor rescue the Undercity population.

THE WEREWOLF

EVERY FULL MOON, cattle on the moors around the Torchwood Estate in Scotland are ripped apart. Locals speak of a giant wolf-like being, and boys vanish without a trace. The clue to these strange events lies nearby in St. Catherine's Glen monastery, where an alien, able to take werewolf form, landed centuries ago and now survives in a succession of human hosts, provided by the monks. When the alien hears that Queen Victoria is visiting the area, it sees its chance to seize power in England by invading her body.

The Torchwood Estate is a place of legend and mystery. Its very name is said to derive from the wood of a lightning-struck gallows—torched wood—used in its construction. Wild rumors were further stoked in the 1800s when the house's eccentric owner, Sir George MacLeish, built a gigantic rooftop observatory.

Landing in Scotland in 1879, the Doctor meets Queen Victoria on her way to Balmoral Castle. Unable to resist the opportunity to make the acquaintance of an English monarch, the Doctor uses his psychic paper to supply him with credentials to tag along to Torchwood House, where the Queen intends to spend the night.

MISTLETOE NECKLACE

The monks craft mistletoe necklaces to ward off the Werewolf.

Sharp claws rip prey apart

FIGHTING STAFF

Rare wood grows locally

Mistletoe worn around neck under robe

Bedeviled Brethren

At the monastery of St. Catherine's Glen, the monks, led by the crazed Father Angelo, have come to worship the power-hungry alien that fell to Earth close to their home in the 1500s. They are even willing to kidnap boys from the local village to provide the alien with the human hosts it needs to survive.

In the Torchwood House cellar, Rose finds a strange caged prisoner that the monks have placed there. To her, as a seasoned space-time traveler, its eyes betray the unmistakable presence of a life form that is not from Earth.

Before the Queen and the Doctor arrive at Torchwood House, the monks take over the house, overpowering and imprisoning the staff using their impressive martial arts skills.

Habit conceals orange fighting robes

Informed of Queen Victoria's movements by the monks, and desperate to infect itself into a being of real power, the alien commands the monks to transport it—in its human host—to Torchwood House. All it needs is for the full moon to provide the power to transform it to its werewolf form.

FATHER ANGELO

Super-sensitive ears

Inhuman eyes betray alien presence inside

Sharp teeth rip apart flesh

Thick skin deflects bullets

Powerful hind legs allow short bursts of fast running or jumping

Royal Secrets

Official records remain silent on the strange events at the Torchwood Estate. Yet it is perhaps no coincidence that shortly afterward, Queen Victoria secretly established the Torchwood Institute to research and fight Britain's enemies "beyond imagination."

ROYAL ATTACHÉ CASE

Official emblem of state

Lock is sign of top secret contentst

QUEEN VICTORIA

In the rooftop observatory at Torchwood House, there is a telescope with an unusual array of prisms. As the current owner, Sir Robert, is obsessed with werewolf legends and the heavens. The Doctor speculates that these prisms might have a secret function.

Prowling Beast

To locals, the Werewolf is simply a creature of terror. But the Doctor recognizes it as a lupine wavelength haemovariform—an alien species that requires the specific wavelength of bright moonlight to change its form.

Objective lens cell

Tube ring

Focusing knob

Eyepiece

CENTRAL TUBE OF TELESCOPE

Unwilling to break through a door smeared with mistletoe, the Werewolf reveals an odd weakness—fear of the parasitic plant.

Light Weapon

Just as the alien needs moonlight to transform, the Doctor realizes that too much light can kill it. He deduces that the prism array in Sir Robert's telescope can project a super-intense beam of light, powerful enough to destroy both the alien parasite and, tragically, its innocent human host.

GELTH

PITY THE GELTH! These formless creatures have been trapped in a gaseous state ever since the Time War, but they long to have physical existence again. An advance party of Gelth make their way to 19th-century Cardiff where they ask a young girl for help. But it soon becomes apparent that the Gelth have an ulterior motive for seeking a physical form.

Blue eyes turn red once the Gelth are through the Rift

The Rift

The city of Cardiff is the location of a weak point in space and time. Known as the Rift, it is where connections are formed with other eras and places and is the cause of the many ghost stories circulating in the area. Having grown up on the center of the Rift, servant girl Gwyneth has become part of it. It has given her "the sight"—the ability to read minds.

The Rift is weakest at 7 Temperance Court, home to Sneed and Co. undertakers. Here, the Doctor communicates with the Gelth via psychic Gwyneth. He allows them use of the corpses, just until he can find them a new home.

Walking Dead

Decomposing human bodies at the funeral parlor produce gas, which forms the perfect home for the gaseous Gelth. When they animate cadavers, the Gelth stimulate the human's dead brain so the corpse becomes aware of details of its former life.

Form changes when Gelth cross the Rift

Bridge Between Worlds

When the truth is revealed—that there are billions of Gelth and they plan to take over Earth—Gwyneth, who is their link across the Rift, sacrifices herself by blowing up the room full of gas.

GELTH FACTS

- The Gelth need a gaseous atmosphere to survive—19th-century gas pipes provide an ideal environment.

- It takes three months of hijacking Sneed's corpses before the Gelth manage to communicate their request to Gwyneth at a seance.

- Without a proper bridge across the Rift, the weakened Gelth are only able to inhabit corpses for short periods of time.

- The Doctor agrees to help the Gelth animate human corpses temporarily, intending that he would later help them find permanent bodies elsewhere.

KRILLITANES

A COMPOSITE RACE, the carnivorous Krillitanes pick the best physical elements from the creatures they conquer, and incorporate them to create an improved form. When the Doctor first met the race, they appeared human, apart from having very long necks. But the next time he encounters them, they have become bat-like.

Wings can lift considerable weight

The Krillitanes have had wings for nearly ten generations, ever since they invaded the planet Bessan, where they killed a million of that planet's winged species in one day.

Jaws ideal for eating children

Claws can rip flesh

Bad Bats

The Krillitanes resemble bats in more ways than just their wings. They sleep hanging upside down and have very sensitive hearing, which means that they dislike loud noises. Their slim, sinuous bodies are capable of great feats of strength.

BROTHER LASSAR

A Krillitane named Brother Lassar takes on the human form of Mr. Finch, principal of Deffry Vale High School. Twelve other Krillitanes impersonate staff at the school, aiming to harness the brains and imaginations of the pupils in order to crack the Skasis Paradigm—which would give them control of time, space, and matter.

The Krillitanes cannot change their physical appearance like shape-shifters, but they can use a simple morphic illusion to cloak themselves in human form. However, it takes barely a moment to shrug off their disguise, should they need to make a flying getaway.

KRILLITANE FACTS

- When there is no fresh flesh to feed on, the Krillitanes sustain themselves with vacuum-packed rats.

- The Krillitanes use Krillitane oil to enhance the intelligence of the pupils under their control.

- Due to overuse and continued physiological alterations, Krillitane oil is now toxic to them.

- As well as physical attributes, the Krillitanes steal technology from other races, such as the means to create a deadlock seal.

SS MADAME DE POMPADOUR

THE SS *MADAME DE POMPADOUR* is one of the great energy trawlers of the 51st century. Purposed to retrieve dark matter energy deep in space, it was originally crewed by humans assisted by clockwork repair robots. However, when Rose, Mickey, and the Doctor arrive onboard in the TARDIS, the robots are the only life form left. Programmed to repair the ship at all costs, the robots used parts of the crew to fix the ship when it was damaged in an ion storm.

Energy Trawler

In the 51st century, humans are dependent on dark matter to fulfill their energy needs. Dark matter is an invisible form of energy that is only identified by its gravitational effects. Until it and its computer is damaged, the SS *Madame de Pompadour* is perfectly equipped for collecting this dark matter: rotating arms scoop it up out of space, and it is then stored in the ship's central hub.

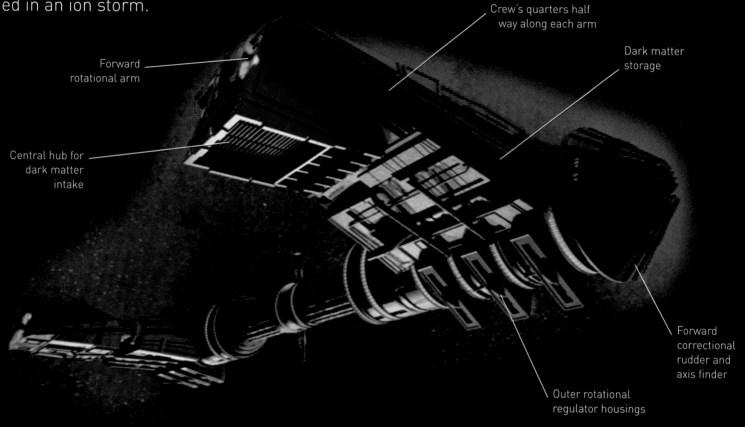

Forward rotational arm

Crew's quarters half way along each arm

Dark matter storage

Central hub for dark matter intake

Forward correctional rudder and axis finder

Outer rotational regulator housings

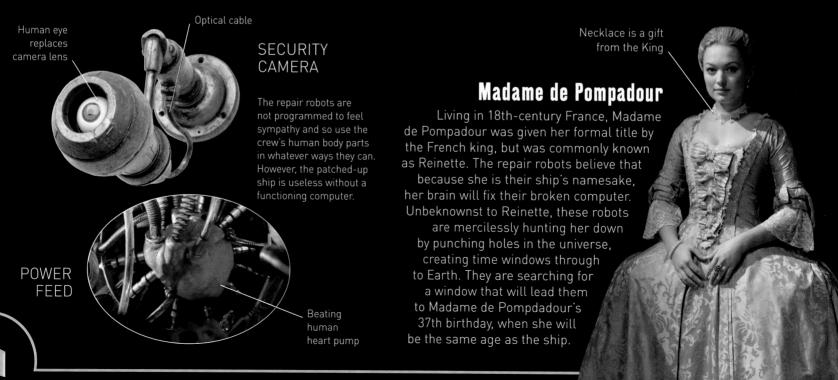

Human eye replaces camera lens

Optical cable

SECURITY CAMERA

The repair robots are not programmed to feel sympathy and so use the crew's human body parts in whatever ways they can. However, the patched-up ship is useless without a functioning computer.

POWER FEED

Beating human heart pump

Necklace is a gift from the King

Madame de Pompadour

Living in 18th-century France, Madame de Pompadour was given her formal title by the French king, but was commonly known as Reinette. The repair robots believe that because she is their ship's namesake, her brain will fix their broken computer. Unbeknownst to Reinette, these robots are mercilessly hunting her down by punching holes in the universe, creating time windows through to Earth. They are searching for a window that will lead them to Madame de Pompdadour's 37th birthday, when she will be the same age as the ship.

Using their ship's powerful, undamaged warp engines, one of the robots' time windows eventually opens to reveal a ballroom in 18th-century Versailles. Without these portals, the droids have no way of fixing their ship and therefore no reason to carry on existing.

SS MADAME DE POMPADOUR FACTS

■ **The ship's arms generate an artificial gravity field, as well as a negative magma field that drives the ship forward.**

■ **The ship boasts antiquated sigmus-style warp engines in case its other power sources fail. These are used to create the windows through time and space.**

Clockwork Repair Robot

Although their costumes and masks give them the appearance of French courtiers, a loud ticking noise reveals the repair robots for what they truly are. To match the time zone they have entered, the robots have attempted to disguise themselves accordingly. Each deadly android has a sharp blade hidden in its sleeve, can read humans' minds, and even teleport short distances.

Wig typical of those worn at French court

Mask conceals clockwork head

Sharp, retractable blade

Silk stockings cover mechanical legs

REPAIR ROBOT

When the repair robots anesthetize Rose and Mickey and strap them to surgical gurneys, it looks like they, too, will be integrated into the ship's systems.

The repair robots contain 51st century clockwork technology. Old-fashioned, reliable Swiss clockwork techniques are integrated with sophisticated space-age computer chips.

Using the fireplace portal, the Doctor first meets Reinette as a child and saves her from the clockwork "monster." She calls him her "fireplace man" and holds onto the belief that he will rescue her when she needs help. When the Doctor accesses the same portal seemingly a few minutes later he is surprised to discover that Reinette has grown into a beautiful young woman. To the Doctor, time passes much more quickly than for Reinette.

The repair robots are able to scan Reinette's mind to work out when her brain is "complete." The Doctor uses telepathy to find out what the robots are looking for but he is shocked when Reinette is also able to read his mind, presumably due to her exposure to his Time Lord abilities, and discover the secrets of his lonely childhood.

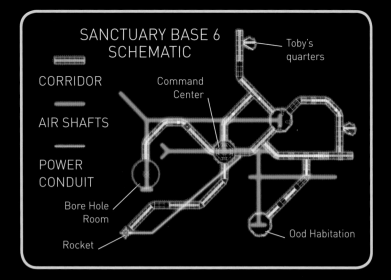

SANCTUARY BASE 6
SCHEMATIC

CORRIDOR

AIR SHAFTS

POWER
CONDUIT

Toby's
quarters

Command
Center

Bore Hole
Room

Rocket

Ood Habitation

THE BEAST

B ENEATH A DRILLING STATION on a planetary
exploration base, an ancient, trapped evil called
the Beast is stirring. Scripture from a pre-human
civilization marks the walls, and the planet is orbiting
a black hole—going against the laws of physics. The
base's crew is drilling to the center of the planet to
harness the mysterious power that keeps it in orbit,
but as they mine, it becomes clear that the source is
more terrifying than they could ever have imagined.

Base Floorplan

One of many identical bases used in deep space exploration, Sanctuary
Base 6 is constructed from pre-fabricated kits. Separate segments
allow the oxygen field to be contained in different parts of the base,
and areas can be sealed off in the event of a hull breach. This enables
the team to enact "Strategy 9"—sheltering in a locked-down safe
area and opening the base's airlocks, sucking invaders into space.

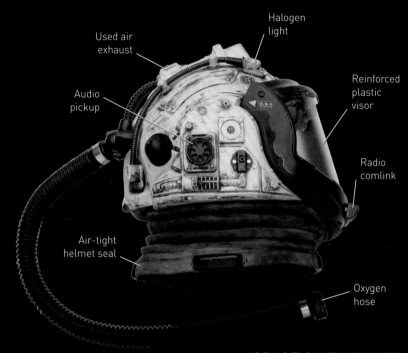

Somehow, the planet is generating
enough power to keep it in
perpetual geostationary orbit
around black hole K37 Gem 5.
The Doctor calculates that
such a power would need an
inverted self-extrapolating
reflex of 6 to the power
of 6 every 6 seconds—a
theoretically impossible figure.

Halogen
light

Used air
exhaust

Audio
pickup

Reinforced
plastic
visor

Radio
comlink

Air-tight
helmet seal

Oxygen
hose

Command Center

The central desk of the command centre controls all the base's
essential functions, including the oxygen field, internal gravity
system, and rocket link. From here the captain tracks everyone's
location from their biochip signals. Overhead shields can be
opened to monitor black hole activity.

SPACE SUIT HELMET

-00373
-00.7
091%

Screens inside the command
center monitor the mining
capsule's rate of descent into
the mineshaft.

Drilling Platform

The planet's solid-rock crust is
excavated with robot drills and
the base crew painstakingly cut a
mineshaft 10 miles beneath the
surface in a bid to reach the planet's
mysterious energy source—
an energy giving readings of over
90 Statts on the Blazen scale.
The enslaved race, the Ood, does
all the dangerous maintenance
work on the drilling platform.

Protective space suits and
helmets must be worn on the
surface because the planet
lacks atmosphere and gravity. At
night, the drills are shut down by
the maintenance trainee, and
the base's computer shuts off
access to the surface.

Black hole

Sanctuary Base 6

Drilling platform

Capsule

Drilled mineshaft

Gravity globe

Carved monolith of demon

The Perfect Prison

The Doctor realizes that the planet is an ingenious prison. If the Beast escapes from the pit, the energy source keeping the planet in orbit will collapse, and the planet will be sucked into the black hole. The air in the pit was supplied by the Beast's gaolers so a traveler could stop the Beast's escape by smashing the power source.

Sealed Trapdoor

Two stone monoliths, standing guard before a circular seal set into the floor, are revealed to be a trap door. Sensors indicate that the Base's power source lies beneath. Without warning, the cavern shakes as the trap door's segments slide back to reveal a deep, black chasm. A voice booms from the darkness: "The pit is open and I am free!"

Ancient drawings

Seal over trap door

Starlight shines through pothole

CAVE MARKINGS

The voice of the Beast tells the Doctor of a people called the Disciples of Light, who rose up against him in a time before the universe was created—something the Doctor finds impossible to believe. As if in confirmation of the devil's words, the Doctor finds cave drawings recording a victory over the Beast and his imprisonment in the pit.

The Doctor

TARDIS

Ancient Creature

A vast cavern beneath Sanctury Base 6 forms the prison home of the Beast—an ancient creature akin to the devil. The proximity of the people drilling above it has meant that it has easily been able to possess some of their minds—such as crewmember Toby Zed—in a bid to escape.

The horrific monster facing the Doctor is the empty body of the Beast. The Doctor uncovers him when he investigates the Base's power source, and has only seconds to destroy the planet and foil the Beast's escape.

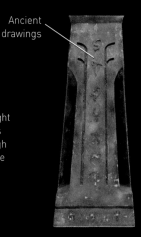

RACNOSS

THE ARACHNID-TYPE ALIEN Racnoss are born with a raging hunger, and will devour anything, from people to planets. In the Dark Times, near the beginning of the universe, the Fledgeling Empires went to war against the ravenous Racnoss, wiping them out—or so it was thought. One group managed to escape, but the energy emitted by their ship exerted such a gravitational pull that passing rocks began to mass around it, gradually forming a planet—Earth—and leaving the fugitive Racnoss survivors trapped in their ship at its center.

The Empress

The Empress is not just the leader of the Racnoss, but is also their mother, as all Racnoss have hatched from her eggs. By reviving the Racnoss hibernating in the Earth's core, the Empress will be freeing her children, who will then be able to satisfy their hunger with human flesh! But her plans are foiled by the Doctor. When he tries to bargain with her by offering the Racnoss safe passage to a new home, she rejects his proposal, condemning her entire race to extinction, as she and the newly awakened Racnoss are then all wiped out.

RACNOSS FACTS

- Each Racnoss can produce miles of strong, thick protein strands that are used to form webs and bind their prey.

- The Racnoss can hibernate without sustenance for billions of years, but when they stir, they are ravenous.

- The Racnoss have mastered teleportation, so do not need to land their ships on the planets they wish to visit.

Webstar of Wonder

A star-shaped object blasting bolts of deadly electricity from its eight "limbs" spreads terror as it flies over London's streets on Christmas Eve. This is the Webstar ship of the Racnoss Empress, which had been hiding undetected at the edge of the universe. Racnoss technology is powered by Huon particles that were long ago destroyed by the Time Lords for being too dangerous—but reactivated by the Empress in her mission to free the rest of her kind from within the center of the Earth.

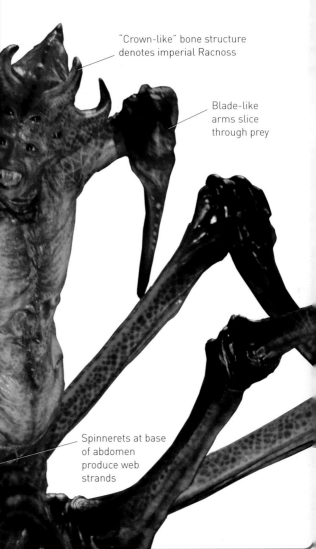

"Crown-like" bone structure denotes imperial Racnoss

Blade-like arms slice through prey

Tough outer skin is shed when outgrown

Pedicle enables free movement of thorax

Spinnerets at base of abdomen produce web strands

PLASMAVORES

PLASMAVORES ARE AN alien species who live off the vital life-juices of other creatures. While necessary to their survival, blood-sucking is also an addictive pleasure, and many Plasmavores travel the universe searching for rare species to sample. This mania for blood can lead to psychosis and a severe disregard for the lives of others.

Drone Bodyguards

The Plasmavore calling itself Florence Finnegan is guarded by two Slab henchmen disguised as motorcycle couriers. These basic slave drones are genetically reared for combat and strong-arm work.

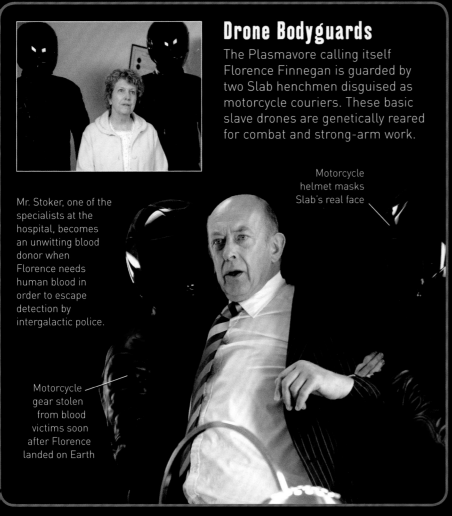

Motorcycle helmet masks Slab's real face

Mr. Stoker, one of the specialists at the hospital, becomes an unwitting blood donor when Florence needs human blood in order to escape detection by intergalactic police.

Motorcycle gear stolen from blood victims soon after Florence landed on Earth

Faced with capture by interplanetary police, Florence uses her criminal knowhow to turn an MRI scanner into a lethal weapon. She resets the machine's magnet to send out a massive magnetic pulse that will fry the brainstems of all other living things within a 200 – 50,000 mile (320 – 80,000 kilometer) radius—leaving her unharmed.

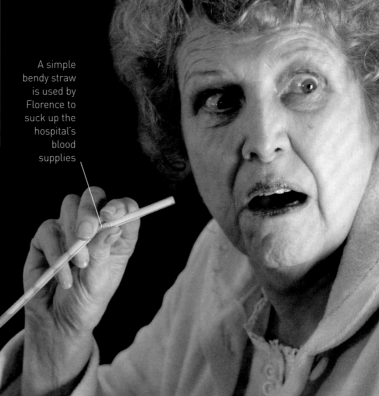

A simple bendy straw is used by Florence to suck up the hospital's blood supplies

Plasmavore in Hiding

Plasmavores are shape-changers who can assimilate the genetic material of any species whose life-juice they drink. One such Plasmavore has taken on the persona of frail 70-year-old Florence Finnegan in the Royal Hope Hospital in order to hide on Earth. "Florence" is on the run from intergalactic law enforcers, the Judoon, after murdering the Child Princess of Padrivole Regency Nine on a whim.

THE JUDOON

THROUGHOUT THE UNIVERSE, police authorities come in many shapes, sizes, and species. One of the most feared is the private paramilitary security force organized by the thick-skinned, twin-horned species called the Judoon. Each Judoon police officer has the power to administer swift justice: he can arrest, charge, judge, sentence, and execute a suspect in a matter of seconds.

Hired Thugs

Judoon police have a reputation of being little more than hired thugs. Their methods are certainly authoritarian and brutal, and carried out without emotion. They focus only on their objective and let nothing stand in the way of their justice being done. As they say, "justice is swift." Among other clients, the Judoon enforce laws for the intergalactic regulatory body, the Shadow Proclamation.

Ears with selective hearing

Small eyes betray no emotion

Magnetic seal activates when pressurized helmet is worn

Military fastenings

Language identification scanner

Twin horns for intimidating suspects

Thick skin impervious to most forms of attack

Decayed teeth due to poor diet

Powerful lungs ensure long-lasting stamina

Voice emitter for use when battle helmet is worn

Bulletproof armor padding

Armored wrist guard

Weapons and equipment attached to utility belt

BATTLE ARMOR, WITH HELMET, SIDE VIEW

Battle helmet with breathing equipment

One-way viewing slit

The Judoon's battle armor provides maximum impact protection and functions as a pressurized life-support system for use in toxic environments or on planets with non-breathable atmospheres.

Thick soles provide protection on uncertain terrain, including toxic spills

Distinctive boot fastenings – Judoon are said to sleep with their boots on as a sign of their dedication to the job

Reinforced knee guard used offensively and defensively in combat

Elaborate military boots

Bioengineered metal plates reinforce boots, adding extra power to bone-shattering kicks

Studded kilt is a symbol of a warrior in Judoon culture

Memory chips hold most known languages

Holster for blaster

JUDOON BLASTER

Muzzle guard

Cooling unit

Trigger

Blaster gas cartridge chamber

Igniter pin

Grip for Judoon hand

Power cell housing

SPECIES SCANNER

Indelible branding tip

DNA scan emitter

LANGUAGE IDENTIFICATION SCANNER

Judoon police carry high-powered blasters, which they are empowered to fire at their own discretion. A single blast of the energy beam can obliterate a person in a flash. Judoon also carry various scanners that allow them to identify and catalog suspects by species. Another scanner can sample and assimilate the languages of most known species—ensuring that the Judoon's orders are clearly understood.

Although the Judoon have no official jurisdiction over Earth, this does not stop them from attempting to capture a Plasmavore suspect hiding on the planet. They use an H2O scoop to suck an entire Earth building onto the surface of the Moon, where they do have authority.

JUDOON FACTS

- **The Judoon are organized along military lines, with troops led by commanders.**

- **The Judoon travel in gigantic tube-shaped spaceships. Originally built as military battleships, these intimidating vehicles were chosen by the Judoon for their ability to strike fear in others.**

- **The Judoon's sense of justice has led them to fight both for and against the Doctor. They are among the army that imprisons him in the Pandorica in order to save the universe, but at the battle of Demon's Run, they are outraged by the theft of Amy Pond's baby and come to his aid.**

THE CARRIONITES

MOTHER BLOODTIDE

LILITH

Face can transform into that of a beautiful human

Wrinkled skin of the eldest Carrionite

Spread "wings" of cloak help witch float in the air

AT THE BEGINNING OF the universe, foul witch-like creatures known as the Carrionites flew the skies of the Rexel Planetary System. They used special powers that were derived from the manipulation of specific words to dominate the universe. When the infinitely powerful elemental beings the Eternals discovered which words could control the Carrionites, they banished them to the Deep Darkness. The Carrionites remained trapped in their prison for millions of years.

Toil and Trouble

The Carrionite wraiths long to escape and take over a world for themselves. They possess the power to harness the energy of strongly expressed emotions and plan to use this skill to pull themselves out the Deep Darkness. Tuning into the intense grief and near madness expressed by the famous wordsmith William Shakespeare when he loses his son, they exploit the energy they derive from this source to try to break free. Three Carrionites escape by this means and are drawn to Shakespeare on Earth in 1599.

Carrionites use a special magical science, based upon the power of words, in their attempts to control people and establish a new Empire on Earth. It closely resembles witchcraft, and employs formulae made out of significant words and shapes to exert its power.

The Carrionites' cauldron is used to communicate, to view the past and to brew potions. The fumes from the witches' brew can control a man's actions, without him being aware of it.

A broomstick aids a Carrionite in her flight, although she is able to fly without one.

Along with their word-based science, Carrionites use a crystal ball to control events on Earth. The are eventually trapped in it by the Doctor.

MOTHER DOOMFINGER

Finger can kill with a touch to the chest

The Globe Theatre was built with fourteen sides to match the Rexel Planetary Configuration. The theater's architect, Peter Streete, was influenced by the Carrionites to design the building this way, so it would be the perfect shape to act as a portal for their escape.

Billowing black robes resemble a crow when in flight

Carrionites can kill by using a poppet—a simple doll resembling their intended victim. Stabbing the poppet's chest stops the victim's heart, and breaking the poppet in two ensures the victim's death. By attaching a lock of a victim's hair to a poppet, a Carrionite can then control the victim completely.

Roughly formed humaoid shape

POPPET

Jail Breakers

When the Carrionite-inspired last lines of Shakespeare's play *Love's Labour's Won* are spoken, the Globe acts as an energy converter, opening a portal to the Deep Darkness and releasing all the Carrionites from their prison. Only Shakespeare—with a little help from Martha—can find the words to close the portal and send the Carrionites back to their eternal jail.

CARRIONITE FACTS

- **All Carrionites are female.**

- **Carrionites try to keep their names secret. They can be harmed when addressed by their true name. However, this works only once. On all subsequent occasions, this has no effect.**

- **When a Carrionite forges a link with a victim's mind, she is able to see through his or her eyes.**

- **Until the Carrionites appeared on Earth in 1599, many races—even the Time Lords— thought they were a myth.**

Shakespeare has met the Doctor before, but the playwright does not recognize him because he has since regenerated.

THE FAMILY OF BLOOD

The TARDIS chooses to hide the Doctor in 1913 among the pupils of Farringham School. The boys are being prepared for war, but when the Family comes, they take up arms earlier than expected.

THE FAMILY OF BLOOD are alien predators with an acute sense of smell, whose life span is only three months. In their natural form, they are merely balls of gas, but they are able to take the bodies of other intelligent beings and gain their strength and physical abilities. However, these feeble forms are soon expended, so they are seeking the Doctor's body, which will give one of them the many lives of a Time Lord.

Family of Mine

The Family's bond is strong and the nameless aliens refer to themselves only in terms of kinship: Father of Mine, Mother of Mine, Son (or Brother) of Mine, Daughter (or Sister) of Mine. Son of Mine is the natural leader and favored child—he is the one for whom the Family seek immortality.

Body Snatchers

When their hunt for the Doctor brings them to England, each Family member takes on a human shape. The mind of each victim is entirely consumed—memory traces may survive, but not enough to enable the Family to pass as their assumed species without arousing suspicion.

A vortex manipulator stolen from a Time Agent allows the Family to track the Doctor. Once on Earth, their spaceship is concealed by an invisibility shield.

Schoolboy Jeremy Baines's body becomes the human host for Son of Mine. Jeremy is fetching illicit beer from Blackdown Woods when he stumbles across the Family and fatally decides to investigate.

Martha suspects something is wrong with maid Jenny at Farringham School when she agrees to share a teapot of gravy. Jenny was snatched by the Family's scarecrow soldiers and consumed by Mother of Mine.

THE FAMILY FACTS

- The Family's strong sense of smell is just as keen within their human bodies. Yet it can be fooled by olfactory misdirection, or "ventriloquism of the nose," an elementary trick of the Doctor's.

- Family members communicate telepathically. In moments of extreme trauma, they feel each other's pain.

- The laser gun is the Family's weapon of choice. It shoots energy bolts that disintegrate its targets instantly.

The scarecrows, who have been turned by the Family into moving soldiers, are sent to locate a body for Father of Mine. They find Farmer Clark in his field at Oakham Farm.

Little Lucy Cartwright is happily walking along with her balloon when the scarecrows take her. She is the perfect host for Daughter of Mine.

MOTHER OF MINE

Gaseous form enters human through eyes

SON OF MINE

Pupil's body allows access to Farringham school

DAUGHTER OF MINE

Childlike appearance disarms foes

FATHER OF MINE

Respectable appearance allays human suspicion

Scarecrow Soldiers

Scarecrows are not uncommon in rural Herefordshire, England—but these scare more than just crows. Son of Mine fashions rough humanoid shapes out of inanimate materials to create a scarecrow army. He gives them basic motor and sensory abilities using the process of molecular fringe animation.

"Eyes" allow limited vision

SCARECROW SOLDIER

Clothes keep straw in humanoid shape

Following the Family's orders, the scarecrow foot soldiers march inexorably toward the schoolboys' guns. Straw men feel no pain, but they are unable to mend themselves if they lose their humanoid form.

The Doctor goes to great lengths to make himself human to hide from the Family, not just for his sake, but also to protect them from punishment at his hands. But when the Family tracks down the Doctor and threatens the village, Martha—helped by psychic schoolboy Tim Latimer—has to bring the Time Lord back before the Family causes any more deaths.

Straw filling provides bulk of scarecrow

Shoes give firm base for straw-filled legs

Eternal Life

The Family wanted to live forever, so the Doctor, left with no alternatives by their actions, makes sure they do. Father of Mine is trapped eternally underground, wrapped in unbreakable chains that were forged in the heart of a Dwarf Star.

The Doctor tricks Mother of Mine into the event horizon of a collapsing galaxy. She is drawn irresistibly into an inescapable black hole, through which she will fall, screaming, for all eternity.

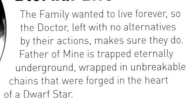

Inside every mirror, occasionally glimpsed but rarely fully seen, is Daughter of Mine. She can never leave her looking-glass prison, where the Doctor visits her once a year.

Son of Mine is suspended in time in a living death, eternally aware but unable to move. The Doctor puts him to work as a scarecrow, guarding the fields of England forever.

THE MASTER

THE MASTER WAS one of the Doctor's oldest friends, but he became his most bitter enemy. They attended the Time Lord Academy together, but eventually both tired of Gallifreyan life and became exiles. The Master's evil schemes were frequently foiled by the Doctor, and he met his final end when he was sucked into the Eye of Harmony in the TARDIS—or so the Doctor thought.

Respectable appearance conceals a psychopath

Hidden in Time and Space

The Master used up all of his lives pursuing diabolical schemes and the Doctor's destruction. However, during the Time War, the Time Lords remembered the Master's battle mania and resurrected his body so that he could fight alongside them. Instead, he ran away scared, eventually reaching the planet Malcassairo where he hid as Professor Yana.

Gallifreyan children are made to stare into the Untempered Schism, a gap in the fabric of reality. The sight sent the Master mad, filling his head forever with the pounding sound of drums.

Professor Yana

To escape the ravages of the Time War, the Master hides himself as a human called Professor Yana at the end of the universe. Using techniques similar to those used when the Doctor became human in order to escape the Family of Blood, the Master's transformation from Time Lord to a human is total.

Laser Screwdriver is now the Master's weapon of choice

The Master's Time Lord self is contained in a pocket watch that is identical to the Doctor's. A perception filter within the watch prevents him from noticing it and realizing his real identity. On opening it, the Master's biology, personality, and memories return. One heart becomes two, his body temperature lowers, and his respiratory bypass system is restored.

Restored Time Lord

Professor Yana becoming the Master again reveals the meaning behind the Face of Boe's prophetic "You are not alone" message to the Doctor; the Doctor is not the last of his kind as he previously thought. The restored Time Lord escapes to Earth in the Doctor's TARDIS.

Tip shoots deadly
laser beam

Isomorphic controls
allow only the Master
to use them

LASER SCREWDRIVER

The Master's laser screwdriver is similar to the Doctor's sonic screwdriver, but its technology is based on laser beams rather than on focused sound waves.

Harold Saxon

After his release from the pocket watch, the Master arrives on present-day Earth. He assumes the identity of "Harold Saxon." He convinces the world that he is a Cambridge graduate and a novelist who became Minister of Defense. He rose to fame after shooting down the alien Racnoss. He is then elected Prime Minister of Great Britain.

Roedean-educated Lucy Saxon appears to be Harold's devoted wife and companion, but his cruel treatment slowly destroys her, and she is the one who finally shoots him dead.

SIGNET RING

This ornate ring with Gallifreyan engravings is worn on the Master's right hand. It contains the Master's genetic code and is rescued from his funeral pyre by a woman named Miss Trefusis.

The Archangel Network

Harold Saxon launches the Archangel Network. This worldwide cell-phone network, carried by 15 satellites, transmits a rhythm that gives the Master hypnotic control over the entire population.

As part of the Archangel Network, the whole of the south coast of England is turned into a rocket shipyard. Rockets are built out of scrap metal by slave labor, in preparation for the Master declaring war on the universe. Each rocket contains a Black Hole Converter.

THE MASTER FACTS

- **The Master has used up his 13 regenerations, but has inhabited at least 17 bodies to stay alive, including Consul Tremas of Traken and an ambulance driver called Bruce.**

- **As well as "Professor Yana" and "Harold Saxon," the Master's aliases have included country vicar Reverend Magister, time-meddling scientist Professor Thascales, and thirteenth-century French knight Sir Gilles Estram.**

- **YANA's name—"You Are Not Alone"— is not the only clue left for the Doctor: "Magister" and "Thascales" both translate as "Master," and "Estram" is an anagram.**

The Last of the Time Lords?

When the Master is defeated, the compassionate Doctor will not let him be executed, but knows that the Master cannot be allowed to go free. As the only other apparent Time Lord in existence, the Master is his responsibility—the Doctor plans to keep him in the TARDIS and care for him. But betrayed Lucy shoots the Master and he refuses to regenerate, preferring death to eternal imprisonment with the Doctor. The Master seems to die with no hope of returning, leaving the Doctor believing he is the last of the Time Lords once more.

The distraught Doctor takes the Master's body to a deserted beach, and places it on a funeral pyre.

THE TOCLAFANE

PRIMITIVE CREATURES wired into mechanical shells represent the final evolution of humanity. In the year 100 trillion, the nothingness at the end of time drove humans to regress into these spherical beings known as the Toclafane. They were then rescued by the Master, who transported them back from the future to invade present-day Earth.

The Toclafane are the Master's enforcers, enabling him to cover the Earth in work camps, and churn out rockets for waging war.

The Master's Secret Weapon

Malevolent Time Lord the Master befriends the vulnerable and impressionable Toclafane. Loyal to him without question, they carry out his every destructive instruction. The Master uses them to conquer Earth and enslave the human race—the first stage in his plan to found a Time Lord Empire across the universe.

Merciless killing machines, the Toclafane speed through the air after their victims. They have lasers for long-range attacks and blades for up-close slicing and dicing.

Blades cause extra damage when the sphere rotates

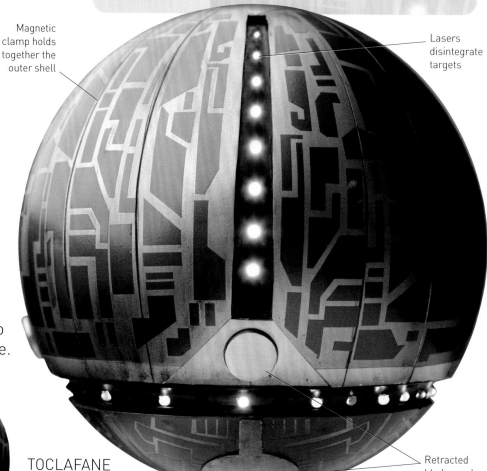

Magnetic clamp holds together the outer shell

Lasers disintegrate targets

Retracted blades and spikes

TOCLAFANE SPHERES

Tough metallic shell can fly through space undamaged

Human head is wired into the sphere

INSIDE THE TOCLAFANE SPHERE

The Paradox Machine is a device the Master created by reconfiguring the TARDIS. It forms a temporal paradox that allows the universe to continue, despite an apparent contradiction. The machine allows the Toclafane to kill their ancestors without wiping out their own existence.

Each sphere houses a withered head—the last remnant of the Toclafane's human form. All six billion Toclafane share a collective memory of the final thoughts and experiences of the last humans. They are haunted by the never-ending darkness and cold of the end of time.

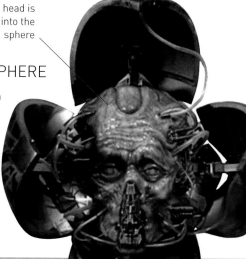

The Utopia Project

In the year 100 trillion, when the universe was coming to an end, the last humans fled the planet of Malcassairo in search of Utopia—a perfect place, believed to have been built by the Science Foundation as part of the Utopia Project in order to preserve humankind. But Utopia was just a myth, and the travelers found nothing but oblivion. Despair led them to evolve into the Toclafane.

Insectoid exoskeleton

Mandibles evolved from insects

Chantho helps the humans to flee Malcassairo by working on the space shuttle as Professor Yana's assistant. She nurtures unrequited feelings for him, quashed when she discovers he is the Master working in disguise.

The spacecraft for the journey used an experimental engine, built using whatever was available to hand, including gluten extract as a binding agent.

CHANTHO

Chantho is the very last of the insectoid Malmooth race, native to the planet Malcassairo. Malmooth bodies survive by drinking their own internal milk, and social conventions dictate a very polite and fomulaic way of speaking. Chantho's every sentence must begin with "chan" and end in "tho."

The Futurekind

A fierce humanoid race, the Futurekind were feared to be the final future of the human race. Humanity's actual fate—becoming the Toclafane—was no better. In order to leave Malcassairo, the last humans had to escape the Futurekind.

Billions of Toclafane spill into the sky from the future, programmed to destroy

Mass Destruction

On the Master's orders, the Toclafane kill one tenth of Earth's population on first contact. Under his regime, they use terror to maintain order among the population, before the Doctor succeeds in returning them to the future.

Sound of drums beats constantly in head

Sense of smell can track the Doctor

Hands ripple with electricity, and can shoot bolts of energy

THE MASTER RACE

ONE MASTER POSES a serious threat to the universe. But six billion of them would be catastrophic. After the Master was shot by his wife, Lucy Saxon, the Doctor made sure that his body was burned. However, someone stole the Master's ring—containing his genetic code. Through this ring, the Master returns and finds a way to turn every human being into himself, so that he can take over the whole universe.

Life-giving Elixir

An underground cult loyal to the Master performs a ritual and creates an elixir to bring him back from the dead. The key ingredients for this potion are the Master's ring, the sacrifice of their own lives, and a catalyst unwittingly provided by the Master's former wife, Lucy Saxon—a tissue with an imprint of her lips, which holds his biometric signature.

A New Body

The Master's body may look the same as when he was Harold Saxon, but it is flawed, because his spurned wife, Lucy, sabotaged the resurrection process. Her actions fail to prevent the Master's return, but do reduce his body's stability. With new supernatural power and strength, the crazed Master seems unstoppable, but he is slowly and surely using up his life force.

The Immortality Gate

The Immortality Gate is a medical device to cure people by transmitting a template that rebuilds cells. Rather than treating one person at a time, it can cure the populations of whole planets at a time. Driven by the desire to give his daughter immortality, Naismith enlists the Master to fix the machine. However, the Time Lord has his own plans for it.

The Gate runs on nuclear power that is controlled via specialist isolation booths. The feed is manned 24 hours a day and cannot be left unattended: the locking mechanism means that a technician cannot leave one side of the booth until the other side is occupied.

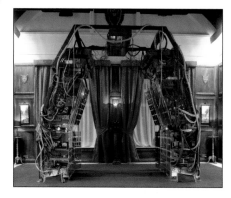

The green-skinned Vinvocci originally built the Immortality Gate, which was later commandeered by billionaire Joshua Naismith. In order to claim it back, two Vinvocci, using shimmer devices to appear human, went to work for Naismith.

The Naismiths

Joshua Naismith is a ruthless billionaire who owns his own private army and will stop at nothing to get what he wants. His daughter, Abigail, is as vain as he is rich, and both are meddling in alien technology that they do not understand. Joshua is aware of the Master's dangerous reputation, but he arrogantly believes that he can control him.

Body language displays close father-daughter relationship

ABIGAIL AND JOSHUA NAISMITH

Cellular Transformation

The Master hijacks Joshua Naismith's plan for the Immortality Gate and uses it to turn everyone on Earth into himself. People become not just genetic copies of the Master, but him in entirety. All six billion Masters share the same mind. In essence, the human race no longer exists.

Heroic Wilf

Wilf was drawn into the world of the Doctor through his granddaughter Donna, and he has his own role to play in saving Earth. The old soldier has one more battle left. He uses his old RAF piloting skills to control an asteroid rocket, ducking and diving the missiles the Master's armies fire at him and the Doctor.

The Doctor's former companion Donna is not affected by the cellular transformation because she is not strictly human after she became part Time Lord in a past incident. However, if she remembers anything about her life with the Doctor, her head will overload and she will die. The Doctor left her with a self-defense mechanism: when her head starts to heat up, she collapses, but remains alive.

TRINITY BEFORE POSSESSION

TRINITY AFTER POSSESSION

Six Billion Masters

By possessing every politician, soldier, and military leader on Earth, as well as others, such as American newscaster Trinity Wells, the Master gains control of all the planet's resources and weapons. Six billion crazed warmongers now prowl Earth and plan to turn it into a giant warship to wage war across the universe.

Clothes suitable for newsreading role

Time Lord Pawn

The Master believes that he is now in charge, but he doesn't realize that he is being manipulated. When he finds out that he is merely a pawn in the plans of other Time Lords, he is quick to take his revenge on Rassilon, Lord President of the High Council of Time Lords.

THE HEAVENLY HOST

Razor-edged halo can be thrown as weapon

Wings stretch out to fly

ONBOARD THE luxury Max Capricorn Cruiseliner *Titanic*, a group of tourists are served by angelic-looking robots known as the Heavenly Host. En route from the planet Sto in the Cassavalian Belt to Earth to experience primitive cultures, the tourists soon discover that the golden creatures—and things onboard the *Titanic*—are not exactly shipshape.

Sinking the Ship

Max Capricorn Cruiseliners are advertised as "the fastest, the furthest, and the best." Their *Titanic* was named after Earth's most famous ship and is owned by Capricorn himself. He has a secret agenda to destroy the ship, kill the passengers and crew, and wipe out life on Earth.

Capricorn bribes the dying Captain Hardaker to sabotage the ship to cause it to crash. By magnetizing the ship's hull, it attracts meteoroids, which damage the Nuclear Storm Drive engines and cause the *Titanic* to plummet toward Earth. If the ship hits the planet, the nuclear engines will explode and destroy all human life.

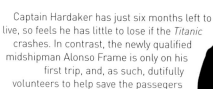

MIDSHIPMAN FRAME

Metal hand can deliver karate-style blows

Captain Hardaker has just six months left to live, so feels he has little to lose if the *Titanic* crashes. In contrast, the newly qualified midshipman Alonso Frame is only on his first trip, and, as such, dutifully volunteers to help save the passegers

Angels of Death

The robotic Heavenly Host's usual job is to provide tourist information and assistance. However, they follow orders from Max Capricorn, and he has reprogrammed them to kill everyone onboard the *Titanic*. When a Host is asked to fix a passenger's necklace, it nearly breaks her neck!

HEAVENLY HOST FACTS

- **Each Host has the strength of ten men.**
- **The Host's robotics can be temporarily deactivated by an electromagnetic pulse.**
- **The Doctor initiates Security Protocol One, which overrides any previous instructions and compels a Host to answer three questions.**

The Host's default position is standing straight, with hands together and head bowed

When the TARDIS crashes into the ship, the Doctor stows away on board. He realizes that the ship is in danger, but the Host try to stop him from saving it.

CAPTAIN HARDAKER

The Doctor and the Waitress

Astrid Peth dreams of seeing the stars—and the Doctor makes her dreams come true by taking her to the alien planet Earth. He recognizes a kindred spirit in the feisty young waitress, and helps her see that nothing is impossible.

Astrid yearns to travel and see the entire Universe. Before getting her job on the *Titanic*, she spent three years as a waitress at a spaceport diner.

Uniform based on 1920s waitress

Smart tweed suit

Chest replaced by cybernetics following accident

ASTRID PETH

BANNAKAFFALATTA

MR. COPPER

Bannakaffalatta, a Red Zocci cyborg, and Mr. Copper, the *Titanic's* historian, help the Doctor defeat the Host. Bannakaffalatta dies, but his bravery enables the Doctor and other survivors, including Mr. Copper, to reach the safety of Earth.

Head is only remaining organic part

Protective casing contains oxygen field

Closed mouth conceals golden flashing tooth

Device can control the *Titanic's* engines

TELEPORT BRACELET

Wrist-worn bracelets like this one can transport passengers between the *Titanic* and Earth.

LIFEBELT

Life-support system constructed in secret on Max's homeworld of Sto

London is deserted—except for Wilfred Mott and the Royal Family. The Queen escapes just as the Doctor pilots the *Titanic* safely over Buckingham Palace.

MAX CAPRICORN

Vengeful Cyborg

Before being ousted by his board and vowing revenge on all those involved, cyborg Max Capricorn ruled his company with a rod of iron for 176 years. He believes that he is the victim of anti-cyborg prejudice and hopes that using the *Titanic* to destroy Earth will ruin the company and land his former colleagues in jail for mass murder. In the meantime, Max has set up offworld accounts and plans to use these secret funds to retire to the beaches of planet Penhaxico Two.

Astrid falls to her death while saving the Doctor. Her molecules are held in stasis and the Doctor sends them to the stars.

ADIPOSE INDUSTRIES

THE BREEDING PLANET ADIPOSE 3 has been stolen by the Daleks, so the Adipose must find a new way to reproduce. Hired "nanny," Matron Cofelia, needs a planet with high levels of obesity and she finds Earth, where she sets up Adipose Industries. The company's unwitting customers think they are buying a miracle diet product—but really they are forming baby Adipose out of their own flesh!

Observation windows

Hover function enables stationary orbit

NURSERY SHIP

"Seeding" a Level Five planet like Earth—using it to grow another species—is against galactic law. While the nursery ship collects the newborn Adipose, the Adiposian First Family murders Matron Cofelia to cover its tracks.

One million customers in Greater London sign up to the Adipose Industries special offer: £45 ($75) for three weeks' supply of weight-loss pills, plus a free gift of an 18-carat gold pendant.

PENDANT

The Adipose

Formed from human fat, new baby Adipose are created at 1:10am every day. These baby Adipose may appear friendly and sweet, but some of them have already killed, albeit unwittingly. In a crisis, Adipose are programmed to consume their entire human host rather than just their fat.

Capsule bio-tunes itself to its owner so as to affect only that person

The gold pendant may be advertised to new customers as a free gift, but it actually attracts fat, binds it together, and galvanizes it to form a body.

Miss Foster

Matron Cofelia of the Five-Straighten Classabindi Nursery Fleet adopts the alias Foster when she is employed by the Adiposian First Family to facilitate the birth of a new generation of Adipose. Her devotion to her charges is matched only by her callousness toward the humans she utilizes in her plans. She will kill to achieve her goals.

FAT-EATING PILL

WATCH

This wrist watch doubles as a communicator between Miss Foster and her minions.

Miss Foster's pen has similar properties to the Doctor's sonic screwdriver.

SONIC PEN

ADIPOSE FACTS

- **Each Adipose consists of exactly 2.2 pounds (1 kilogram) of living fat.**

- **In a crisis, Adipose can form themselves from body parts other than fat, but converting bone, hair, and internal organs makes them sick.**

- **Newborn Adipose are small enough to fit through cat flaps.**

The Adipose Industries building is converted into a Levitation Post, ready to float ten thousand baby Adipose up to the nursery ship.

Although prized as a priceless gem, the Firestar crystal is in fact a Vespiform Telepathic Recorder. It holds the essence of the alien's identity, and can instantly transfer knowledge, emotions, and even a particular mindset to a Vespiform.

VESPIFORM

THIS ANCIENT AND WISE race of shape-shifting insectoid creatures comes from the Silfrax Galaxy. A lone, curious Vespiform left his hive homeworld to come to Earth in 1885. It took on a human form called Christopher in order to learn more about the human race.

Giant Wasp

In its natural form, the body of an adult Vespiform is around eight feet (2.4 meters), which makes it a formidable opponent to a human, especially when buzzing with a fierce temper. However, Vespiform biology is susceptible to insecticides such as piperine, found in pepper. Drowning in water is also a real risk as their wings disintegrate and their spindly legs are too weak to swim.

Powerful wing

Giant antenna sense touch, smell, and taste

Compound eye combines multiple angles for wide field of vision

Long legs for landing and crawling

Insectoid exoskeleton

Stinger full of deadly poison

LADY CLEMENCY EDDISON

Firestar was a gift from Christopher

STINGER

Loss of a Vespiform's stinger renders it temporarily helpless. However, the stinger can be regrown within hours.

AGATHA CHRISTIE

An Insect Romance

Shape-shifting Vespiform are able to interbreed with other species. In Delhi, India in 1885, Christopher met British Aristocrat Lady Clemency Eddison. She conceived his child, but not before Christopher drowned in a monsoon, leaving her heartbroken.

Body can take on the Vespiform wasp-like form, when the Reverend is angry

Hidden Vespiform

Local village vicar Reverend Golightly was adopted, so he has no idea that he is half-human and half-Vespiform. Vespiform offspring remain in their birth form until a strong emotion breaks the genetic lock. One day in 1926, anger, and the proximity of the Firestar, trigger Arnold's transformation into a poisonous wasp. With his emotions raging, he goes on a murderous rampage.

Eddison Hall, home to Lady Clemency, and its estate are passed down the female line, along with the Eddison title.

Reverting to the natural Vespiform state creates a pink-purple haze. This genetic re-encoding also leaves traces of morphic residue—a viscous by-product of the transformation process.

REVEREND ARNOLD GOLIGHTLY

In 1926, the well-known murder-mystery writer Agatha Christie disappeared mysteriously for eleven days. Doctors diagnosed amnesia, but some suggest it was a publicity stunt or revenge on her cheating husband—or perhaps the result of an attack by an alien Vespiform.

Fiery breath can incinerate humans

PYROVILES

EARTH FEELS THE HEAT when the fire-loving stone Pyroviles wake up! After their escape pod crash-landed on Earth, these alien creatures lay dormant for thousands of years under Mount Vesuvius—a volcano near the city of Pompeii in Italy. In 62CE, an earthquake heralds their awakening. With much of their technology still intact, the Pyroviles plan to return to their planet, Pyrovillia, or alternatively, convert Earth into their new home.

Hot stone form can be shattered by cold water

PYROVILE FACTS

■ While the Pyroviles lay beneath the Earth's crust, their homeworld Pyrovillia was stolen by the Daleks.

■ Vesuvius's eruption is so powerful that it cracks open a rift in time. Ripples from the explosion radiate back to the start of the Pyrovillian timeline—the earthquake in 62CE.

The magma creatures travel from the heart of Vesuvius to Pompeii via an underground network of hot springs.

Magma flows through body

Stone exoskeleton

Reconstituted Rock Creatures

With their original bodies smashed into dust when their ship crashed, the Pyroviles need a new form. Inhaled as tiny particles by the citizens of Pompeii, they then force themselves inside the human brains, where they use psychic talent to bond with their host's body, gradually transforming it into stone.

Pyrovile dust is contained in the vapors from Vesuvius's hot springs, which are breathed in by the mystics of Pompeii, in the belief that it aids their visions.

Inside Vesuvius, the Pyroviles blaze with ideas. Their energy converter will harness the power of the lava in the volcano to create a fusion matrix and speed up the conversion of humans into Pyroviles. In their new Empire, the Earth will burn and the oceans will boil.

Pompeii was a popular holiday destination for Romans, until Mount Vesuvius erupted with the force of 24 nuclear bombs on August 23, 79CE. It's unknown exactly how many of the town's 20,000 inhabitants died, but the scale of the disaster was unprecedented.

The Sibylline

The name "Sibyl" is given to women thought to be possessed by the god Apollo and thus granted the gift of prophecy. Joining the Sibylline Sisterhood is a life-long commitment and considered a prestigious and honorable occupation for Roman women. They wear painted eyes on their hands as a symbol of their foresight, but stubbornly refuse to listen when Donna Noble tries to tell them about the impending volcanic eruption.

Entire body has become stone

The High Priestess

As head of the Sibylline Sisterhood, the High Priestess is highly respected. However, she too succumbs to the Pyrovile dust and begins to speak with the voice of the Pyrovile. Halfway between human and Pyrovile, she thinks that her painful transformation is a blessing from the gods.

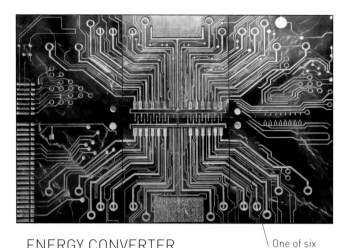

ENERGY CONVERTER

One of six circuits, each carved from marble

This energy converter is designed to convert humans the world over into Pyroviles. The plans for it came to Lucius Dextrus in a dream inspired by the Pyroviles themselves.

The Doctor's Dilemma

Pompeii or the world? The Doctor has to choose. Vesuvius's lava will be used up in the Pyroviles' plan, but by stopping the aliens, the eruption goes ahead and the whole of Pompeii is destroyed.

THE DOCTOR'S WATER PISTOL

The Doctor's pocket water pistol is the perfect weapon to use against the hot Pyroviles. Water causes them pain and makes their molten bodies solidify and then shatter.

Pyrovillian Prophet

Toga conceals stone right arm

Lucius Petrus Dextrus is Pompeii's Chief Augur— a type of Roman priest. Having inhaled Pyrovile dust, he is slowly turning to stone. The crack in time caused by the eruption gives Pyrovile-infected citizens, like Lucius, the ability to see echoes of the future.

LUCIUS PETRUS DEXTRUS

Not even the Pyroviles' escape pod could survive the eruption of Vesuvius. But as it is programmed to evade danger, it removes itself from the heart of the volcano and lands safely nearby with Donna and the Doctor.

The Caecilius Family

Caecilius is a marble dealer living in Pompeii with his wife, Metella, son, Quintus, and daughter, Evelina, when Vesuvius erupts. History states that those who stayed in Pompeii died. Technically, there is therefore nothing that the Doctor can do to stop Caecilius and his family from perishing. However, Donna encourages the Doctor to look beyond the letter of the law. He can surely save one family without changing history entirely, and so he chooses the Caecilius family.

SONTARANS

AN AGRESSIVE HUMANOID SPECIES from the planet Sontar, Sontarans care about nothing but war. They have been fighting their deadly enemy, the Rutans, for 50,000 years, and there is no end in sight. Their every action serves to further their cause, whether it's searching for a strategically advantageous position or increasing the number of Sontaran warriors to take part in the conflict. Combat is glorious for Sontarans, and to die heroically in battle is their ultimate goal.

Probic vent is a Sontaran's only weak spot

Staal enlists the help of teen genius scientist Luke Rattigan and his students to lay the foundations of a clone world on Earth. However, he has nothing but contempt for these human helpers and proposes to use them for target practice when their usefulness is at an end.

Three-fingered hands

General Staal, the Undefeated

General Staal of the Tenth Sontaran Battle Fleet is charged with turning Earth into a clone world to create more Sontaran warriors. When the Doctor disrupts this plan, vengeful Staal prepares to wipe out the human race. He is proud to enter the fray with his troops, and when the Doctor gives him the choice between death or defeat, he refuses to submit, even though it costs the lives of himself and all his soldiers.

Body weighs several tons on the high-gravity planet Sontar

Attack of the Clones

All Sontarans look similar because they are clones. At their military academy on the planet Sontar, one million battle-hungry Sontaran clones are hatched at every muster parade. Under the charge of Sontaran High Command, each warrior is immediately given a rank and dispatched on a battle mission.

Muscles designed for load-bearing rather than leverage

Commander Skorr, the Bloodbringer

Second-in-command Skorr leads the Attack Squad to Earth, relieved to finally be facing combat. He welcomes his death in battle at the hands of UNIT's Colonel Mace, as an honorable warrior's death, regretting only that he will not see the Sontarans victorious.

SONTARAN FACTS

- Sontarans have a strict code of honor. As warriors, nothing offends them more than accusations of cowardice.

- The probic vent on the back of a Sontaran's neck is its major Achilles heel. However, Sontarans consider it a strength as it means they must always face their enemies during battle.

- Sontarans are vulnerable to Coronic acid, which causes a quick but agonizing death in seconds.

Sontaran Spacecraft

The Tenth Sontaran Battle Fleet consists of a Command Ship and a number of detachable capsules that can be moved into position when Battle Status is enjoined. Sontaran ships are impervious to nuclear missiles and the separate Scout Ships are small enough to avoid detection by radar.

Spherical Scout Ship capsules detach from main ship

COMMAND SHIP

Sphere spins through space

Single Sontaran pilot

SCOUT SHIP

"skinned" battle pose

Sontaran blaster gun is never far from Strax's hands

As Madame Vastra's unconventional butler, Strax finds it difficult adapting to a life of servitude. While he accepts Vastra's role as the leader of the Paternoster Gang, he still harbors a healthy mistrust of any being that isn't a Sontaran.

Red light indicates grenade is activated

Activation button

STRAX'S GRENADE

This Sontaran grenade is one of Strax's favorite weapons, as it brings the added satisfaction of blowing things up. Strax has little patience for stealth tactics, preferring to engage the enemy directly with every weapon at his disposal— whether they're actually needed or not.

Point fires a disabling beam that can temporarily render a person useless

Baton emits an energy pulse that can repair systems like teleport pods

SWAGGER STICK

The Sontarans' love of warfare drives their desire to invent ever more methods to destroy their enemies. From blasters and beam guns to grenades and gas attacks, the clone warriors have a weapon for every occasion.

Clips onto handheld blaster to make it a rifle blaster

Attaches to Sontaran's belt

CLIP-ON BLASTER EXTENSION

Barrel emits laser beams that kill instantly

Display indicates power usage

Nurse Strax

Strax is a disgraced Sontaran forced to work as a nurse during the Battle of Zaruthstra in 4037 as punishment, for crimes he has never confessed. Indebted to the Doctor, who saved his life, Strax later helps his Time Lord ally in the fight against the Headless Monks at Demon's Run. He appears to die a glorious death during the battle, but is brought back to life by Silurian Madame Vastra. What Strax lacks in brains, he more than makes up for with brawn

Trigger designed for three-fingered grip

BLASTER GUN

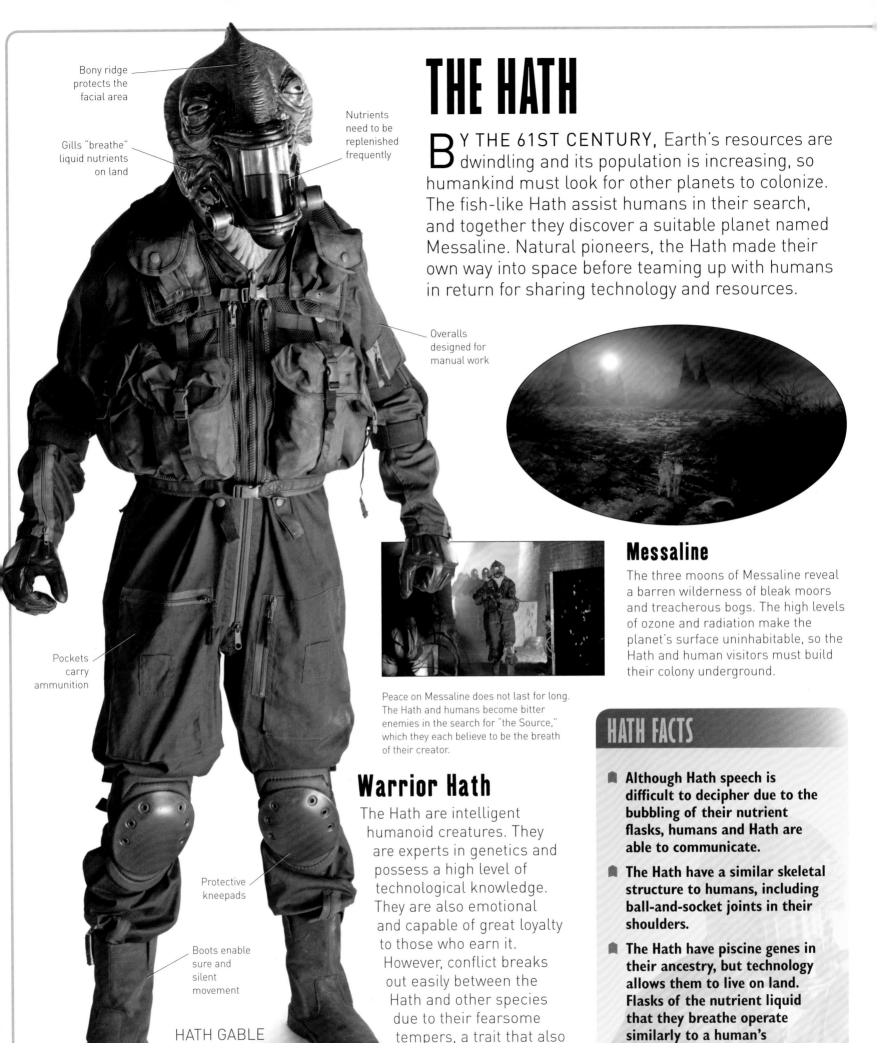

Bony ridge protects the facial area

Gills "breathe" liquid nutrients on land

Nutrients need to be replenished frequently

Overalls designed for manual work

Pockets carry ammunition

Protective kneepads

Boots enable sure and silent movement

HATH GABLE

THE HATH

BY THE 61ST CENTURY, Earth's resources are dwindling and its population is increasing, so humankind must look for other planets to colonize. The fish-like Hath assist humans in their search, and together they discover a suitable planet named Messaline. Natural pioneers, the Hath made their own way into space before teaming up with humans in return for sharing technology and resources.

Messaline

The three moons of Messaline reveal a barren wilderness of bleak moors and treacherous bogs. The high levels of ozone and radiation make the planet's surface uninhabitable, so the Hath and human visitors must build their colony underground.

Peace on Messaline does not last for long. The Hath and humans become bitter enemies in the search for "the Source," which they each believe to be the breath of their creator.

Warrior Hath

The Hath are intelligent humanoid creatures. They are experts in genetics and possess a high level of technological knowledge. They are also emotional and capable of great loyalty to those who earn it. However, conflict breaks out easily between the Hath and other species due to their fearsome tempers, a trait that also makes them formidable opponents in battle.

HATH FACTS

- Although Hath speech is difficult to decipher due to the bubbling of their nutrient flasks, humans and Hath are able to communicate.

- The Hath have a similar skeletal structure to humans, including ball-and-socket joints in their shoulders.

- The Hath have piscine genes in their ancestry, but technology allows them to live on land. Flasks of the nutrient liquid that they breathe operate similarly to a human's underwater oxygen tank.

GENERAL COBB

Unyielding mission commander General Cobb leads the human army. His inability to work alongside the Hath triggers a generations-long war between the two species as they quarrel over who should assume control of Messaline. As a result, colonists divide into rival factions.

Holstered gun used in "shoot first, question later" approach

The colonists need extra workers, so the Hath create the progenation machine, which takes genetic material from the original pioneers and uses it to form fully grown beings of the same race.

Two hearts, like a Time Lord

DETONATOR

Originally designed for building work, this detonator is used as a weapon by the humans.

Progenation Machine

The humans on Messaline reprogram the progenation machines to create soldiers—embedding military history and tactics in the generations that spring from them. When the TARDIS lands on Messaline, a soldier forces the Doctor's hand into one of the machines. A tissue sample is extrapolated and accelerated, and within minutes the Doctor genetically becomes a father!

Genetic Anomaly "Jenny"

The Doctor's daughter is genetically a Time Lord, but has been engineered to be a soldier. Donna calls the blond teenager "Jenny" because she is a "genetic anomaly." Despite their physiological likeness, the Doctor claims there is no real relationship between them. However, he grows to care for his "daughter," and Jenny learns compassion and wanderlust from her "father." When she is shot, her Time Lord DNA enables her body to restore itself.

A doctor treats anyone, and when you are a space-traveler, that includes aliens. Martha resets Peck's dislocated shoulder and gains the trust of the injured Hath and his colleagues.

Weapon of Hath design

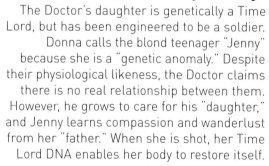

Super-temp Donna realizes the mystery numbers on the walls are the building completion dates. This means that, despite having been on Messaline for "generations," the colonists have actually been there for only seven days!

Ammunition magazine

HATH PECK

In return for Martha helping him, Hath Peck bravely insists on accompanying her across the perilous surface of Messaline. He ends up rescuing Martha from a deadly swamp.

The Source

Tales of the Source have been passed down through generations of colonists. It turns out to be a terraforming machine—a device used to make bare planets habitable. The gases it releases into the atmosphere accelerate evolution on Messaline, rejuvenating the ecosystem, creating abundant plant life and restoring peace between humans and Hath.

VASHTA NERADA

BY THE 51ST CENTURY, there are many ways to experience narratives—holovids, direct-to-brain downloads, fiction mist—but people still love books. The Felman Lux Corporation creates a planet-sized Library controlled by a computer called CAL. However, the company doesn't realize that the newly printed books have been made from trees containing microspores of the deadly alien Vashta Nerada. Over time, more than a million of these microscopic, flying carnivores hatch inside the Library.

The Library

When the human-hunting Vashta Nerada hatch in the Library, it seals itself, leaving a single message: "the lights are going out." The Library's creator, Felman Lux, cannot decode the seals and enter, but he exhorts his descendants to keep trying and to safeguard CAL.

100 years before the Doctor arrives, the Vashta Nerada enter their deadly hatching cycle. There are 4022 humans in the Library at the time, and nowhere is safe for them to be teleported to, so CAL saves them all to her hard drive.

A group of expeditioners led by River Song venture into the Library, but many fall prey to the Vashta Nerada. The swarms devour human flesh, then animate the remaining skeletons.

Space Piranhas

The name "Vashta Nerada" means "the shadows that melt the flesh" because they strip their victims to the bone in seconds. They are also known as "piranhas of the air." After devouring one of the visitors to the library, a swarm of the carnivores animate the leftover spacesuit and use its neural relay to communicate a ghostly, deadly message.

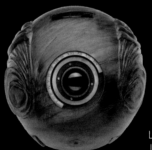

SECURITY CAMERA

CHARLOTTE ABIGAIL LUX (CAL)

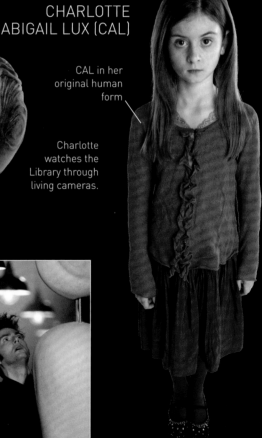

CAL in her original human form

Charlotte watches the Library through living cameras.

VASHTA NERADA FACTS

- The Vashta Nerada are found on a billion worlds, including Earth, where they live mainly on roadkill.

- The creatures hunt by latching onto a living food source and keeping it fresh until they devour it.

- The tiny beings normally live in the darkness, but can also be seen as the dust in sunbeams.

The Doctor brokers a deal with the Vashta Nerada: he will allow them free reign over the Library for eternity, but in exchange they must give him a day's grace to evacuate everyone trapped on CAL. He plans to sacrifice himself to stabilise the power to CAL, but River Song insists on taking his place.

Book-loving Charlotte Abigail Lux was terminally ill, but her father, Felman Lux, wouldn't let her die. Instead, her mind became the main command node of the Library, which Lux built for her eternal pleasure.

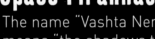

THE FLOOD

HUMANITY'S EXPLORATION of the stars makes a leap forward in the year 2058 with the first human settlement on Mars. The pioneering crew on Bowie Base One studies the planet to see if a colony is viable. They tap into an underground glacier in the Gusev Crater for water supplies, unaware that the water holds a viral life form known as the Flood. A faulty filtration system leads to some of the crew becoming possessed.

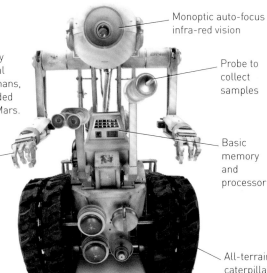

Strong-minded Captain Adelaide Brooke leads the team on Bowie Base One. She pursued a dream of space travel after she saw a Dalek as a child. Thanks to her intellect and determination, she was the first non-American NASA candidate, the first woman on Mars, and is famous for her research. The Doctor greatly admires Adelaide, calling her the "woman with starlight in her soul."

Possessed eyes

Watery Nightmare

Six of the nine crew on Bowie Base One, including Tarak Ital, fall victim to the Flood virus and have their bodies transformed: their mouths crack, their teeth blacken, and their eyes turn a haunting light-blue. Controlled by a hive mind, the zombie-like creatures try to infect the rest of the crew, using them to reach water-rich Earth.

Water drips constantly from the body

The Flood virus spreads through water. Nowhere is safe: water can wait and seep through the tiniest of cracks or build up pressure to break through the strongest of defenses.

THE FLOOD FACTS

- The Flood virus infects a victim through contaminated water. It possesses and transforms a person's body and mind, leaving no trace of their personality.

- Infected people gush an endless supply of water from their mouths and hands.

- The possessed can survive on the surface of Mars without protective suits or oxygen.

- Host bodies are driven to perpetuate the Flood by infecting more people and hunting out new sources of water.

TARAK ITAL
POSSESSED
BY THE FLOOD

Self-destruct

When Adelaide realizes that the crew is doomed, she arms the base's nuclear self-destruct to stop the Flood from reaching Earth. Those infected perish in the explosion, but the Doctor steps in to rescue the remaining healthy crew in the TARDIS.

SAN HELIOS

HALFWAY ACROSS the universe in the Scorpion nebula, the civilization of San Helios has been wiped out by scavenging stingrays who devour everything in their path. And their next stop is planet Earth! All that stands in their way is a handful of passengers on a London bus that has fallen through a wormhole and landed on San Helios. But these are no ordinary passengers—one of them is the Doctor, and he'll do anything to get them all home.

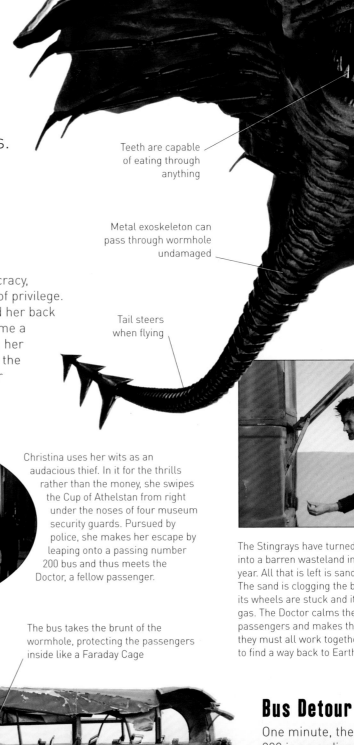

Teeth are capable of eating through anything

Metal exoskeleton can pass through wormhole undamaged

Tail steers when flying

Lady Christina de Souza

Stylish, fashionable attire

A minor member of the British aristocracy, Lady Christina is bored with her life of privilege. Seeking adventure, she has turned her back on her dull upbringing and become a notorious jewel thief. However, her subsequent adventures with the Doctor bring her far greater excitement than any of the heists she has pulled off.

Close-fitting clothes for ease of movement

Christina uses her wits as an audacious thief. In it for the thrills rather than the money, she swipes the Cup of Athelstan from right under the noses of four museum security guards. Pursued by police, she makes her escape by leaping onto a passing number 200 bus and thus meets the Doctor, a fellow passenger.

Sturdy and silent rubberized boots

The Stingrays have turned San Helios into a barren wasteland in less than a year. All that is left is sand—lots of it! The sand is clogging the bus's engine, its wheels are stuck and it is out of gas. The Doctor calms the panicking passengers and makes them see that they must all work together, if they are to find a way back to Earth.

The bus takes the brunt of the wormhole, protecting the passengers inside like a Faraday Cage

Unbeatable global call tariffs

Bus Detour

One minute, the number 200 is an ordinary London bus, entering a tunnel in traffic. The next, it is battered and stranded on the sandy world of San Helios. It fell through a wormhole, but returning to Earth is not so simple: the driver tries to walk through and is fried to a skeleton.

Ravenous Stingrays

Body is size of a small car

These scavenging stingrays swarm in their billions and travel from world to world consuming everything in their path. When a planet is stripped bare, they fly in a massive formation, circling at high speed until they rupture space and create a wormhole. Then they pass through to another unsuspecting world and repeat the cycle.

Bones reinforced with metal creature has consumed

Stingrays travel in vast swarms, which look like a sandstorm to the untrained eye. But the Doctor soon realizes that stingrays are approaching, and knows that Earth will be history if they reach the wormhole they created.

Cup of Athelstan

Solid gold

This cup was given to King Athelstan of England at his coronation in 924CE. Gold is an excellent conductor of electricity, so the Tenth Doctor uses the cup to forge a device to get the bus home—destroying it in the process.

Scientific Advisor

Professor Malcolm Taylor is a top scientific advisor at UNIT. A computer genius, he devises a program that will seal the wormhole created by the stingrays. Determined to save the lives of all those stranded, he bravely defies orders to use it until the number 200 bus, carrying the Doctor, Christina, and their fellow passengers, is safely back in London. Only after his new best friend the Doctor calls and tells Malcolm to close the wormhole, does he run his program—just ahead of the pursuing stingray swarm.

UNIT-issued lab coat

PROFESSOR
MALCOLM TAYLOR

Tritovores

Two Tritovores—a race of green-skinned humanoids with heads similar to thoses of flies—are also stranded on San Helios. They arrived in one of their large, hi-tech spaceships, hoping to trade, but soon realized that the stingrays had wiped out all life on the planet. Believing the number 200 bus is a weapon that caused their ship to crash, the Tritovores capture the Doctor and Christina. But they soon realize that the stingrays are responsible and join forces. Unfortunately, before the two Tritovores can reach the bus, they fall prey to a stingray.

Compound eyes just like flies

Mouth sucks up organic waste

Telepathic translator

Moving mandibles make clicking sounds used to communicate

Impulse laser pistol

Tritovores technology is very advanced and the Doctor is pleased to find anti-gravity clamps, which, when attached to the wheels of the bus, help the bus fly home.

- **The first time Prisoner Zero duplicates someone with whom it has formed a psychic link, they fall into a deep coma. They stay unconscious until the link is broken.**
- **Prisoner Zero can create perception filters to stop it from being seen. It can also use them to conceal anything it chooses.**
- **Multi-forms can live for millennia.**

Prisoner Zero is extremely dangerous. Amy narrowly escapes death when she discovers it in her house.

PRISONER ZERO

A HIGHLY DANGEROUS creature, known as Prisoner Zero, has escaped from an alien police race known as the Atraxi. A crack in space allows the fugitive to flee to Earth where it hides in the house of young girl Amy Pond. The creature remains concealed there for twelve years using its shape-shifting abilities to avoid detection. But it's only a matter of time before the Atraxi locate it— with grave consequences for Earth.

Shape-shifter's natural form

Malevolent yellow eyes have vertical slit pupils

Gelatinous, snake-like body

Internal organs glow below the translucent skin

Mouth has razor-sharp teeth and a ridged tongue

Escape Route

Prisoner Zero flees through the crack in space and time in Amy's room and creates a perception filter to hide within her house for 12 years. From the other side of the crack, a voice could be heard saying, "Prisoner Zero has escaped." It takes the Doctor's arrival to uncover that the disembodied voice is an Atraxi prison guard, who then warns him that Prisoner Zero is hiding on Earth.

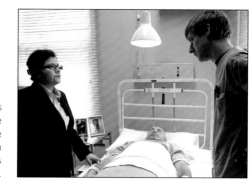

Nurse Rory Williams suspects something is amiss when he sees supposed comatose patients out in the English town of Leadworth. He uses his phone to take photos of them.

Escaped Prisoner

The escaped alien convict Prisoner Zero is an inter-dimensional multi-form, meaning it can change its shape and even copy the identities of more than one creature at a time. To adopt another form, Prisoner Zero must first create a psychic link with a living, dormant creature, so the patients in Leadworth Hospital's coma ward provide numerous guises for the escapee.

The Atraxi

The Atraxi are a sophisticated race of aliens that use advanced technology to search for Prisoner Zero on Earth. They scan the entire planet to detect alien life, but miss their escapee because it has taken human form. The fugitive is dangerous, so the Atraxi are willing to destroy Earth to stop it from fleeing. They break Article 57 of the Shadow Proclamation when they surround Earth, seal off its atmosphere, and threaten to boil the planet if Prisoner Zero does not surrender.

Giant eyeball used to see and speak

Ship contains enough firepower to incinerate Earth

Crystalline structure is similar to a snowflake

ATRAXI SHIP

Prisoner Zero bares its teeth when threatened, giving away its true identity.

PRISONER ZERO AS COMA PATIENT AND DAUGHTERS

Patient Impersonator

Prisoner Zero's psychic link with its victims enables it to take the form of anything the victim dreams about. When Amy and Rory find a terrified mother and her two daughters in the coma ward, Amy soon realizes that they are actually Prisoner Zero impersonating a patient dreaming of her daughters. The shape-shifter's disguise is ruined when it confuses their voices and one of the girls speaks with the mother's voice.

The Doctor tries to alert the Atraxi by using his sonic screwdriver, but it breaks before they detect its signal, so he must find another way to get their attention. Using Rory's phone, he creates a computer virus to reset every counter on Earth to zero.

RESET CLOCK

0 00

Clock counters turned to zero as the computer virus takes hold

With the help of Earth's space and alien experts, the Doctor's reset virus spreads across the world. The Atraxi trace Rory's phone to find the Doctor and Prisoner Zero's location.

Duplicate Doctor

The Doctor transmits photos of the coma patients on Rory's phone to the Atraxi to identify Prisoner Zero, but it now has a psychic link to Amy. She dreams of herself as a child with the Doctor, so Prisoner Zero impersonates them both. The real Doctor gets her to dream of Prisoner Zero's true form. It is then easily identified and recaptured, saving Earth.

Demonic red eyes strike fear into the heart of anyone who looks into them

Head rotates to show three different faces: smiling, frowning, and angry

SMILERS

IN THE CLASSROOMS, in the elevators, in the streets—the android Smilers are everywhere on the *Starship UK*. As the monumental ship travels between the stars in the 33rd century, Smilers keep watch over the British population, letting them know what is good and what is bad. Any lawbreakers discover that the smiling law enforcers have a very nasty side to them!

Long purple robe hides a mechanical body

MANDY

Young schoolgirl Mandy explains to the Doctor and Amy about the Smilers and life on *Starship UK*.

Terrifying Presence

The Smilers are an extension of the *Starship UK*'s security system, observing life and activity onboard in an attempt to maintain order. The British people live in fear of them: no one walks too near their booths, and while the starship is battered, untidy and filthy, the Smilers' booths are spotless—kept clean by frightened citizens. It's one more clue that something is not quite right about life on board the ship.

Onboard the *Starship UK*, people travel by Vators. These are vast elevators operated by Smilers that travel through district blocks.

SMILER BOOTH

Plaque on the booth reads "Smiler"

Smilers are located all over the *Starship UK* in specially designed Smiler booths. People know whether their behavior meets with approval or not from the expression on the Smiler's face. If displeased, a Smiler can open the front of its booth and step out in order to deal with lawbreakers.

The Smiler's face is happy and placid, as long as citizens obey the rules

A frown is a warning that laws are being broken, and that bad behavior must cease.

This feared expression is a final warning before punishment is meted out.

Liz Ten

Liz Ten is really Queen Elizabeth the Tenth, supposed ruler of the *Starship UK*, which, in actuality, is controlled by the government. She is about 300 years old, but her body clock has been adjusted, so that she lives the same ten years over and over again, making her effectively immortal. She is unaware of all this, as at the end of each ten-year time block, her memory is wiped clean.

Winders

The Winders are the police force of the *Starship UK*. They wind up the Smilers and are the only people to know the terrible truth about the *Starship UK*— that it's not a working spaceship at all but a ship built upon a suffering Star Whale. They take an oath to keep this secret and they uphold the tyrannical system that stops people from asking questions.

The Winders are so devoted to serving the *Starship UK* system that they have become cyborgs—part human, part Smiler.

Ring contains knock-out gas

Wind-up key

Winders wear long dark robes with hoods that conceal their "Smiler" side until they choose to reveal it.

WINDER

Porcelain mask allows Liz to walk inconspicuously among her subjects

WIND-UP KEY BOX

Key

On the *Starship UK* many things, such as the street lamps, are wind-up operated. The Winders patrol the streets and have keys for all of them.

Shape is perfectly molded to face

Mainspring provides power, when wound up with the key

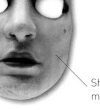

LIZ TEN'S MASK

Gun barrel

Energy blast converter

Sighting

Energy focus

Isomorphic trigger

Liz Ten's gun fires energy blasts that can stop the formidable Smilers, but only temporarily because they are able to repair themselves.

LIZ TEN'S GUN

Battery compartment in grip

On/off switch

High-definition display

Camera

Eternal momentum battery

Liz Ten communicates with her government officials through her PDA. The high-tech device can also be used to track people. Liz gives her PDA to the Doctor to track Amy, who's been kidnapped by Smilers. Finding the PDA later abandoned, Liz tracks the Doctor with it.

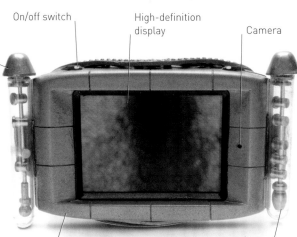

Sumptuous red velvet cape is a clue to Liz's regal identity

Gold plating

LIZ TEN'S PDA

Wireless connector

STAR WHALE

WHEN EARTH WAS being devastated by solar flares, the planet's nations fled to the stars—all except for the United Kingdom. Hearing the cries of the country's children, a Star Whale arrived to help them. However, the creature's kindness was mistaken for a lucky coincidence and the beast was captured by Britain's leaders. They built a ship upon its back and cruelly forced it to carry the nation through space.

Each massive tower block houses an entire county

Gentle Giant

Star Whales are giant alien creatures with several flippers and tentacles that trail behind them. They also have numerous tendrils along their chins and undercarriages. Over the years the Star Whale population has declined—in fact the one carrying the *Starship UK* is the last of its kind.

Friend Not Foe

In the Tower of London, where the Star Whale is "piloted," Mandy and Timmy see a huge tendril emerge from a hole in the floor. They learn that it is part of the Star Whale. Instead of attacking, it strokes them affectionately. Amy sees this and pieces together the clues: the creature is ancient, kind, and hates to see children harmed—it deliberately came to Earth to try to save them and didn't need to be coerced into helping.

Dinner Time!

After the Doctor presses the "Protest" button in the voting booth, the floor below disappears and he and Amy fall down into the Star Whale's mouth. To escape, the Doctor makes the monster vomit—it's not dignified but it works!

The Doctor had been unable to detect an engine on the *Starship UK*. After landing in the monster's mouth, he finally understands how the spaceship flies without one.

STAR WHALE FILM

Voting booths are equipped with monitors, showing a film about the capture and enslavement of the Star Whale that carries *Starship UK*.

Voting Booth

In the name of democracy, every five years people over the age of 16 find out the truth about the *Starship UK* in a film shown to them in voting booths. Afterward, they are given a choice: to protest about what they have learned or to forget it. Most choose to forget; those who protest are fed to the beast.

Like her subjects, Liz Ten is shown the truth about *Starship UK*, but every ten years instead of every five. As Queen, she must choose to forget what she has been told or abdicate by pressing the appropriate button in her voting booth. Every time she has chosen to forget.

FORGET BUTTON

ABDICATE BUTTON

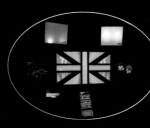

At Winder Division 1, the Winders and Hawthorne, *Starship UK*'s head of government, watch the citizens—and the Queen herself— on huge television monitors as they vote.

The exterior of the *Starship UK* was designed with an extended shelf to conceal the Star Whale below it

The Driving Force

Builders of *Starship UK* didn't understand the benevolence of the Star Whale and thought it would only carry them under duress. They accessed the Star Whale's brain and blasted it with energy bolts to make the creature fly faster. This cruel practice has been taking place ever since.

STAR WHALE FACTS

- Star Whales communicate using sounds that are too high pitched for the human ear.

- According to legend, Star Whales helped the first human space travelers to navigate their way through space safely.

- Star Whales are bioluminescent creatures and have glowing spots on their tentacles and tendrils.

SATURNYNES

ONE WOMAN AND THOUSANDS of her male children are the only surviving members of a race of vampire fish fleeing from their planet of Saturnyne, lost through a crack in space and time. The woman and her eldest son settle in 16th century Venice as humans named Rosanna and Francesco Calvierri. They establish a desirable school for young ladies, the House of Calvierri, and plot to restore their race. Meanwhile Rosanna's other children are lying in wait in the canals.

Vampiric Fish

The vicious Saturnynes are amphibious anthropod aliens who need constant hydration when on land. In their natural form, behind their perception filters, they have four insectoid legs and a thick tail. With their razor-sharp teeth, they feed in swarms like piranhas.

Respiratory system can both breathe air and extract oxygen from water

Razor-sharp teeth for tearing through flesh

Scales overlap downwards to reduce drag in the water

It would be easy to mistake the Calvierri girls for vampires with their fangs, aversion to sunlight, and the fact that mirrors don't show their reflections. In fact they are worse—Saturnynes. A perception filter manipulates the brainwaves of anyone looking so they see humans. Their fangs cannot be hidden because self-preservation overrides the mirage, while their brains become confused by mirrors, causing the absence of a reflection.

Isabella's dowdy clothes from before joining the House of Calvierri

Legs sprout from the abdomen, rather than the thorax, like Earth's insects

Aristocratic Aspirations

Impoverished 17-year-old Isabella joins the House of Calvierri at her boat-builder father Guido's urging, in the hope that she will gain a better position in society as a result. When she goes out walking beneath a perception filter and doesn't recognize him, Guido becomes convinced that something sinister has happened.

Isabella betrays the Calvierris by helping the Doctor to escape from them. She pays for her treachery with her life—she is fed to the Saturnynes in the canal.

ISABELLA

Multi-jointed legs end in bladelike bones that pierce prey

The House of Calvierri

Rosanna Calvierri is a fearsome matriarch who carries the sole responsibility for ensuring the future of her race. She is converting the girls at her school into Saturnynes by drinking their human blood and replacing it with her own. Her hope is that they will become suitable mates for her male children. Her son Francesco is a ferocious predator with a cruel streak, but he is also fiercely devoted to his mother.

FRANCESCO CALVIERRI

Reticella lace ruff reflects fish quills of natural form

Opulent attire denotes wealth and stature

ROSANNA CALVIERRI

Crustaceous exoskeleton molts as the creature grows

Broad tail helps keep heavy body stable on land

When on land, body needs constant hydration

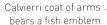

Calvierri coat of arms bears a fish emblem

Control hub for elements manipulator

Alien Technology

Rosanna receives visitors to the palatial House of Calvierri while sitting on a grand throne. It is a symbol of her opulent life, but the intricate gold work and rich velvet also hide advanced Saturnyne technology. The chair is the control hub for a complex system of circuits that can manipulate the weather.

CALVIERRI THRONE

Orbs open to reveal controls

With a flick of a switch on a high-speed rotating cog, the Doctor ends the storm and saves Venice.

ELEMENTS MANIPULATOR

Rosanna can control the weather with this elements manipulator, situated on the spire of the House of Calvierri. It forms dark clouds, creates rain, and causes the sky to boil. It can whip up storms violent enough to trigger earthquakes and tidal waves that will swamp Venice.

Device is disguised as decorative sphere on building spire

On/off switch hidden on cog

Wheels and spheres rotate around the central spike

Two halves of orb close to conceal the inner workings

Rosanna uses her influence in Venetian society to seal the city under the pretense of protecting it from the Plague. She plans to use the elements manipulator to sink Venice, kill all its human inhabitants, and create a new Saturnyne colony.

When Rosanna fails to ensure the future of her race, she jumps into a canal in human form and is devoured by her children. The Doctor tries to save her, but she is determined to die.

SILURIANS

LONG BEFORE HUMANS evolved, a humanoid reptilian race called Silurians ruled Earth. When an apocalypse was predicted, the Silurians retreated deep underground to hibernate until it was safe to return to the surface. In the meantime, evolution moved on and now human beings believe they own Earth. The Silurians disagree, but have also become divided amongst themselves.

In the Welsh hamlet of Cwmtaff, a patch of blue grass has led a scientific research team to drill deep into Earth's crust. Since this project began, strange things have been happening: bodies vanish from graves, pets go missing, and steam pours from holes in the ground. Continued drilling reveals the perpetrators to be the Silurians, awakening within their vast underground city.

Silurian City

Bathed in an orange glow from the Earth's molten core, the Silurian city spreads majestically over a wide valley. Buildings hewn from rock and granite are sealed together with cooled lava. The settlement has its own self-sufficient ecosystem, processing carbon dioxide and providing food. Geothermal power is used to split water from deep-crust minerals into hydrogen and oxygen, which is stored in pockets above the city for a fresh air supply.

Eyes are wizened with age but still sparkle

MALOHKEH

Malohkeh, a brilliant scientist, has been monitoring changes to life forms on Earth's surface for 300 years, while his fellow Silurians sleep. Driven by the quest for scientific discovery, he has no sentimentality toward the creatures that he studies and torments— including humans—but he doesn't intend them any malice.

Leader's ceremonial robes

Eldane

Old and wise, Eldane is the tribal elder of the Silurians. Like the Doctor, Eldane sees the potential for good in humanity and believes homo sapiens and homo reptilia can live peacefully side-by-side. But his argument that the military's role is to protect not provoke falls on deaf ears.

Family of Fear

Mo Northover works on the drilling project at Cwmtaff. Along with his wife, Ambrose, and son, Elliot, he is astonished to discover the existence of the Silurians. When Ambrose's father is injured by the Silurians and Elliot is kidnapped, they display the worst of human nature and respond with violence. Their fear and anger is born out of love and desperation to protect their family, but it derails the peace process.

Family gathers in a protective huddle

AMBROSE, MO, AND ELLIOT

Silurian Lab

The Silurians have built an advanced society thanks to their exploration of science. In a high-tech laboratory, Malohkeh conducts his experiments on the creatures he collects from the surface. His living database includes hedgehogs, domestic pets, a woolly mammoth, and even a human child. The control station for these activities is powered by geothermal energy, and can be programmed to release toxic fumes.

A laser scalpel can make highly accurate incisions. It is used for living autopsies—without anesthetic!

LASER SCALPEL

Built-in power supply

Activation switch

CENTRAL LAB CONTROL

Monitor displays vital life signs

Database contains 300 years worth of specimens

Organic fluid-control technology

Battle-scarred face

Warrior dress

Clothing denotes high military rank

Heat-ray gun

Human-like fingers

RESTAC

Restac is Alaya's gene-twin, but as a military commander, she outranks her sister. She is charged with the security of the hibernating population. Some argue for peace and cohabitation with humans, but Restac has no time for that—she thinks executing the Doctor is a good way to send a message to the "apes."

Thirteen-year-old dyslexic Elliot is the latest addition to Malohkeh's list of experiments. His life cycle is slowed to one millionth of the normal rate, leaving him unresponsive and with a blank stare. Tubes of green fluid keep him alive with essential nutrients.

Shape designed to fit human specimens

ALAYA

Dedicated to ridding Earth of humanity, Alaya is a soldier happy to die for her cause. In fact, she taunts Ambrose into killing her. She believes her murder will trigger a human-Silurian war, enabling her race to reclaim Earth's surface.

Shackles hold wrists and ankles

STRETCHER

Those unfortunate enough to find themselves on Malohkeh's study list are strapped to a stretcher for "decontamination." This process neutralizes harmful bacteria and viruses.

SILURIAN WARRIORS

THE FIERCELY PROTECTIVE Silurian race established a warrior caste to keep its cities safe from the dinosaurs that roamed Earth at that time. For these warriors, nothing is more important than the survival of their reptilian species. Now awake after eons hibernating underground, the warriors are furious that humanity has overrun "their" home. They see humans as vermin—just like the primitive apes they encountered millennia ago.

Sisters in Arms

With special training and fearsome armor, Silurian warriors such as Restac and Alaya are creatures of precision, beauty, and absolute deadliness. With superior Silurian technology, these humanoid, cold-blooded reptiles believe they can reclaim the surface of Earth. For these soldiers, violence is always the answer.

Tough ridges of bone protect Silurian skull

Venom glands take 24 hours to refill

Hole in battle mask for forked tongue to lash out and strike opponents

Military uniform of the Silurian warrior caste

Tailor-made armor fits tight to body

Chain mail forged from underground metals

HEAT RAY GUN

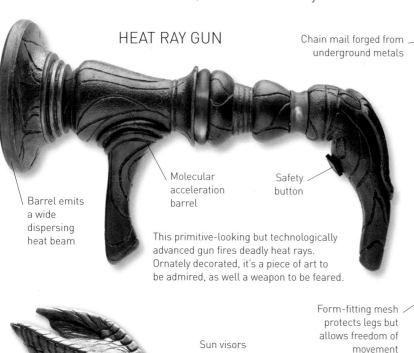

Barrel emits a wide dispersing heat beam

Molecular acceleration barrel

Safety button

This primitive-looking but technologically advanced gun fires deadly heat rays. Ornately decorated, it's a piece of art to be admired, as well a weapon to be feared.

Sun visors shield eyes used to living underground

Mouth fixed in a sinister expression

Form-fitting mesh protects legs but allows freedom of movement

Heavy boots needed for tough underground terrain

BATTLE MASK

As a sign of honor and also for protection, Silurian warriors wear battle masks that are molded to fit closely to the very fronts of their faces. A flexible armored gorget protects their vulnerable neck area.

RESTAC

ALAYA

MADAME VASTRA

A NOBLE SILURIAN WARRIOR, Madame Vastra was awoken from hibernation by London Underground workers, who accidentally caused the deaths of her sisters. Vastra was in the process of avenging them when the Doctor intervened, after which she chose a different path. Now, instead of working to destroy humanity, she lives in Victorian England, solving strange and disturbing crimes as leader of the Paternoster Gang.

Bandolier for extra weapons

A Noble Warrior

An intelligent and capable warrior, Vastra is not only effective at armed combat, but her battle experiences have also developed her skills as a master strategist. She is highly intuitive, relying on instinct to predict her enemies' actions.

Known informally as the "Veiled Detective," Vastra specializes in seemingly unsolvable cases. One of her great successes is the capture of the infamous serial killer, Jack the Ripper, whose body Vastra then devoured.

Over the years, Vastra has developed great affection for the Doctor. In the Eleventh Doctor's hour of need, when his death seems close at hand, she gathers those close to him, determined to protect her old friend.

Gently curved long sword for battle

Dagger for short-range fighting

During the epic battle of Demon's Run, Vastra and Jenny display their incredible sword-fighting prowess against the Headless Monks in a bid to protect Amy Pond and her baby, Melody.

Victorian-inspired corset

A Silurian, a Sontaran, and a human make up the Paternoster Gang—an unlikely trio of amateur sleuths. Stubbon Vastra, weapons-obsessed Strax, and feisty, sarcastic Jenny investigate the murky underworld of Victorian England, dispensing their version of justice to both local criminals and aliens alike.

Jenny Flint

Jenny is Madame Vastra's dedicated and trustworthy maid. Over time, the pair have become close and are now married, working together as they carry out their investigations. Like Vastra, Jenny is an expert fighter, as skilled in hand-to-hand combat as she is wielding a sword.

Skintight leather combat clothing often worn beneath Victorian dress

Tough leather combat boots

THE PANDORICA

LEGEND HAS IT THAT the Pandorica is a box designed as a prison to hold the most feared thing in all the universe: a nameless, terrible monster soaked in the blood of a million galaxies. The Doctor is familiar with the tale, but he never imagined that the description could fit him, and that he is the intended inhabitant of the Pandorica. The Doctor, River Song, and Amy Pond find the Pandorica in an ancient weathered chamber beneath Stonehenge.

Center pin pops out to allow the sections to rotate

The patterns on the side of the Pandorica are made up of intricately carved stone pieces that interlock like a 3-D puzzle box. When the unlocking process is triggered from inside, these layers of locks move apart and rotate.

Hand can drop away to reveal Auton gun-stick

Realistic period clothing

The Pandorica Opens

A gleaming black cube 10 feet (3 meters) square, the Pandorica is a formidable fortress with layers of security protocols: deadlocks, time-stops, matter lines. It has been waiting for the Doctor in an old dark chamber called the "underhenge" hidden below Stonehenge. It takes only one scan of the biometric data from the Doctor's handprint for it to unlock itself. The Doctor is curious to know what is inside, unaware that the Pandorica is opening to receive him.

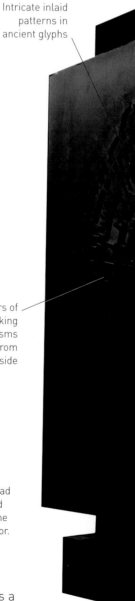

Intricate inlaid patterns in ancient glyphs

Layers of locking mechanisms unlock from the inside

AMY'S BOOKS

Information from books that Amy read as a child—about Pandora's Box and the Romans—inform the scenario the Nestene create to ensnare the Doctor.

Fake Romans

Above the Pandorica, it appears to be Roman Britain, but everything is a fabrication created as a trap by the Nestene Consciousness, formed from an imprint of Amy's memories. The Roman Army is the greatest human military machine ever known, but these centurions are not human, let alone Roman.

AUTON GUN-STICK

Gun can shoot or vaporize targets

Jointed fingers solidify when gun activated

Box emits an energy forcefield that can extend over the whole of Stonehenge

Chair forces prisoner to stay alive

The Auton Deceit

The Roman soldiers are Autons—living plastic in a human shape controlled by the Nestene Consciousness. Soldiers appear human until they glaze over, turn in unison, and raise their hands to reveal considerably more firepower than a sword or bow and arrow.

The illusion created by the Nestene is highly convincing, with a full Roman encampment near Stonehenge. However, a scan reveals that energy weapons have been used here.

While the Pandorica is open, time energy is eating up the universe, wiping many races from existence. Some turn to stone, as after-images of creatures that now never existed.

The Anomaly Exhibition

After 2,000 years, the Pandorica turns up at the Anomaly Exhibition, a display of impossible things at the National Museum in London. Surrounded by myth and legend, it was discovered under Stonehenge in 107AD and taken back to Rome. Stolen by Goths, and sold by Marco Polo, it was later recovered from the Aegean seabed. During the Blitz in World War II it was rescued from a burning warehouse in London.

THE ALLIANCE

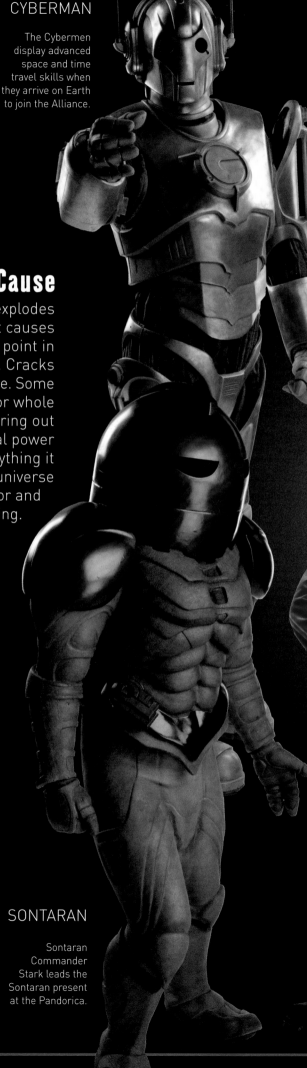

CYBERMAN

The Cybermen display advanced space and time travel skills when they arrive on Earth to join the Alliance.

O VER THE CENTURIES, many aliens have crossed swords with the Doctor. Daleks, Cybermen, and many other races join in an unlikely alliance to build the Pandorica to put an end to the Doctor once and for all. When the Pandorica opens, they all receive notification from a transmission boosted by Stonehenge. They gather in the skies over Earth in their billions to see the Doctor locked in the prison.

At first, the Doctor is bemused that the prison is for him. He is astonished that it took such an alliance to entrap him and that he is seen as a great warrior. But when the gravity of the situation becomes clear, he is angry and then remorseful. He feels the pain he has inflicted while saving one species from another.

Allies with a Cause

In a far future event, the TARDIS explodes and the Eye of Harmony within it causes temporal energy to burn at every point in time and space simultaneously. Cracks begin to appear across the universe. Some are tiny and some are big enough for whole planets to fall through. The light pouring out the cracks carries so much temporal power that it wipes from existence anything it touches—so all species across the universe come together to lock up the Doctor and prevent this event from ever happening.

The Cyber Sentry

The Cybermen posted to watch over the Pandorica have stood guard for so long that their organic parts have rotted. However, their metal components are still active and are just as deadly. Although dismembered, their wires spread around the underhenge, searching for fresh meat to replace their decayed organs.

CYBERHEAD SENTRY

The Pandorica chamber also contains petrified Cybermen parts. Time energy seeping from cracks in the Universe have caused the Cybermen to cease to exist, leaving just a stone imprint of their memory.

STONE CYBERMAN SENTRY

SONTARAN

Sontaran Commander Stark leads the Sontaran present at the Pandorica.

JUDOON

The armed Judoon,
led by their captain,
personally help
force the Doctor
into his prison.

ROBOFORM

Roboforms are scavengers
that normally accompany
other races on invasions.

SUPREME DALEK

Daleks are not known for
cooperating, but their hatred
of the Doctor is greater than
their hatred of other races.

SILURIAN

A small group of Silurians
reveal that they still count
the Doctor as their enemy
when they turn up at
Stonehenge.

AUTON

The Nestene Consciousness
uses Auton slaves disguised
as Roman soldiers to trick
the Doctor and guard the
Pandorica prison.

UVODNI

The Uvodni are a
humanoid race with
insectoid faces from
the Spiral Cluster of
the Dragon Nebula.

SYCORAX

Some Sycorax warriors
also obey the summons
to join the Alliance.

PEG DOLLS

To BEGIN WITH, the Peg Dolls are ordinary wooden dolls inhabiting a dollhouse, which belongs to a young boy named George. However, George is not a regular human child, but part of an alien species called the Tenza. George uses his psycho-kinetic powers to send all his fears into the dollhouse—which causes the Peg Dolls to come to life and transform anyone they touch into living dolls as well.

George has taken on the appearance of a regular human child

GEORGE THE TENZA

Like other Tenza, George hatched in space then sought out foster parents for himself. However, he believes the human parents he chose are rejecting him, and as a result, is subconsciously trapping all his worst fears in the dolls' house.

Old-fashioned toy soldier uniform

Long, straggly hair sprouts from victim's head

Painted face is chipped and cracked

Limbs lumber and walk in awkward fashion

Wooden arms open wide to ensnare more victims

George's Dad

George's foster dad Alex is desperate to help his son overcome his fears and seeks medical help. However, he doesn't realize that George thinks the "Doctor" has come to take him away—escalating the young Tenza's terror, and causing the Doctor and Alex to enter the dollhouse.

As George himself enters the dollhouse and is about to be transformed by the Peg Dolls, Alex tells his son that he'll never send him away—allaying George's fears and restoring everything to normality.

Living Dolls

When a person is turned into a Peg Doll, their body parts grow larger bit by bit, swiftly changing into wood. With all trace of personality lost, the end result is a terrifying toy that lumbers around the doll-house in a state of living death.

HANDBOTS

THE CLINICALLY WHITE HANDBOTS are medical robots designed to look after people suffering from the fatal Chen 7 plague in the Two Streams Facility on the planet Apalapucia. Limited in intelligence and physical agility, the robots are equipped with hypodermic needles and darts for administering medicine. They lack eyes in the conventional sense, instead using their hand sensors to "see" where they're going.

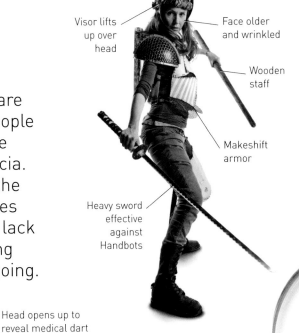

Visor lifts up over head

Face older and wrinkled

Wooden staff

Makeshift armor

Heavy sword effective against Handbots

THE GIRL WHO WAITED

Trapped in the accelerated time stream of plague-infested Apalapucia while the Handbots believe she needs anesthetizing, one version of Amy Pond waits 36 years for the Doctor and Rory to rescue her. She becomes embittered and careworn in the process.

Hand delivers anesthetic by touch

Head opens up to reveal medical dart

Chest compartment stores hypodermic syringes

Glass resembles oversized magnifying glass

TIME GLASS

In the Two Streams Facility, infected patients with only 24 hours to live are placed in a faster time stream, allowing them to "live" their full lives in a single day. A Time Glass syncs the faster time stream with the normal world, allowing visitors to communicate with the patients. Rory and the Doctor use it to reach Amy.

Two-way communication interface

Rorybot

Starved of human friendship, the trapped, aging Amy creates her own companion by disarming a Handbot and drawing a smiley face on it. She names it Rory after the boyfriend she thinks she'll never see again.

Organic Robots

The Handbots have sensitive organic skin grafted onto their hands for sensing bacteria in their surroundings. As well as delivering anesthetic, the robotic hands can complete detailed scans of their environment and even register the presence of bacteria on a patient.

The Handbots are limited and unable to sense that Amy's human body would be unable to cope with their medicine. To prevent them from giving her what could be a lethal injection, she becomes something of an expert at disabling and reprogramming the machines.

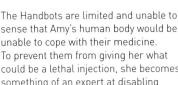

THE *FANCY*

A GHOSTLY GREEN APPARITION is terrorizing the crew of the becalmed pirate ship the *Fancy*. Its captain, Henry Avery, believes they are being attacked by the mythical Siren, a beautiful being which rises from the ocean each time one of his men is injured. Lulled by the Siren's haunting singing, Avery's crew members are being atomized one by one.

The Black Spot

Every time someone is wounded, a black spot suddenly appears on the palm of his hand. The pirates believe this means just one thing: that the Siren has marked her latest victim for death.

Black spot on the hand of pirate McGrath

Mop used as makeshift weapon against Siren

17th century pirate dress

Tricorn sailor's hat

Keys to ship's armory and store-rooms

Flintlock pistol

FLORRES

DANCER

CAPTAIN AVERY

BOATSWAIN

The Siren

The Siren is really a virtual doctor from a spaceship trapped in a parallel reality. Since the ship's alien crew was destroyed by a human virus, the ghostly doctor has been teleporting Avery's crew aboard in order to heal them.

Captain Avery

Formerly a respected naval officer, Avery turned to piracy and abandoned his wife and young son, Toby. When he realizes that Toby has stowed away onboard, he is unable to admit what he has become and believes he's an unfit father for the boy.

When Rory accidentally cuts himself, he suddenly finds the Siren's eerie song utterly irresistible. His friends have to hold him back to stop him from trying to touch the creature.

Avery's son has typhoid fever, and so, Avery decides to stay and care for him under the Siren's medical protection. Along with his pirate crew, he sails the *Fancy* out into space.

MINOTAUR

A TERRIFYING, HORNED CREATURE, the Minotaur stalks the corridors of a strange hotel full of people's worst nightmares. At first, it seems the Minotaur is feeding on the fear of those trapped in the hotel, but when it starts killing people, the Doctor realizes that the beast is actually feasting on their faith—literally draining the life from its victims.

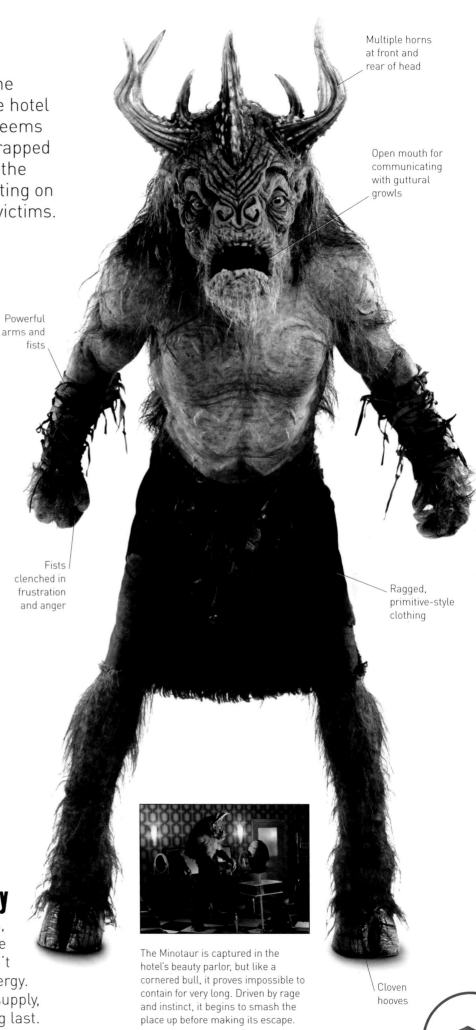

Multiple horns at front and rear of head

Open mouth for communicating with guttural growls

Powerful arms and fists

Fists clenched in frustration and anger

Ragged, primitive-style clothing

Cloven hooves

The hotel is actually an automated spaceship prison, built by a race that had once worshipped the Minotaur before turning against it and casting it off into space. The prison is programmed to trap other life forms and convert their faith into food for the creature.

Each "hotel room" in the prison ship contains a disturbing vision for every being that's become trapped there. Amy Pond's room is probably the most terrifying of all—it contains Weeping Angels.

Unable to stop the Minotaur hunting people down and killing them, the Doctor decides to go on the offensive instead. With everyone's help, he devises a plan to corner the beast and interrogate it.

Overthrown Deity

After being imprisoned for thousands of years, all the Minotaur longs for is death. However, the beast's survival instinct is too strong and it can't help but feast on each new source of faith energy. Eventually, the Doctor succeeds in severing its supply, giving the Minotaur the space it needs to die at long last.

The Minotaur is captured in the hotel's beauty parlor, but like a cornered bull, it proves impossible to contain for very long. Driven by rage and instinct, it begins to smash the place up before making its escape.

In order to mentally control their Gangers, the Morpeth Jetsan miners remain in a dormant state. If this link is broken, it is possible for the Gangers to become independent beings.

GANGERS

IN THE 22ND CENTURY, duplicates of humans known as Gangers (shortened from "Doppelgängers") are used in environments that are too dangerous for real people to work in. Formed from an artificial substance called the Flesh, the beings are telepathically controlled by their human counterparts. Whenever a Ganger gets damaged or destroyed, another duplicate can be created with ease.

Flashlight for low-light mining conditions

Logo of acid-mining company, Morpeth Jetsan

White face shows that Ganger has not fully stabilized

Metallic implements used as weapons

Gangers wear the same clothes as their original human counterparts

DICKEN

MIRANDA CLEAVES

JIMMY WICKS

BUZZER

Rebel Flesh

When a solar tsunami hits an acid mine on a remote island, the link between the human miners and their duplicates is severed and the Gangers become independent, with their own thoughts and feelings. Humans and Gangers are mistrustful of the other, and the threatened Gangers plot to kill the humans in order to ensure their own survival.

Ganger Creation

Creating a Ganger is a complex technological process. First, a special harness scans the molecular structure of a human. Next, a vat of Flesh slowly fills up a human-sized tank until it is brimming with the gooey white substance. Slowly, facial features begin to form, the process continues until a perfect Ganger copy has been created.

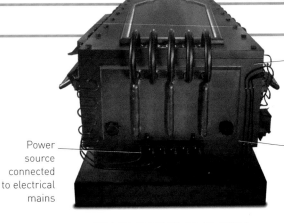

Thick metal walls to prevent leakage

Power source connected to electrical mains

Length of tank allows it to contain whole human being

TANK FOR THE FLESH

When the Doctor scans the Flesh, it somehow makes a mental connection with him. He realizes that the substance is sentient in a way no one else can comprehend.

Doctor Ganger

A Ganger version of the Doctor is accidentally created after the real Doctor leaves a genetic imprint on the Flesh. Behaving much like his alter ego, the Ganger fools even Amy Pond into believing he is the real Doctor.

JENNIFER LUCAS

Cloned face

A solar storm wreaks havoc on the acid mine. Not only does it cause the power surge that creates the rebel Gangers, but it also causes the mine's pipes to crack, leaking lethal acid everywhere.

Unstable Flesh molecules allow for unnatural flexibility

Recovering from the infighting at the mine, three Gangers, including Miranda Cleaves and Dicken, survive. Thanks to the TARDIS's energy, they fully stabilize as people. They now face the daunting task of making everyone understand the plight of Gangers across the world.

Ganger Jennifer

The multiple Ganger versions of Morpeth Jetsan worker Jennifer Lucas are less stable than those of her colleagues'. Not remembering that the humans on the island were once her fellow workers, she plots to kill them by causing the mine's acid to explode—after which, she intends to inspire a Ganger revolution worldwide. She eventually transforms into a deranged Flesh monster, and is destroyed by the Ganger Doctor.

Amy Substitute

As awareness of Gangers is spread across the universe, it opens up the possibility that people might use them for evil. The Order of Silence, led by Madame Kovarian, kidnaps a pregnant Amy Pond and replaces her with a Ganger copy, which the Doctor eventually destroys. They plan to keep her safe until her baby is born, at which point they substitute the baby too, hoping to brainwash her into becoming the Doctor's killer.

THE ORDER OF SILENCE

THE SILENCE IS A RELIGIOUS ORDER dedicated to preventing the Doctor from reaching the planet Trenzalore. They believe that his presence there would allow the Time Lords to return to the universe, causing the Time War to begin all over again. The Silence therefore decide to travel back along the Doctor's time stream, going to desperate lengths in their attempts to kill him.

Madame Kovarian

A key figure in the Kovarian Chapter of the Silence, Madame Kovarian is ruthlessly dedicated to bringing about the Doctor's destruction. Her main task is to kidnap Amy Pond's baby, Melody, and brainwash her into becoming the Doctor's killer—a psychopath otherwise known as River Song.

Eye-drive enables wearer to remember the memory-proof Silents

Expecting trouble from the Doctor, the Silence have amassed a vast army of Clerics—highly trained soldiers who are dedicated to ensuring that their overriding mission is successful.

When Madame Kovarian is captured in an alternative timeline, she is horrified to discover that she has become dispensable to the Silence and is killed by her own electrified eye-drive.

During one assassination attempt on the Doctor, Kovarian and the Silence kidnap the grown-up River Song and place her in an armed, automated spacesuit beneath Lake Silencio in Utah. They believe they have engineered a fixed point in time. However, when River rises from the lake, she refuses to gun down the Doctor and time itself unravels.

One of many smart, crisp business suits, normally worn in black

Fiercely sharp high heels

ORDER OF SILENCE FACTS

- ■ The Order of Silence was created by Tasha Lem, Mother Superior of the Papal Mainframe.

- ■ Members of the Order have the power to time travel.

- ■ In one attempt to kill the Doctor, they blew up the TARDIS, unwittingly causing the universe to collapse.

- ■ Also calling themselves the "Sentinels of History," the Order's core belief is that "Silence must fall." It means that the Doctor must never be allowed to speak his name and free the Time Lords, thus potentially restarting the Time War.

The Silents

Tall, skeletal humanoids, the Silents are confessional priests, genetically engineered by the Papal Mainframe to be memory-proof so that people would forget everything they'd told them. A group of the creatures travels back in time with Madame Kovarian to help her attempt to kill the Doctor. They are a dangerous enemy to have: they can absorb electricity from their surroundings into their bodies, before discharging it again through their fingers. The resultant blast is powerful enough to reduce a human to charred cinders.

Mouth opens wide during electrical absorption

Sunken eyes within hollow, terrifying faces

Kovarian Chapter Silents wear shirt and tie

Elongated fingers, from which lightning bolts can be discharged

After looking away from a Silent, people forget that the creature ever existed. One way to record an encounter with a Silent is to draw tally marks while still looking at it—to act as a reminder of how many times the aliens have been encountered.

The Silents have influenced the world throughout history, using their powers of post-hypnotic suggestion to make humanity do their will. They even inspired mankind's desire to go to the Moon so that it would develop spacesuit technology. Even US President Nixon becomes involved in the quest to stop them.

The Silents are devious creatures. In an alternative timeline, they allow themselves to be imprisoned inside glass tanks, but far from being dormant, they are really lying in wait for the Doctor.

The Doctor encounters the Silents creatures again on the planet Trenzalore. In that final battle, they actually join forces with the Doctor against the Daleks, proving that old enemies can fight side by side.

DEMON'S RUN

A REMOTE ASTEROID, Demon's Run is the Order of Silence's secret military base and the scene of a great battle in which the Doctor attempts to rescue his companion Amy Pond and her baby, Melody. The asteroid's name hails from a prophetic poem containing the line "Demons run when a good man goes to war." Assuming himself to be that man, and calling in some old debts, the Doctor gathers together an unlikely band of fighters to help overcome the massed forces of the Silence.

The Headless Monks

One of the Silence's principal allies, the Headless Monks are a deeply religious order who choose to decapitate themselves as they believe in following their hearts rather than their minds. On Demon's Run, the Monks do not register as alive on scanning equipment—an advantage that allows them to mount surprise attacks.

Loose skin left from removal of head twisted into a knot

Hood normally raised to cover headless state

Hands outstretched for shooting balls of energy

Simple monks' robes

Before a fight, the Headless Monks chant a sacred attack prayer. During battle they fire lethal blasts of energy from their hands and fight with electrified swords.

Insignia denoting rank of Colonel

Colonel Manton

Colonel Manton is in charge of military operations on Demon's Run, determined to boost his troops' morale in preparation for an attack by the Doctor. However, when the Doctor tricks Manton's forces into disarming themselves, he tells the Colonel to order his men to run away, hoping that the disgraced leader will be forever known as "Colonel Runaway."

LORNA BUCKET

Lorna met the Doctor briefly when she was a little girl. She believed him to be a great warrior and so joined the Church's army of clerics in the hope of encountering her hero again. On Demon's Run, she switches sides and joins the Doctor's army of allies, but is tragically killed by the Headless Monks.

Some of the Doctor's closest allies are Madame Vastra, her partner, Jenny, and Strax the Sontaran nurse. They bravely defend Amy and her baby against the Headless Monks' brutal attack, which results in Strax's apparent death.

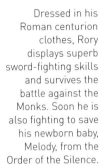

Dressed in his Roman centurion clothes, Rory displays superb sword-fighting skills and survives the battle against the Monks. Soon he is also fighting to save his newborn baby, Melody, from the Order of the Silence.

The Doctor's influence stretches far and wide. He calls on the Silurians and Judoon to help his friends take on the Silence. He even gets his old pal Winston Churchill to send a squadron of space-faring Spitfires to take out Demon's Run's communications array.

Media chip implanted in head can receive wi-fi

Bright blue skin

Opulent robes and expensive jewelry

Dorium Maldovar

A fat, blue-skinned alien, Dorium is a wealthy wheeler dealer who always has his ear to the ground. He sells the Headless Monks the security software they need to imprison Amy's child, but later switches sides when the Doctor calls on him to repay an old debt. During battle, he attempts to sweet-talk the Headless Monks into sparing him, but instead they chop off his head.

A shifty alien named Gantok is a servant to the Silence, but he agrees to take the Doctor to Dorium Maldovar's head in the underground tunnel of skulls. Only the wealthiest can afford boxes for their severed heads. The walls of the tunnels are lined with loose, mean-spirited, skulls capable of devouring a man.

The Headless Monks place Dorium's head in box and store it in the Seventh Transept. Dorium remains alive in this state and is able to tell the Doctor about the Silence and their reasons for wanting to prevent him from reaching Trenzalore.

TRENZALORE

A LEVEL TWO HUMAN COLONY, Trenzalore is a world of enormous significance to the Doctor. It is a planet he finds himself defending in order to prevent the Time War beginning anew between the Time Lords and the rest of the universe. In an alternative timeline, it is also the place where the Doctor discovers that his body is buried.

Physiogonomy is probably mostly human

Body does not age

Clothes are a holographic projection

A Crack in the Universe

In the town of Christmas on Trenzalore, the Doctor finds a familiar-looking crack in a wall—the last remaining tear in the skin of reality. Trapped in a pocket universe, the Time Lords are beaming a truth field and an endlessly repeating question, "Doctor who?", through the gap. The Doctor realizes that if he answers with his real name, the Time Lords will know it's safe to come through and return, possibly triggering a new Time War.

The Papal Mainframe

As the security hub of the known universe, the Papal Mainframe seeks to prevent war from breaking out. This "church" is both mysterious, and, at times, controversial. It consists of different, often heavily armed, factions, including more violent groups that have broken away—such as the Doctor's old foe Madame Kovarian.

When the Daleks invade the Papal Mainframe as a means to reach Trenzalore, they slaughter Tasha Lem before harvesting information from her body. She is turned into a Dalek puppet, but the Doctor manages to restore strong-minded Tasha's true personality once again, turning her against her Dalek masters.

Tasha Lem

Otherwise known as the Mother Superious, Tasha Lem is an old friend of the Doctor's and the powerful head of the Church of the Papal Mainframe. She protects Trenzalore with a forcefield, realizing that if the Doctor gives his name, the Time Lords will return and the Time War will begin anew. She therefore dedicates her church to a new cause, declaring that "Silence will fall," meaning the Doctor must be prevented from speaking his name at all costs.

A Town called Christmas

Snow-farming villages like Christmas can be found across Trenzalore. The presence of the crack in time and space, however, marks Christmas out to receive attention and bombardment from alien forces. The Doctor decides to become the sheriff of this village in order to protect both his own race, the Time Lords, and his new home on Trenzalore, fighting off alien attempts to invade with the help of the Papal Mainframe.

The friendly villagers of Christmas welcome the Doctor, and will always answer any question honestly, due to the truth field imposed by the Time Lords.

Woolen cap wards off cold

Colorful clothes of Christmas residents

Shorts worn by junior citizens

BARNABLE

A young boy named Barnable is one of the many human villagers that the Doctor befriends over the centuries. He and the Doctor become very attached to one another after the Doctor saves Barnable's father's barn from destruction.

Countless alien races travel in their spaceships to Trenzalore to investigate the potential Time Lord threat, including the Daleks, Sontarans, and the Cybermen.

Wood untouchable by the Doctor's sonic screwdriver

Flamethrower weapon built into arm

WOODEN CYBERMAN

The Papal Mainframe places technology sensors around Christmas to alert the Doctor to the presence of approaching alien enemies. Undeterred, the invading Cybermen downgrade to be made of wood—which doesn't set off the sensors.

The Doctor is prepared to grow old and die defending Trenzalore, even when the Daleks send for reinforcements and break through the Papal Mainframe's defenses. In events that rewrite time, the Time Lords gift the Doctor new regenerations, ensuring his survival, the safety of the people of Trenzalore, and the Daleks' defeat.

The Doctor's Grave

In an alternative timeline, Trenzalore is a desolate battlefield graveyard and the location for the Doctor's tomb. In this version of events, the Doctor pays his first visit to the planet after his friends in the Paternoster Gang are kidnapped by the Great Intelligence. His grave is marked by a damaged future version of his TARDIS, which has grown to an enormous size. Fortunately, this timeline is aborted when the Time Lords change the future and grant him a new set of regenerations.

KAHLER

A TECHNOLOGICALLY GIFTED race, the Kahler suffered a terrible war which wiped out half of their planet. Tasked with restoring peace, a team of scientists including Kahler-Jex experimented on innocent volunteers, turning them into cyborg killers who defeated the enemy. However, one of the cyborgs, Kahler-Tek, wants revenge on its creators and tracks Jex to the American town of Mercy.

Distinctive Kahler markings

Cybernetic eye with in-built sensors

Spare energy cells for laser weapon

Arm replaced with high-intensity laser weapon

Clothing damaged during combat

The people of Mercy, a small town in 1870s America, face a dilemma—either they hand over Kahler-Jex to the Gunslinger, or they face starvation.

Isaac is Mercy's brave and wise sheriff. When he is accidentally gunned down by Kahler-Tek, the sheriff hands his badge to the Doctor, telling him to protect both Jex and his town.

Kahler-Jex

Although he saved millions of lives, scientist Jex regrets performing the cruel experiments that turned people into monsters. To atone for his crimes, he saves the townsfolk of Mercy from cholera, and gives them electricity.

Kahler-Jex uses his crashed spaceship as a generator to bring electricity to Mercy. The Doctor probes its data banks to reveal the truth about Jex's past.

Thanks to its cybernetic eye, Kahler-Tek has an automatic targetting mode, making the cyborg a highly efficient killer.

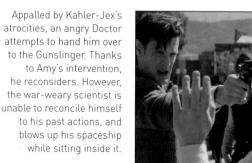

Appalled by Kahler-Jex's atrocities, an angry Doctor attempts to hand him over to the Gunslinger. Thanks to Amy's intervention, he reconsiders. However, the war-weary scientist is unable to reconcile himself to his past actions, and blows up his spaceship while sitting inside it.

Kahler-Tek

Otherwise known as the Gunslinger, Kahler-Tek is half-man, half-machine. Determined to kill Kahler-Jex for his monstrous experiments, he places Mercy under siege and demands that they hand over the war criminal—or face certain death themselves.

SHAKRI

THE SHAKRI ARE mysterious beings who the Doctor mistakenly believed were only a myth to keep the young of Gallifrey in their place. Known as the pest controllers of the universe, the Shakri see humans as dangerous vermin who must be wiped out before they can colonize space.

Aged appearance

Somber black robes

Long, sharp fingernails

Deadly Cubes

Serving an entity known as "the Tally," the Shakri deposit millions of small black boxes all over Earth to gather information about its inhabitants. When activated, each one sends out an electrical surge to stop the heart of the nearest human.

The Shakri have seven spacecraft in another dimension, connected to Earth via seven portals. The Doctor locates a portal in a nearby hospital where he also finds an outlier droid in the form of a young girl, used by the invaders to monitor the vicinity.

Orderlies

Silent, creepy humanoids with grills for mouths, the Orderlies' function is to kidnap hospital patients and take them aboard the Shakri spaceship. They defend themselves with large hypodermic syringes.

The automated Shakri interface is helpless when the Doctor disrupts the Shakri computer systems and manages to disconnect the Shakri craft from their portals, leaving them drifting in dark space. Even better, the Doctor uses the cubes to turn their victims hearts on once again.

Automated Interface

The Doctor is denied knowledge of what the Shakri really look like. When he finally makes contact with the Shakri ship responsible for dumping the black cubes on Earth he is greeted by a hologram taking the form of a black-cloaked humanoid. This sinister apparition warns that the Shakri plan to release a second wave of cubes and cause further deaths.

AKHATEN

A PARASITIC, SENTIENT PLANET, Akhaten is treated fearfully as a vengeful god by the Sun-singers of Akhet—the inhabitants of the seven neighboring worlds. Known as the "Old God," Akhaten has been kept asleep for millions of years, thanks to "The Long Song"—a never-ending lullaby sung by successive generations of Sun-singer choristers.

A host of aliens have gathered on the orbiting asteroid Tiannamat, including Panbabylonians, Hooloovoos, Ultramantas, and Terraberserkers. They have all come for the Festival of Offerings, where each creature presents a treasured gift to the "Old God" Akhaten.

High-domed skull

Ancient, emaciated appearance

Queen of Years

The title of the "Queen of Years" has been bestowed on a young girl named Merry. In this role, she is expected to sing to the Old God, and know every song, poem, and legend from the Sun-singers' history. Merry, however, is ignorant of the Queen of Years' other duty— to be sacrificed. The locals believe it is their job to sacrifice the queen to Akhaten. Otherwise, Akhaten will feed on the souls of everyone on the seven planets, and then in the universe beyond.

Garland presented during the Festival of Offerings

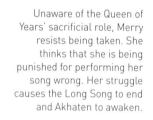

Unaware of the Queen of Years' sacrificial role, Merry resists being taken. She thinks that she is being punished for performing her song wrong. Her struggle causes the Long Song to end and Akhaten to awaken.

MERRY GEJELH

The Vigil are mysterious beings with telekinetic powers who stand guard in the Mummy's temple. Once Akhaten awakens, it has no further use for its servants. The Vigil vanish into thin air, and the Mummy starts dying inside its shattered cell.

Long talons and powerful arms for breaking down cell

The Doctor confronts Akhaten, hoping to overload the parasite with his countless memories. Clara then joins the fight, offering it a precious leaf which represents all the days her mom could have had, if she hadn't died young. Overwhelmed, Akhaten implodes.

The Mummy

Trapped in a glass cell within a pyramid-shaped temple on an orbiting asteroid, the Mummy serves as Akhaten's alarm clock. A primitive, savage creature, it communicates with guttural snarls and growls. Placed to warn the Old God when the Long Song ends, the beast sends a signal, causing it to awaken.

SWEETVILLE

IN 1893, MRS. GILLYFLOWER is recruiting people to live in the idyllic Yorkshire, England community of Sweetville, although she seems interested only in the fittest, brightest, and most beautiful applicants. Advertised as a safe haven where people have a chance to survive a coming apocalypse, Sweetville turns out to be a front for Mrs. Gillyflower's plan to create a "perfect" world.

Mr. Sweet is a tiny red leech from the time of the dinosaurs and Silurians, which has somehow managed to survive. A parasitic creature, it has attached itself to Mrs. Gillyflower's chest. In return for sustenance, it provides her with the deadly venom she needs and has become physically dependent upon. She refers to him as her "silent partner".

Slow-moving body

MR. SWEET

Modest dress of a Victorian puritan

Outer garments conceal Mr. Sweet

Black widow's gown

It may look like the perfect place to live, but nobody residing in Sweetville is ever seen again.

To aid her recruitment drive, Mrs. Gillyflower issues sermons full of warnings of the End of Days, neglecting to mention it is she who intends to destroy mankind.

Scarred face and blindness caused by leech venom

ADA GILLYFLOWER

The gentle and devoted daughter of Mrs. Gillyflower, Ada is the victim of her mother's experiments with red leech venom in her attempts to discover an antitoxin. Ada is devastated when she learns she is not part of her mother's plan for the new "perfect" world.

Winifred Gillyflower

A prize-winning chemist and mechanical engineer, Mrs. Gillyflower is a puritan with an insane vision for humanity. She plans to load the venom produced by Mr. Sweet onto a rocket, explode it in the atmosphere, and bring about an apocalypse. She will then create a new world, populated only by her chosen, beautiful recruits.

Mrs. Gillyflower's chosen people, including Clara, are preserved beneath giant bell jars. The jar will protect them from the venom that will be showered over Earth.

Sweetville's rejects are cast into a nearby canal, their dead bodies glowing a suspicious bright red. The Doctor is amongst these, but his Time Lord body survives the toxic process that was meant to kill him.

Mrs. Gillyflower builds the rocket to fire the leech venom herself. As her plan progresses, she activates the rocket's firing mechanism—but is thwarted thanks to Madame Vastra and Jenny, who have removed its lethal cargo.

ICE WARRIORS

Natives of the planet Mars, Ice Warriors are reptilian beings with a strong instinct for war. More than seven feet tall, the Martians developed mechanized armor to allow them to survive when their home planet turned cold. Inside a bulky protective shell is a wiry and cunning creature that is able to leave its armor and wreak havoc with astonishing agility.

LIEUTENANT STEPASHIN

Hammer and sickle emblem of the Soviet Union

Black Soviet naval uniform

Three stripes and star on sleeve insignia indicate Stepashin's rank

A fiercely patriotic Soviet naval officer, Stepashin attacks the Ice Warrior Skaldak by electrocuting him. Stepashin remains loyal to his country by attempting to form an alliance with the Ice Warrior. But the Soviet officer underestimates Skaldak, and is killed by him.

Ice Warriors are naturally bloodthirsty. In a dangerous or unknown situation, their immediate response is to fight. When Grand Marshal Skaldak finds himself bound in chains onboard a Soviet submarine, he sends out a distress call to his fellow Ice Warriors. When he receives no reply, his thoughts turn to vengeance.

Like his fellow Ice Warriors, Skaldak has a strong sense of honor. He instinctively understands the concepts of war—and the merits of mercy. Skaldak arms the Soviet submarine's nuclear warheads, but is halted by the Doctor, who begs the Ice Warrior to act like a soldier, not a murderer.

Beneath their bio-armour, the Ice Warriors have a reptilian humanoid form. Skaldak has red glowing eyes, scaly skin, and rows of tiny, razor-sharp fangs.

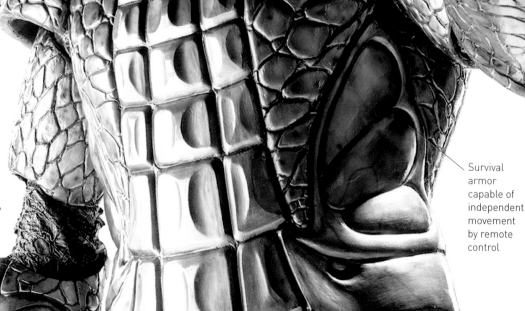

Helmet flips upward to reveal face of occupant

Sonic weapon built into arm

Survival armor capable of independent movement by remote control

The Ice Warriors travel through space in huge ships. When they receive a distress call from Earth, they come as fast as they can. The center of the ship has an opening through which Skaldak is teleported aboard, before returning to Mars.

Grand Marshal Skaldak

The greatest Ice Warrior hero of all, Skaldak has been sleeping in the ice on Earth for over 5,000 years. When he's awoken and attacked by the crew of a Russian sub, the proud warrior honors his ancient Martian code by declaring war on humanity.

ZYGONS

SHAPE-SHIFTING ZYGONS have been waiting hundreds of years to invade Earth—ever since their own planet, Zygor, was destroyed during the Time War. With high-domed heads and sucker-covered skin, the creatures use their advanced body-print technology to copy and impersonate humans, making it easy for them to gain power by means of infiltration.

Adept at manipulating the technology of other races, the Zygons succeed in hiding inside stasis cubes—Time Lord paintings, which are really frozen instants of time. The Zygons lie in wait for hundreds of years, then invade when Earth is sufficiently advanced and suitable for conquest.

When a Zygon changes back into its natural form, it spews out a red mucous from its mouth.

Regal Elizabethan dress emblazoned with jewels

Venom sacs located in tongue

Suckered body

Stingers in hands can stun, maim and even kill

QUEEN ELIZABETH I

As the most powerful person in England, Queen Elizabeth attracts the attentions of the Zygons, becoming the primary target of their invasion attempt. A Zygon duplicate of the Queen attempts to kill her and take control of the country. However, the real Elizabeth kills her impersonator and infiltrates the Zygons' base. The Zygons realize that the time is not yet right to conquer Earth.

Zygon mimicry is so convincing, the Tenth Doctor finds it impossible to tell Queen Elizabeth apart from her Zygon double—even after kissing both of them!

The Zygons believe that alien artifacts contained within the secret vault at UNIT will help them conquer Earth. They impersonate UNIT's chief scientific officer, Kate Stewart, and succeed in infiltrating the so-called Black Archive.

Invasion Party

The homeless Zygons plan to enslave humanity and alter Earth's climate in a bid to recreate the conditions of their home planet. Their attempt to invade through paintings is not their first—the aliens were once aided by a creature called the Skarasen, which was mistaken for the Loch Ness Monster!

Thick, muscular legs lend huge strength to torso

Human brain held within metal exoskeleton

Some metalwork dates back to Roman times

Detachable hand capable of independent movement

Flame-emitting weapon concealed inside sleeve

Movement accompanied by sound of cogs in motion

THE HALF-FACE MAN

LIKE A ROBOTIC VERSION of the infamous Frankenstein's monster, the Half-Face Man is a nightmarish cyborg that stalks the streets of Victorian London, hunting for human body parts. In reality, he is a repair droid from the SS *Marie Antoinette*, a spaceship from the 51st century that crash-landed on Earth millions of years ago. Along with the rest of his kind, the Half-Face Man has been constantly rebuilding himself with cannibalized organs ever since.

Control Droid

The Half-Face Man is the control node for his fellow repair droids—when he comes to life, the others do too. Despite the fact that his ship has been buried underground for countless centuries, he has been determined to carry on functioning, requiring a fresh and constant supply of organs in order to remain operational. When asked about his true purpose, however, the robot gives the same strange answer— to reach the "Promised Land."

The repair droids will stop at nothing to ensure their continued survival. Much to the Doctor's horror, they even destroy a huge T-Rex in order to extract its optic nerve, which they then use to repair their computer systems.

REPAIR DROID FACTS

- The SS *Marie Antoinette* is the sister ship of the SS *Madame de Pompadour*, which was run by similar repair droids.

- The Half-Face Man has replaced every mechanical and organic component of himself so many times, there is no longer any trace of the original left.

- When the Half-Face Man is destroyed, the other repair droids stop functioning as well.

Mask made of real human skin

Plain black and white outfit, suitable for use in Mancini's restaurant

THE DOCTOR IN DISGUISE

The Doctor disguises himself as a repair droid by putting on one of their creepy human masks. Not only does the ghoulish disguise deceive the robots, but it also fools Clara.

The Half-Face Man is the manager of Mancini's restaurant, although the building is merely a front for the repair droids' gruesome operations. The upstairs area is populated with decoys—grotesque robotic diners who never eat anything but are equipped with multifunctional control devices disguised as pens. Used to scan other life forms, innocent people are then taken prisoner and sent down to the spaceship below, where their body parts are extracted.

The robotic droids recognize humans—a source of potential new body parts—by sensing their breath. Clara and the Doctor find themselves in mortal peril when catapulted from Mancini's restaurant into the heart of the robots' underground spaceship. Clara succeeds in holding her breath for a painfully long time in order to fool them—a ruse that works for a while, until she's found out and brought before the Half-Face Man for a terrifying interrogation.

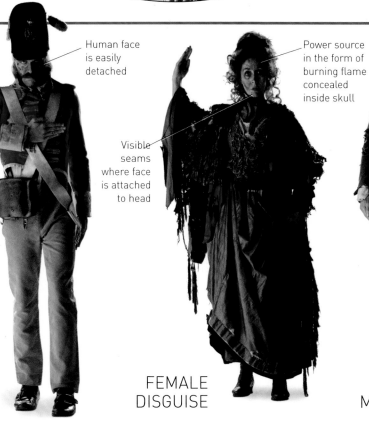

The droids' restaurant is held within an escape pod—the only part of the spaceship that is still able to fly. When the roof opens up, a huge balloon made out of patches of stretched human skin begins to inflate, carrying the capsule up into the sky.

Droid Army

The robots' underground ship is populated with dozens of sinister robots, each one dressed in ragged Victorian clothing.

DROID DRESSED AS VICTORIAN SOLDIER

Unlike the droids in the restaurant, these are battle-ready, each with a lethal sword concealed in its sleeve, ready to slide out automatically.

Human face is easily detached

Visible seams where face is attached to head

Power source in the form of burning flame concealed inside skull

Blank, zombie-like expression

Extracted human organs in constant process of decay

FEMALE DISGUISE

MALE DISGUISE

ROBOTS OF SHERWOOD

AFTER A SPACECRAFT crash-lands in Nottingham, England in the Middle Ages, both the ship and its robotic crew set about adapting to their new environment. The ship itself transforms into a twelfth-century castle, and while the robust robots seek to repair their craft, they take on the guise of knights in armor and seek out a new master to serve— the infamous Sheriff of Nottingham.

Sheriff of Nottingham

An arrogant tyrant, the Sheriff is just as cruel and bloodthirsty as legend has portrayed him. Seriously injured when the spaceship fell to Earth, the robots reconstructed him using metallic components, to the extent that he is now a cyborg—half man, half robot. Not content with terrorizing the unfortunate inhabitants of Nottingham, the Sheriff has greater ambitions. He wants his robots to repair their spaceship so that he can fly to London and kill his unappreciative master, Prince John, claim the throne for himself and rule the entire world.

Cyborg head

Body capable of movement even when headless

Gold regarded as valuable by the robots, as it can be used to fix their ship

Tunic conceals device for controlling robots

Sword armed and dangerous

Robot Knights

Thanks to their advanced technology, the robots have successfully adapted to blend seamlessly into their medieval surroundings. They appear to be ordinary knights in metal armor, but when they switch to battle mode, their true alien features are revealed and they begin to unleash their lethal firepower.

When lowered, helmet conceals metallic facial features

Boar traditionally symbolizes bravery and a willingness to fight to the very end

Hidden blasters fire purple-colored laser bolts

Armor protects robotic circuitry

KNIGHT WITH MECHANICAL FACE REVEALED

Soon after arriving in Sherwood Forest, the Doctor meets the legendary outlaw Robin Hood and his band of merry men—Will Scarlet, Friar Tuck, Alan-a-Dale, and Little John, all equally cheerful. The Doctor has a hard time believing that they actually exist, theorising he must have materialized inside either a miniscope, or possibly some kind of futuristic theme park.

MECHANICAL MEN FACTS

■ Just like the robotic Half-Face Man, the Sheriff's robots were also on their way to the mysterious "Promised Land" when they crash-landed on Earth.

■ The robots' energy beams can be deflected with shiny objects such as shields or mirrors. Aiming this beam at the robots can destroy them.

■ The Sheriff has a hand-held device giving him complete control over his robot followers.

The damaged engines on the robots' spaceship are causing an odd effect. Radiation is leaking into the surrounding countryside—creating a temporary micro-climate where everything looks extra green and perfect. To repair the craft, the Sheriff sends his robots to steal gold from the locals, then melts it down to seal the engine breach. He doesn't realize, however, that the vessel is so badly damaged that it will explode on lift-off—taking half of England with it.

As good a swordsman as Robin is, he is no match for the Doctor and a small piece of cutlery. When Robin tries to steal the TARDIS from him, the Doctor fights back with his metal spoon, tripping Robin up and sending him sprawling into a nearby stream.

GOLDEN ARROW

The prize of the Sheriff of Nottingham's archery contest, the golden arrow is rightfully won by skilled archer Robin. It serves another purpose when the outlaw fires it at the robots' spaceship as it takes off. The arrow weighs just the right amount to help the crippled ship reach orbit, where it explodes harmlessly.

Straight shaft allows archer to achieve deadly accuracy

Pure gold from head to fletchings

Bow for use in archery competitions

Felt cap worn to disguise face when in public

Long hair regarded as ridiculous by Doctor

Lightweight armor does not inhibit in combat

Green is perfect camouflage for hiding in Sherwood Forest

The Legendary Robin Hood

The permanently grinning Robin Hood is instantly disliked by the Doctor. Not only is he annoyed by Robin's constant laughing, but he also believes that the outlaw is too physically perfect to be real and deduces that he must be another of the Sheriff's robots. Much to the Doctor's astonishment, however, Robin turns out to be a real-life flesh and blood human. He really is Robert, Earl of Loxley—a man who is determined to be a hero for those who have suffered under the Sheriff's tyrannical rule.

KARABRAXOS

O N A BLEAK, DESERT WORLD is a single city, dominated by the pyramid-shaped building of the Bank of Karabraxos. It is supposedly the most dangerous bank in the galaxy and completely impregnable, thanks to the sophisticated security protocols that protect its precious contents. High above the arid surface, a solar storm is brewing in the planet's atmosphere, threatening to disrupt the banks' security systems. Below ground, the bank's vaults and passageways stretch down to the very core of the planet and harbor many sinister secrets.

Professional, perfectly styled coiffure

Outfit conceals activating button that allows access to the bank's public address system

The main bank vault is protected by multiple time-delayed locking codes, which must be cracked individually to obtain access. One of the vault's security protocols is a supposedly unbreakable atomic seal which is eventually tripped when the solar storm strikes an antenna on top of the building. Inside the vault are thousands of metal safes, which the Doctor discovers have also been opened by the solar disruption.

Ms. Delphox

Cold and aloof, Ms Delphox is Head of Security at the Bank of Karabraxos. Together with her terrifying Teller creature, she deals with potential criminal activity with ruthless efficiency, determined to reinforce her bank's reputation of impregnability. Despite her powerful position, Ms Delphox lives in constant fear of being fired by the bank's owner, her elusive boss, Karabraxos—who uses identical clones of herself, including Ms Delphox, to ensure the safety of her bank. Karabraxos is not averse to firing her minions when they let her down, which she does literally, by having them thrown into an incinerator.

Expensive tailored clothes

At first, the Doctor thinks a manipulative being known as the Architect has forced him into robbing the Bank of Karabraxos, along with Saibra and Psi. He eventually realizes, however, that he is the Architect himself, and that he's sent himself on a mission to infiltrate the bank in order to rescue the imprisoned Teller creatures.

THE TELLER

Hard exoskeleton

Antennae project waves of invisible, paralyzing energy

Straitjacket prevents escape

Straps and buckles bind captive in a cage with jungle-like conditions

Cloven hoof

SAIBRA

Saibra is afflicted with a mutant gene, which means she transforms into an exact replica of any life form that touches her bare skin. She, therefore, keeps herself covered up as much as possible, a situation that distresses her since it means she is always alone. Desperate to rid herself of her condition, Saibra agrees to help rob the Bank of Karabraxos in order to obtain a suppressant that will destroy her mutant gene once and for all.

Wrap keeps skin covered to avoid direct contact

All-black clothes suitable for robbing bank

Diodes and cables in head allow Psi to interface with other electronic systems

Data streaming visible in eyes during download

Fingertips project information

PSI

An augmented human, Psi is a hacker-turned-bank-robber whose body has been upgraded with artificial parts. He once underwent a prison interrogation, and, worried that he might unwittingly endanger the lives of his friends and family, decided to wipe all memory of them from his mind. Now, like Saibra, he is after something precious that's stored deep within the vault of Karabraxos—a neophyte circuit that can retrieve lost data from any computer system, and will, therefore, restore his lost memories.

Endangered Creature

One of only two surviving members of its species, the Teller is held captive in enforced hibernation by Ms. Delphox. When a security breach occurs, the Teller is woken up and forced to hunt down guilty intruders, using its telepathic powers to detect incriminating thoughts. The creature then paralyzes would-be robbers with a massive telekinetic charge, liquefying their brains and reducing them to brainless vegetables. In the end, thanks to the Doctor, the Teller is reunited with its mate, who has also been cruelly caged against its will.

BBC
DOCTOR WHO
CHARACTER ENCYCLOPEDIA

WRITTEN BY
JASON LOBORIK, ANNABEL GIBSON,
MORAY LAING, AND EMMA GRANGE

CONTENTS

ABZORBALOFF
GREEDY SHAPE-SHIFTING HUMANOID

The Abzorbaloff is a vile green alien from Clom, the twin planet of Raxacoricofallapatorius. The creature can absorb people into his body simply by touching them—feasting on their life force and experiences in the process. He is determined to find the Doctor, believing the Time Lord would be the greatest feast of all.

A STICKY END
The Abzorbaloff disguises himself as a human called Victor Kennedy and takes charge of LINDA, a motley band of people searching for the Doctor. The Abzorbaloff plans to use the TARDIS to return home in triumph.

CANE CONTAINING LIMITATION FIELD

DATA FILE

HOMEWORLD:
CLOM

SPECIAL ABILITIES:
ABSORBING OTHER LIFE FORMS, DISGUISING HIS APPEARANCE

DOCTORS MET:
10TH

ABSORBED FACE OF LINDA MEMBER URSULA BLAKE

The Abzorbaloff carries a cane that creates a protecting limitation field. When the cane is broken, the Abzorbaloff's absorbing abilities can no longer be controlled, and he messily disintegrates in front of the Doctor!

NATURAL ABZORBALOVIAN FORM

ACE
TEARAWAY COMPANION

Ace is a tough, streetwise teenager who is transported in a time storm to Iceworld where she meets the Seventh Doctor. Embarrassed by her real name Dorothy, she assumes the nickname Ace. She becomes a close companion of the Doctor, whom she calls "Professor", even though he disapproves of her tendency to blow things up with Nitro 9—her homemade brand of explosives.

BASHING DALEKS
One Dalek becomes the unlucky recipient of Ace's violent streak. Determined to defend herself, Ace bashes it to bits with a baseball bat powered by the Hand of Omega, knocking off its eye stalk in the process!

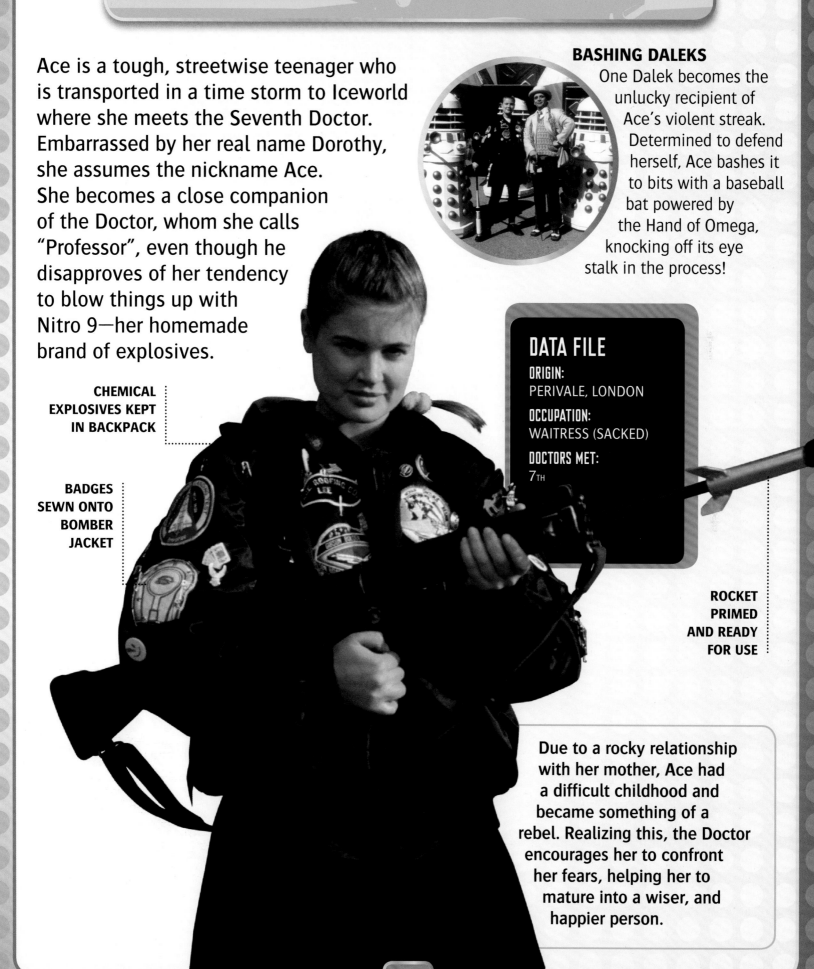

CHEMICAL EXPLOSIVES KEPT IN BACKPACK

BADGES SEWN ONTO BOMBER JACKET

DATA FILE

ORIGIN:
PERIVALE, LONDON

OCCUPATION:
WAITRESS (SACKED)

DOCTORS MET:
7TH

ROCKET PRIMED AND READY FOR USE

Due to a rocky relationship with her mother, Ace had a difficult childhood and became something of a rebel. Realizing this, the Doctor encourages her to confront her fears, helping her to mature into a wiser, and happier person.

ADAM MITCHELL
SHORT-TERM COMPANION

Adam is a young, day-dreaming genius who works for Henry Van Statten, a billionaire and collector of alien artifacts. Adam's job is to catalog each strange object and work out its purpose. After surviving a lone Dalek's killing spree, he briefly joins the Ninth Doctor on his travels.

CASUAL HOODIE

HOLE IN THE HEAD
In the year 200,000, Adam has surgery aboard the Satellite Five space station to install an infospike, an advanced computer interface port, into his forehead. When he clicks his fingers, the center of the device opens up, exposing his brain and allowing it to receive vast amounts of advanced information.

Adam steals secrets from the future and plans to profit from them when he returns to the 21st century. The Doctor is furious when he finds out and immediately takes Adam back home, warning him to keep his infospike a secret.

ALIEN ARTIFACTS
Before meeting the Doctor, Adam studies alien artifacts in a bunker belonging to Henry Van Statten.

DATA FILE

ORIGIN:
ENGLAND, EARTH

OCCUPATION:
GENIUS, SCIENTIFIC RESEARCHER

DOCTORS MET:
9TH

ADELAIDE BROOKE
COMMANDER OF BOWIE BASE ONE

Captain Adelaide Brooke is the leader of the first human colony on Mars. She tells the Doctor that as a ten-year-old girl, she saw a Dalek appear at her window, then fly away. She knew one day she would follow it into space.

HAIR WORN OFF FACE

DATA FILE

ORIGIN:
FINCHLEY, NORTH LONDON, EARTH

OCCUPATION:
COMMANDER

DOCTORS MET:
10TH

Adelaide is a tough, intelligent, and single-minded authority figure. However, she cares deeply about her crew and is devastated when she realizes she will be unable to save them.

GREEN COMBAT UNIFORM

WATERTIGHT BOOTS

FLOOD ALERT
In November 2059, Adelaide is plunged into a terrifying crisis when infected water starts leaking through the roof—turning her crew into zombies called the Flood.

A FIXED POINT IN HISTORY?
Adelaide's death would inspire her descendents to travel into space, but the Doctor decides to change history and save her life. When Adelaide realizes this, she tells him he was wrong and takes her own life.

ADIPOSE
LIVING FAT MONSTERS

The Adipose are cute, friendly aliens made of human fat. When dieting, humans take a pill made by Adipose Industries. Baby Adipose then grow inside their bodies before bursting out of their skin, taking their hosts' excess fat with them. To the world, it seems like the ultimate cure for obesity!

SMOOTH, WHITE BODY

MATRON COFELIA
Calm, arrogant Matron Cofelia goes to Earth undercover as "Miss Foster" trying to find obesity. She needs to breed a new generation after the Adipose nursery planet was lost.

The Doctor learns that the Adipose are being bred illegally by Matron Cofelia, an intergalactic super-nanny who is working for the Adiposian First Family. Eventually, a huge spaceship appears to take the cute creatures back to the stars.

SHORT ARMS

SMALL, WIDE FEET

MONSTERS ON THE MOVE
One night, many thousands of baby Adipose leave their host bodies and begin marching through the streets of London, much to the astonishment of passersby.

DATA FILE
ORIGIN:
ADIPOSE 3

SPECIAL ABILITIES:
CAN CONVERT MOST HUMAN TISSUE INTO ADIPOSE

DOCTORS MET:
10TH

ADRIC
GENIUS COMPANION

Adric is a teenage genius from the planet Alzarius, whose own people once gave him a badge for mathematical excellence. When his brother Varsh is killed by Marshmen, Adric stows aboard the TARDIS, although he sometimes finds it hard getting along with his fellow travelers and often feels like an outsider.

BADGE AWARDED FOR MATHEMATICAL EXCELLENCE

DATA FILE

HOMEWORLD:
ALZARIUS, E-SPACE

OCCUPATION:
UNKNOWN

DOCTORS MET:
4TH, 5TH

YELLOW TABARD

BAGGY UTILITARIAN PANTS

LAYING TRAPS

Following the Fourth Doctor's regeneration, Adric is kidnapped by the Master. He uses the boy's mathematical skills to create a space-time trap for the Doctor—the bizarre city of Castrovalva.

After fighting the Terileptils, Urbankans, and the Mara, Adric's final battle is against the Cybermen. He tries to stop them from crashing a spaceship into Earth but sadly dies in the attempt, never to know that the explosion was responsible for wiping out the dinosaurs.

AGGEDOR
ROYAL BEAST OF PELADON

Originally found roaming around on the troubled planet of Peladon, the powerful, furry Aggedor creatures were hunted by the Pel people to the point of extinction. Considered as the Royal Beast of Peladon, legends refer to Aggedor one day returning and the great danger that will follow as a result.

ROYAL EMBLEM
Imagery of Aggedor appears throughout the Citadel of Peladon. Aggedor's head is also the royal emblem and its fur is used on royal clothing.

The Pels worship the spirit of Aggedor and are unaware that one of the creatures lives on in the caves of Peladon. It is used to scare off the Galactic Federation.

SHARP HORNS

THICK FUR

DATA FILE

HOMEWORLD:
PELADON

SPECIAL ABILITIES:
STRENGTH, ABLE TO SCARE

DOCTORS MET:
3RD

THE ALLIANCE
MASSIVE MONSTER ARMY

The Alliance is a confederation of the Doctor's deadliest enemies. Normally bitter foes, these monsters unite in their desire to stop the Doctor from destroying the universe. Millions of them gather in spaceships above Stonehenge when a prison box called the Pandorica opens to trap the Doctor inside.

The Alliance includes Daleks, Cybermen, Autons, Uvodni, Roboforms, Terileptils, Slitheen, Chelonians, Nestene, Drahvins, Sycorax, Haemogoths, Zygons, Atraxi, Draconians, Silurians, Sontarans, Judoon, Hoix, and many others!

CYBERMAN

SONTARAN

JUDOON

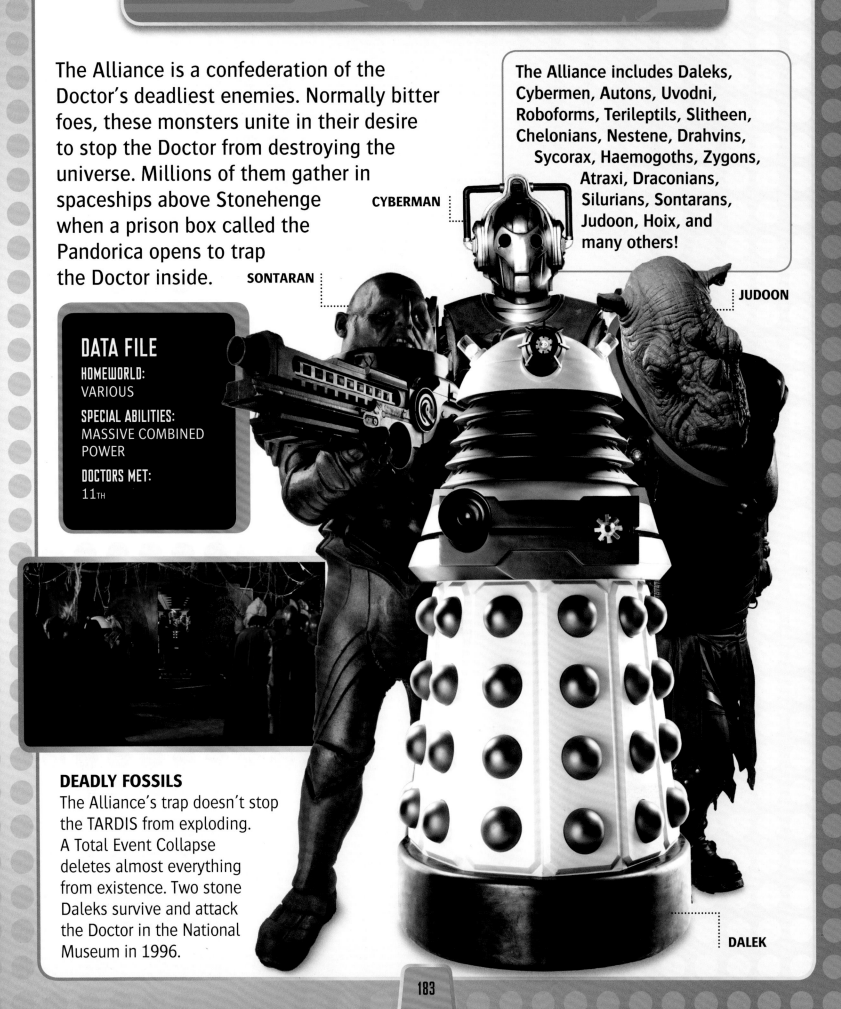

DATA FILE

HOMEWORLD:
VARIOUS

SPECIAL ABILITIES:
MASSIVE COMBINED POWER

DOCTORS MET:
11TH

DEADLY FOSSILS
The Alliance's trap doesn't stop the TARDIS from exploding. A Total Event Collapse deletes almost everything from existence. Two stone Daleks survive and attack the Doctor in the National Museum in 1996.

DALEK

ALPHA CENTAURI
SIX-ARMED ALIENS

Instantly recognizable by their one huge, bulbous eye, these creatures have a distinctive high-pitched voice, green skin, and six arms. They are a nervous race, which shows in their uneasy demeanor. One of them is an alien delegate working on behalf of the Galactic Federation.

LARGE PROTRUDING EYE

ALIEN DELEGATES
Alpha Centauri is just one of the alien delegates sent to Peladon. Other delegates include Ice Warriors, Arcturus, and two delegates from Earth (who are actually the Doctor, and his companion Jo Grant).

The Doctor calls Alpha Centauri a "hermaphrodite hexapod"—it is neither male nor female. The poor creature appears to be quite timid and shrieks with panic when scared. And when Sarah Jane Smith meets Alpha Centauri, the strong, young journalist is frustrated by its treatment of women—it considers females to be unimportant.

LONG YELLOW CAPE

THE ALPHA SPECIES HAVE LONG TORSOS WITH SIX ARMS

DATA FILE
HOMEWORLD:
ALPHA CENTAURI

CHARACTER TRAITS:
FRIGHTENING HUMANS (UNINTENTIONALLY)

DOCTORS MET:
3RD

AMY POND
GUTSY COMPANION

Amy's real name is Amelia. Witty, feisty, and just a little stubborn, Amy had a difficult childhood, and was raised by her Aunt Sharon after a space-time crack in her bedroom wall swallowed up both her parents. She eventually marries her childhood friend, Rory Williams, and they travel together with the Doctor.

DATA FILE

ORIGIN:
SCOTLAND, EARTH

OCCUPATION:
FORMER KISSOGRAM AND MODEL, TRAVEL WRITER

DOCTOR MET:
11TH

LEATHER JACKET SHOWS HER TOUGH SIDE

RAGGEDY FRIEND

Amy first meets the Eleventh Doctor when he crash-lands the TARDIS in her back yard and fixes the space-time crack in her bedroom wall. Dazzled by her "Raggedy Doctor", she has to wait 14 years before getting a chance to travel with him, but when she does they become close friends.

When a Weeping Angel zaps Rory back in time, Amy makes the emotional decision to let the angel send her back as well, meaning she won't ever see the Doctor again. She ends up living out her life with Rory, her beloved husband.

RIVER'S REVELATION

During the Battle of Demon's Run, a distraught Amy loses her daughter Melody to The Silence. However, she's even more shocked when River Song announces that she is Melody, all grown up!

STURDY BOOTS PERFECT FOR ANY ADVENTURE

ASTRID PETH
BRAVE *TITANIC* WAITRESS

Astrid Peth, citizen of Sto, becomes a waitress on the *Titanic* spaceship to see the universe. When starliner owner Max Capricorn sabotages his own ship, Astrid teams up with the Doctor to fight Max's Heavenly Host robots and stop the *Titanic* from crashing into Earth.

CURLY BLONDE UPDO

DRINKS TRAY

DATA FILE
HOMEWORLD:
STO

SPECIAL ABILITIES:
QUICK THINKING, BRAVERY

DOCTORS MET:
10TH

WAITRESS UNIFORM

Astrid spends three years working at a spaceport diner before joining the crew of the *Titanic*. She dreams of traveling to other worlds, but it isn't until the Doctor sneaks her onto Earth that she stands on a different planet.

RELEASED TO THE STARS
Astrid is wearing a teleport bracelet when she falls. The Doctor tries to save her body but the system is too badly damaged. All that is left is an echo of her consciousness, which he releases to fly among the stars.

FALLING FAST
On learning of Max Capricorn's plans to destroy Earth, Astrid drives a forklift truck into his life-support system, plunging them both into the Nuclear Storm Drive.

ATRAXI
ALIEN POLICE FORCE

The Atraxi are large crystalline-shaped wardens in charge of an extra-dimensional prison. They come to Earth in search of Prisoner Zero, a shape-changing alien who has escaped through a crack in time. The Atraxi send out a short but terrifying message, warning humanity that the entire planet will be incinerated unless Prisoner Zero is returned to them.

CRYSTALLINE STRUCTURE RESEMBLES SNOWFLAKE

EXTENDABLE SINGLE EYE

THE DOCTOR'S WARNING
After tracking down Prisoner Zero himself, the newly regenerated Doctor summons the Atraxi and tells them to leave Earth alone in the future, warning them that the planet is well defended.

The Atraxi possess advanced technology. They manage to seal off Earth's atmosphere with a force field and are also able to take control of TVs, and radios across the world—using them to broadcast their scary message in multiple languages.

AUTONS
KILLER STORE MANNEQUINS

The Autons are the blank-faced servants of the Nestene Consciousness, a disembodied alien entity that has made several attempts to conquer Earth. The Consciousness has the ability to bring any form of plastic to life and uses its murderous mannequins to clear the way for invasion.

PLASTIC BODIES, AND FACES

DATA FILE

HOMEWORLD:
UNKNOWN

SPECIAL FEATURES:
HIDDEN WEAPONRY IN THEIR HANDS

DOCTORS MET:
3RD, 9TH, 11TH

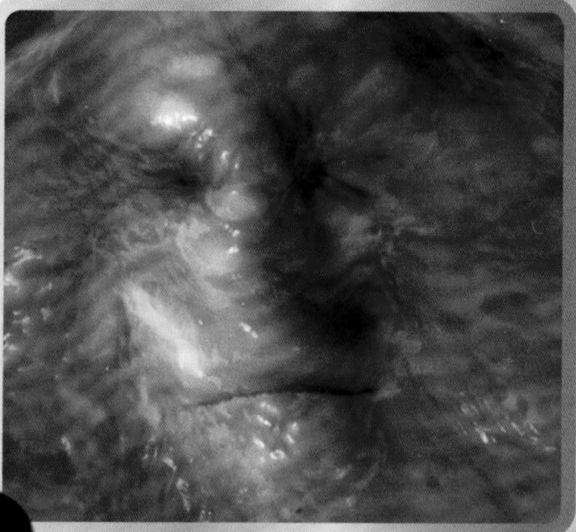

NESTENE
The Nestene Consciousness's real body is originally multi-tentacled. However, after the stresses of a war, it becomes liquid with a humanoid face.

SMART SUITS FROM HIGH STREET STORE

DUMMIES ON THE LOOSE
As part of the Nestene plan to turn Earth into a source of food, hordes of Autons burst from store windows all over the world and gun down innocent passers-by!

While most Autons are crude-looking mannequins, some are plastic copies of living people who look and sound like the real thing. In order to maintain a copy, the Nestene Consciousness needs to keep the original human alive.

AXONS
PARASITE RACE

This race of beautiful, gold-skinned humanoids first appears to be made up of four kind aliens with genuinely peaceful intentions. Their large organic ship contains an adult male and female with two child Axons. They tell Earth that their homeworld has been destroyed.

METALLIC FACE

LUMINOUS GOLD AND SILVER SKIN

AXON SECRET
The gold-humanoid aliens are hideous, red-tentacled monsters in disguise. "Axonite" and the monsters are actually one giant creature called "Axos". The parasitic race is after just one thing—the energy of Earth.

DATA FILE

HOMEWORLD:
AXOS

SPECIAL ABILITIES:
SHAPE-CHANGING, ENERGY ABSORBING

DOCTORS MET:
3RD

The Axons offer a substance called Axonite—a material that can bring world famine to an end—to the people of Earth. The gift proves to be too good to be true.

MASTER PLANS
The Axon creatures capture the Doctor's old enemy, the Master, as well as his TARDIS. The renegade Time Lord brings them to Earth so they can feed from the planet and drain its energy.

AZAL

LAST OF THE DÆMONS

Azal is the last of the powerful Dæmons from the planet Dæmos. He arrived on Earth thousands of years ago, influencing humanity's development as part of a great experiment performed by his race. Azal's image is familiar to humans, and he is partly responsible for humans' idea of the Devil.

DATA FILE

HOMEWORLD:
DÆMOS

SPECIAL ABILITIES:
CAN CHANGE SIZE RAPIDLY, CREATE HEAT BARRIERS

DOCTORS MET:
3RD

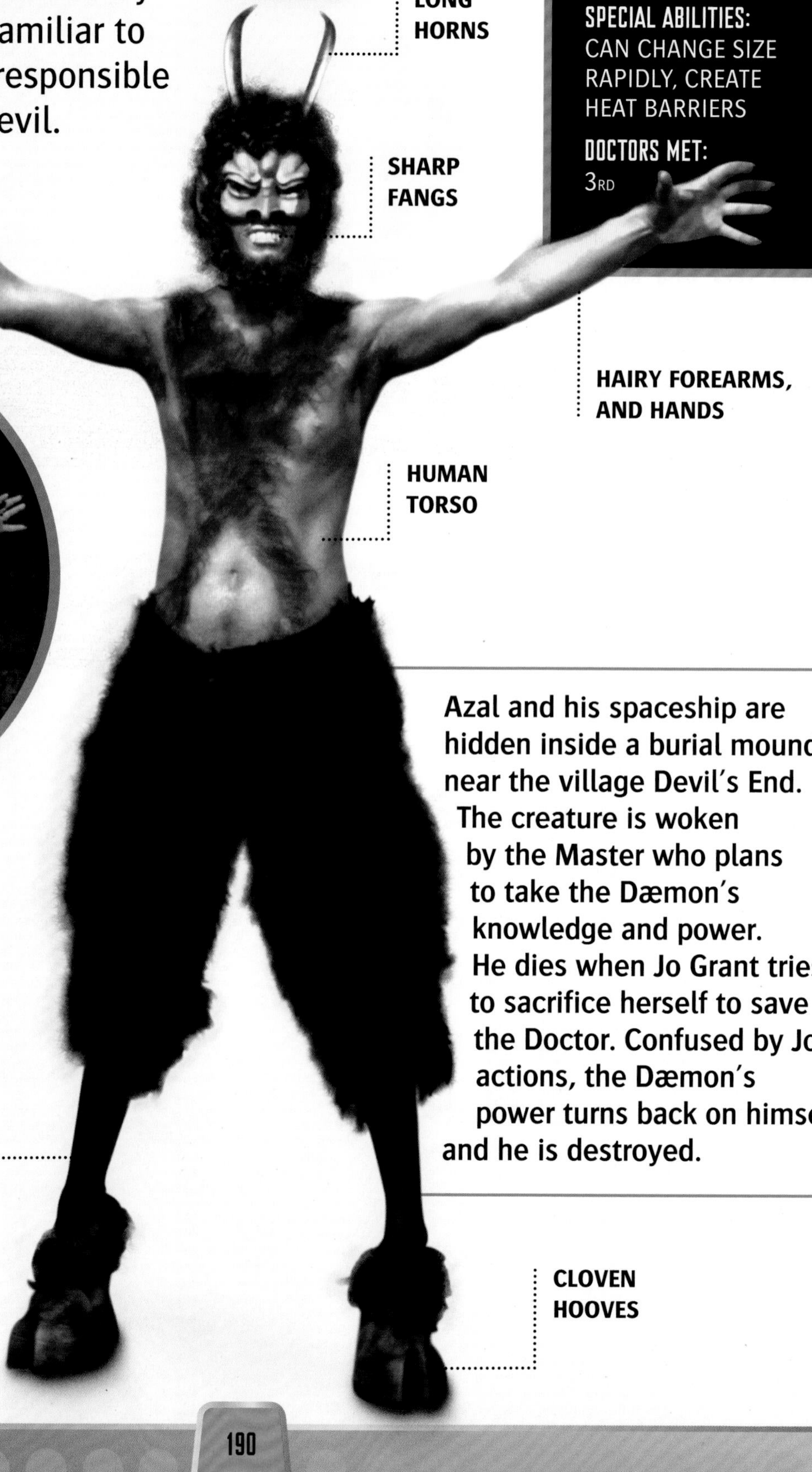

LONG HORNS
SHARP FANGS
HAIRY FOREARMS, AND HANDS
HUMAN TORSO
33 FEET (10 METERS) TALL
CLOVEN HOOVES

Azal and his spaceship are hidden inside a burial mound near the village Devil's End. The creature is woken by the Master who plans to take the Dæmon's knowledge and power. He dies when Jo Grant tries to sacrifice herself to save the Doctor. Confused by Jo's actions, the Dæmon's power turns back on himself and he is destroyed.

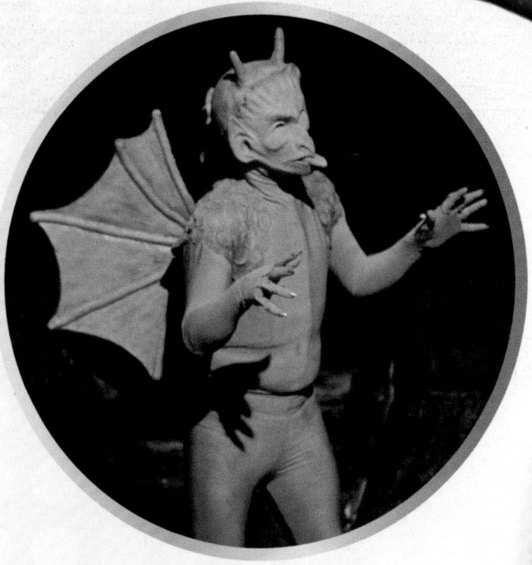

STONEY FACE

Bok is a stone gargoyle brought to life by Azal's power. Bok helps the Master at Devil's End and when Azal dies, the gargoyle returns to stone.

BANNAKAFFALATTA
ZOCCI *TITANIC* PASSENGER

Bannakaffalatta is a Zocci who travels on the *Titanic* spaceship. The Doctor says he looks like a "talking conker" and worries that he may start a riot when they teleport to Earth. Bannakaffalatta is actually a cyborg, the result of an accident years earlier on the planet Sto.

SPIKY ZOCCI SKIN, SIMILAR TO THAT OF HIS VINVOCCI COUSINS

Spiky by shape and by nature, Bannakaffalatta doesn't like his name being shortened to Banna. But while he is small and grumpy, he is also very brave.

CYBORG SECRET
Bannakaffalatta only admits to Titanic waitress Astrid Peth that he is a cyborg because he has a crush on her. He makes her promise to keep his secret, then asks her to marry him!

GLOVED HANDS

SMARTLY DRESSED AS IF FOR THE *TITANIC*

FATAL BLAST
Bannakaffalatta is embarrassed to be a cyborg, but the EMP device implanted in his chest gives him tremendous power. He uses it to save his friends when they are under attack by the Host. But the blast uses up all his energy and he dies.

DATA FILE
HOMEWORLD:
STO

SPECIAL ABILITIES:
ELECTROMAGNETIC PULSES (EMP), SQUEEZING THROUGH SMALL HOLES

DOCTORS MET:
10TH

BARBARA WRIGHT
CONSIDERATE COMPANION

Barbara is a history teacher from London and one of the Doctor's first human companions. Gentle and wise, she is determined to keep an open mind about the many alien life forms she encounters, and her knowledge of history proves invaluable whenever the TARDIS journeys into Earth's past.

DATA FILE
ORIGIN:
LONDON, ENGLAND

OCCUPATION:
HISTORY TEACHER

DOCTORS MET:
1ST

NEAT HAIRSTYLE
SMART CLOTHING FOR TEACHING
HISTORY TEXTBOOK

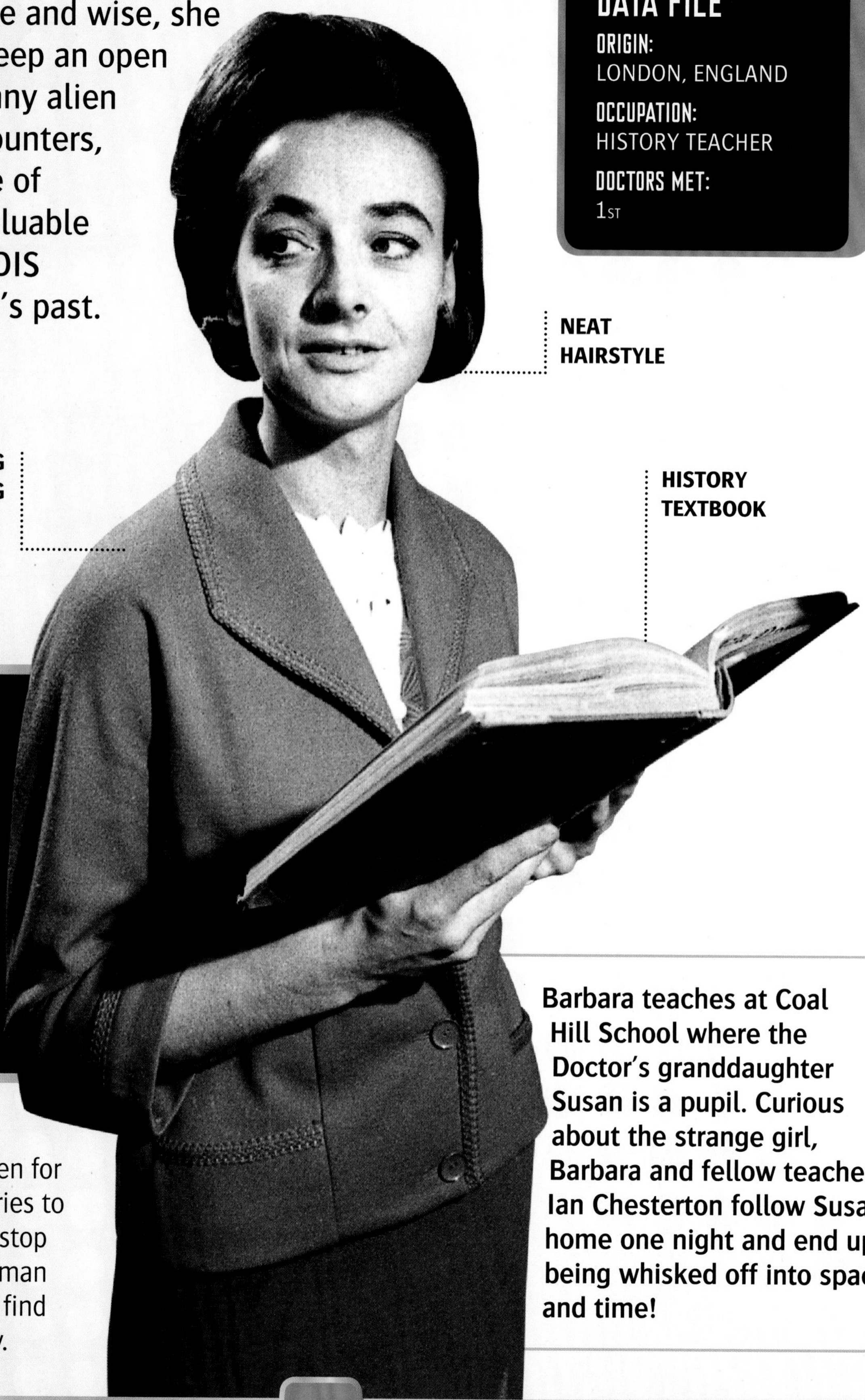

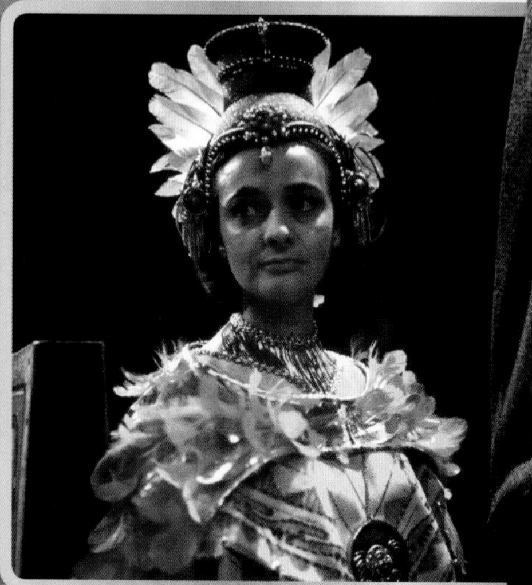

CHANGING HISTORY
When Barbara is mistaken for an Aztec goddess, she tries to use her divine status to stop the Aztec practice of human sacrifice, but is upset to find she can't change history.

Barbara teaches at Coal Hill School where the Doctor's granddaughter Susan is a pupil. Curious about the strange girl, Barbara and fellow teacher Ian Chesterton follow Susan home one night and end up being whisked off into space and time!

THE BEAST
LEGENDARY EVIL ENTITY

Before time itself existed, the Disciples of Light imprisoned a gigantic demon beneath the surface of Krop Tor. They placed the planet in perpetual orbit around a black hole, knowing that should the creature ever escape its bonds, the planet would immediately fall into the black hole, destroying the Beast in the process.

FEROCIOUS APPEARANCE INSPIRED LEGENDS OF DEVILS AND EVIL ACROSS THE UNIVERSE

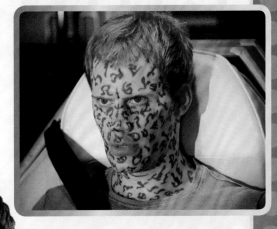

POSSESSED BY THE BEAST
The Beast possesses all of the Ood on Krop Tor. And when a human expedition arrives at Sanctuary Base, it plans to escape its prison by also taking over the mind and body of crewmember Toby Zed.

OVERSIZED, CURVED HORNS

DATA FILE

ORIGIN:
BEFORE TIME BEGAN

SPECIAL ABILITIES:
POSSESSION, TELEKINESIS, BREATHING FIRE

DOCTORS MET:
10TH

The Beast is defeated when Rose Tyler causes the possessed Toby Zed to be ejected into space. The black hole swallows him up, and the creature's body also perishes when Krop Tor itself is sucked into the black hole.

BEN JACKSON
COURAGEOUS COMPANION

A young cockney sailor, Ben meets the First Doctor in 1960s London and becomes caught up in WOTAN's attempt to take over the world with its lethal war machines. Practical, down-to-Earth, and full of fight, Ben is not afraid of risking his own life, especially if his fellow companions are in danger.

DATA FILE

ORIGIN:
LONDON, ENGLAND, EARTH

OCCUPATION:
ROYAL NAVY SAILOR

DOCTORS MET:
1ST, 2ND

UNINVITED GUEST

Ben's life changes forever when he and his new friend Polly follow the Doctor into the TARDIS. Ever the realist, Ben takes some convincing that he has barged aboard a space-time machine.

NEAT NAVY
HAIRCUT

SAILOR
UNIFORM

Ben goes on some incredible adventures, fighting the likes of the Daleks, Cybermen, and crab-like Macra. Eventually, the TARDIS takes him back to Earth and he is delighted to discover that he has arrived on the same day he had left!

BLACK GUARDIAN
GUARDIAN OF DARKNESS AND CHAOS

The Black Guardian is a dangerous being that thrives on evil and darkness in the universe. As powerful as the White Guardian, the Black Guardian will appear in times of great chaos. He can appear out of thin air and manipulate people so they do what he wants.

BLACK BIRD HEADDRESS

The Black Guardian will always dress in black. However, he can change his appearance to trick people and once pretended to be the White Guardian to confuse the Doctor.

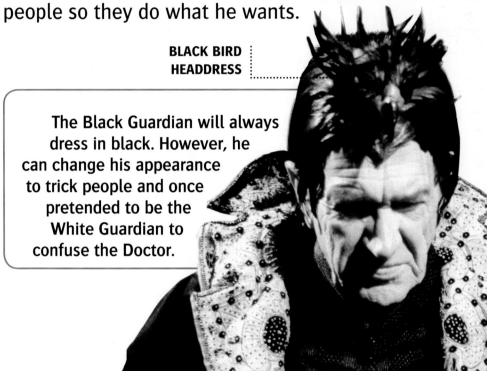

GUARDIAN AGENTS
The Black Guardian, like all Guardians, does not act directly. He has many agents who work for him, including the Shadow, a mysterious cowled figure.

ORNATE BLACK ROBES

DATA FILE
HOMEWORLD:
UNKNOWN

SPECIAL ABILITIES:
SHAPE-SHIFTING, MIND CONTROL

DOCTORS MET:
4TH, 5TH

BLON FEL-FOTCH PASAMEER-DAY SLITHEEN
CALCIUM-BASED CRIMINAL

Blon is a particularly devious member of the Slitheen family. She kills MI5 officer Margaret Blaine and hides in her skin in order to infiltrate government. Her true form is an 8-feet (2.5-meters) tall green alien. Like all Slitheen, she is a wanted criminal, obsessed with money and prone to extreme flatulence.

HIDDEN ZIP IN FOREHEAD

WARMONGER
Blon tries to start World War III. When her plot fails and her entire family are blown up, she plans a nuclear meltdown in revenge.

Blon was made to carry out her first kill at age thirteen. If she had refused, her father would have fed her to the Venom Grubs. She loves the thrill of hunting humans and the last thing Blon wants is to return to Raxacoricofallapatorius where she faces execution.

DATA FILE

HOMEWORLD:
RAXACORICOFALLAPATORIUS

SPECIAL ABILITIES:
HIDING AS A HUMAN, IMMENSE STRENGTH, MANIPULATION

DOCTORS MET:
9TH

HUMAN SKIN SUIT

BORUSA
CORRUPT TIME LORD

Borusa is a Time Lord, who has held various positions within the High Council on Gallifrey. At first a kind and gentle man, one of his pupils at the Prydon Academy was the Doctor, and the two Time Lords were great friends. He later regenerates into a more dangerous character.

EMBELLISHED HEADDRESS

DATA FILE
HOMEWORLD:
GALLIFREY

SPECIAL ABILITIES:
REGENERATION

DOCTORS MET:
4TH, 5TH

LOVE-HATE RELATIONSHIP
Until the end, the Doctor always has great respect for Borusa—in many ways, the Doctor looks up to him. However, the Doctor is surprised to find out that his old friend would later put all his lives in danger.

TIME LORD TRAP
To gain access to Rassilon's tomb, President Borusa takes various incarnations of the Doctor out of space and time and places them in the Death Zone.

As Lord President of Gallifrey, Borusa decides he wants immortality. As punishment, he is turned into living stone inside Rassilon's tomb in the Death Zone.

BRIAN WILLIAMS
RORY WILLIAMS' FATHER

Rory's dad Brian is a conservative 50-year-old with a limited world view. He hates traveling, never venturing further than the newspaper shop or the golf course. But that changes when the TARDIS materializes around him and whisks him into space for an adventure with dinosaurs!

Although Brian is often critical of Rory, he is very protective of him. When pterodactyls swoop at Rory, Brian fights them off with a trowel, and he makes the Doctor promise to bring Rory and Amy back safely.

JACKET WITH MANY USEFUL POCKETS

TRICEY, FETCH!
Brian is astounded to find dinosaurs on a spaceship, and even more so to ride one! When the Doctor can't find a way to get the Triceratops moving, quick-thinking Brian chucks his golf balls and it runs after them.

PRACTICAL CLOTHING FOR GARDENING

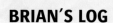

BRIAN'S LOG
Brian's horizons are massively broadened by his space adventure. When millions of cubes appear all over Earth, Brian is full of ideas of what they might be and records his observations of them in a video log.

DATA FILE
ORIGIN:
ENGLAND, EARTH
HOBBIES:
GARDENING, DIY
DOCTORS MET:
11TH

BRIGADIER LETHBRIDGE-STEWART
FORMER COMMANDER OF UNIT

The Brigadier has been one of the Doctor's greatest allies and a close friend. The pair first meet when Lethbridge-Stewart is a Colonel and together they work to defeat the invading Great Intelligence. Some years later, the newly promoted Brigadier dedicates himself to defending Earth as head of UNIT.

EMBLEM OF THE BRITISH ARMY

MILITARY UNIFORM

NESTENE INVASION
With the Doctor as his scientific advisor, the Brigadier helps prevent countless alien invasions, including an attempt by the Nestenes and the Master to conquer Earth.

DATA FILE

ORIGIN:
SCOTLAND, EARTH

OCCUPATION:
HEAD OF THE UK CONTINGENT OF UNIT

DOCTORS MET:
1ST, 2ND, 3RD, 4TH, 5TH, 7TH

UNIT
UNIT stands for Unified Intelligence Taskforce (previously United Nations Intelligence Taskforce). It is a military group set up to investigate and counter paranormal threats to Earth. A number of different incarnations of the Doctor have had close involvement with the organization, and with Brigadier Lethbridge-Stewart.

As a military man, the Brigadier is fiercely patriotic and his first instinct is to blow up anything he sees as a threat, much to the Doctor's annoyance. Although the Doctor leaves UNIT, the pair remain friends and meet up several times.

CANTON EVERETT DELAWARE III
AGENT WITH ATTITUDE

Canton Everett Delaware III is an ex-FBI agent recruited by President Nixon to investigate some cryptic phone calls. He meets the Doctor in the Oval Office and is immediately impressed by his skills of deduction. They join forces to solve the mystery calls and fight The Silence.

MEANS BUSINESS

FIGHTING THE SILENCE
Canton is not afraid to break the rules. He pretends to re-join the FBI to hunt down Amy, Rory, and River but is actually helping them halt the Silent invasion.

DATA FILE

HOMEWORLD:
EARTH

HOBBIES:
RULE-BREAKING

DOCTORS MET:
11TH

CLASSIC
BLACK SECRET
AGENT SUIT

The FBI kicked Canton out for wanting to marry a man. A rebel by nature, he takes it as a compliment when Nixon says he has a problem with authority.

LAKE SILENCIO
Canton remains loyal to the Doctor even into his old age, fulfilling one final task for him. He gives River gasoline to burn the Doctor's body at Lake Silencio.

SHOES
IMPRACTICAL
FOR DESERTS

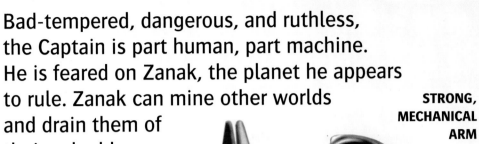

THE CAPTAIN
CYBORG PIRATE

Bad-tempered, dangerous, and ruthless, the Captain is part human, part machine. He is feared on Zanak, the planet he appears to rule. Zanak can mine other worlds and drain them of their valuable mineral wealth.

STRONG, MECHANICAL ARM

PET ROBOTIC PARROT CALLED POLYPHASE AVATRON

The Captain was wounded when a spaceship he was on crashed into Zanak. One of very few survivors, he needed extensive surgery, including a replacement, cybernetic arm.

THE CAPTAIN'S NURSE
The Captain is actually controlled by the ancient Queen Xanxia. She uses the energy from ruined planets to stay alive. A projection of her appears by his side as his "nurse".

PIRATE PLANET
The Captain travels around the whole universe with his pirate planet Zanak, capturing and destroying other worlds.

DATA FILE

HOMEWORLD:
ZANAK

HOBBIES:
PIRACY, MINING, SHOUTING

DOCTORS MET:
4TH

CAPTAIN JACK HARKNESS
IMMORTAL COMPANION

Originally a Time Agent manipulating history to remove "rogue elements," Captain Jack meets the Ninth Doctor in war-torn London and joins the TARDIS crew when the Doctor saves him from his exploding spaceship. Cheeky and flirtatious, he throws himself into his adventures and helps stop a Slitheen from destroying Earth before defending Satellite Five against a Dalek invasion.

A 51st century time-traveling con man, Jack takes on the identity of an American Royal Air Force volunteer, Captain Jack Harkness, who had died in action earlier in 1941. Jack eventually ends up working for the Torchwood Institute, which protects the British Empire from extraterrestrial threat.

DATA FILE

ORIGIN:
BOESHANE PENINSULA

OCCUPATION:
FORMER TIME AGENT AND CON MAN, TORCHWOOD AGENT

DOCTORS MET:
9TH, 10TH

GUN IN HOLSTER

1940S MILITARY COSTUME

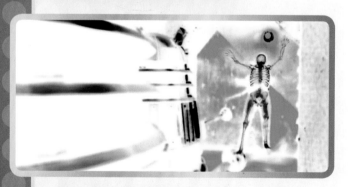

IMMORTAL SKILLS
Jack's immortality makes him the perfect companion to help the Tenth Doctor when the Master conquers Earth. Jack also helps stop Davros and the Daleks from destroying the universe with their reality bomb.

BROWN LEATHER SHOES

LIVING FOREVER
After Jack is exterminated by the Daleks, Rose Tyler uses the power of the Time Vortex to bring him back to life, making him immortal in the process. It may be his destiny to become the Face of Boe...

CAPTAIN MIKE YATES
THE BRIGADIER'S SECOND-IN-COMMAND

Charming and easy-going, Captain Yates is the Brigadier's efficient right-hand man. Despite years of good service, his idealistic nature eventually leads to his involvement with a project that will see Earth revert to prehistoric times. Having betrayed his friends, he is allowed to take extended sick leave and resign from UNIT.

DATA FILE

ORIGIN:
ENGLAND, EARTH

OCCUPATION:
FORMER UNIT CAPTAIN

DOCTORS MET:
3RD

CAPTAIN'S CAP

BRITISH ARMY UNIFORM

GIANT SPIDERS
After leaving UNIT, Yates ends up in a Buddhist meditation center, but soon realizes something is wrong when his fellow meditators make contact with the spiders of Metebelis III.

During his time at UNIT, Yates helps defend Earth against a stream of alien invaders, including the Autons, Axons, and Daleks. He also goes undercover to investigate a chemical company whose pollutants have created a race of giant maggots!

CARRIONITES
SHAPE-CHANGING ALIEN WITCHES

In their true form, the Carrionites are hideous wraiths. Using a word-based science often mistaken for witchcraft, they are able to transform themselves into humanoids, and can also warp reality.

The Carrionites were once banished into the Deep Darkness. However, the grief of playwright William Shakespeare is strong enough to allow three of them to come to Earth in the late 1500s.

SKIN WRINKLED FROM ENERGY EXPELLED MAINTAINING HUMAN FORM

CLAWED HANDS

DATA FILE

ORIGIN:
REXEL PLANETARY CONFIGURATION

SPECIAL ABILITIES:
SHAPE-CHANGING, MANIPULATING MATTER USING WORDS

DOCTORS MET:
10TH

ESCAPE ATTEMPT
During the performance of one of Shakespeare's plays, three Carrionites use their "magic" to help the rest of their kind descend to Earth. They want to destroy the entire human race.

WILLIAM SHAKESPEARE
Just as it is Shakespeare who brings the Carrionites to Earth, it is his combination of words that sends them back into the Darkness. The three on Earth become trapped in their own crystal ball, which the Doctor decides to stow aboard the TARDIS for safekeeping.

MOTHER DOOMFINGER

CELESTIAL TOYMAKER
DANGEROUS GAME PLAYER

A mysterious figure, the Celestial Toymaker has lived forever in a strange world outside of the known universe. The Toymaker gives people challenges through a series of childish and potentially fatal games. If a player loses, they become trapped in the Toymaker's world for the rest of time.

DRIVEN TO INSANITY BY PROLONGED ISOLATION

CHINESE MANDARIN STYLE CLOTHES

The Celestial Toymaker cheats, lies, and does not like to lose. He makes it difficult for players to leave his world—and losers become his toys.

HELPING HAND
Two dolls, Clara and Joey, are brought to life by the Toymaker to help him with his traps. They play games with the Doctor and his companions.

SINISTER GAMES
The Doctor's companions Dodo and Steven find themselves playing for their lives—including a game of deadly musical chairs and electrified hopscotch.

CLARA OSWALD
THAT IMPOSSIBLE GIRL

For a long time, Clara is an enigma. She appears as a Victorian governess, a Cockney barmaid, and a Dalek and looks the same and says the same phrase to the Doctor hundreds of years apart. Smart, sassy, and determined, she tracks down the Doctor, and refuses to leave until he explains who he is—and who she is!

The Doctor finds Clara maddening and intriguing in equal measure. He can't explain how she keeps reappearing in his life after he watched her die at the hands of the Ice Governess and as a Dalek.

TERRIBLE TRUTH
In the far future, a version of Clara called Oswin Oswald crashes onboard the *Alaska* ship on an Asylum planet. She is so intelligent that the Daleks perform a full conversion on her. Unable to face the horror of what she has become, she lives in a dream world. But when the Doctor confronts her with the truth, her Dalek nature takes over.

CLARA MULTIPLIED
After traveling with the Eleventh Doctor, Clara is distraught to be with him at his apparent end on Trenzalore. In order to save him, she jumps into his time stream—causing versions of herself to appear at key moments in his time line when he most needs help.

THICK SOLES CAN ENDURE LOTS OF RUNNING

DATA FILE
ORIGIN:
EARTH

OCCUPATION:
TEACHER, NANNY, GOVERNESS, BARMAID

DOCTORS MET:
ALL

CRAIG OWENS
THE DOCTOR'S LANDLORD

Craig Owens is a call center worker, married to Sophie and father to baby Alfie (aka Stormageddon). He becomes friends with the Eleventh Doctor when the Time Lord moves in as his lodger. Together they fight an alien spaceship disguised as the top half of Craig's house and stop a Cyber invasion.

COZY CARDIGAN

Dubbed "Mr. Sofa Man" by the Doctor, Craig hates traveling. But, of all his friends, it's Craig that the Doctor visits before he is due to die at Lake Silencio. The two are very close and both like to use the phrase "geronimo."

AVATAR ATTACK!
Initially too shy to tell Sophie he has a crush on her, Craig declares his love for her while fighting the spaceship's avatar. Their kiss causes the ship to implode!

COMFORTABLE PANTS FOR WATCHING TV

CYBER CONVERSION
Craig is a loyal friend to the Doctor. He even attempts to rescue him from the Cybermen and is almost converted into a Cyber Controller in the process.

DATA FILE

ORIGIN:
ENGLAND, EARTH

SPECIAL ABILITIES:
FIGHTING CYBERMATS, EXPLODING CYBERMEN

DOCTORS MET:
11TH

CYBERMEN
STEEL SOLDIERS

Cybermen are one of the Doctor's most enduring enemies. They are near indestructible cybernetic beings with living brains jammed into metal bodies. Inside their super-strong casings, an emotional inhibitor suppresses all human feelings. They have one goal—to upgrade all other beings into Cyberkind.

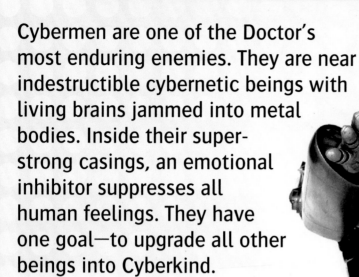

ENORMOUS STRENGTH AND POWER

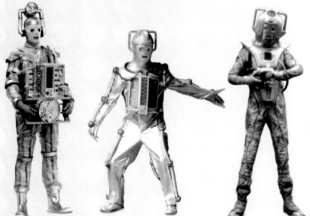

The first Cybermen came from the planet Mondas and had cloth faces and human hands. Their shape has evolved repeatedly.

PARALLEL-EARTH CYBERMEN
A new army of deadly Cybermen is created on a parallel Earth by Cybus Industries' owner, John Lumic. They believe they are Human Point Two, and everyone must become like them.

METAL EXOSKELETON

CYBERKING   CYBERSHADE

In 1851, Cybermen built the CyberKing—a massive, dreadnought-class battleship—and also experimented on animals to create Cybershades.

Cybermen relentlessly seek to upgrade themselves and mankind, and are merciless to those who refuse. Chanting "Delete!", they electrocute victims with their hands or blast them with lasers.

DALEKS
THE DOCTOR'S DEADLIEST ENEMY

Daleks are the stuff of nightmares. Inside their almost indestructible dalekanium shells lies a foul one-eyed Kaled mutant. Genetically engineered by Davros to be empty of all emotions but hate, they seek to destroy all other "less superior" life forms, and electrocute their victims with the terrifying cry of "EXTERMINATE!"

EYESTALK

PLUNGER

The animosity between the Daleks and the Doctor predates the Time War that apparently destroyed all Time Lords and Daleks. The Daleks both hate and fear the Doctor, calling him "the Oncoming Storm" and "the Predator."

The Daleks have assumed many guises over the years. The Doctor has fought many types, including:

ORIGINAL DALEK

IRONSIDE

DALEK SEC

THE SUPREME

DEATH RAY

DALEK PARLIAMENT
When the Daleks summon the Doctor before the Dalek Parliament, they hope to use him then destroy him. But Oswin Oswald erases their databases, leaving the Doctor's archenemies with no memories of him!

DATA FILE

HOMEWORLD:
SKARO

SPECIAL ABILITIES:
EXTERMINATING, EXTRACTING DATA FROM HUMAN MINDS

DOCTORS MET:
ALL

DAVROS
CREATOR OF THE DALEKS

A crippled and deranged scientist, Davros is obsessed with the survival of his race, the Kaleds, following centuries of chemical and nuclear warfare. He creates the Daleks and programs them with the instinct to destroy all other life forms in the universe.

BLUE LENS REPAIRS SIGHT

DALEK DESTRUCTION
When the Tenth Doctor destroys all the Daleks, Davros is left burning. The Doctor offers to save him, but bitter Davros declines, believing the Doctor to be "The Destroyer of Worlds."

REALITY BOMB
Davros comes up with crazy schemes, such as his construction of a massive reality bomb. He plans to use the bomb to destroy all matter in the universe, leaving nothing but the Daleks and himself.

LIFE-SUPPORT CHARIOT

Davros has an uneasy relationship with his own pitiless creations. The Daleks once tried to kill him, believing in their own superiority. But when their own survival is threatened they often return to him for help.

DATA FILE
HOMEWORLD:
SKARO

SPECIAL ABILITIES:
CAN FIRE ENERGY BOLTS FROM HIS FINGERTIPS

DOCTORS MET:
4TH, 5TH, 6TH, 7TH, 10TH

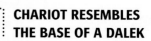

CHARIOT RESEMBLES THE BASE OF A DALEK

THE FIRST DOCTOR
TARDIS THIEF

The Doctor is a Time Lord, an extraterrestrial leader from the planet Gallifrey, who travels through space and time. He is part-warrior, part-conflict resolver. The First Doctor is a tetchy, eccentric old man who steals a TARDIS (time machine) and travels through the universe. Occasionally stubborn, aloof, and absent-minded, he mellows as he gets used to traveling with a succession of long-suffering human companions.

The Doctor regenerates, or transforms, when his body becomes old or mortally wounded. This changes him physically and alters his personality. After an epic battle, the First Doctor announces that his old body has at last worn out. His features change into those of a much younger man!

AZTEC LOVE
Cameca is an Aztec lady to whom the Doctor unknowingly proposes in the 15th century. She is the Doctor's first known love interest.

DEFEATING THE DALEKS
The Doctor first meets the Daleks when he accidentally lands the TARDIS on Skaro, where the ruthless Daleks are planning to wipe out their enemies, the Thals.

MONOCLE

DATA FILE
SPECIAL ABILITIES:
POWER OF HYPNOSIS (WITH THE HELP OF HIS SIGNET RING)

REASON FOR REGENERATING:
EXHAUSTION AND OLD AGE

THE SECOND DOCTOR
CUNNING CLOWN

Compared with the stern figure of the First Doctor, the Second Doctor is more like a batty uncle. He bumbles around and often panics in dangerous situations. His nature often fools his enemies into underestimating him—he has the same razor-sharp intelligence as ever before.

DATA FILE

INTERESTS:
PLAYING THE RECORDER

REASONS FOR REGENERATION:
FORCED TO CHANGE HIS APPEARANCE BY THE TIME LORDS

RECORDER

DOCTOR ON TRIAL
The Time Lords finally catch up with the Second Doctor and put him on trial for interfering in galactic affairs. As punishment, he is forced to regenerate and live as an exile on planet Earth.

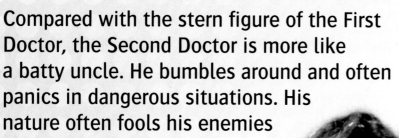

PLAID PANTS

CYBER RISING
It is in this incarnation that the Doctor first encounters the Cyber Controller and Cybermats, deep within the Cyber-Tombs on the planet Telos. With the help of Jamie and Victoria, the Doctor fights off what are believed to be the very last of the Cybermen.

The Second Doctor believes it is his duty to fight the many evils in the universe. In his time he battles both Cybermen and Daleks, the robotic Yeti, and the reptilian Ice Warriors—he even encounters a scary seaweed creature.

THE THIRD DOCTOR
EARTH EXILE

Charming and flamboyant, this version of the Doctor is a dashing action hero with a fondness for fast vehicles and cool gadgets. During his exile, he reluctantly joins UNIT as its scientific advisor, but he soon tires of defending Earth against alien invaders and longs to roam the universe once more.

DOCTOR TIMES THREE
When the Time Lords come under attack, they bring the first three Doctors together to help save them. As a reward, the Third Doctor's exile is finally lifted.

DATA FILE

INTERESTS:
VENUSIAN AIKIDO

REASONS FOR REGENERATION:
RADIATION SICKNESS

FRILLED SHIRT

CAPE WITH RED LINING

Alongside Brigadier Lethbridge-Stewart and companions Liz Shaw, Jo Grant, and Sarah Jane Smith, the Third Doctor fights various menaces from Autons to Axons and dinosaurs to Daleks. He also battles the Master who is as determined as ever to destroy humanity.

SPIDER DOOM
The Third Doctor's life ends when he and Sarah Jane run into giant spiders on Metebelis III. In the course of confronting the eight limbed Great One, the Doctor consumes a lethal amount of radiation, triggering his regeneration.

THE FOURTH DOCTOR
EAGER EXPLORER

At times madly eccentric, at others mysterious and moody, the Fourth Doctor is the most unpredictable. He has a wild spirit of adventure, an offbeat sense of humor, and loves filling his pockets with random objects.

WILD, CURLY HAIR

BRIGHTLY COLORED SCARF

DOCTOR ASSASSIN
Freed from his exile on Earth, the Fourth Doctor is able to travel the universe once more. He is even summoned back to Gallifrey, where he apparently steals some ceremonial Time Lord robes and murders the Time Lord President—before it is revealed to have all been another of the Master's plots.

A DOCTOR'S DILEMMA
This Doctor has the chance to destroy the Daleks at the point of their creation. He struggles with the decision, questioning if he has the right to commit genocide.

FROCK COAT WITH MANY USEFUL POCKETS

Some of the Fourth Doctor's closest companions are Sarah Jane Smith, the savage Leela, and Time Lady Romana. He saves Gallifrey from the invading Sontarans and also goes on an epic mission to assemble the Key to Time, restoring harmony to the universe.

DATA FILE

INTERESTS:
YO-YO TRICKS

REASON FOR REGENERATION:
FALLS FROM THE TOP OF AN ENORMOUS RADIO TELESCOPE

THE FIFTH DOCTOR
PEACE-SEEKING PACIFIST

With his love of cricket, the younger-looking Fifth Doctor possesses a manic, nervous energy, which often leads him to rush about and talk too fast, while his vulnerable nature means he occasionally doubts himself. But when faced with a dangerous enemy, he is every bit as determined and heroic as his previous selves.

EDWARDIAN CRICKETER'S OUTFIT

The Fifth Doctor becomes close to his companions, including the gentle Nyssa, stubborn flight attendant Tegan, and Turlough— a Black Guardian agent who is secretly out to kill him. He is deeply upset by the tragic loss of young Adric, who dies while trying to save Earth.

NOBLE SACRIFICE
The Doctor and his companion Peri Brown contract an illness called spectrox toxaemia on Androzani Minor. The Doctor gives up his share of the cure to save her life, but as a result he regenerates for the fifth time.

PANAMA HAT

STRIPED PANTS

FIVE DOCTORS
As part of a cruel game organized by the Time Lord Rassilon, all five incarnations of the Doctor meet in order to save their past, present, and future lives. The Fifth Doctor is offered the position of President of Gallifrey for the role he plays, but prefers to return to a life of traveling.

THE SIXTH DOCTOR
COLORFUL CHARACTER

Stubborn, self-centered, with a loud manner and even louder dress sense, the Sixth Doctor is difficult to like at first. Happily, though, his dedication to fighting evil remains as strong as ever, and the more extreme aspects of his personality mellow as time goes by, revealing a surprisingly caring Doctor beneath the bluster.

The Sixth Doctor travels with botany student Peri and computer expert Mel. As well as Daleks and Cybermen, he fights the slug-like Gastropods and the money-loving Mentors, until he meets his end at the hands of the Rani.

QUESTION MARKS SEWN ON SHIRT COLLAR

DATA FILE
INTERESTS:
ENJOYS RECITING POETRY

REASONS FOR REGENERATION:
THE RANI'S LASER ATTACK ON THE TARDIS

CAT-SHAPED BROOCH

MISMATCHED, MULTICOLORED CLOTHES

ON TRIAL AGAIN
The Doctor has faced being prosecuted on more than one occasion and in several incarnations. The Sixth Doctor faces a dark version of himself in the shape of the villainous Valeyard.

DOCTOR TIMES TWO
The Sixth Doctor has to rescue the Second Doctor, who has been kidnapped by the Sontarans and Androgums. They want to operate on him to discover the secret of time travel!

THE SEVENTH DOCTOR
DARKER DOCTOR

As eccentric as any of his predecessors, the Seventh Doctor is a wiry, off-the-wall character at first, given to acting the clown and spouting mangled proverbs. Over time, though, he reveals a darker side to his nature, coming across as a master chess-player, who is forever one step ahead of his enemies.

QUESTION MARK-SHAPED UMBRELLA USED TO DISARM FOES

DATA FILE

INTERESTS:
PLAYING THE SPOONS, MAGIC TRICKS, CHESS

REASONS FOR REGENERATION:
BULLET WOUNDS AND SUBSEQUENT HEART SURGERY

The Seventh Doctor's closest friend is a rebellious teenager called Ace. He enjoys educating her as they travel the universe fighting menaces such as Cybermen, Cheetah people, Husks, and Haemovores. However, he is not opposed to manipulating her to get his own way.

DALEK DESTROYER
After allowing Davros to steal a deadly device called the Hand of Omega, the Seventh Doctor tricks him into activating it. The pre-programed Hand then destroys Skaro, the Daleks' homeworld!

PATTERNED CLOTHES DISGUISE DARKER NATURE

UNITED
The Seventh Doctor is pleased to be reunited with an old friend when the Brigadier comes out of retirement to help UNIT deal with an alien invasion.

BROWN AND WHITE BROGUES WORN BENEATH TWEED PANTS

THE EIGHTH DOCTOR
PARADOXICAL PSYCHIC

A more human version of the Doctor, this eighth incarnation has a childlike playfulness coupled with an infectious zest for life and adventure. Warm, witty, and charming, he also has the uncanny knack of being able to predict events in people's personal futures—a talent none of his other selves has possessed.

Following his regeneration, the Eighth Doctor steals a fancy dress costume to wear—similar to clothes worn by 19th century gunfighter Wild Bill Hickok. He is assisted by heart surgeon Grace Holloway.

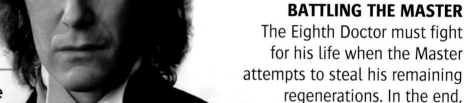

BATTLING THE MASTER
The Eighth Doctor must fight for his life when the Master attempts to steal his remaining regenerations. In the end, his deadly enemy is absorbed into the TARDIS's power source.

19TH CENTURY- LOOKING VELVET JACKET

EMBROIDERED VEST

ELIXIR OF LIFE
After crashing and dying on Karn, the Sisterhood of Karn resurrect the Doctor and give him the chance to regenerate and bring an end to the Time War. The Doctor chooses to embody characteristics of a Warrior.

DATA FILE

SPECIAL ABILITIES:
PREDICTING THE FUTURE

REASON FOR REGENERATING:
DRINKS THE ELIXIR OF LIFE TO BECOME THE WAR DOCTOR

THE NINTH DOCTOR
WAR-WEARY WANDERER

The Ninth Doctor is left emotionally scarred in the aftermath of the Time War, a catastrophic event in which the Time Lords are destroyed. As the last of his kind, this Doctor needs a human companion more than ever before, and is relieved to meet Rose Tyler, a feisty shopgirl from London.

SONIC SCREWDRIVER

WELL-WORN LEATHER JACKET

DATA FILE

SPECIAL ABILITIES: INCREDIBLE TIMING— HE ONCE MANAGED TO STEP THROUGH THE BLADES OF A MASSIVE SPINNING FAN

REASON FOR REGENERATING: CELLULAR DEGENERATION AFTER ABSORBING THE TIME VORTEX

This Doctor deals ruthlessly with his enemies if they choose not to heed his warnings. He refuses to save the villainous Cassandra, launches a missile attack against the Slitheen, and even orders the last Dalek in the universe to destroy itself.

ACQUIRING ASSISTANCE
The Doctor acquires a new companion when he travels back to World War II. Captain Jack Harkness is a con man from the 51st century dressed as an air force pilot.

SAVING ROSE
When Rose absorbs the whole of the Time Vortex, the Ninth Doctor bravely draws it into his own body to save her life, knowing full well it would trigger a regeneration.

THE TENTH DOCTOR
LAID-BACK LONER

This version of the Doctor is empathetic, confident, and quirky, with a real zest for adventure. More talkative and laid-back than his predecessor, he revels in his voyages through space and time. Towards the end of his life, though, he grows sad at the loss of so many friends, and decides to travel alone once more.

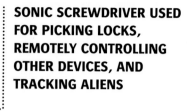

SONIC SCREWDRIVER USED FOR PICKING LOCKS, REMOTELY CONTROLLING OTHER DEVICES, AND TRACKING ALIENS

With his loyal companions, the Tenth Doctor battles an array of adversaries, from Cat Nuns and Carrionites to the Sycorax and Sontarans. He even manages to stop the Time Lord Rassilon's attempt to bring about the end of time itself after he was previously assumed killed in the Time War.

OLD TIMER
As a warning to Martha and humanity, the Master uses his laser screwdriver to age the Doctor's body to his real age of over 900!

BROWN PINSTRIPE SUIT

DATA FILE

SPECIAL ABILITIES: CAN ANALYZE SUBSTANCES BY TASTING THEM

REASON FOR REGENERATING: RADIATION POISONING

SCRUFFY PLIMSOLES

FAREWELL ROSE
One of the Tenth Doctor's toughest moments is saying goodbye to Rose at Bad Wolf Bay. She becomes trapped in a parallel universe and he believes he has lost her forever.

THE ELEVENTH DOCTOR
BABY-FACED BRAINIAC

The most youthful-looking Doctor of all, the Eleventh Doctor has one of the most alien and eccentric personas yet. Like an excitable kid at times, he doesn't always appear to take dangerous situations seriously, but when confronting his enemies, he is capable of showing a colder, and even ruthless, side to his nature.

STYLISH QUIFF

QUIRKY BOW TIE, BECAUSE "BOW TIES ARE COOL"

TWEED JACKET

BIG BANG TWO
When the universe all but collapses, the Eleventh Doctor achieves the impossible—he flies the Pandorica prison box at his exploding TARDIS, miraculously managing to reboot the entire universe!

DATA FILE

INTERESTS:
PLAYING SOCCER, HATS AND BOW TIES

REASON FOR REGENERATING:
OLD AGE

DRAINPIPE PANTS

This incarnation of the Doctor faces greater challenges than ever before. His biggest enemy is The Silence, a religious order that is desperate to prevent the revelation of the Doctor's real name—something known by very few people, one of whom is River Song.

DEFENDER OF CHRISTMAS
At the end of his life, the Eleventh Doctor spends several centuries protecting the town Christmas on the planet Trenzalore. His enemies are poised ready to attack the Time Lords, who are trying to emerge through a crack in time.

LEATHER BROGUES

THE TWELFTH DOCTOR
GRAY-HAIRED GENIUS

Wearing an older, sterner face than seen for many regenerations, the Twelfth Doctor has left behind his younger incarnations. He is tougher round the edges, but still ultimately trying to be a good person—for which he needs his friends more than ever before.

AN IMPOSSIBLE HERO
The Doctor knows how dangerous it is for him to travel alone and comes to see that he needs his Impossible Girl more than ever before. Clara helps him to believe in hope and in himself again—once she accepts that this strange, gruff man is still her Doctor.

INTENTIONALLY MINIMALIST LOOK

DATA FILE
SPECIAL ABILITIES:
HORSERIDING, ABLE TO DISARM OPPONENTS USING JUST A SPOON

REASON FOR REGENERATING:
HAS NOT YET REGENERATED

Over 2,000 years old, the Doctor no longer sees the need to seek acceptance from humans in quite the same way he did before. Having wandered the universe for millennia, he is tired of witnessing death and destruction.

STURDY, POLISHED LACE-UP SHOES

NEW OLD FACE
Having chosen his new face, the Doctor can't remember why. He doesn't like his facial features—in particular his eyebrows, which seem to be independently cross!

DOCTOR SIMEON
SERVANT OF THE GREAT INTELLIGENCE

As a child, Walter Simeon's only friend is the snowman he makes in his yard. Walter pours his darkest dreams into it, and they become telepathically linked. As an adult, Doctor Simeon sets up the GI Institute and becomes the devoted servant of a disembodied alien called the Great Intelligence.

.... TOP HAT

.... MERCILESS AND EMOTIONLESS

CARNIVOROUS SNOWMEN
The Great Intelligence is an extremely powerful alien who longs to take human form. Using carnivorous alien snow, it plans to create a world full of living ice people.

Ruthless to his core, Doctor Simeon thinks nothing of feeding his workers to the savage Snowmen. He gathers alien ice samples from all over London to help his master learn about Earth.

DEVOTED TO HIS MASTER ....

FUR-LINED COAT FOR STAYING WARM IN SNOWY CLIMES

ICE COLD
When his mind is erased by a Memory Worm, Doctor Simeon becomes possessed by the Great Intelligence and transforms into an ice-faced zombie who tries to freeze the Doctor.

DATA FILE

ORIGIN:
EARTH

SPECIAL ABILITIES:
PSYCHIC LINK WITH THE GREAT INTELLIGENCE

DOCTORS MET:
11TH

DONNA NOBLE
TEMPERAMENTAL COMPANION

Funny, feisty, and fiery-tempered, Donna is one of the Doctor's more outspoken companions. She adores traveling in the TARDIS—even though she once believed she'd never be able to cope with the Doctor's dangerous lifestyle—and her incredible adventures open up her mind to the wonders of the universe.

FIERY RED HAIR

WARM JACKET FOR TRAVELING

DATA FILE
ORIGIN:
LONDON, EARTH
OCCUPATION:
OFFICE TEMP
DOCTORS MET:
10TH

During a battle with the Daleks, Donna is transformed by the Doctor's regeneration energy, which gives her the consciousness of a Time Lord. She uses her new-found great intelligence to save the universe from Davros's reality bomb!

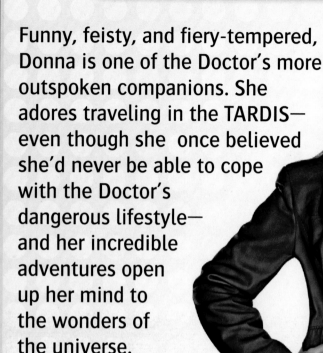

SPACE BRIDE
Donna first meets the Doctor when she is accidentally transported into his TARDIS on her wedding day. She initially declines his invitation to join him on his travels, but soon realizes that her ordinary, everyday life is dull in comparison.

DOCTOR DONNA
Tragically, the Time Lord part of Donna's brain is too much for her and the Doctor is forced to erase her mind in order to save her life. He takes her back to Earth, where she eventually meets and marries her husband, Shaun Temple.

DORIUM MALDOVAR
BLUE-SKINNED BAR OWNER

A big blue alien of dubious morals, Dorium owns a space bar called the Maldovarium in the 51st century. He dabbles in the black market and sells the Headless Monks security software with which to kidnap Amy Pond. Dorium is always in the know.

The Doctor summons Dorium to repay a debt by helping him rescue Amy from Demon's Run. But he is killed by Headless Monks and his head is placed in the Labyrinth of Skulls.

BRIGHT BLUE SKIN

LAVISH RICHES ACCUMULATED THROUGH MARKETEERING

FOND OF SENTIENT MONEY

SILENCE WILL FALL
Although bodiless, Dorium's head remains well-informed. He provides the Doctor with data on The Silence and reveals to him the question that must never be answered on the fields of Trenzalore.

DATA FILE

HOMEWORLD:
UNKNOWN

SPECIAL FEATURES:
WI-FI FITTED TO MEDIA CHIP IN HEAD

DOCTORS MET:
11TH

DOROTHEA CHAPLET
CHEERFUL COMPANION

Dorothea Chaplet (nicknamed "Dodo" at school) becomes the First Doctor's companion by chance after stumbling into the TARDIS, thinking it is a real police box. Fun-loving and carefree, she has few qualms about joining the Doctor, who took something of a shine to her, thanks to her striking resemblance to his granddaughter Susan Foreman.

BEARS RESEMBLANCE TO SUSAN FOREMAN

SMART WOOL COAT

AMAZING ADVENTURES
Dodo's time with the Doctor is short, but during her travels she visits a giant space ark, fights against the evil Toymaker, and even sees her dream come true when she meets legendary lawman Wyatt Earp in the Wild West!

In one of Dodo's more frightening exploits, her mind was taken over by the mad supercomputer WOTAN. The Doctor successfully breaks its hypnotic control, but after recovering from the ordeal, Dodo decides to stay on Earth.

DATA FILE

ORIGIN:
ENGLAND, EARTH

INTERESTS:
THE WILD WEST

DOCTORS MET:
1ST

DRACONIANS
HUMANOID REPTILES

The Draconians are an intelligent, civilised, and honorable race of reptilian humanoid creatures. In the 26th century, as the Earth and Draconian Empires expanded, a misunderstanding led to a war between the two races. Separate borders were agreed—creating a frontier in space.

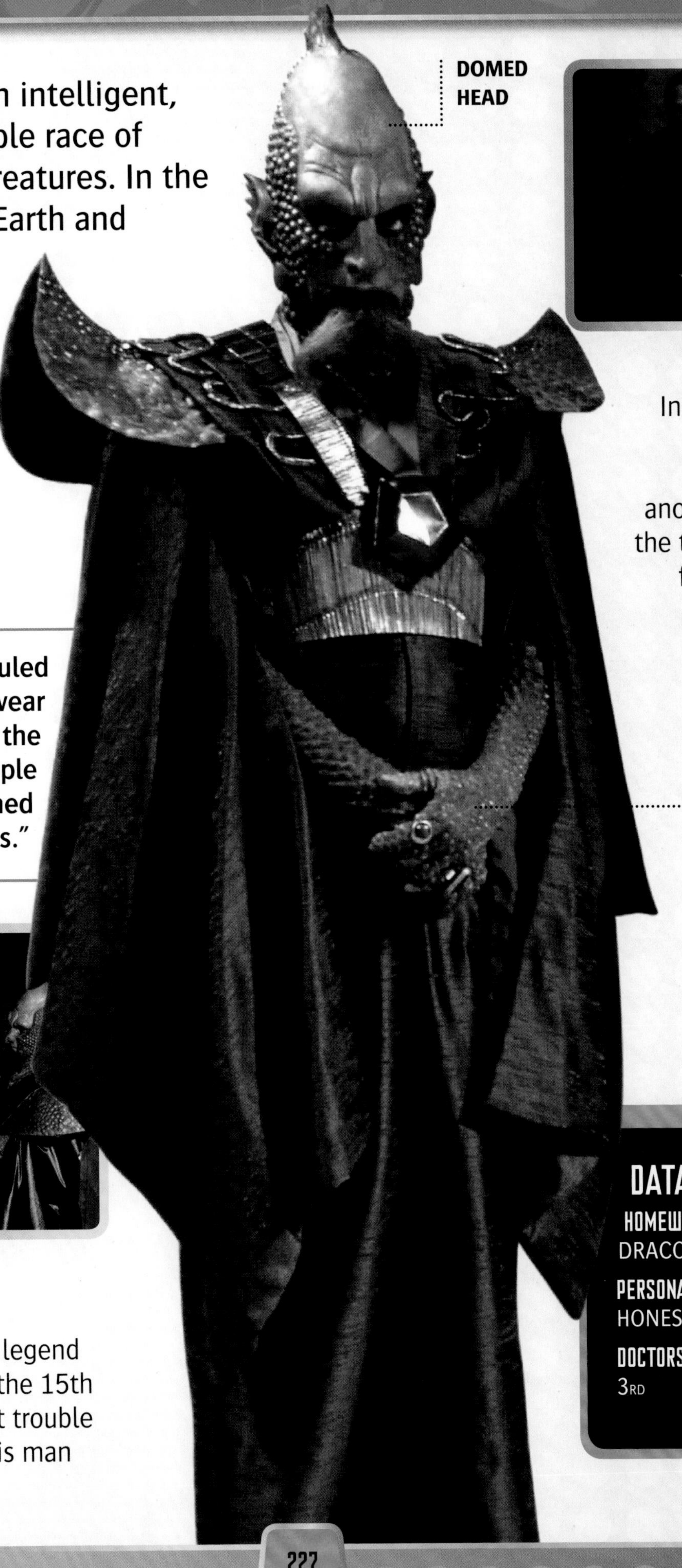

The Draconians are ruled by an Emperor. They wear long, green robes. In the 26th century, people cruelly nicknamed them "dragons."

DOMED HEAD

MASTER PLANS
In 2540, the Master and the Daleks attempt to cause another war between the two empires. They fail thanks to help from the Doctor.

REPTILIAN SKIN

THE DOCTOR AND THE DRACONIAN
There is an old Draconian legend about a man who helped the 15th Emperor at a time of great trouble during a space plague. This man was the Doctor.

DATA FILE
HOMEWORLD:
DRACONIA

PERSONALITY TRAITS:
HONESTY, HONOR

DOCTORS MET:
3RD

THE DREAM LORD
THE DOCTOR'S DARK ALTER-EGO

The Dream Lord is created when specks of psychic pollen from Karass Don Slava become trapped in the TARDIS's time rotor. A mind parasite, the pollen feeds on the dark areas of people's psyche and it uses the Doctor's mind to create a villainous version of the Time Lord.

DANGEROUS AND MISCHIEVOUS MIND

INVADING THE TARDIS
Appearing in the TARDIS, the Dream Lord asks the Doctor, Amy and Rory to choose which of two worlds is real, and which is only a dream. The wrong choice will kill them!

DIFFICULT CHOICES
The Dream Lord's two worlds are equally unattractive: freezing to death in a TARDIS slowly spinning into a cold star, or being obliterated by the alien Eknodines. When Rory is killed, it is at first unclear whether he will also be dead in the real world.

CLOTHES REFLECT THE ELEVENTH DOCTOR'S STYLE

Taunted by the Dream Lord, the Doctor eventually realizes that neither world is real and wakes up safely back in the TARDIS. The Dream Lord is defeated, but the Doctor catches one last glimpse of him, reflected in the TARDIS console...

DATA FILE
ORIGIN:
THE DOCTOR'S MIND

SPECIAL ABILITIES:
CONTROLLING PEOPLE'S DREAMS

DOCTORS MET:
11TH

EKNODINES
POSSESSED PENSIONERS

A proud and ancient race of creatures who were driven from their planet by upstart neighbors, the Eknodines flee to Earth and take possession of the elderly residents of Rory Williams' hometown Leadworth. A single green eyeball hides in the mouths of their human hosts.

LIVES INSIDE PENSIONER FROM UPPER LEADWORTH'S OLD PEOPLE'S HOME

HUMAN HOST MRS. HAMIL'S BODY AND CLOTHING

VENGEANCE

Bitter at their own destruction, the Eknodines plan to do the same to other races, starting with mankind. Their eyeballs squirt out venom that can reduce a human to dust in seconds.

FRAIL APPEARANCE HIDES GREAT STRENGTH

DATA FILE
HOMEWORLD:
UNKNOWN

SPECIAL ABILITIES:
DISGUISE, STRENGTH, DEADLY VENOM

DOCTORS MET:
11TH

JUST A DREAM

The Doctor, Amy, and Rory encounter the Eknodines in a dream world conjured up by the mischievous Dream Lord. Whether they exist in reality somewhere in the universe is unknown.

The Eknodines have been living in the bodies of pensioners for many years, unnaturally prolonging their lifespan. They look old and frail, but are actually very strong, effortlessly picking up humans and throwing them aside.

THE FACE OF BOE
THE LAST OF BOE-KIND

A huge head in a glass tank, the Face of Boe is a mysterious being who is believed to be billions of years old. It is said that he has watched the universe grow old and that one day, just before his death, he will reveal a great secret to a lonely wanderer.

HUMANOID HEAD

DATA FILE

ORIGIN:
THE SILVER DEVASTATION

SPECIAL ABILITIES:
TELEPATHY, SELF TELEPORTATION

DOCTORS MET:
9TH, 10TH

MESSAGE FOR THE DOCTOR
Sacrificing himself to save the people of New Earth, the Face of Boe's dying words are "you are not alone"—a warning that the Doctor's archenemy, the Master, is still alive.

The Face of Boe can teleport himself through the power of his will. He mostly grunts, but is also able to communicate telepathically, and in his dying days, sings ancient songs in the mind of his devoted cat nurse, Novice Hame.

SENSORY ORGANS

THE FAMILY OF BLOOD
GREEN, GASEOUS ALIENS

The Family of Blood are gaseous beings with short life spans. They go after the Doctor, realizing his Time Lord essence will enable them to live for much longer. Following him to England in 1913, they take over the bodies of four local people and use their own keen sense of smell to hunt him down.

After hiding away in human form, the Doctor eventually confronts the Family and their soldiers, the Scarecrows, and pretends to surrender. In reality, he has tricked them into letting him rig their ship to blow itself up!

JEREMY BAINES (SON OF MINE)

JENNY (MOTHER OF MINE)

MR. CLARK (FATHER OF MINE)

LUCY CARTWRIGHT (SISTER OF MINE)

ETERNAL PUNISHMENT
The Doctor devises prisons for each member of the Family. He binds Father of Mine in unbreakable chains, freezes Son of Mine in time, throws Mother of Mine into a collapsing galaxy, and traps Sister of Mine in every existing mirror!

DATA FILE

ORIGIN:
UNKNOWN

SPECIAL ABILITIES:
ACUTE SENSE OF SMELL, TAKING OVER OTHER LIFE FORMS

DOCTORS MET:
10TH

FENRIC
ANCIENT EVIL

Fenric is the name given to a powerful force as old as the universe. In the third century AD, the Doctor manages to trap Fenric inside a flask after winning a game of chess. Despite being imprisoned, Fenric is still able to use his Haemovores and manipulated humans to help with his eventual escape thousands of years later.

STOLEN BODY OF MATHEMATICIAN DR JUDSON

DATA FILE
ORIGIN:
THE DAWN OF TIME

SPECIAL ABILITIES:
POSSESSING PEOPLE'S BODIES

DOCTORS MET:
7TH

CAPTAIN SORIN
The Russian soldier Captain Sorin is on a mission to steal a code-breaking machine during World War II when he becomes Fenric's latest victim. But Fenric's possession ends when the Haemovores turn on him and destroy him.

In Norse mythology, "Fenrir" is a wolflike figure that will destroy the world. This ancient curse is passed down through generations, as the flask carrying his being is buried in an English village by the Vikings. Fenric continues to use people as his pawns until he escapes, at which point he kills and possesses the first person he finds—the wheelchair-bound Dr Judson.

WORLD WAR II ERA WHEELCHAIR

THE FLOOD
WATERY MARS MONSTERS

A highly contagious viral life-form found in the water on Mars, the Flood was possibly once frozen under the planet's surface by the Ice Warriors. When an exploratory mission to colonize the red planet uses the water from a contaminated ice field, the Flood possess the crew.

The Flood virus is highly contagious. If just one drop of infected water touches your skin you will become one of them. Human beings are about 60 per cent water, making them the perfect host.

WATER POURS CONTINUOUSLY FROM BODY

MILKY WHITE EYES

CONTAMINATED CARROT
The crew of Bowie Base One catch the Flood virus when their Bio-Dome becomes contaminated by Flood-infected water. One bite of a carrot turns crewmember Andy into a Flood monster and he starts converting the rest of the humans.

A NEAR ESCAPE
Six members of Bowie Base One become Flood. The Doctor and Captain Adelaide Brooke are among the few to escape infection. They know that the only way to stop the Flood reaching Earth is to blow up the base.

DATA FILE
HOMEWORLD:
MARS

SPECIAL ABILITIES:
WATER-SPRAYING, CONVERTING OTHERS, HIVE MIND

DOCTORS MET:
10TH

FUTUREKIND
SAVAGE CANNIBALS

Near the end of the universe, in the year one hundred trillion, a wild, snarling race called the Futurekind appear on the planet Malcassairo. The Futurekind resemble humans, but have developed fangs to help them slice through human flesh—their favorite food— and mark their faces with tribal patterns and metal piercings.

FILTHY HAIR

FACES PAINTED WITH WOAD

"HUUUUMAN!"
On their arrival on Malcassairo, the Doctor, Martha, and Jack encounter the Futurekind chasing a terrified human called Padra. The only way to escape them is by running to the safety of Silo 16—the desginated safe zone for non-Futurekind on Malcassairo.

BRAVE CHANTHO
In an attempt to kill the Doctor, the Master lowers the defenses of the Silo to let the Futurekind in. His assistant Chantho, the last of the Malmooth, tries to stop him, but the Master kills her and the Futurekind stream inside.

The Futurekind are a primitive race who communicate using a basic hissing language. They are led by a Chieftain and hunt as a pack, yelling bloodthirsty war cries as they chase their prey.

DATA FILE

HOMEWORLD:
MALCASSAIRO

SPECIAL ABILITIES:
HUNTING, RUNNING, EATING RAW FLESH

DOCTORS MET:
10TH

GANGERS
LIVING FLESH MONSTERS

In the 22nd century, cloned body doubles are used to perform tasks that are too dangerous for humans. These Gangers look exactly like their human controllers, but are made from programable matter called Flesh. Humans think Gangers don't feel pain, but they can, and they are determined to live a normal existence.

WAXY, BLOODSHOT FACE

DATA FILE
ORIGIN:
EARTH

SPECIAL ABILITIES:
COPYING HUMANS, MUTATION, STRETCHY BODIES

DOCTORS MET:
11TH

MORPETH JETSAN UNIFORM

UNSTABLE FORM OF JENNIFER LUCAS' GANGER

Gangers are consumed by rage and a desire to punish mankind for their ill-treatment at their hands. This is especially true for Jennifer Lucas' Ganger, which mutates into a massive human-gobbling monster!

DOCTOR GANGER
A Ganger of the Doctor is created during a solar storm. Amy is disturbed by it, believing it to be inferior, not realizing the two Doctors have actually swapped places.

TRICKED TWICE
Gangers make such convincing copies that even the Doctor is fooled when Amy is swapped for one. The mysterious Madame Kovarian plays the same trick on the real Amy, kidnapping and replacing her baby with a Ganger.

GELTH
BODYSNATCHING GAS CREATURES

Having lost their bodies in the Time War, some of the gaseous Gelth use the Cardiff space-time rift to come to 19th-century Earth. They want a physical form once more, and convince the Doctor to allow them to come through in force so they can possess the bodies of dead people.

GASEOUS FORM

DATA FILE
HOMEWORLD:
UNKNOWN

SPECIAL ABILITIES:
AFFINITY WITH GAS

DOCTORS MET:
9TH

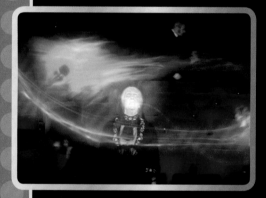

GELTH INVASION
Using psychic maid Gwyneth as a gateway, billions of Gelth begin to descend to Earth. They reveal they are planning to kill the human race and take over their corpses!

EYES TURN FROM BLUE TO RED ONCE THE GELTH'S TRUE NATURE IS REVEALED

In their disembodied form, the Gelth are glowing, wraithlike beings. They emerge from gas pipes and swirl through the air before entering dead people's bodies. Gwyneth sacrifices herself by causing an enormous explosion that destroys the Gelth.

MAKE GHOSTLY SCREAMS

CHARLES DICKENS
After his reading of *A Christmas Carol* is interrupted by a Gelth manifestation, Charles Dickens helps the Doctor to discover more about the creatures. He even takes part in a séance, during which the Gelth reveal their plight.

GIANT MAGGOTS
LARGE INFECTED GRUBS

Huge giant maggots are the result of pollution from Global Chemicals' factory in Wales. Feeding on the slimy green chemical waste causes ordinary maggots to dramatically increase in size and become deadly. Their bite and touch infects humans, causing the victim to glow bright green and eventually die.

Found in a coal mine in Wales, the maggots are virtually indestructible. Bullets and fire do not have any effect on them. However, they are susceptible to a type of edible fungus discovered by Professor Clifford Jones.

MASSIVE BODY

SHARP FANGS

SLIMY SKIN

MAGGOT MISSION

The Doctor pulls in the help of UNIT and the RAF to destroy the maggots. Like a normal maggot, the larvae creatures will turn into flies—giant flies. Only one transforms and is downed by the Doctor's cape.

DATA FILE

ORIGIN:
EARTH

SPECIAL ABILITIES:
INFECTING OTHERS, METAMORPHOSIS

DOCTORS MET:
3RD

GODS OF RAGNAROK
ENTERTAINMENT SEEKERS

Easily bored and hard to please, the Gods of Ragnarok crave one thing—entertainment. If they are not happy with what they see, they become angry and kill. They take over the Psychic Circus, also called "The Greatest Show in the Galaxy," and make people perform for their lives. Creepy clowns and robots help organize talent shows to keep the Gods amused.

THE PSYCHIC CIRCUS
Calling itself the Greatest Show in the Galaxy, the Psychic Circus travels from planet to planet. The Doctor turns the Gods' powers back on themselves, destroying them and blowing up the circus.

DATA FILE

HOMEWORLD:
SEGONAX

SPECIAL ABILITIES:
PSYCHIC POWER, ABLE TO EXIST IN TWO TIME ZONES

DOCTORS MET:
7TH

The Gods exist in two different dimensions. In their true time, they are living stone statues. On Segonax, the three Gods look like a mother and father with their small daughter.

STONE APPEARANCE

HEAVY MASKED FACE

GRACE HOLLOWAY
CLEVER COMPANION

A witty and intelligent heart surgeon, Grace helped the Eighth Doctor defeat the Master on the eve of the new millennium. The Master had opened the Eye of Harmony, the TARDIS's dangerous power source, in an attempt to steal the Doctor's lives, but Grace succeeded in jump-starting the ship before the Eye could destroy Earth.

COMPETENT SURGEON

REGENERATION
Grace operates on the fatally injured Seventh Doctor, not realizing he has two hearts. He appears to die in theater, but later regenerates as the Eighth Doctor. Grace drives the Doctor to her house for safety.

ALL CHANGE
The newly-regenerated Doctor returns to the TARDIS with Grace, only to face the power of his bitter enemy, the Master.

DATA FILE
ORIGIN:
SAN FRANCISCO, USA

OCCUPATION:
CARDIOLOGIST

DOCTORS MET:
7TH, 8TH

It took a while for Grace to believe the eccentric Eighth Doctor was really an alien from another planet. Even though they became close, Grace decided she couldn't face traveling in the TARDIS and decided to stay on Earth.

GRAYLE
AMERICAN CRIME BOSS

Julius Grayle is a powerful and wealthy crime magnate who lives in 1930s New York. Private investigator Garner describes him as the scariest guy he knows. Yet Grayle lives in fear of the mysterious Weeping Angels, with bars on the windows and locks on the doors of his mansion.

Grayle is a collector. His house is packed with priceless artifacts. But the jewel of his collection is a captured Weeping Angel, which he keeps chained up behind a curtain in his study.

SILK
POCKET
SQUARE
REFLECTS
WEALTH

A DANGEROUS OBSESSION
The Weeping Angels have fascinated Grayle all his life. He is obsessed with discovering what they are. He sends Garner to find out where they live, but the private investigator never returns.

PINSTRIPE
BUSINESS SUIT

ANGEL'S GRIP
Grayle has River Song from the Angel Detective Agency captured because he craves information about the Angels. His Angel prisoner grips her tightly and River breaks her own wrist as she escapes.

DATA FILE
ORIGIN:
NEW YORK, USA

SPECIAL ABILITIES:
CRUEL MANIPULATIONS

DOCTORS MET:
11TH

HAEMOVORES
VAMPIRE MUTATIONS

Haemovores were once human. These creatures are dependent on blood and live in water. At first their appearance is not unlike vampires, with pale skin and sharp claws, but eventually they turn into hideous mutations. Fenric, an ancient evil, uses them to aid his escape from the Doctor's trap.

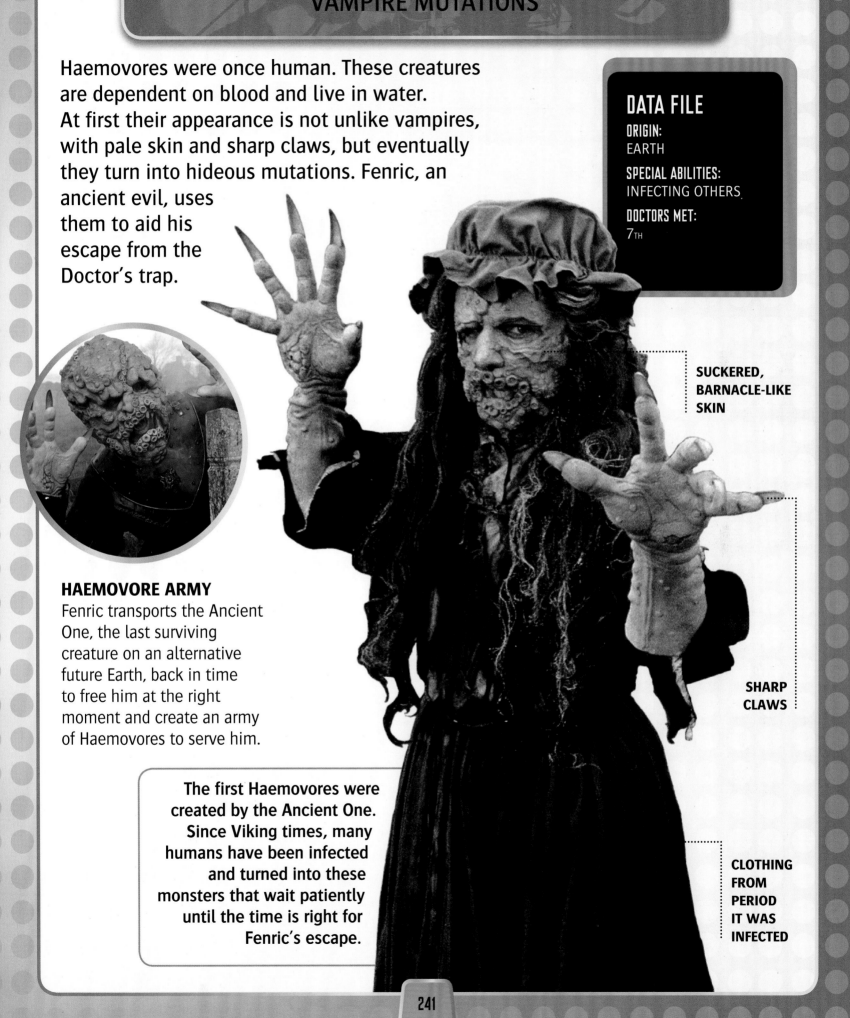

DATA FILE
ORIGIN:
EARTH

SPECIAL ABILITIES:
INFECTING OTHERS

DOCTORS MET:
7TH

SUCKERED, BARNACLE-LIKE SKIN

SHARP CLAWS

CLOTHING FROM PERIOD IT WAS INFECTED

HAEMOVORE ARMY
Fenric transports the Ancient One, the last surviving creature on an alternative future Earth, back in time to free him at the right moment and create an army of Haemovores to serve him.

The first Haemovores were created by the Ancient One. Since Viking times, many humans have been infected and turned into these monsters that wait patiently until the time is right for Fenric's escape.

HANDBOTS
AUTOMATED MEDICAL ROBOTS

The Handbots look after sufferers of the deadly Chen7 virus in the Two Streams Facility on Apalapucia. Slow-moving and of limited intelligence, the blank-faced robots use their hands to "see" where they are going, and carry hypodermic needles and darts for administering medicine.

NO FACIAL FEATURES

DATA FILE
HOMEWORLD:
APALAPUCIA

SPECIAL ABILITIES:
DELIVERING ANAESTHETIC BY TOUCH

DOCTORS MET:
11TH

Handbots have synthetic, organic skin which has been grafted onto their hands. Using their hands, they can even see types of bacteria on a person and administer anaesthetic.

SENSORS IN HANDS

CHEST COMPARTMENT FOR STORING SYRINGES

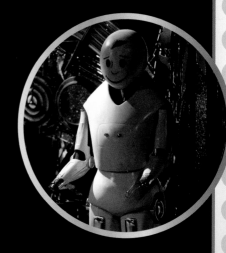

RORYBOT
Alone for many years, Amy ended up keeping one of the Handbots for company. She literally disarmed it by chopping off its hands, and drew a smiley face on its head. She even gave her robot pet a name—Rory!

BATTLE WITH THE HANDBOTS
When Amy becomes trapped with the Handbots, she realizes their medical injections could kill her. In order to survive she has to learn how to reprogram, and occasionally destroy, the well-meaning machines.

HARRIET JONES
FORMER UK PRIME MINISTER

Harriet Jones is a quirky politician who meets the Doctor during the Slitheen's attempt to cause a nuclear war. Thanks to her role in defeating the aliens, Harriet is made Prime Minister. However, a furious Doctor later brings about her political downfall as punishment for her decision to destroy a retreating Sycorax spaceship.

INTELLIGENT AND MODEST

PASS PLEASE

Harriet always assumes no one has heard of her. She introduces herself with a flash of her ID card, prompting the inevitable response, "We know who you are"—even from the Daleks and Sycorax!

DEFYING THE DALEKS

Following a Dalek invasion, Harriet uses her sub-wave network to bring the Doctor's friends together in an attempt to reach the Time Lord. Tragically, the Daleks detect her signal and exterminate her!

SMART OUTFIT AS BEFITS POLITICIAN

Harriet is not afraid to make difficult decisions. She orders the Doctor to organize a missile strike that will destroy all the Slitheen invaders—and at great risk to herself.

DATA FILE

ORIGIN:
ENGLAND, EARTH

OCCUPATION:
MP FOR FLYDALE NORTH, UK PRIME MINISTER

DOCTORS MET:
9TH, 10TH

HARRY SULLIVAN
CLUMSY COMPANION

Brave, if a little old-fashioned, Harry Sullivan is a medical officer at UNIT who does his best to look after an erratic Doctor following his third regeneration. Once the Doctor has recovered, Harry ends up joining him aboard the TARDIS. The Doctor often becomes exasperated by the young man's clumsiness.

CLUMSY AND UNSUBTLE

GET READY
The Fourth Doctor and his companions sometimes travel by transmat (matter transmitter) as well as by TARDIS. It doesn't always get them to where they want to go!

SMART BLAZER

DATA FILE
ORIGIN:
ENGLAND, EARTH

OCCUPATION:
ROYAL NAVY
SURGEON LIEUTENANT

DOCTORS MET:
4TH

SEEING DOUBLE
When the shape-shifting Zygons capture Harry, they use his body print to enable them to copy his form. Some time later, the Kraals make their own android duplicate of him!

Harry encounters some of the Doctor's most notorious enemies during his short time in the TARDIS. He meets a Sontaran on a ravaged Earth, battles the Cybermen on Voga, and even witnesses the birth of the Daleks on Skaro!

HATH
AMPHIBIOUS HUMANOIDS

The Doctor meets the fish-like Hath on the colony planet of Messaline. Once allies of the human settlers, the Hath initially helped them adapt the planet so that both races could establish a new society. Sadly, a war broke out and both sides used special progenation machines to replace their massacred troops.

BONY HEAD

FLASK OF NUTRIENT LIQUID

In order to breathe properly, the Hath wear special masks filled with a form of liquid. This has the unfortunate effect of distorting their speech, and the resulting bubbling and gurgling noises make the creatures difficult to understand!

PROTECTIVE GLOVES

TOUGH BOILERSUIT

HATH HERO
After being captured by the Hath, Martha befriends one of their troops, Peck. He manages to save her from drowning in a swamp, but tragically loses his own life in the process.

DATA FILE
HOMEWORLD:
UNKNOWN

SPECIAL ABILITIES:
CONSIDERABLE STRENGTH AND STAMINA

DOCTORS MET:
10TH

HEADLESS MONKS
WARRIOR MONKS

The Headless Monks belong to a religious order who cut off their heads for their faith. Applicants are selected from visiting armies. Although headless, they are skilled warriors, and if they think anyone is trying to look under their hoods they will kill on the spot.

CLOAK HIDES TWISTED SKIN AT TOP OF NECK

HUNGRY SKULLS
The skulls of the monks are stored in the Seventh Transept, a catacomb under their temple. The skulls eat rats and intruders.

DATA FILE

HOMEWORLD:
UNKNOWN

SPECIAL ABILITIES:
COMBAT-TRAINED, ARMED WITH ELECTRICITY AND SWORDS

DOCTORS MET:
11TH

BODIES DO NOT REGISTER AS LIVING LIFE-FORMS

HANDS CAN SHOOT BOLTS OF ELECTRICITY

UNDER THE HOOD
It is a Level One Heresy punishable by death to look under a Headless Monk's hood. Colonel Manton is granted special permission from the Papal Mainframe to unhood them in a public ceremony. It isn't pretty!

The Headless Monks form an uneasy alliance with the Clerics and Madame Kovarian in order to capture the pregnant Amy Pond and baby Melody. The Doctor disguises himself as one of the Headless order and infiltrates Demon's Run to save them.

HENRY AVERY
17TH CENTURY PIRATE CAPTAIN

Henry Avery was a respected naval officer who turned to piracy because of his greed for gold. The Doctor arrives on Avery's ship, *Fancy*, when it becomes the target of the mysterious Siren. Despite their misunderstandings, the Doctor comes to respect Avery and even calls on him for help on another occasion.

PIRATE HAT

SHAGGY BEARD

DATA FILE

ORIGIN:
EARTH

INTERESTS:
SAILING AND SWASHBUCKLING

DOCTORS MET:
11TH

ARMED WITH A PISTOL

An obsession with stealing treasure keeps Avery at sea, away from his wife and son, Toby, for three years. He promises to return but doesn't keep his word, so Toby stows away on his father's ship.

PLANK WALK
Avery is very suspicious of the Doctor. He refuses to believe the Doctor's TARDIS is a proper ship, thinks he is a stowaway, and forces him to walk the plank.

THE SIREN
Avery discovers his crew are being held in stasis on the Siren's spaceship. They think the Siren is a sea monster, but she turns out to be a virtual doctor, who is programed to heal sick people.

HENRY VAN STATTEN
ARROGANT AMERICAN BILLIONAIRE

Henry Van Statten is a powerful businessman who owns the internet and a secret museum full of alien artifacts. For years he has profited from alien technology that has fallen to Earth. He keeps a Dalek as a pet in his dungeon, completely unaware of how dangerous it is!

COMPUTER GENIUS MIND

DATA FILE
ORIGIN:
EARTH

INTERESTS:
MAKING MONEY, COMPUTER PROGRAMING, WIPING MINDS

DOCTORS MET:
9TH

METALTRON
The prize of Henry's collection is the "Metaltron"—a battle-scarred Dalek. He arrogantly thinks it will never escape its cage. But one touch from Rose Tyler frees it and it goes on a rampage.

Henry has agents around the world looking to recruit geniuses for his company. But he often fires them on a whim and wipes their memories. Even the president is at his mercy!

EXPENSIVE GOLD SIGNET RING

ALIEN MUSEUM
Van Statten has spent a fortune on his collection, which contains moondust, meteorites, parts of the Roswell spaceship, a stuffed Slitheen arm, and a Cyberman's head.

IAN CHESTERTON
COMPETENT COMPANION

Like his fellow teacher, Barbara Wright, Ian Chesterton stumbles aboard the TARDIS one night, unaware of the incredible adventures to come. Honest and loyal, Ian is a practical man, and his logical mind helps him escape numerous dangers. He is also not afraid of standing up to the cantankerous First Doctor!

SIR IAN OF JAFFA
One of the highlights of Ian's travels is when he is knighted by Richard the Lionheart. The King sends Ian as his emissary in search of the kidnapped Barbara.

Although he enjoys his travels in the TARDIS, Ian always longs to return to his own time. Both he and Barbara risk their lives to travel back to 1960s London using one of the Daleks' time machines.

SUSAN FOREMAN'S TEACHER

MICROSCOPE FROM CLASSROOM C3

DATA FILE

ORIGIN:
LONDON, ENGLAND

OCCUPATION:
SCIENCE TEACHER

DOCTORS MET:
1ST

ICE WARRIORS
MARTIAN CREATURES

Originally from the planet Mars, the Ice Warriors are a powerful warrior race of reptilian humanoids. They have attempted to invade Earth several times, wanting to transform its atmosphere into one more suitable to their biology, before becoming peaceful and joining the Galactic Federation.

HELMET CONCEALS SCALY SKIN AND SHARP REPTILIAN TEETH

The Ice Warriors' greatest weakness is heat, which can leave them gasping for breath until they eventually die. Most of their large body is armor that protects the creature inside.

HUGE, BULKY FRAME

ARMORED BODY WITH BUILT-IN WEAPONRY

DATA FILE
HOMEWORLD:
MARS

SPECIAL ABILITIES:
STRENGTH, SONIC WEAPONRY

DOCTORS MET:
2ND, 3RD, 11TH

FUTURE ICE AGE
During an Ice Age in Earth's future, an Ice Warrior is found frozen in a glacier. When it thaws out, the creature captures Victoria, the Doctor's companion. It wants her to help find the rest of its comrades who are still trapped inside the glacier.

GRAND MARSHAL SKALDAK
Believing he is the last of his kind, a vicious Ice Warrior goes on a vengeful rampage onboard a Soviet submarine. The Doctor appeals to his sense of honor to stop him obliterating humanity.

IDRIS
HUMANOID HOST FOR THE TARDIS

Before Idris is filled with the soul, or Matrix, of the Doctor's TARDIS, she is a Patchwork Person who lives on a sentient asteroid, called House. Her only companions are two other Patchwork People and Nephew, a green-eyed Ood. Being possessed by the TARDIS makes Idris behave like she's mad—when the Doctor arrives, she bites him!

MESSY HAIR

RAGGED PARTY DRESS

VICTORIAN-STYLE OUTFIT

BRAIN DRAIN
On House's orders, Nephew empties Idris's mind from her body and then fills it with the TARDIS Matrix. It's extremely painful and her human body does not survive for long.

Idris often muddles tenses and talks about things that haven't happened yet. However, she clearly remembers all the adventures the TARDIS has shared with the Doctor.

JUNK TARDIS
When House steals the Doctor's TARDIS, Idris helps the Time Lord build a junk one to pursue him. She uses her power to energize it, but when the Matrix merges back with the TARDIS, Idris dies.

DATA FILE
HOMEWORLD:
HOUSE

SPECIAL ABILITIES:
HOST TO THE TARDIS MATRIX, SENDING TELEPATHIC MESSAGES

DOCTORS MET:
11TH

JABE
MEMBER OF A NOBLE TREE-PEOPLE

Three representatives from the Forest of Cheem arrive onboard Platform One to witness the destruction of Earth. They are led by Jabe, a kind and flirtatious tree-woman who takes an instant liking to the Doctor. She does her best to console him when she discovers he is the last of his kind.

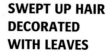

SWEPT UP HAIR DECORATED WITH LEAVES

BEJEWELED COLLAR

RICH EMBROIDERY

LUTE AND COFFA
Tree-forms Lute and Coffa are very loyal to Jabe. They are visibly distraught when the Ninth Doctor informs them of her death.

FAMILY TREE
Jabe offers the Doctor a cutting of her grandfather as a peace offering. She also reveals her reasons for coming to pay her respects to Earth, as a direct descendant of the planet's tropical rainforests.

LUXURIOUS ROBE

DATA FILE
ORIGIN:
UNKNOWN

SPECIAL ABILITIES:
JABE COULD SHOOT A LIANA FROM HER WRIST

DOCTORS MET:
9TH

Jabe bravely helps the Doctor to re-activate Platform One's sun filters, but tragically dies when her wooden body catches fire in the space-station's ventilation chamber.

JACKIE TYLER
ROSE TYLER'S MOTHER

Hairdresser Jackie Tyler becomes a widow and single mum aged just 19. She lives with her daughter Rose in a council flat on the Powell Estate in London, until the Doctor arrives and turns their lives upside down. She is torn between wanting Rose to be happy and wanting to keep her safe.

MOUTHY

DATA FILE

ORIGIN:
LONDON, EARTH

SPECIAL ABILITIES:
SLAPPING THE DOCTOR, PROTECTING HER DAUGHTER

DOCTORS MET:
9TH, 10TH

Rose is the most important thing in Jackie's life. She would do anything for her. When the Doctor whisks Rose away to see the universe, Jackie misses her terribly.

FIERCELY PROTECTIVE OF ROSE

BIG FAN OF CLIFF RICHARD

MIGHTY MUM
Jackie's adventures with the Doctor make her stronger and braver. When Rose crosses parallel worlds to find the Doctor, Jackie follows, determined to rescue her from the Daleks before returning to their new life in their alternative universe.

ALIEN FIGHTER
Jackie has witnessed Autons attacking London and was almost killed by a Slitheen. After a battle between Daleks and Cybermen, she becomes trapped in a parallel Earth alongside Rose.

SCRUFFY SNEAKERS

JACKSON LAKE
VICTORIAN WOULD-BE DOCTOR

Jackson Lake is a brave and brash Victorian school teacher who becomes convinced he is an incarnation of the Doctor. With his faithful companion, Rosita, he constructs his own versions of the TARDIS (a hot-air balloon) and a not-so-sonic screwdriver! He also spends time investigating the presence of a group of Cybermen in 19th-century London.

VICTORIAN CLOTHES

POCKET WATCH ENGRAVED WITH LAKE'S INITIALS

DATA FILE
ORIGIN:
SUSSEX, ENGLAND

OCCUPATION:
MATHEMATICS TEACHER

DOCTORS MET:
10TH

MISTAKEN IDENTITY
When the Cybermen kill his wife and kidnap his son, Jackson wants to forget. He finds one of their infostamps—a steel data storage device—but it backfires and makes him believe he is the Doctor.

NICE TO MEET YOU
In a snowy street, the Tenth Doctor meets a man he thinks could be a future incarnation of himself. It's actually Jackson Lake, who believes he himself is the traveling Time Lord.

With the Doctor's help, Jackson recovers his painful memories and true identity. The two manage to defeat the Cybermen who have been building a huge CyberKing using child slaves. Courageous as ever, Jackson helps free the children, including his own son.

JAGRAFESS
EDITOR-IN-CHIEF OF SATELLITE FIVE

TINY EYE

MULTIPLE ROWS OF SHARP FANGS

SLOBBERING DROOL

PURPLE, VEINY FLESH

The Jagrafess's full title is The Mighty Jagrafess of the Holy Hadrojassic Maxarodenfoe. Its fast metabolism means it can only survive in a very cold environment, but thanks to the Doctor's intervention, the creature eventually overheats and explodes!

Resembling a massive slab of meat, the Jagrafess is a vicious, slimy creature which clings to the ceiling of Floor 500 aboard Satellite Five. Installed by the Daleks, it manipulates the news reports broadcast by the station and creates a climate of fear that enables it to control the whole of humanity.

DATA FILE
ORIGIN:
UNKNOWN

SPECIAL ABILITIES:
CAN LIVE UP TO 3,000 YEARS

DOCTORS MET:
9TH

PRISONERS OF THE JAGRAFESS
The Doctor and Rose are captured by the Jagrafess and interrogated by the Editor, its shifty employee. The Editor wants to use the Doctor's TARDIS to rewrite history and prevent humanity from ever developing.

JAMIE MCCRIMMON
FAITHFUL COMPANION

James "Jamie" Robert McCrimmon first met the Second Doctor in the aftermath of the infamous Battle of Culloden in 1746. While he isn't the brightest of the Doctor's companions, he is certainly one of the bravest and most loyal, and he travels with the Second Doctor for a long time.

SHEEP'S WOOL SCARF

When the Time Lords put the Doctor on trial, part of his punishment was the loss of his companions. Jamie returns to Scotland and the Time Lords wipe his memory so he can only recall his first adventure with the Doctor.

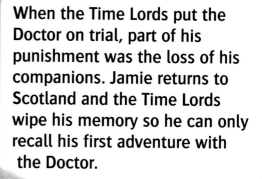

WHITE FRIGHT
When the Doctor activates the TARDIS's emergency unit, the ship is taken out of time and space. Jamie, together with fellow companion Zoe, soon finds himself in a nightmarish void, surrounded by sinister white robots.

SCOTTISH KILT FROM THE HIGHLANDS

FIGHTING DALEKS
Although Jamie is astounded by many of the aliens he meets during his adventures, he isn't fazed by the Daleks. He bravely takes them on and even manages to destroy a couple!

JENNY
THE DOCTOR'S DAUGHTER

Jenny is a generation 5000 soldier created from the Doctor's DNA to fight the Hath on planet Messaline. She is a child of the Progenation Machine and was "born" fully grown, primed to take orders, and ready for combat. Donna Noble names her Jenny because she is a "generated anomaly."

TWO HEARTS, LIKE THE DOCTOR

Jenny and her father don't bond easily. Her natural instinct is to fight, whereas the Doctor wants peace. But their adventure on Messaline reveals how similar they both are.

BITTER WAR
The humans on Messaline are locked in war against the fish-faced Hath. Jenny is born with the knowledge that she must fight the Hath until the war is won.

COMBAT-READY

DYING FOR THE DOCTOR
Jenny takes a bullet to protect the Doctor and dies in his arms. Later, energy from a terraforming device brings her back to life and she sets off to explore the universe.

MILITARY-STYLE BOOTS

DATA FILE

HOMEWORLD:
MESSALINE

SPECIAL ABILITIES:
FIGHTING, ACROBATICS, EXPLOSIVES

DOCTORS MET:
10TH

JENNY FLINT
MEMBER OF THE PATERNOSTER GANG

Alongside her wife Madame Vastra and the Sontaran Strax, Jenny can often be found fighting crime and aliens in Victorian London. Brave and plucky, and quite often sarcastic, Jenny has faced many dangers and fought for the Doctor on several occasions, including some very nearly fatal accidents.

BELT FOR ATTACHING WEAPONS AND GADGETS

KATANA SWORD

DATA FILE
HOMEWORLD:
EARTH

SPECIAL ABILITIES:
HAND-TO-HAND COMBAT, EXCELLENT SWORDSWOMAN

DOCTORS MET:
11TH, 12TH

THE DOCTOR'S ARMY
Jenny's feisty exterior hides a compassionate soul. She has grieved alongside the Doctor's companions, and she was prepared to travel with the Doctor to his end, alongside Madame Vastra and Strax—the rest of the Paternoster Gang.

WARRIOR WOMAN
Beneath her prim and proper Victorian costume, Jenny is always battle-ready! Clad in skin-tight leather, and armed with fierce combat skills, Jenny is more than prepared to take on Winifred Gillyflower's guards and free the Doctor.

Thrown out of her home and ostracized by her family for being different, Jenny was rescued by Madame Vastra and taken on as an employee. Her courage remains undaunted, as does her attitude to change for nobody.

JO GRANT
CREATIVE COMPANION

A loveable scatterbrain, Jo Grant manages to wangle herself a job at UNIT as the Third Doctor's companion, thanks to her powerful uncle at the United Nations. At first the Doctor is horrified at the thought of having such a clumsy assistant around him, but he soon grows very fond of her.

ABLE TO RESIST HYPNOSIS ATTEMPTS

JO JONES
Jo eventually leaves the Doctor after falling in love with Clifford Jones, a brilliant professor who wants to end world hunger, and who reminds Jo of a younger version of the Doctor.

Although she has a knack for putting her foot in it, Jo is always enthusiastic and often very resourceful. She is good at escapology and picking locks, and she even lists cryptology, safe-breaking, and explosives among her repertoire of skills!

NATURALLY ENTHUSIASTIC

CROPPED, LACE-UP JACKET

DATA FILE
ORIGIN:
ENGLAND, EARTH

OCCUPATION:
UNIT AGENT

DOCTORS MET:
3RD, 11TH

JOAN REDFERN
SCHOOL NURSE

Joan Redfern is a kind and helpful matron at Farringham School for Boys. After her husband dies in the Boer War, she falls for an unusual history teacher called John Smith. She has no idea that he is really the Doctor in a human disguise until the sinister Family of Blood hunt him down.

John Smith intrigues Joan. She is fascinated by his Journal of Impossible Things—a dream diary packed full of monsters and other worlds. She never imagines it might all be real.

COME WITH ME
After defeating the Family, the Doctor asks Joan to travel with him. However, she declines as she is unable to reconcile this man, bringing death and destruction in his wake, as being the same man she fell in love with.

REALITY HURTS
Joan and John's blossoming relationship is cut short when the Family attacks the school during a village dance. Joan is heartbroken to realize the man she loves must sacrifice himself to return to his true identity as the Doctor.

1910 ERA
PARTY DRESS

DATA FILE

ORIGIN:
EARTH

SPECIAL ABILITIES:
NURSING, DANCING, BEING BRAVE

DOCTORS MET:
10TH

JOHN LUMIC
CREATOR OF THE CYBERMEN

Lumic is the owner of Cybus Industries on a parallel version of Earth. Wheelchair-bound and suffering from a terminal illness, he is desperate to prolong his own life and so he develops the ultimate upgrade for humanity. His grisly process involves removing a person's brain and placing it in a protective metal exoskeleton.

DATA FILE

HOMEWORLD:
PARALLEL EARTH

OCCUPATION:
OWNER OF CYBUS INDUSTRIES

DOCTORS MET:
10TH

BREATHING APPARATUS

CYBER CONVERSION
When Lumic's life-support systems are damaged, his Cybermen realize he is in pain and force him to undergo the upgrade process. Despite Lumic's objections, they convert him into their Cyber Controller.

Lumic believes his motives are for the good of mankind, reasoning that people would no longer have to suffer from disease or painful emotions. Fortunately, the Doctor manages to stop his insane plan, and Lumic's cyber-form is eventually destroyed.

JOHN RIDDELL
BIG-GAME HUNTER

John Riddell is a big-game hunter on the African plains, originating from early 20th-century England. He is old friends with the Doctor and shares his love of fun and adventure. When a Silurian ark carrying dinosaurs hurtles on a crash-course with Earth, Riddell jumps at the chance to help the Doctor stop it.

LIGHT KHAKI CAMOUFLAGE CLOTHING FOR HUNTING

THRILL-SEEKER
Nothing makes Riddell happier than being in danger! He finds the prospect of fighting Raptors and the strong likelihood of being blown up thrilling.

SHEATHED HUNTING KNIFE

QUEEN NEFERTITI
At first, John Riddell and Queen Nefertiti find each other distinctly annoying, but they soon start flirting. And when Riddell returns to Africa, Neffy joins him.

DATA FILE
ORIGIN:
ENGLAND, EARTH

INTERESTS:
HUNTING, FIGHTING RAPTORS

DOCTORS MET:
11TH

Riddell has hunted big beasts all his life and has to fight his urge to kill all the space-bound dinosaurs. More than anything he wants a dinosaur tooth to take home!

JUDOON
INTERGALACTIC LAW ENFORCERS

The huge and powerful Judoon are police for hire that look like rhinoceroses. As well as being used to bring murderers to justice, they also provide security for the law-making Shadow Proclamation. They aren't known for their intelligence, though, and their predictable methods sometimes lead to mistakes.

TWO HORNS

DATA FILE

HOMEWORLD:
UNKNOWN

SPECIAL ABILITIES:
LARGE LUNGS CAN COPE WITH LOW LEVELS OF OXYGEN

DOCTORS MET:
10TH, 11TH

LARGE LUNGS

HEAVY, BLACK ARMOR

BLASTER SHOOTS OUT RED ENERGY BEAM

SCANNING DEVICE FOR IDENTIFYING LIFE FORMS FROM THEIR GENETIC MAKE UP

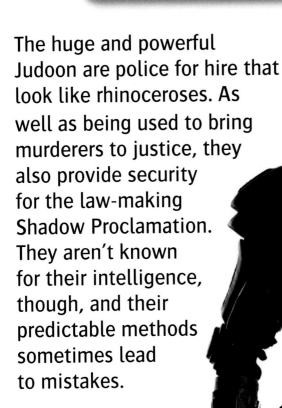

STOLEN HOSPITAL
Hired to eliminate a murdering alien Plasmavore, the Judoon search every floor of the Royal Hope Hospital—but not before they transport the entire building to the Moon, taking Martha Jones with it!

The Judoon possess impressive technology. They travel through space in massive, cylindrical spaceships and can surround buildings with powerful force shields. They use hand-held translator devices that analyze the speech of alien beings, allowing the Judoon to communicate freely.

K-9
ROBOT-DOG COMPANION

Once described by the Doctor as his "second best friend," K-9 is a brilliant super-computer with an endearing personality, even if he sometimes comes across as a bit of a know-it-all. The original K-9 was built in the year 5000 by dog-loving Professor Marius, who gave him to the Doctor as a gift.

DATA FILE

HOMEWORLD:
BI-AL FOUNDATION, ASTEROID K4067

SPECIAL ABILITIES:
ENCYCLOPEDIC MEMORY BANK, VAST INTELLIGENCE

DOCTORS MET:
4TH, 10TH

A PRESENT FOR SARAH JANE
When Sarah Jane met the Tenth Doctor, he was able to temporarily repair her broken K-9 Mk 3. He later built a fourth version for her, complete with two sonic lipsticks and a scanner watch.

SIGNAL BOOSTER TAIL ANTENNA

ROTATING EAR PROBES

PLAID COLLAR WITH IDENTITY TAG

GREEN/GRAY PAINTWORK

TELESCOPIC DATA-COM PROBE

LASER BEAM

K-9 MK 3

K-9 is loyal and fearless, with large memory banks and highly sophisticated sensors. There have been four versions of K-9. Mk 1 stayed on Gallifrey with the Doctor's companion Leela, while Mk 2 was given to the Doctor's friend Romana. Mk 3 and Mk 4 belonged to Sarah Jane.

KAHLER-JEX
ALIEN DOCTOR

Kahler-Jex is a Kahler scientist who experiments on his own people in order to win a war. When one of his cyborg soldiers goes rogue and starts hunting down its makers, Jex flees to Earth. He hides in a town called Mercy where he becomes their doctor.

Jex considers himself to be a war hero, but he is also haunted by guilt. To atone for his crimes, he does his best to help the people of Mercy, saving them from cholera and giving them electricity.

DISTINCTIVE KAHLER FACIAL MARKINGS

THE WAR IS OVER
Knowing his old volunteer Tek will tear the universe apart in order to find him, Jex takes matters into his own hands and ends the war by blowing up his own spaceship.

HUMANOID BODY

DISGUISED IN WILD WEST ATTIRE

LIVING A LIE
The Doctor normally loves the Kahler, calling them "one of the most ingenious races in the galaxy." But on discovering the truth about Jex, he is so horrified he drives him out of town.

DATA FILE
HOMEWORLD:
KAHLER

SPECIAL ABILITIES:
ADVANCED MEDICAL KNOWLEDGE

DOCTORS MET:
11TH

KAHLER-TEK
THE GUNSLINGER

Kahler-Tek was originally a volunteer who signed up for special training, only to be experimented on by Kahler scientist, Jex, who turned Tek into a cyborg assassin by fusing weaponry to his body. Tek and the other cyborg creations were then programed to kill in order to bring an end to the nine-year war on Kahler.

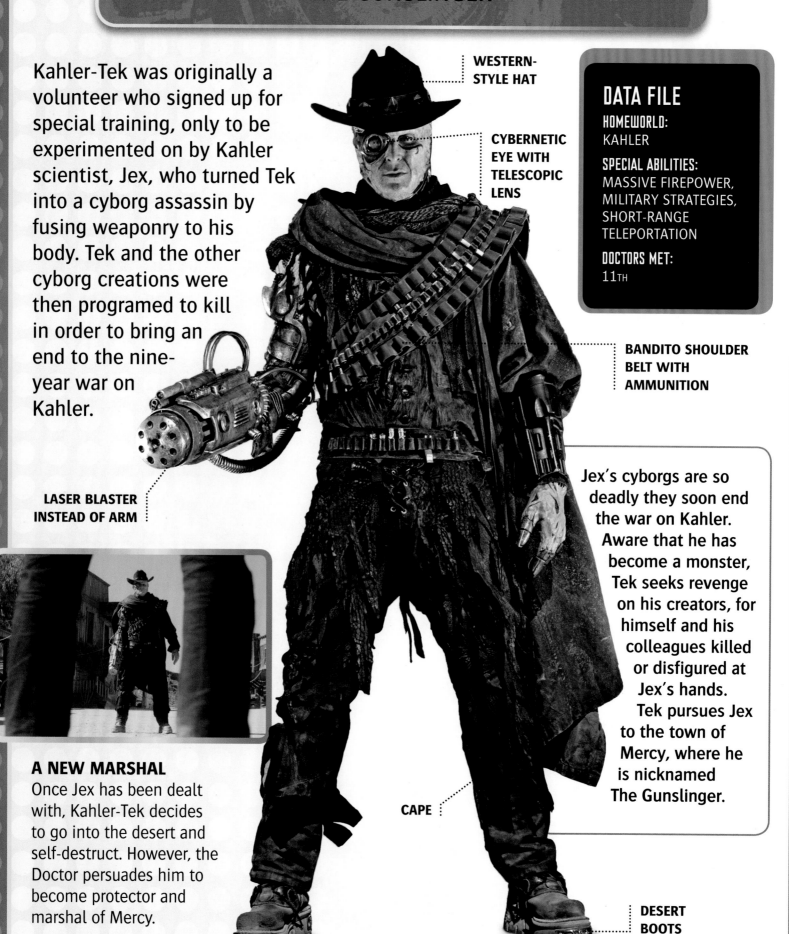

WESTERN-STYLE HAT

CYBERNETIC EYE WITH TELESCOPIC LENS

BANDITO SHOULDER BELT WITH AMMUNITION

LASER BLASTER INSTEAD OF ARM

CAPE

DESERT BOOTS

DATA FILE

HOMEWORLD:
KAHLER

SPECIAL ABILITIES:
MASSIVE FIREPOWER, MILITARY STRATEGIES, SHORT-RANGE TELEPORTATION

DOCTORS MET:
11TH

Jex's cyborgs are so deadly they soon end the war on Kahler. Aware that he has become a monster, Tek seeks revenge on his creators, for himself and his colleagues killed or disfigured at Jex's hands. Tek pursues Jex to the town of Mercy, where he is nicknamed The Gunslinger.

A NEW MARSHAL
Once Jex has been dealt with, Kahler-Tek decides to go into the desert and self-destruct. However, the Doctor persuades him to become protector and marshal of Mercy.

KAMELION
ROBOTIC COMPANION

Kamelion is a shape-changing android originally used by invaders of the planet Xeriphas. When the Master discovers the robot, he uses it to impersonate King John of England with the intention of changing the course of history. The Doctor succeeds in foiling his plan and Kamelion joins him in the TARDIS.

CAN BE CONTROLLED MENTALLY

DATA FILE
HOMEWORLD:
UNKNOWN

SPECIAL ABILITIES:
SHAPE-CHANGING

DOCTORS MET:
5TH

METALLIC APPEARANCE

CAN TAKE ON SHAPE OF DIFFERENT PEOPLE

MASTER MIND
The Master later manages to regain control of Kamelion. The Time Lord had accidentally shrunk himself and needed the android's help to return him to full size!

With Kamelion under the Master's mental control, the Doctor is forced to attack it. He reluctantly induces a reaction in its psycho-circuits—the electronic equivalent of a heart attack. He then uses the Master's own weapon to destroy the damaged robot.

MUSIC MAESTRO
Kamelion is a complex mass of artificial neurons, capable of infinite form. He is controlled by simple concentration and psychokinetics—and can even be made to play musical instruments!

KATARINA
TROJAN COMPANION

A gentle handmaiden to High Priestess Cassandra, Katarina of Troy meets the Doctor when he visits the besieged city in 1184 BC. She joins the TARDIS crew after helping the Doctor's injured companion Steven Taylor inside the ship. With no knowledge of technology, Katarina believes the TARDIS to be the Doctor's temple.

DARK, WAVY HAIR

SELF SACRIFICE
When a crazed criminal tries to blackmail the Doctor by taking Katarina hostage, she saves her friends by opening an airlock door, sending both her and the convict into space.

After entering the TARDIS, Katarina tells the Doctor that she knows she will die. She believes he is Zeus and is taking her to the Place of Perfection. Following her tragic death, a shaken Doctor hopes Katarina has found such a place.

ANCIENT GREEK DRESS

DATA FILE
ORIGIN:
TROY, EARTH

OCCUPATION:
HANDMAIDEN

DOCTORS MET:
1st

KATE STEWART
THE BRIGADIER'S DAUGHTER

Kate Stewart is head of Scientific Research at UNIT. Although it is unusual for a scientist to run the military organization, strong-minded Kate drags UNIT kicking and screaming into the 21st century.
She successfully leads the investigation when millions of mysterious cubes appear across the globe, and again when Zygons start bursting through historical portraits.

DOESN'T WEAR UNIT UNIFORM

TEAM CUBE
Kate enlists the Doctor's help with the Shakri's cube attack. She is delighted to have the opportunity to work with her father's old friend and with his encouragement, her leadership qualities shine.

DATA FILE
ORIGIN:
EARTH

SPECIAL ABILITIES:
LEADERSHIP, INTELLIGENCE, INITIATIVE

DOCTORS MET:
WAR DOCTOR, 10TH , 11TH

FACE-OFF
In UNIT's Black Archive beneath the Tower of London, Kate faces her toughest challenge yet. While she is prepared to detonate the whole of London, the Doctor instead forces her to organize a truce with the invading Zygon race. As an added complication, the Zygons assume the forms of Kate and her colleagues!

Depite being the daughter of former UNIT Commander Brigadier Lethbridge-Stewart, Kate is determined to make her own way in the world. She drops the "Lethbridge" from her name in order to avoid rumors of favoritism.

KAZRAN SARDICK
MISERABLE MISER

Kazran Sardick is a wealthy money-lender who controls the skies of Sardicktown. But years of being on his own have twisted him into a mean old man, just like his father had been. The Doctor travels into Kazran's past to force him to change his cruel ways.

WATCH CHAIN

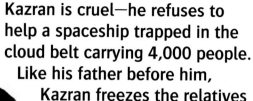

Kazran is cruel—he refuses to help a spaceship trapped in the cloud belt carrying 4,000 people. Like his father before him, Kazran freezes the relatives of people he loans money to and allows fierce Fog Sharks to frighten the Sardicktown citizens—thus maintaining his control over them.

CHRISTMAS DAY
When the older Kazran finally sees the error of his ways, he releases Abigail from the frozen chamber so they can spend one last day together.

FIRST LOVE
As a twelve-year-old boy, Kazran befriends a woman called Abigail Pettigrew. She is kept locked up in a cryo-cylinder in Kazran's father's basement. Every Christmas eve, Kazran and the Doctor visit Abigail and they all go on adventures together in the TARDIS.

SOMBRE VICTORIAN OUTFIT

DATA FILE
HOMEWORLD:
EMBER

SPECIAL ABILITIES:
CONTROLLING THE FOG LAYER, ISOMETRIC CONTROLS

DOCTORS MET:
11TH

KRILLITANES
COMPOSITE ALIEN SPECIES

FLEXIBLE WINGS, LIKE A BAT'S

DATA FILE
HOMEWORLD:
UNKNOWN

SPECIAL ABILITIES:
EVOLVING ANATOMY

DOCTORS MET:
10TH

Once looking like long-necked humans, the Krillitanes improved their physical form over the centuries by taking on the best characteristics of the races they had conquered. In their alien form, they tried to use unwitting school pupils to solve the Skasis Paradigm which would have allowed the Krillitanes control of time, space, and matter.

The Krillitanes had one weakness—they had evolved so much that the oil they used to make the school children more intelligent had become toxic to them. When K-9 exploded a vat of the oil, it sprayed over the creatures and killed them.

ALIEN TEACHERS
Thanks to a simple morphic illusion, the Krillitanes take on the appearance of human schoolteachers to disguise themselves. Their leader Brother Lassar, however, prefers to take an actual human form.

CLAWS FOR TEARING FLESH

BAT BEDROOM
Resembling bats in more ways than one, the Krillitanes sleep upside down and have acute hearing.

KROTONS
CRYSTALLINE LIFE FORMS

Bulky and somewhat clumsy life forms, a group of angry Krotons are found in suspended animation on a planet inhabited by Gonds, a near-human race. After the Krotons' spaceship had crash-landed there, the Krotons set about educating and ruling the Gonds.

TARDIS ATTACK
One Kroton tries to destroy the TARDIS and thinks it succeeds. However, the Doctor had remembered to set the Hostile Action Displacement System controls—and the TARDIS dematerializes to safety.

SPINNING HEAD

BODY CAN BE DESTROYED BY ACID

CLAMPS FOR HANDS

KROTON BLASTER

DATA FILE

HOMEWORLD:
"UNIMPORTANT," AS THE KROTONS WOULD SAY.

SPECIAL ABILITIES:
HARNESSING MENTAL POWER

DOCTORS MET:
2ND

Krotons are unable to see well in daylight and can turn mental power into pure energy. They use energy from the most intelligent Gond students to try to bring their spaceship, the *Dynatrope*, back to life.

KRYNOIDS
HOSTILE ALIEN WEEDS

These monsters are deadly, carnivorous alien plant creatures. The bulky, green form can expand incredibly quickly and is also able to control other plants in close proximity. Contact with Krynoids is fatal to human beings.

LETHAL TENTACLES

PLANT LIFE

HUMANOID SHAPE AFTER INFECTING A HUMAN BODY

Two Krynoid pods are found buried in Antarctic permafrost. One pod reacts to ultraviolet radiation and turns a scientist into a Krynoid creature. A second pod is stolen and taken to the UK— nearly destroying all human life.

DESTRUCTION PLAN
The stolen Krynoid pod rapidly expands in size, and is soon the size of a house. It terrorizes the Doctor and Sarah Jane, and is eventually blown up by an RAF squadron.

DATA FILE

HOMEWORLD:
UNKNOWN

SPECIAL ABILITIES:
RAPID GROWTH, PSYCHIC, UNAFFECTED BY EXTREME HEAT AND COLD

DOCTORS MET:
4TH

LADY CASSANDRA O'BRIEN
SELF-PROCLAIMED LAST HUMAN

Lady Cassandra is one of the guests aboard Platform One come to observe the Earth's destruction. Vain, selfish, and money-grabbing, she describes herself as the "last pure human" alive. However, all that is left of her is a piece of tightly stretched skin, thanks to the 708 surgical operations Cassandra has had to extend her life.

NO WRINKLES

METAL FRAME STRETCHES SKIN

WHAT A NAME!
When Cassandra was younger she was considered to be very beautiful. Her full name is Lady Cassandra O'Brien.Δ17 (pronounced Dot Delta Seventeen).

BRAIN PRESERVED IN A JAR

In her stretched state, Cassandra's skin needs to be moisturized regularly to stop it drying out. When her first piece of skin rips, she simply replaces it with another piece taken from the back of her body!

CASSANDRA'S DEATH
Fed up of being flat, Cassandra tries to find herself a new body. She takes over her devoted servant Chip, but his weak body can't cope and Cassandra finally dies.

HEAVY BASE SUPPORTS FRAME

LADY CHRISTINA DE SOUZA
PROFESSIONAL THIEF

Cheeky and charming, Christina is an aristocrat who gets her kicks from stealing precious artifacts, including the priceless Cup of Athelstan. She tries to escape on a London bus which takes her on the greatest adventure of her life—traveling through a wormhole to the ravaged planet of San Helios.

EXCELLENT EYESIGHT AND QUICK WITS

CLEVER CAT
When she stole the gold Cup of Athelstan from the International Gallery, Christina left a Japanese waving cat statue as her calling card.

FITTED CLOTHES FOR NIMBLE ACROBATICS

DATA FILE

ORIGIN:
ENGLAND, EARTH

SPECIAL ABILITIES:
CAT BURGLARY

DOCTORS MET:
10TH

BLACK CLOTHES GO UNSEEN IN THE DARK

FLYING BUS
Christina's skills as a cat burglar helped her penetrate a crashed spaceship to recover its anti-gravity clamps. The Doctor then used the devices to fly the battered bus back to Earth!

RUBBER-SOLED BOOTS REDUCE SOUND OF FOOTSTEPS

Christina loves her exciting escapade with the Doctor and is eager to join him in the TARDIS. However, the Doctor refuses as he has lost too many companions, and Christina ends up flying away in the bus, heading off on her own adventures.

LEELA
CURIOUS COMPANION

Leela is a warrior of the Sevateem, a tribe of humans on an alien world which has regressed to the point of savagery. Although uneducated and ignorant of technology, Leela is bright and inquisitive and tends to learn quickly. The Fourth Doctor does his best to educate her and attempts to curb her violent tendencies.

PRIMITIVE ANIMAL SKIN OUTFIT

Leela is a creature of instinct and can often tell if danger is nearby. Much to the Doctor's annoyance, she is also familiar with a number of weapons, including hunting knives, crossbows and poisonous darts, called Janis thorns.

CHUNKY CROSSBOW

RAT ATTACK
Although handy in a fight, Leela is helpless against a savage sewer rat that had been made many times larger, thanks to the experiments of war criminal Magnus Greel. She narrowly manages to escape.

LIZ SHAW
STUDIOUS COMPANION

Doctor Elizabeth Shaw is a distinguished Cambridge scientist. She was drafted in by the Brigadier to become UNIT's scientific advisor, despite her initial scepticism about the existence of aliens. When the Doctor is exiled to Earth, Liz's role quickly changes to that of companion as she ends up assisting him on his investigations.

Liz is one of the Third Doctor's most resourceful and intelligent companions. An expert in meteorites, she has degrees in various subjects, including medicine and physics. She eventually decides to leave UNIT and return to her own research at Cambridge.

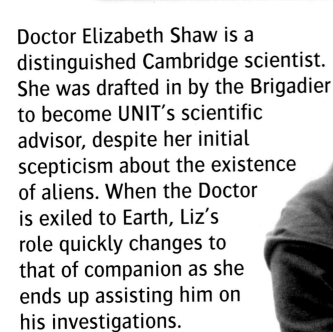

TIED BACK HAIRSTYLE

PARALLEL LIZ
The Doctor has a nasty shock when he accidentally travels to a parallel world and meets Section Leader Shaw—a much stricter and more severe version of his friend.

FASHIONABLE DUFFLE COAT

SENSIBLE LEATHER BOOTS

DATA FILE

ORIGIN:
ENGLAND, EARTH

OCCUPATION:
SCIENTIST

DOCTORS MET:
3RD

LIZ TEN
RULER OF *STARSHIP UK*

Otherwise known as Queen Elizabeth the Tenth, Liz Ten is the ruler of *Starship UK*, a ship that saved her people from devastating solar flares. Cool and collected, she believes her government is hiding a dark secret and is determined to find out how *Starship UK* could appear to fly without engines.

FACE OFTEN HIDDEN BY MASK

ROYAL IDENTITY
In order to carry out her investigations in secret, Liz Ten wears a porcelain mask perfectly sculpted to her facial features. However, she doesn't realize that the mask is hundreds of years old.

STARSHIP SECRET
Liz is horrified when she discovers she has been keeping secrets from herself. She is conditoned to find out every 10 years that the *Starship UK* has been built around a tortured star whale and has repeatedly chosen to forget the painful truth.

PISTOL FOR SHOOTING SMILERS

DATA FILE
ORIGIN:
EARTH

OCCUPATION:
RULER OF
STARSHIP UK

DOCTORS MET:
11TH

Liz Ten believes she is 50 and she has ruled for 10 years. However, the Doctor deduces that her government has slowed down her body clock. She is actually about 300 years old.

ROYAL CLOAK

SENSIBLE, STURDY BOOTS

MACRA
GIANT CRAB CREATURES

Enormous crustaceans, the Macra live in the enclosed Undercity of New New York where they feed on the poisonous exhaust fumes of thousands of gridlocked vehicles. Once intelligent and manipulative creatures, the Macra have devolved over billions of years to become mindless beasts, albeit with a strong instinct for survival.

The Doctor met an earlier form of Macra on a human colony world, a long time before they eventually devolved. These creatures also fed on gas and brainwashed the inhabitants into mining it for them.

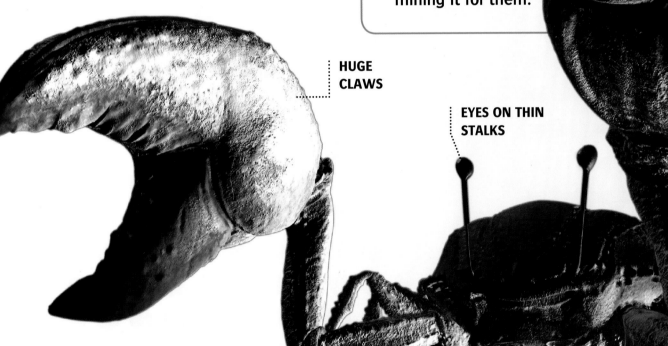

HUGE CLAWS

EYES ON THIN STALKS

DATA FILE

ORIGIN:
UNKNOWN

SPECIAL ABILITIES:
CAN BREATHE TOXIC GAS

DOCTOR MET:
2ND, 10TH

MACRA ATTACK
When the Doctor's companion Martha is kidnapped and taken to the low-level fast lane, the car she is traveling in is attacked by the Macra, who instinctively protect their territory.

MADAME DE POMPADOUR
THE GIRL IN THE FIREPLACE

Madame de Pompadour, known as Reinette, is the mistress of King Louis XV. At the age of seven, she discovered a deadly Clockwork Robot under her bed, but, luckily, is saved by the Doctor. Reinette's bedroom fireplace contains a portal between a 51st-century damaged spaceship and 18th-century Paris.

ALSO KNOWN AS JEANNE ANTOINETTE POISSON

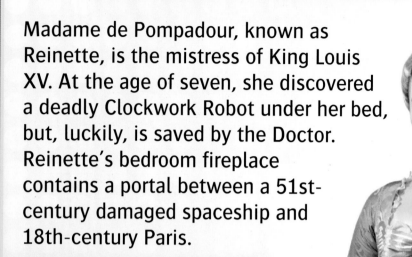

TIMELESS LOVE
Time passes at different speeds for the Doctor and Reinette. A minute for him is years for her. He watches over Reinette her entire life. In turn, Reinette falls in love with her "Fireplace Man."

BRAIN ACHE
When Reinette turns 37, the Clockwork Robots believe her brain can be used to fix their ship and return to take it. Even in danger, Reinette never doubts the Doctor will save her.

EMBROIDERED 18TH-CENTURY DRESS

Reinette becomes involved with the Clockwork Robots because their spaceship, the *SS Madame de Pompadour*, and Reinette share the same name.

DATA FILE

ORIGIN:
EARTH

OCCUPATION:
ACCOMPLISHED ACTRESS, ARTIST, MUSICIAN, AND DANCER

DOCTORS MET:
10TH

MADAME KOVARIAN
HUMANOID ENVOY OF THE SILENCE

EYE DRIVE

This wicked woman serves the religious order known as The Silence. She is charged with creating a weapon to kill the Doctor so that he never reaches the fields of Trenzalore, where "Silence will fall." That weapon is Melody Pond—Amy and Rory's part-Time Lord child, whom Kovarian raises to be a psychopath.

HIGH-HEELS MAKE HER FEEL MORE POWERFUL

DATA FILE

HOMEWORLD:
UNKNOWN

INTERESTS:
TRICKING THE DOCTOR

DOCTORS MET:
11TH

Madame Kovarian trains Melody for a single purpose—to kill the Doctor. When Melody regenerates into River Song, Madame Kovarian forces her to shoot the Doctor at Lake Silencio.

TRICKED TWICE
Madame Kovarian uses trickery to get her own way. She kidnaps Amy so she can watch over her whilst she is pregnant—fooling even the Doctor by leaving a Ganger in her place. Then, when Melody is born, she swaps the baby for another Ganger, much to the unsuspecting Amy's dismay.

TERMINATED
Like all servants of The Silence, Madame Kovarian wears an Eye Drive so that she remembers their existence. She is horrified when The Silence use it to electrocute her.

MADAME VASTRA
SILURIAN SWORDFIGHTER

Madame Vastra is a Silurian warrior who lives in Victorian England with her human wife Jenny. She is a skilled swordfighter who puts her superior intelligence to good use by working for Scotland Yard. She helps them crack cases, hunts down criminals, and eats them for dinner!

REPTILIAN SKIN

WIELS TWO SWORDS IN COMBAT

LAST STAND
The Doctor turns to Madame Vastra for help when trying to rescue Amy and Melody Pond from asteroid Demon's Run. She courageously fights the Headless Monks to protect Amy's baby.

DOCTOR DUTY
Madame Vastra, Jenny, and a Sontaran called Strax watch over the Doctor in Victorian England. She disapproves of his desire to be alone and thinks he needs a companion.

The Doctor and Madame Vastra are old friends. He stops her trying to avenge her sisters by killing innocent tunnel diggers. In return, she protects him and gives him guidance.

WARRIOR OUTFIT

DATA FILE

ORIGIN:
EARTH

SPECIAL ABILITIES:
SWORD-FIGHTING, CRACKING CASES, EATING CRIMINALS

DOCTORS MET:
11TH, 12TH

MADGE ARWELL
NO ORDINARY HOUSEWIFE!

Kind-hearted Madge Arwell is wife to Reg and mother to Lily and Cyril. Her life takes an unexpected turn when she comes to the aid of a spaceman in a field. Promising to repay her kindness, the spaceman (aka the Doctor) returns years later to give her family a Christmas present like no other!

1940S BOB

1940S COAT WORN OVER NIGHTDRESS IN HASTE

MISSING IN ACTION
Reg's Lancaster Bomber is lost during World War II. Madge is devastated and can't bring herself to tell her children their father won't be home for Christmas.

RESCUE MISSION
The Doctor's gift is a portal to another world. When Lily and Cyril vanish through it, Madge follows, determined to rescue them. Her steely resolve saves not only them but also Reg and a whole planet of endangered trees.

In order to protect her children from the London Blitz, Madge takes them to stay in their Uncle Digby's country house—a grand, old building with an eccentric new caretaker called the Doctor!

MARTHA JONES
CAPABLE COMPANION

Martha was a medical student when she first met the Doctor. After saving his life from a blood-sucking Plasmavore, she was invited aboard the TARDIS and soon fell in love with her traveling companion and her new life. Bold and brainy in equal measure, she fought against some of the Doctor's most deadly enemies.

MARTHA'S UNIT CALL SIGN IS "GREYHOUND 6"

BREAKING AWAY
After helping to save the world from the Master, Martha decided to stop traveling to look after her family. She also needed time to get over her unrequited love for the Doctor.

ALL-BLACK UNIT UNIFORM

DATA FILE
ORIGIN:
LONDON, EARTH

OCCUPATION:
DOCTOR, ALIEN HUNTER

DOCTORS MET:
10TH

Martha's adventures continued on Earth when she joined UNIT as a fully qualified doctor. She helped them fight off Dalek and Sontaran invasions, before being persuaded by husband Mickey Smith to become a freelance alien hunter!

THE JONESES
When Martha's father Clive, mother Francine, and sister Tish are arrested and held at gunpoint by the Master, Martha fears for their lives. She also realizes the dangers of being associated with the Doctor.

THE MASTER
ROGUE TIME LORD

Once childhood friends on Gallifrey, the Master grew up to become the Doctor's archenemy. He turned mad when he looked into the Untempered Schism. Like the Doctor, he stole a TARDIS and left to explore the universe. But unlike the Doctor, the Master wants to conquer worlds and wreak destruction.

DEVIOUS MIND

TWO HEARTS, LIKE THE DOCTOR

ARMED WITH AA LASER SCREWDRIVER

After dying, the Master is resurrected by the Time Lords to fight in the Time War. However, he flees to the end of the universe instead and hides as a human.

OLD RIVALS

As Time Lords, and with the ability to regenerate, the Master and the Doctor have faced each other in many incarnations. The Master is constantly tormented by the sound of drums, as a result of looking into the Time Vortex.

VOTE SAXON

Pretending to be likeable politician Harold Saxon, the Master worms his way into Downing Street. Once in control, he orders deadly Toclafane to kill one tenth of mankind.

MAX CAPRICORN
CEO OF MAX CAPRICORN CRUISELINERS

Max Capricorn is a rich and powerful cyborg who owns a luxury starliner business. When his company fails, he is voted out by his own board. In revenge, he plans to crash one of their spaceships, *Titanic*, into Earth, wiping out mankind so that the board members will be jailed for mass-murder.

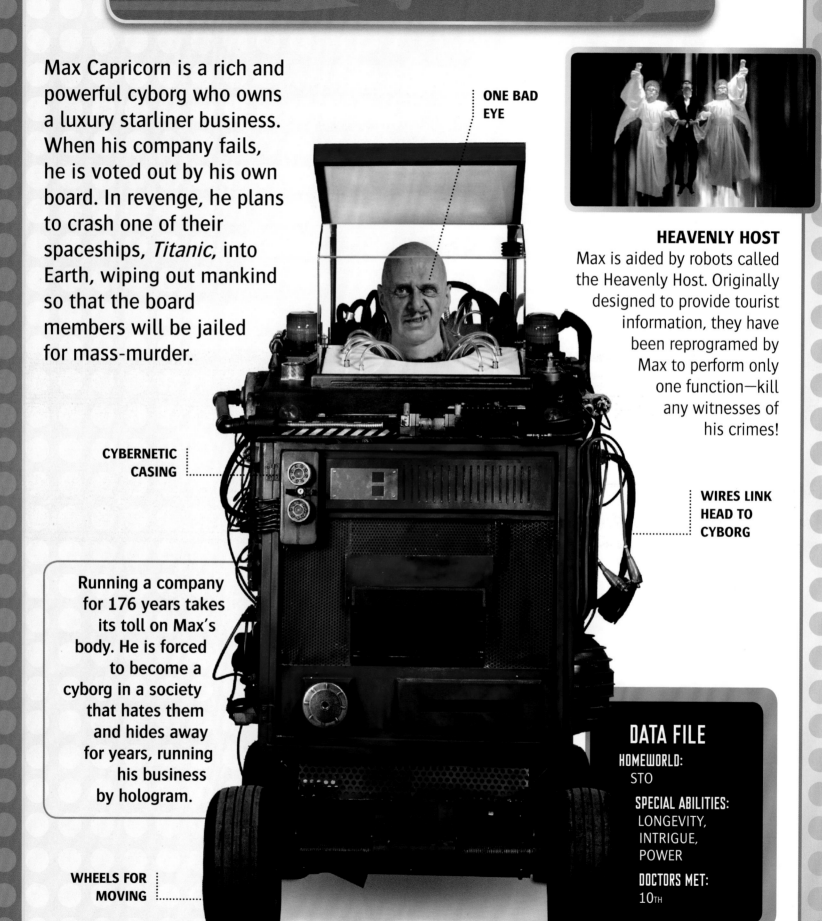

ONE BAD EYE

HEAVENLY HOST
Max is aided by robots called the Heavenly Host. Originally designed to provide tourist information, they have been reprogramed by Max to perform only one function—kill any witnesses of his crimes!

CYBERNETIC CASING

WIRES LINK HEAD TO CYBORG

Running a company for 176 years takes its toll on Max's body. He is forced to become a cyborg in a society that hates them and hides away for years, running his business by hologram.

WHEELS FOR MOVING

DATA FILE
HOMEWORLD:
STO

SPECIAL ABILITIES:
LONGEVITY, INTRIGUE, POWER

DOCTORS MET:
10TH

MEDDLING MONK
TIME TWISTER

The Monk is from the same homeworld as the Doctor, the planet Gallifrey. He likes to break the golden rule of space and time travel and chooses to interfere with the course of history. To teach him a lesson, the Doctor breaks the dimensional circuit of the Monk's TARDIS.

MISCHIEVOUS FACE

BAD HABIT
The Monk keeps a diary of his meddling. One entry talks of meeting the Italian painter and sculptor Leonardo da Vinci and discussing powered flight hundreds of years before the airplane is invented.

TRAPPED
The First Doctor's companion, Vicki, discovers a Viking's helmet. The Doctor deduces that it is 1066, the year of both the Viking and Norman invasions in Britain, and suspects someone is up to no good.

MONK'S HABIT

The Monk delights in changing history. He finds it funny and does not care. It is not known what happens to the Monk after the Time War that wiped out Gallifrey and all the Time Lords.

DATA FILE

HOMEWORLD:
GALLIFREY

SPECIAL ABILITIES:
TIME TRAVEL, MEDDLING IN TIME

DOCTORS MET:
1ST

MELANIE BUSH
ENERGETIC COMPANION

Better known as Mel, Melanie Bush is a young computer expert who relishes her adventures in the TARDIS. Bright and breezy, Mel is always full of energy and has a tendency to look on the bright side of things. She also has a natural curiosity, a trait which often gets her into danger.

DISTINCTIVE HAIR

FIT AND HEALTHY

MULTIPLE MELS
On Lakertya, with the help of the Tetraps, wayward time lady the Rani impersonates Mel in order to gain the trust of the newly-regenerated Doctor. The real Mel has a tough job convincing him she's the real thing!

A fitness fanatic, Mel keeps trying to get the burly Sixth Doctor to eat more healthily and get some exercise. She eventually leaves the TARDIS to travel with lovable rogue, Sabalom Glitz, determined to keep him on the straight and narrow.

MERCY HARTIGAN
CONTROLLER OF THE CYBERKING

UMBRELLA PROTECTS FROM SNOW

Once the matron of a Victorian workhouse, Miss Hartigan forms an alliance with a group of Cybermen. Angry and bitter, she resents men's dominance over women and looks to her "knights in shining armor" to liberate her. However, she is shocked when the Cybermen betray her and turn her into their CyberKing!

ROBOT REVENGE
Instead of losing her human emotions, Miss Hartigan's strong mind dominates the CyberKing. Angry and defiant, she causes the giant robot to stomp all over London!

FESTIVE VICTORIAN OUTFIT

To save millions from being converted into Cybermen, the Doctor breaks Miss Hartigan's mental connection with the CyberKing. She is so horrified at what she has become that she ends up destroying both her Cybermen servants and herself.

DATA FILE
ORIGIN:
LONDON, ENGLAND

SPECIAL ABILITIES:
UNUSUALLY STRONG MIND

DOCTORS MET:
10TH

FULL-LENGTH DRESS

MERRY GEJELH
QUEEN OF YEARS

Young Merry was taken from her family when she was still a baby. Chosen to be the new "Queen of Years" on the asteroid planet Tiannamat, Merry acquired knowledge of all the songs, melodies, and poems ever sung. Conflicted but courageous, Merry puts the safety of her people before herself.

CROWN OF QUEEN OF YEARS

Overwhelmed by the responsibility of her role, and frightened of making a mistake, Merry flees from the Festival of Offerings and runs straight into the Eleventh Doctor and Clara. This encounter comes to free her people from the parasitic sentient planet Akhaten forever.

SINGING SACRIFICE
Every thousand years, at the Festival of Offerings, the Queen of Years sings the Long Song to pacify the Old God to keep him asleep. Unknown to Merry, the queen is then usually sent to the beast as a sacrifice.

CHORISTER'S ROBES

DEFEATING THE OLD GOD
Encouraged by Clara and the Doctor, Merry helps defeat the beast terrorizing her planet. As she sings, the Doctor feeds it a mass of his memories, causing it to implode.

DATA FILE
ORIGIN:
TIAANAMAT

SPECIAL ABILITIES:
BEAUTIFUL SINGING VOICE, LONG MEMORY, TELEKINESIS, AND PSYCHIC POWERS

DOCTORS MET
11TH

MICKEY SMITH
TALENTED COMPANION

Mickey was the devoted boyfriend of Rose Tyler who all but lost her when she went off traveling with the Doctor. A bit of a no-hoper, Mickey is at first timid and cowardly in the face of alien threats, but shows a great talent for hacking into advanced computer systems.

GOOD WITH COMPUTERS

LOVES SOCCER

DELETING CYBERMEN
After fighting the newly created Cybermen on a parallel Earth, Mickey reveals his braver side. He decides to stay behind to help rid the world of the emotionless cyborgs.

CLOCKWORK ALERT
Mickey's first trip in the TARDIS takes him to the SS Madame de Pompadour in the far future. Wandering around the spaceship's corridors, both he and Rose are soon attacked by the vessel's clockwork maintenance robots!

A more heroic and grown-up Mickey eventually returns to our universe where he marries another of the Tenth Doctor's companions, Martha Jones. The pair hunt down dangerous aliens on Earth.

THE MINOTAUR
PRISONER IN SPACE

A huge, horned beast, the Minotaur stomps through the corridors of a strange hotel. In reality, the building is an automated prison, built by a race that had once worshipped the creature before turning against it. The prison is programed to trap other life forms, converting their faith into food for the Minotaur.

MANY HORNS

After being trapped for thousands of years, the Minotaur wants to die, but is unable to as its instinct to feed is too strong. In the end, the Doctor manages to sever its source of faith energy, allowing the creature to die at last.

BULL-LIKE HUMANOID

CLASSICAL-STYLE GARMENT

NIGHTMARE HOTEL
Desperate not to become another of the Minotaur's victims, the Doctor and his companions hide in the hotel's rooms, each of which contains someone's worst nightmare!

SKIN COVERED IN BOVINE HAIR

HOOVES

DATA FILE
HOMEWORLD:
UNKNOWN

SPECIAL ABILITIES:
FEEDS ON FAITH ENERGY

DOCTORS MET:
11TH

MORBIUS
TIME LORD WAR CRIMINAL

A Time Lord from the planet Gallifrey, Morbius was a ruthless dictator. Originally he once led the High Council of the Time Lords, and he wanted to use their powers to conquer planets rather than just observe them. He had millions of followers and admirers.

MORBIUS' BRAIN IN TEMPORARY PLASTIC CASE

MADE UP OF HUMAN, MUTT, AND BIRASTROP, AMONG OTHER SPECIES

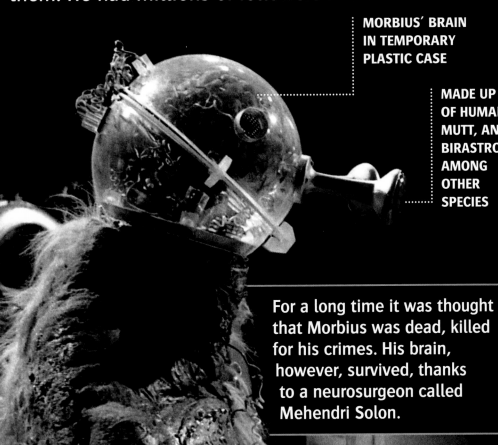

For a long time it was thought that Morbius was dead, killed for his crimes. His brain, however, survived, thanks to a neurosurgeon called Mehendri Solon.

THE CULT OF MORBIUS
The Doctor recognizes a model of Morbius' head when the TARDIS arrives on the planet Karn. Morbius and his followers—known as the Cult of Morbius—had come to Karn to steal the Elixir of Life so that they could be immortal.

SURGEON SOLON
Solon is a brilliant Earth neurosurgeon who hides away on the planet Karn. He is responsible for piecing together a new body to host the brain of Morbius.

DATA FILE

HOMEWORLD:
GALLIFREY, ORIGINALLY

SPECIAL ABILITIES:
REGENERATION

DOCTORS MET:
4TH

MOVELLANS
BEAUTIFUL ANDROIDS

The Movellans are a race of androids that generally hide the fact that they are not human. Physically striking, they are all incredibly strong and can lift great weights without any effort at all. For many years, the Movellans were locked in a war with the Daleks.

A design fault of these androids is the visible power pack attached to their bodies. It is easy to remove and without it, the Movellan is powerless and will collapse.

SILVER DREADLOCKS

DATA FILE

ORIGIN:
STAR SYSTEM 4X ALPHA 4

SPECIAL ABILITIES:
LOGICAL, PHYSICAL STRENGTH

DOCTORS MET:
4TH

EXTERNAL POWER PACK

CONE-SHAPED PINK GUN FOR KILLING OR STUNNING

FORM-FITTING WHITE UNIFORM

DUEL WITH DALEKS
The logical machine minds of the Movellans are their downfall when it comes to fighting the Daleks. Both races are, however, unable to beat the other due to their logical tactics.

MOVELLAN SPACESHIP
The Movellans spaceships are striking, as the Doctor and Romana discover. When landing on a planet, part of the ship will drill down into the earth as a form of camouflage and also defense.

THE MOXX OF BALHOON
OBSERVER OF EARTHDEATH

A representative of the solicitors Jolco and Jolco, the Moxx of Balhoon is one of the many distinguished guests aboard Platform One who have come to witness the natural destruction of planet Earth. A shriveled, goblin-like creature, the Moxx is unable to walk and floats around on a special anti-gravity chair.

SPITTING SURPRISE
As a formal greeting, the Moxx of Balhoon gives the gift of bodily saliva. Unfortunately for Rose, she is the one who ends up with spit in her eye.

Although the Doctor eventually succeeds in rectifying Lady Cassandra's sabotage of Platform One, he is sadly unable to save the Moxx. With its shields down, the station's exoglass begins to crack and he is killed by the sun's unfiltered rays.

SPEEDY ANTI-GRAVITY CHAIR

DATA FILE

HOMEWORLD:
BALHOON

SPECIAL ABILITIES:
BODILY FLUIDS REPLACED BY HIS CHAIR EVERY 25 MINUTES

DOCTORS MET:
9TH

CRIPPLED LEGS

MUTTS
MUTANT INSECTOID SOLONIANS

The humanoid Solonians on the planet Solos are undergoing a long evolutionary process, unknown to themselves. One stage in the terrifying transformation produces insect-like mutant creatures, who become known as "Mutts," by those who look down on and don't understand them.

MENACING CLAWS

BIG EYES

THE MUTANT STAGE LEADS TO LOWERED INTELLIGENCE AND AN INABILITY TO SPEAK

SOLONIAN STRUGGLES
When the Doctor arrives on Solos, the planet is in turmoil. Many humans in the Solos-based Earth colony, and some Solonians, despise the Mutts, believing them to be diseased, and want them wiped out.

A new evolutionary stage in the life of an Insectoid Solonian occurs every five hundred years, as the seasons on Solos alter. In the summer, the "Mutt" will eventually change into a beautiful and powerful super-being.

INSECT BODY

DATA FILE
HOMEWORLD:
SOLOS

SPECIAL ABILITIES:
METAMORPHOSIS

DOCTORS MET:
3RD

NIMON
PARASITIC BULL CREATURES

The imposing Nimon treat whole populations of planets as their food supply. Typically, a Nimon will arrive on a planet, set itself up as a god to be worshipped and then start demanding sacrifices. On Skonnos, the planet's leader Soldeed serves the Nimon. He believes that the creature will give him power and riches in return for his help.

HORNS THAT EMIT
AN ENERGY BEAM

BULL
FACE

The Nimon are a technically advanced race. They are able to create black holes linked to any planet they choose, and travel between worlds in transmat capsules.

DATA FILE

HOMEWORLD:
SEVERAL, INCLUDING SKONNOS AND CRINOTH

SPECIAL ABILITIES:
CONVERTING HUMANS INTO ENERGY, INTERGALACTIC TRAVEL

DOCTORS MET:
4TH

RESEMBLES
MINOTAUR
FROM GREEK
LEGENDS
ON EARTH

SACRIFICES
The Nimon claim humans as sacrifices and drain their life force for energy to sustain them. Once depleted, all that is left of the human is an empty husk.

NYSSA
TRAKENITE COMPANION

The Fourth Doctor meets Nyssa on Traken, a peaceful world that had been invaded by the dying Master who was desperate to prolong his life. The gentle daughter of an eminent scientist called Tremas, Nyssa inherits her father's intellect and helps the Doctor rid her world of the renegade Time Lord.

ADVANCED SCIENTIFIC KNOWLEDGE

COLORFUL OUTFIT

After traveling with both the Fourth and Fifth Doctors, it is Nyssa's caring nature that influences her decision to leave him. She chooses to stay on Terminus and use her scientific skills to develop a cure for the fatal Lazar's disease.

PRACTICAL CLOTHING FOR HER TIME ON EARTH

MEETING THE MASTER
When her father disappears, Nyssa goes in search of him. She is horrified to discover that not only had the Master taken over his body, but he had also destroyed her entire world, meaning Nyssa is the last of the Trakenites.

DATA FILE
HOMEWORLD:
TRAKEN

OCCUPATION:
BIOELECTRONICS EXPERT

DOCTORS MET:
4TH, 5TH

OGRI
BLOODTHIRSTY STONES

The Ogri are large silicon-based life forms from the repulsive swamp planet Ogros. Resembling large standing stones, they can live for centuries, living off amino acids. While on Earth, the Ogri need blood globulin to survive. An Ogri can absorb the blood of a human in seconds.

Three Ogri arrive on Earth with a criminal called Cessair of Diplos. They end up forming part of a stone circle called the Nine Travellers, confusing people because their number changed between surveys.

IRREGULAR
SHAPE ⋯⋯⋯⋯⋯

CESSAIR OF DIPLOS
Wanted for murder and theft, Cessair of Diplos comes to Earth to avoid capture. She assumes a number of identities across centuries, while the Ogri serve and carry out her commands.

DATA FILE

HOMEWORLD:
OGROS IN THE TAU CETI SYSTEM

SPECIAL ABILITIES:
DRAINING LIFE FORMS OF BLOOD

DOCTORS MET:
4TH

OGRONS
UNINTELLIGENT SERVANT RACE

The Ogrons are lumbering ape creatures with little intelligence, making them loyal servants to their masters. Living in scattered communities on one of the outer planets, they act as a simple and effective police force. They are honest and have very simple needs.

In the 22nd century, the Daleks use the Ogrons to keep humans under control. Centuries later, the Master works with them to start a war between humans and Draconians—reptilian humanoids from Draconia.

BULKY BODY

DATA FILE
HOMEWORLD:
THE OUTER PLANETS

SPECIAL ABILITIES:
STRENGTH, STAMINA

DOCTORS MET:
3RD

STURDY BOOTS

DICTATOR DALEKS
Daleks probably use the stupidity of the Ogron race to their advantage. An Ogron will never reveal any Dalek plans and will carry out orders without question.

SO LONG, OGRON
The Third Doctor escapes the clutches of the Ogrons at Auderly House, where a world peace conference was due to be held.

OMEGA
BETRAYED TIME LORD

Omega is the Time Lord regarded as a hero for giving the people of Gallifrey the ability to travel through time. It was widely believed that the stellar engineer died when he blew up a star in order to harness its power for time travel, but in fact he lives on, trapped inside a lonely anti-matter universe. Alone and abandoned, he seeks revenge.

DATA FILE
HOMEWORLD:
GALLIFREY, ORIGINALLY

SPECIAL ABILITIES:
STELLAR ENGINEERING

DOCTORS MET:
3RD, 5TH

ELABORATE HEADPIECE

GELL GUARDS
In his anti-matter world, Omega commands Gell Guards—horrific anti-matter creatures of his own creation. The beings invade UNIT HQ and take the building and the Doctor back to Omega's world.

BODY COPY
In another attempt to return to the positive-matter world, Omega steals the Doctor's biodata from the Matrix on Gallifrey. His return is short-lived as Omega is destroyed on Earth.

Driven insane from his exile in his anti-matter world, Omega plans to return to the proper universe. But as anti-matter himself, he is unable to exist in a positive-matter universe.

ANTI-MATTER BODY

THE OOD
HIVE-MINDED HUMANOIDS

A race of gentle, tentacle-faced telepaths, the Ood lived in peaceful harmony until the arrival of the Halpen Family. These entrepreneurial tycoons enslaved the Ood and sold them throughout the Human Empire. They were set free by the Doctor in 4126 AD.

TRANSLATOR DEVICE

TENTACLES

Each Ood is born with an external hindbrain containing the creature's memories and personality. Unlike the forebrains in their heads, the Ood carry their delicate hindbrains in their hands.

THE NEPHEW
An Ood known as Nephew was transported to a living asteroid called House and came under the entity's psychic control. Nephew has the scary ability to drain people's minds from their bodies!

FUNCTIONAL WORK-WEAR

RED EYE
On Krop Tor, the Ood's telepathic field comes under the psychic possession of the Beast. Somehow, as a sign of their possession, their eyes glow red and they act in ways that, for a peaceful race, are unnaturally violent.

DATA FILE

HOMEWORLD:
OOD SPHERE

SPECIAL ABILITIES:
TELEPATHY, POWER OF PROPHECY

DOCTORS MET:
10TH, 11TH

PATCHWORK PEOPLE
TIME LORD TRAPPERS

Auntie and Uncle are Patchwork People. Their bodies are Frankenstein-like collections of Time Lord body parts that have been crudely stitched together. They live in a TARDIS junkyard on a talking asteroid called House and act as his servants.

EYES OF A 20-YEAR-OLD

CLOTHES PATCHED TOGETHER WITH MISMATCHED FABRICS

HUNGRY HOUSE
The Patchwork People see House as their saviour. He mends and nourishes them and in turn they do his will, luring Time Lords to their doom so House can eat their TARDISes.

TIME LORD'S ARM

OLD CAST-OFFS

Auntie and Uncle were once travelers who came through the Rift. But they have been patched up so many times that nothing recognizable remains of their original selves.

TWO LEFT FEET

DATA FILE
HOMEWORLD:
HOUSE

SPECIAL ABILITIES:
TRICKING TIME LORDS

DOCTORS MET:
11TH

PEG DOLLS
LIVING TOYS

The Peg Dolls were brought to life by the psycho-kinetic powers of a young boy called George. Really an alien Tenza, George has the ability to send everything he's afraid of into a doll's house in his cupboard. The dolls hunt down people and transform them into dolls.

The transformation into a Peg Doll is quick. First, the victim's hands get bigger and turn to wood, followed by the rest of the body. When Amy and Rory find themselves in the doll's house, Amy is caught and becomes a doll—ending up in a state of living death.

18TH-CENTURY SOLDIER'S UNIFORM

VICTIM'S CLOTHING MODIFIED

WOODEN LIMBS

DATA FILE
ORIGIN:
EARTH

SPECIAL ABILITIES:
TRANSFORMING OTHER BEINGS INTO DOLLS

DOCTORS MET:
11TH

NO MORE NIGHT TERRORS
After George himself appears in the doll's house, the toys surround him and threaten to transform him. When his Dad reassures him that he is loved, though, his fears disappear and everyone is returned to normal.

PERI BROWN
AMERICAN STUDENT COMPANION

While on holiday in Lanzarote, American botany student Perpugilliam "Peri" Brown is saved from drowning by the Doctor's companion, Turlough. Adventurous Peri gleefully accepts the Doctor's invitation to travel with him and Turlough.

BRIGHT AND INTELLIGENT

SIXTH DOCTOR
Peri finds it tough going when the Doctor regenerates into his explosive and unstable sixth incarnation. Luckily, the Doctor eventually settles down and the pair become good friends.

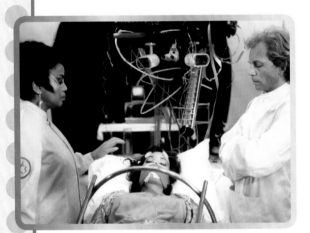

BRAIN TRANSFER
Put on trial by the Time Lords, the Doctor is shown evidence that his meddling has led to Peri's death. The brain of Mentor Kiv has seemingly been transplanted into her body!

COLORFUL VACATION OUTFIT

DATA FILE
ORIGIN:
USA, EARTH

OCCUPATION:
STUDENT

DOCTORS MET:
2ND, 5TH, 6TH

After their many adventures fighting the likes of Cybermen, Gastropods, and Sontarans, the Doctor is distraught at his companion's death. Happily, he later discovers that the evidence had been faked—Peri had in fact married the boisterous warrior King Yrcanos!

PETE TYLER
ROSE TYLER'S FATHER

Rose's Dad Pete dies in a car crash when she is just six months old. She grows up hearing stories from her mum Jackie about how clever and brilliant he was. But in truth he is a hopeless dreamer whose daft money-making schemes never work.

PARALLEL WORLD VERSION OF PETE TYLER

REUNITED
Pete meets his grown-up daughter when she goes back in time and saves his life. But it causes a wound in time that can only be healed by his death.

PETE'S WORLD
In a parallel universe, Pete is a successful and wealthy businessman. He works undercover to stop Cybus Industries creating Cybermen and saves Rose from being sucked into the Void.

Jackie is always telling Pete he's useless. He wishes he could be a proper businessman and a better husband and father. However, when Jackie meets the parallel world version of Pete, the two are given a second chance together. They fall in love again and go on to have a son—Tony.

DATA FILE

HOMEWORLD:
EARTH, PARALLEL EARTH

SPECIAL ABILITIES:
SELF-SACRIFICE, FIGHTING CYBERMEN

DOCTORS MET:
9TH, 10TH

PIG SLAVES
HOG-FACED HENCHMEN

Pig Slaves are the savage servants of the Daleks. They are the horrific result of a genetic experiment in which the Daleks merged humans with pigs in the sewers of New York City. Their job is to kidnap other humans for the Daleks to experiment on as part of their quest for evolution and survival.

CAN ONLY GRUNT OR SQUEAL

SHARP TEETH FOR CUTTING FLESH

HUMANOID WITH PORCINE FLESH

FUNCTIONAL BOILER SUIT

DATA FILE

ORIGIN:
EARTH

SPECIAL ABILITIES:
KIDNAPPING, KILLING, FOLLOWING DALEK ORDERS

DOCTORS MET:
10TH

Daleks select the least intelligent humans to become Pig Slaves, saving clever people to become Dalek-Human soldiers. Once converted, they forget their humanity and act like wild beasts.

LUCKY LASZLO

Laszlo is working at a theater in New York when he is ambushed by Pig Slaves. They take him to the Daleks to be converted into a Pig Slave, but Laszlo escapes before they take his mind and he can still talk.

THE CULT OF SKARO

The Pig Slaves' masters are an elite group of Daleks known as the Cult of Skaro. Pig Slaves obey these Daleks without question, dragging people down into the New York sewers to be transformed.

PLASMAVORES
BLOOD-SUCKING SHAPE-SHIFTERS

The Plasmavores are a vicious race of shape-changing aliens who survive by draining the blood of other life forms, leaving them for dead. By assimilating their blood, they have the ability to mimic the internal structure of their victims' bodies—a talent which enables the creatures to avoid detection.

DRAINING THE DOCTOR
With the Judoon on her trail, Florence drinks the Doctor's blood, believing it will make her appear human, thus hiding her real identity. She gets a shock when the Judoon's scanners say otherwise!

JUDOON ARMY
The Judoon invade Royal Hope Hospital on Earth in their search for a rogue criminal Plasmavore operating under the alias of Florence Finnegan. She is accused of murdering the Child Princess of Padrivole Regency Nine.

Florence is assisted by two Slabs—solid leather drones who hold down her victims while she feasts on their blood. However, she cannot run from the Judoon for long, and is eventually executed by them for her crimes.

X INDICATES FLORENCE HAS SUPPOSEDLY BEEN APPROVED AS BEING HUMAN BY THE JUDOON

DATA FILE

ORIGIN:
UNKNOWN

SPECIAL ABILITIES:
MIMICKING OTHER LIFE FORMS

DOCTORS MET:
10TH

POLLY WRIGHT

CONFIDENT COMPANION

A bright, fun-loving girl from 1960s London, Polly is the secretary to Professor Brett, the creator of WOTAN. When the supercomputer decides to take over humanity, Polly is one of many who is hypnotized into constructing its war machines. Luckily she survives the ordeal, and stays with the First Doctor after helping him defeat WOTAN.

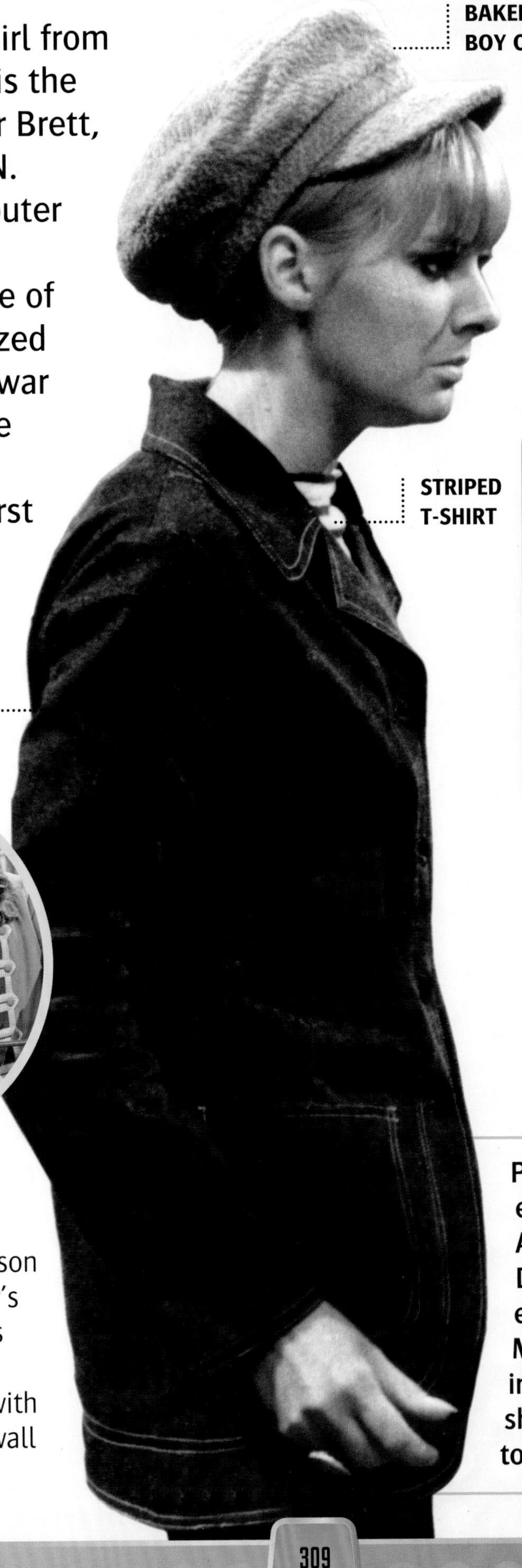

BAKER-BOY CAP

STRIPED T-SHIRT

DENIM JACKET

DATA FILE

ORIGIN:
ENGLAND

OCCUPATION:
PERSONAL ASSISTANT

DOCTORS MET:
1st, 2nd

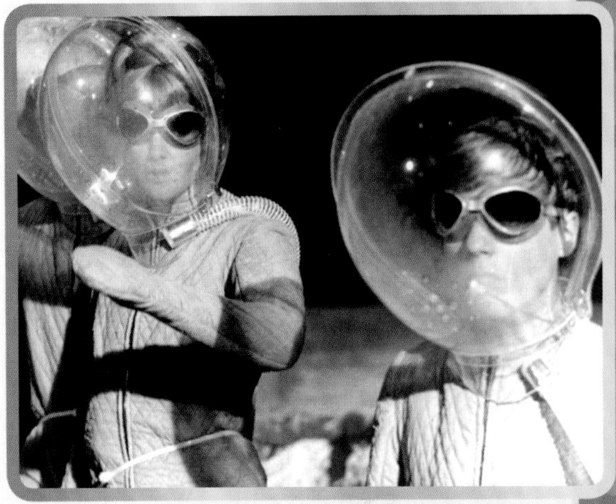

MOONWALK
When the TARDIS lands on the moon, Polly is excited about taking a walk across the lunar surface. It's not long though before she comes up against the invading Cybermen.

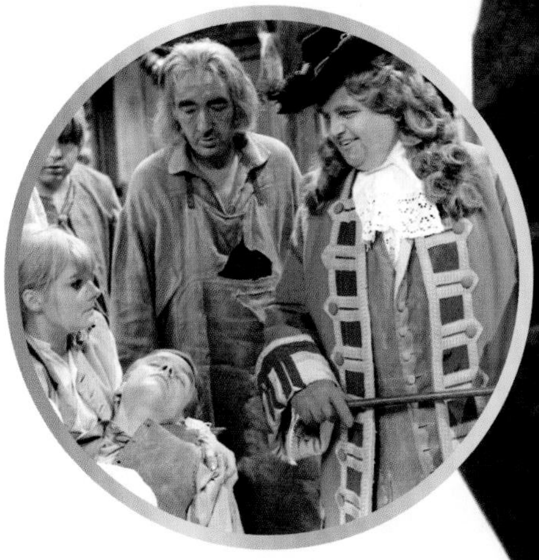

TALL TALES
Polly first sneaks aboard the TARDIS with Ben Jackson in order to test the Doctor's tales about his adventures in space and time. They soon become embroiled with a smuggling ring in Cornwall in the 17th century!

Polly copes with many strange experiences during her travels. After witnessing the First Doctor's regeneration, she encounters the malevolent Macra and is nearly turned into a fish person. In the end, she leaves the Doctor to return to a normal life in London.

PORRIDGE
DEFENDER OF HUMANITY

Emperor Ludens Nimrod Kendrick called Longstaff XLI considers his role to be the loneliest in the universe. Tired of being viewed as a ruler and not as an individual, he shrugs off his responsibilities, assumes the name "Porridge" and flees to Hedgewick's World of Wonders—the galaxy's biggest and best, but abandoned, amusement park.

CHESS MACHINE
When the Doctor and his companions first encounter Porridge, he looks nothing like an Emperor. Instead, he is operating a supposedly unbeatable chess-playing Cyberman from the inside.

BOMBER HAT

FACE APPEARS ON IMPERIAL COINS AND OFFICIAL STATUES

DATA FILE
ORIGIN:
UNKNOWN

SPECIAL ABILITIES:
EXCELLENT CHESS PLAYER

DOCTORS MET:
11TH

WARM SHEEPSKIN COAT

PROPOSAL
Despite the Doctor's disapproval, Porridge issues Clara with a marriage proposal, having been struck by her intelligence during the battle with the Cybermen. He takes her refusal with good grace, before turning his imperial spaceship for home.

As Emperor, Porridge is responsible for protecting the universe from Cybermen attacks. Forced to make difficult decisions, such as detonating whole galaxies in order to ensure the destruction of the Cybermen, Porridge maintains his sense of humor throughout.

PRISONER ZERO
SHAPE-SHIFTING ALIEN CRIMINAL

A prisoner of the Atraxi, Prisoner Zero is a gelatinous serpent creature that escapes to Earth through a crack in time, hiding out in the house of Amy Pond. As a shape-shifting multi-form, it can copy the identities of more than one creature at the same time, thus avoiding capture.

ONE MAN AND HIS DOG
When the Doctor draws Amy's attention to a room concealed by a perception filter, Prisoner Zero shows itself, disguised as an angry man with an equally ferocious-looking dog.

VICIOUS
SERPENTINE
YELLOW EYES

PRISONER ZERO'S
NATURAL FORM

FIERCELY
SHARP
TEETH

Before it can copy another life form, Prisoner Zero needs to link with it psychically. This proves simple to achieve with the unconscious patients in a nearby coma ward. Prisoner Zero can even assume the form of a creature that is being dreamt about.

DATA FILE

ORIGIN:
UNKNOWN

SPECIAL ABILITIES:
ASSUMING THE APPEARANCE OF OTHER BEINGS, CREATING PERCEPTION FILTERS

DOCTORS MET:
11TH

PROFESSOR EDWARD TRAVERS
BRITISH EXPLORER

Professor Edward Travers is an explorer. He is searching for the Yeti in the Himalayas when he becomes caught up with the robot Yeti attacks and the Great Intelligence. Forty years later he reactivates a Yeti and ends up fighting the Great Intelligence again in London's Underground, alongside his daughter Anne—who is a scientific advisor for the British army.

THERMAL HAT

YETI ATTACK
Forty years after his first encounter with the Yeti and the Doctor, Travers sells one of the unanimated Yeti to a museum. When he reactivates one of the control spheres, he brings back the threat of the Yeti to Earth.

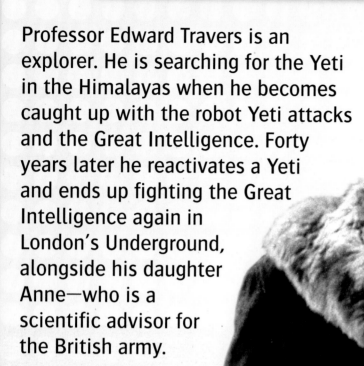

Travers has always believed that the Abominable Snowman exists. Quick to judge, when his friend is killed on an expedition, he initially thinks it is the Doctor who did it.

THICK LAYERS FOR HUNTING IN COLD CLIMES

HUNTING RIFLE

DATA FILE
ORIGIN:
EARTH

SPECIAL ABILITIES:
EXPLORING

DOCTORS MET:
2ND

PROFESSOR LAZARUS
CREATOR OF THE GMD

An elderly scientist, Professor Richard Lazarus uses his great invention, the Genetic Manipulation Device (GMD), to make himself thirty years younger. During the process, however, he unwittingly brings to the surface a series of molecules in his DNA which had stayed dormant throughout humanity's evolution. As a result, Lazarus is transformed into a savage, multi-limbed monster.

PROFESSOR IN ORIGINAL, AGED FORM

DINNER SUIT

DATA FILE

ORIGIN:
EARTH

SPECIAL ABILITIES:
MUTATING BETWEEN HUMAN AND ARTHROPODAL FORMS, DRAINING PEOPLE'S LIFE FORCE

DOCTORS MET:
10TH

30 YEARS YOUNGER
Professor Lazarus may have made himself younger, but the process produces disastrous consequences.

DINNER TIME
With its DNA fluctuating wildly, the Lazarus creature needs huge amounts of energy to maintain its mutated form. To satisfy its appetite, it sucks the life force from its victims, leaving behind a shrunken husk.

WALKING STICK

In monster form, Lazarus chases Martha and Tish inside Southwark Cathedral. The Doctor uses his sonic screwdriver to magnify the resonance of a pipe organ, causing the creature to plummet to its death.

PYROVILES
FIRE-BREATHING ROCK MONSTERS

Huge creatures composed of rock and lava, the Pyroviles landed on Earth thousands of years ago, shattering on impact. On reawakening, they start reconstituting themselves by causing humans to breathe in their dust, transforming them into living stone. They plan to convert millions more, by using the power of the volcano Vesuvius.

SHOOTS FLAMES FROM MOUTH

FORM MADE OF ROCK AND LAVA

VERY HOT

The Doctor faces a terrible dilemma. He can either allow the Pyroviles to take over the human race or destroy the creatures by triggering an eruption. In the end, he causes Vesuvius to erupt and the city of Pompeii is destroyed.

CAN BE OVER 33 FEET (10 METERS) TALL

DATA FILE

HOMEWORLD:
PYROVILLIA

SPECIAL ABILITIES:
TURNING OTHER BEINGS INTO PYROVILES, BREATHING FIRE AND TURNING PEOPLE TO ASH

DOCTORS MET:
10TH

STONE SISTERS
In Pompeii, the Doctor encounters the High Priestess of the Sibylline Sisterhood. He discovers she is halfway to becoming a Pyrovile and has almost completely turned to stone.

RACNOSS
SEMI-HUMANOID SPIDER CREATURES

Born starving, the Racnoss are ten-limbed omnivores from the Dark Times who were believed to have been wiped out during a war with the Fledgling Empires. The last of their kind, the Racnoss Empress, returns to Earth billions of years later, eager to free her children—who have been asleep at the center of the planet all this time.

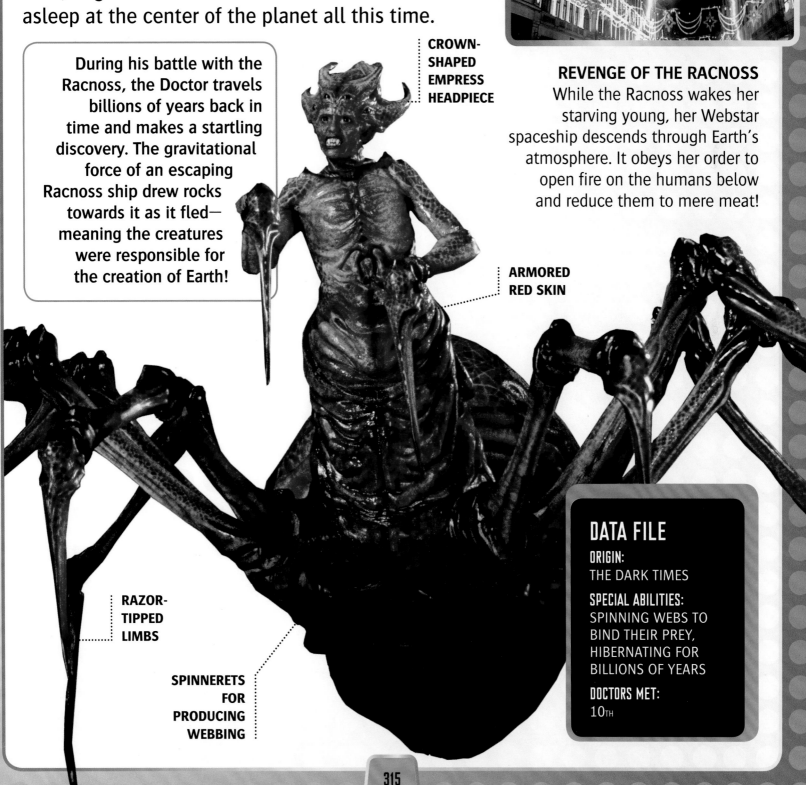

During his battle with the Racnoss, the Doctor travels billions of years back in time and makes a startling discovery. The gravitational force of an escaping Racnoss ship drew rocks towards it as it fled—meaning the creatures were responsible for the creation of Earth!

CROWN-SHAPED EMPRESS HEADPIECE

REVENGE OF THE RACNOSS
While the Racnoss wakes her starving young, her Webstar spaceship descends through Earth's atmosphere. It obeys her order to open fire on the humans below and reduce them to mere meat!

ARMORED RED SKIN

RAZOR-TIPPED LIMBS

SPINNERETS FOR PRODUCING WEBBING

DATA FILE

ORIGIN:
THE DARK TIMES

SPECIAL ABILITIES:
SPINNING WEBS TO BIND THEIR PREY, HIBERNATING FOR BILLIONS OF YEARS

DOCTORS MET:
10TH

THE RANI
DANGEROUS TIME LADY

The Rani is a scientific genius. A Time Lady from Gallifrey, she is exiled when one of her experiments—an enlarged mouse—bites the President and also eats his cat. She has a TARDIS, but what happens to her after the Time War is unknown.

TETRAPS
The Rani uses Tetraps as servants when she is on their home planet of Lakertya. These hairy, bat-like creatures eventually capture their mistress and take her back to their home planet.

COPY CAT
This Time Lady has a sense of humor. To baffle the newly regenerated Seventh Doctor, the Rani dresses up as his companion Mel. For a short time, this confuses the Time Lord.

EVIL SMILE

EYE-CATCHING JACKET

COMMUNICATION AND STORAGE DEVICE

The Rani cares about one thing only—herself. Stylish and incredibly beautiful, she rules the planets Miasimia Goria and Lakertya, using the natives in her experiments.

DATA FILE
HOMEWORLD:
GALLIFREY

SPECIAL ABILITIES:
REGENERATION, CHEMISTRY, DISGUISE

DOCTORS MET:
6TH, 7TH

RASSILON
FOUNDER OF TIME LORD SOCIETY

One of the greatest figures in Time Lord history, Rassilon was originally an engineer and architect who brought the nucleus of a black hole to Gallifrey. Known as the Eye of Harmony, it became as legendary as Rassilon, providing the Time Lords with the eternal energy source they needed for their time-travel.

HEADDRESS OF THE LORD PRESIDENT

THE ULTIMATE SANCTION
Rassilon intends to end the Time War by initiating the "Ultimate Sanction" and bringing about the End of Time. Only the Time Lords will survive, becoming creatures of consciousness alone. Luckily, the Doctor succeeds in stopping him.

PRESIDENTIAL ROBES

CEREMONIAL STAFF OF OFFICE

GAUNTLET

Brought back to life by the Time Lords, Rassilon is their leader during the Time War. He even finds a way to avoid Gallifrey's seemingly inevitable destruction, eventually confronting the Doctor on Earth.

DATA FILE
HOMEWORLD:
GALLIFREY

SPECIAL ABILITIES:
GAUNTLET WITH UNUSUAL POWERS

DOCTORS MET:
1ST, 2ND, 3RD, 5TH, 10TH

RASTON WARRIOR ROBOTS
PERFECT KILLING MACHINES

Raston Warrior Robots are the most perfect killing machines ever created. Reacting to the slightest movement, the silver androids can move short distances in the blink of an eye in order to attack their prey. Conveniently, weapons such as sharp arrows and discs are built into their arms. A quick movement will then shoot the chosen armament directly from their hand.

SILVER BULLET-LIKE HEAD

DATA FILE

HOMEWORLD:
UNKNOWN

SPECIAL ABILITIES:
INCREDIBLE SPEED, KILLING CYBERMEN, CAN REFORM WHEN BLOWN UP OR DECAPITATED

DOCTORS MET:
3RD

WEAPONS CONCEALED INSIDE ARMS

SMOOTH, FEATURELESS BODY

CYBERMEN MASSACRE
While trapped in the Death Zone on Gallifrey, one lone Raston Warrior Robot destroys a whole troop of Cybermen all by itself.

To move from one place to the next, Raston Warrior Robots leap momentarily into the air and reappear almost instantaneously behind their victims, ready to attack. They can feed on atomic radiation—meaning they never run out of energy.

SILVER BOOTS WITH SPECIAL POWERS

REAPERS
TIME PREDATORS

Terrifying dragon-like creatures, the Reapers search out time paradoxes and "sterilize" the rips in the fabric of time by devouring everyone in sight. The Doctor comes face to face with the predators after Rose Tyler changes history by preventing her dad, Pete, dying in a car accident.

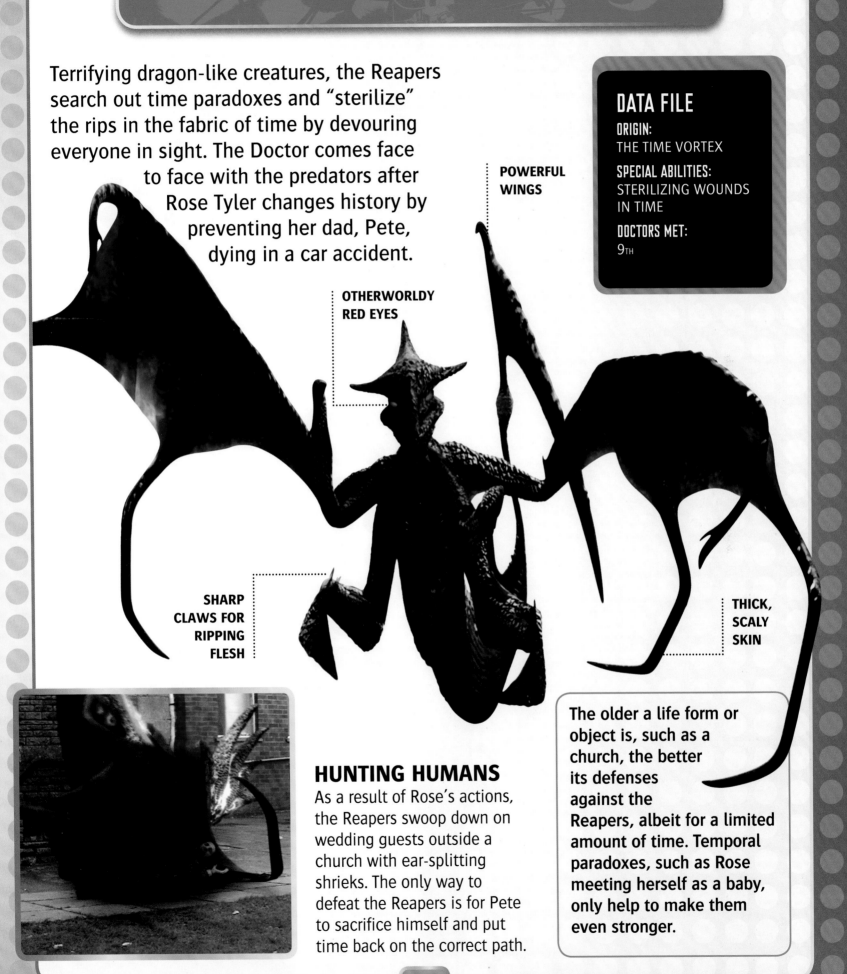

POWERFUL WINGS

OTHERWORLDY RED EYES

SHARP CLAWS FOR RIPPING FLESH

THICK, SCALY SKIN

DATA FILE

ORIGIN:
THE TIME VORTEX

SPECIAL ABILITIES:
STERILIZING WOUNDS IN TIME

DOCTORS MET:
9TH

HUNTING HUMANS

As a result of Rose's actions, the Reapers swoop down on wedding guests outside a church with ear-splitting shrieks. The only way to defeat the Reapers is for Pete to sacrifice himself and put time back on the correct path.

The older a life form or object is, such as a church, the better its defenses against the Reapers, albeit for a limited amount of time. Temporal paradoxes, such as Rose meeting herself as a baby, only help to make them even stronger.

RIVER SONG
THE DOCTOR'S WIFE

Enigmatic and flirtatious, River Song is a time-traveling archaeology professor constantly meeting the Doctor in the wrong order. He eventually learns that she is Rory and Amy's daughter— the "child of the TARDIS"—so can regenerate, among other Time Lord skills. She is also conditioned to be responsible for the Doctor's death, due to her upbringing at the hands of his enemies Madame Kovarian and The Silence.

When River first learns what kind of man the Doctor is, she gives up her remaining regenerations to save him. Although she is imprisoned for later seemingly killing him, she is eventually pardoned and continues on her own adventures, sometimes alongside her Time Lord husband.

RIVER GETS MARRIED
Having overcome her conditioning, River refuses to kill the Doctor and causes time itself to split apart. She ends up marrying him in a resultant alternative time line, and helps him to cheat death.

VORTEX MANIPULATOR

GUN HOLSTER

SPOILERS!
To keep track of her muddled-up adventures with the Doctor, River Song keeps a special time-traveler's diary. She is careful not to let him read about events in his own future though— in case he comes across spoilers!

ROBOFORMS
ROBOTIC SCAVENGERS

Roboforms are silent scavengers who travel through space alongside more powerful life-forms. On Christmas Day 2006, the Roboforms are attracted by the Doctor's regeneration and try to abduct him, intending to use him as a power source. A year later, they are used by the Racnoss Empress to track down and kidnap Donna Noble.

In 102 AD, several undisguised Roboforms the join Pandorica Alliance —a group that wants to trap the Doctor in the Pandorica underground prison, believing that they will stop him from destroying the universe.

DATA FILE
HOMEWORLD:
UNKNOWN

SPECIAL ABILITIES:
TELEPORTATION

DOCTORS MET:
10TH, 11TH

SINISTER SANTAS
Posing as a band of Santas, the Roboforms make an attempt to eliminate the Doctor's defenses. They open fire on Rose and Mickey using weapons disguised as musical instruments.

BLACK CLOAK HIDES ALL BUT THEIR FACES

ROSE & MICKEY
The Roboforms send a robotic Christmas tree to Rose and Mickey. It can only be stopped using a sonic screwdriver.

ROMANA
TIME LORD COMPANION

Romanadvoratrelundar is a Time Lord sent by the White Guardian to help the Doctor assemble the Key to Time, a mythical artifact used to control the universal order. Haughty and conventional, she's initially critical of the Doctor's unusual methods and lack of academic achievement, causing much friction between the two travelers.

After locating the Key, Romana forms a close bond with the Doctor, respecting his knowledge and experience. Ultimately, she realizes she has to be her own person and she leaves him to help free the enslaved Tharil race in E-Space.

FLOWING WHITE GOWN

GLAMOROUS FUR STOLE

ROMANA MK 2
Deciding to regenerate, Romana cheekily models herself on Princess Astra of Atrios, much to the Doctor's annoyance. Luckily, he ends up getting on better with this more playful version of Romana.

DATA FILE

HOMEWORLD:
GALLIFREY

SPECIAL ABILITIES:
CAN CHOOSE WHICH FORM SHE REGENERATES INTO

DOCTORS MET:
4TH

RORY WILLIAMS
CARING COMPANION

Amy Pond's long-suffering childhood sweetheart Rory ends up traveling with her aboard the TARDIS. At first rather timid and suspicious of the Doctor, Rory's confidence soon grows and he becomes a more willing adventurer —even though he is apparently killed and brought back to life many times!

Caring and sensitive, Rory remains devoted to Amy and eventually marries her. Together they take on everything from Pirates and Peg Dolls to Silurians and Silents.

CASUAL,
SCRUFFY
JEANS

DATA FILE
ORIGIN:
LEADWORTH, ENGLAND

OCCUPATION:
NURSE

DOCTORS MET:
11TH

CYBERMAN STAND-OFF
When Amy is kidnapped by Madame Kovarian, Rory stops at nothing to get her back. Armed only with the Doctor's sonic screwdriver, he confronts a group of Cybermen and demands to know his wife's whereabouts!

STUCK IN TIME
Rory's travels with the Doctor come to a tragic end when he is zapped back in time by a Weeping Angel. Amy follows him, despite knowing that they will never be able to see the Doctor again.

ROSE TYLER
COMPASSIONATE COMPANION

Rose was an ordinary shopgirl who met the Ninth Doctor after she was attacked by a horde of murderous store mannequins. After helping the Doctor defeat the Nestene Consciousness and its Auton servants, she couldn't resist joining him on his travels. Over time, she grows very close to the battle-scarred Time Lord.

After an epic battle against the Daleks and Cybermen, Rose becomes trapped in a parallel universe. Determined as ever, she finds a way to return and ends up living her life with a part-human version of the Tenth Doctor.

CARING AND KIND-HEARTED

DEATH TO THE DALEKS
With the power of the Time Vortex running through her head, Rose once atomized an entire Dalek fleet and its Emperor. She also uses her temporary powers to make Captain Jack immortal!

STREETWISE LONDON ORIGINS

ROSE BECOMES TOUGHER AFTER HER TRAVELS WITH THE DOCTOR

A HUMAN TOUCH
Rose's compassionate nature is displayed when she is drawn to touch the last Dalek, kept in chains in Henry Van Statten's museum. It is her emotions that then save her when the Dalek escapes, as it cannot bring itself to kill her.

DATA FILE
ORIGIN:
LONDON, ENGLAND

OCCUPATION:
STORE ASSISTANT, TORCHWOOD AGENT

DOCTORS MET:
9TH, 10TH

SALAMANDER
ENEMY OF THE WORLD

Salamander is a dangerous and cunning inventor and politician. He is a potential world dictator from Mexico who makes natural disasters happen in order to get what he wants. Coincidentally, he looks identical to the Second Doctor.

ASTRID FERRIER

Astrid discovers the Doctor on an Australian beach and rescues him from pursuers in her mini-helicopter. She helps him overthrow the dangerous plans of Salamander. Like everyone else the Doctor meets, she is startled at the resemblance.

COPYCATS

The Doctor impersonates Salamander to bring about his downfall, but Salamander also pretends to be the Doctor. He operates the TARDIS controls while the doors are still open and he is ejected into space.

STRIKING RESEMBLANCE TO THE SECOND DOCTOR

Salamander is popular and considered a saviour. Many people call him "the shopkeeper of the world" because he invented Sun Store, which collects rays from the sun to force-grow crops.

DATA FILE

ORIGIN:
EARTH

SPECIAL ABILITIES:
INVENTING

DOCTORS MET:
2ND

SALLY SPARROW
THE COMPANION THAT NEVER WAS

Sally Sparrow is a photographer who discovers a message written in 1969 by the Doctor to her, with a warning about the Weeping Angels. When her best friend Kathy is zapped into the past by the stone statues, she teams up with Kathy's brother to stop them stealing the TARDIS.

CLEVER AND COURAGEOUS

WARM COAT FOR NIGHTTIME PHOTOGRAPHY SHOOTS

Sally is bright, brave, and a little bit dangerous. She's not put off by keep-out signs, doesn't like to be patronized, and is furious that the Angels have taken her friend.

WEEPING ANGELS
It's up to Sally to figure out how to stop the Weeping Angels from getting the TARDIS and return it to the Doctor. She faces them with incredible courage and succeeds in beating them.

"DON'T BLINK"
The Doctor and Martha are stuck in 1969 without the TARDIS. They need Sally to rescue them, but the only way they can communicate is through pre-recorded messages on DVDs.

SARAH JANE SMITH
CLOSE COMPANION

Sarah Jane Smith is one of the Doctor's closest companions. A trained journalist, her curious nature and nose for a good story often gets her into some sticky situations. She fought a host of aliens—Ice Warriors, Daleks, Cybermen, and Sontarans—before being left on Earth by the Doctor.

DATA FILE

ORIGIN:
FOXGROVE, ENGLAND

OCCUPATION:
JOURNALIST,
DEFENDER OF EARTH

DOCTORS MET:
1ST, 2ND, 3RD, 4TH, 5TH,
10TH, 11TH

SONIC LIPSTICK KEPT CLOSE BY

SCHOOL REUNION

Later in her life, Sarah Jane has an emotional reunion with the Doctor while investigating strange goings-on at a school. She reveals how hurt she has been that he has never returned for her.

MODERN CLOTHES

Sarah Jane continues to fight aliens on Earth with robot dog K-9, super-computer Mr. Smith, and a team of young investigators. Working from her attic, she bravely takes on all manner of menaces and has helped save the world countless times.

STOWAWAY SARAH JANE

Soon after her first meeting with the Doctor, Sarah Jane is determined to investigate the mysterious disappearance of a group of scientists. She stows aboard the TARDIS which takes her back to the Middle Ages where Linx, a Sontaran, is holding the scientists captive.

THE SATURNYNS
VAMPIRIC SPACE FISH

The Saturnyns are a race of fish-like aliens that drink blood. When their planet is lost to alien species The Silence, they flee to Earth through a crack in the universe. They establish a new home in 16th century Venice and set about turning it into Saturnyne Mark II.

SENSITIVE TO UV LIGHT

Rosanna and Francesco wear perception filters that make them appear human to onlookers. However, they still have vampire-like fangs and their reflections cannot be seen in mirrors.

NEED WATER TO SURVIVE

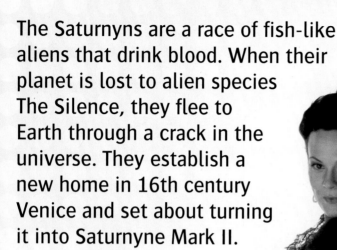

BLOOD SUCKERS
In their true form, Saturnyns look like a cross between a lobster and a fish. They convert young women into Saturnyns, also known as Sisters of the Water, by draining their blood and replacing it with their own.

OPULENT CLOTHES SHOW WEALTH AND HIGH STATUS

DATA FILE
HOMEWORLD:
SATURNYNE

SPECIAL ABILITIES:
SHAPE-SHIFTING, CONVERSION

DOCTORS MET:
11TH

SCARECROW SOLDIERS
SERVANTS OF THE FAMILY OF BLOOD

The Scarecrows are the foot soldiers of the Family of Blood, used in their quest to hunt down the Doctor. Stuffed with straw and of limited intelligence, they are the creations of Son of Mine who brought them to life using molecular fringe animation. They are a scary sight as they lurch menacingly towards their victims.

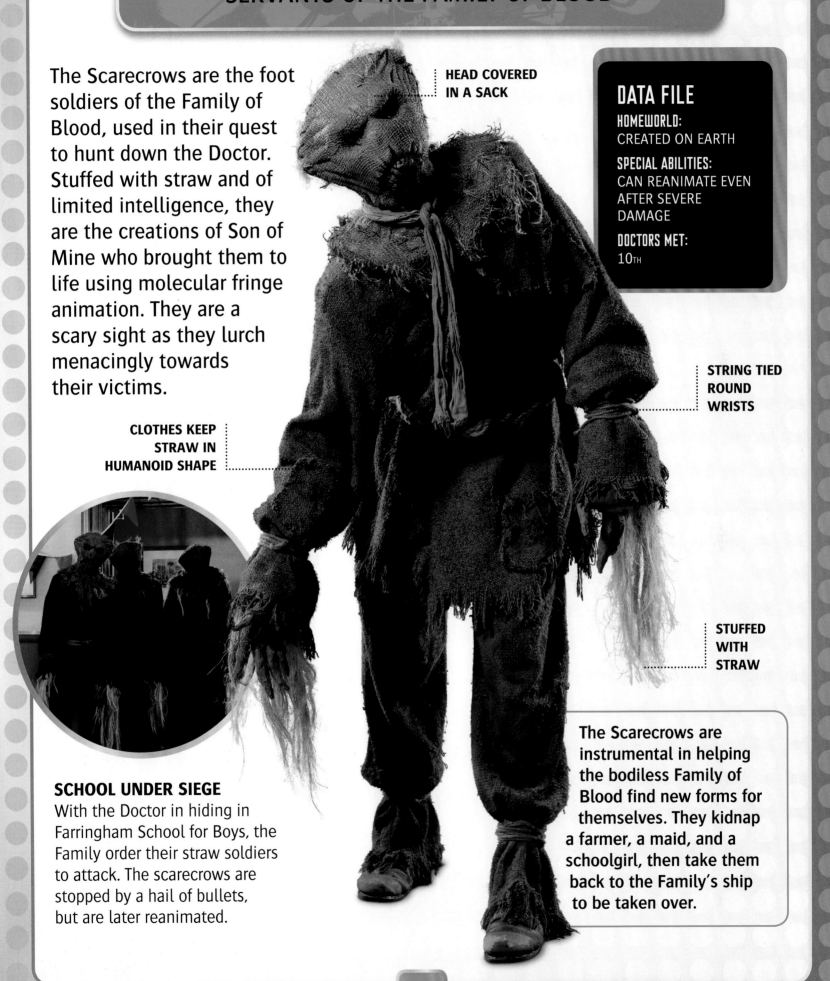

HEAD COVERED IN A SACK

STRING TIED ROUND WRISTS

CLOTHES KEEP STRAW IN HUMANOID SHAPE

STUFFED WITH STRAW

DATA FILE
HOMEWORLD:
CREATED ON EARTH

SPECIAL ABILITIES:
CAN REANIMATE EVEN AFTER SEVERE DAMAGE

DOCTORS MET:
10TH

SCHOOL UNDER SIEGE
With the Doctor in hiding in Farringham School for Boys, the Family order their straw soldiers to attack. The scarecrows are stopped by a hail of bullets, but are later reanimated.

The Scarecrows are instrumental in helping the bodiless Family of Blood find new forms for themselves. They kidnap a farmer, a maid, and a schoolgirl, then take them back to the Family's ship to be taken over.

SCAROTH
LAST OF THE JAGAROTH

The Jagaroth was a race of highly advanced, vicious, and war-like creatures that existed millions of years ago. When their pilot, Scaroth, tried to leave prehistoric Earth, the Jagaroth spaceship blew up and the race was wiped out, apart from Scaroth. He was splintered into twelve identical bodies that are connected through time.

Scaroth is a revolting creature with green skin and a single, unblinking eye. For most of his time on Earth, Scaroth chooses to hide his alien features beneath a realistic human mask.

UNNERVING EYE

HORRIFIC FACE (USUALLY COVERED WITH MASK)

CHANGING HISTORY
Scaroth wants to go back in time to stop his ship blowing up in order to save his people. The radioactive explosion it creates triggers the start of life on Earth.

DRESSED AS COUNT SCARLIONI THE ART DEALER

DATA FILE

HOMEWORLD:
PLANET OF THE JAGAROTH RACE

SPECIAL ABILITIES:
HUMAN DISGUISE, TIME TRAVEL, INVENTING, TELEPATHY

DOCTORS MET:
4TH

SEA DEVILS
UNDERWATER MENACE

The Sea Devils are an intelligent race of reptile creatures. Their species are related to the Silurians and are incredibly advanced. They ruled Earth when man was just an ape and have many colonies, each containing thousands of their kind, all over the world.

When Sea Devil astronomers falsely predicted a great catastrophe that would end all life on Earth, the reptilian humanoids hid underground and went into hibernation. Waking up millions of years later, they want to reclaim the planet.

REPTILIAN FACE

GUN FROM THEIR LARGE STASH

WARRIOR ARMOR

AWAKENING
The Master uses a sonar device to wake a group of Sea Devils hibernating in the English Channel. The Doctor's old enemy wants them to rule Earth again.

POSSIBLE PEACE
The Doctor recognizes the Sea Devil race. He tries to persuade them to share the planet with humans and make them live in peace. The Sea Devils consider the possibilty.

DATA FILE
HOMEWORLD:
EARTH

SPECIAL ABILITIES:
SWIMMING, HIBERNATING

DOCTORS MET:
3RD, 5TH

SENSORITES
TELEPATHIC RACE

The Sensorites are a species of advanced and telepathic aliens. A quiet race, they are afraid of what might happen to their planet when Earth discovers them. Sensorites are afraid of the dark and react badly to loud noises. They live near the Ood home planet, Ood-Sphere.

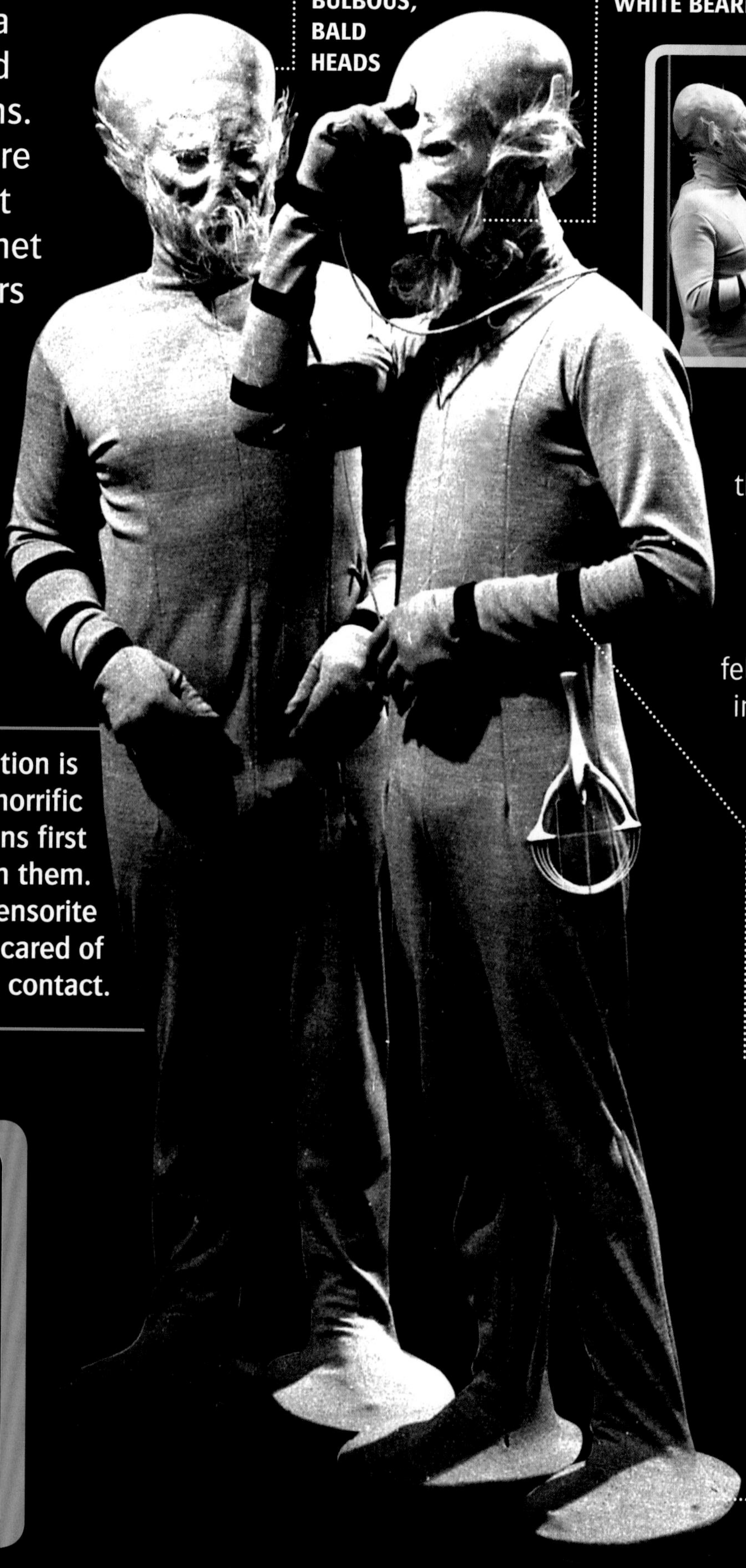

BULBOUS, BALD HEADS

WHITE BEARD

The Sensorite population is endangered by a horrific plague when humans first make contact with them. After this, the Sensorite people are scared of human contact.

TRAPPED
Wary of outsiders, the Sensorites steal the lock of the TARDIS, briefly trapping the Doctor and his fellow time travelers in the 28th century.

THREE BLACK SASHES ON ARM INDICATE SENSORITE IS A WARRIOR—THE LOWEST SENSORITE RANK

DATA FILE

HOMEWORLD:
SENSE-SPHERE

SPECIAL ABILITIES:
TELEPATHY, LOCK PICKING

DOCTORS MET:
1ST

LARGE FEET

SERGEANT BENTON
ASSOCIATE OF UNIT

Benton is a friendly, down-to-earth member of UNIT who aids the exiled third Doctor in his battles against alien invaders. He is reliably loyal and brave, although he occasionally finds himself outwitted by UNIT's enemies. In such situations, he inevitably finds himself on the receiving end of the Brigadier's exasperated put-downs!

TARDIS TRAVEL
When the first three Doctors unite to fight the insane Omega, Benton gets his first—and only—trip in the TARDIS, finding himself on Omega's desolate anti-matter world.

DATA FILE
ORIGIN:
ENGLAND, EARTH

OCCUPATION:
UNIT SERGEANT

DOCTORS MET:
2ND, 3RD, 4TH

LOYAL TO THE DOCTOR

When he first meets the Doctor, Benton is a Corporal, before being promoted to the rank of Sergeant. Around the time of the Doctor's third regeneration, he becomes a Warrant Officer, but ultimately leaves UNIT to sell second-hand cars.

MILITARY OUTFIT

SHAKRI
PEST CONTROLLERS OF THE UNIVERSE

The Doctor was told about the Shakri as a child but assumed they were a myth to keep young Gallifreyans in their place. The Shakri exist in all of time, serving something called the Tally. They view mankind as pests that must be erased before they colonize space.

APPEARS AS HOLOGRAM TO THE DOCTOR

CLEVER CUBES
The Shakri send millions of cubes to Earth. They appear to be doing nothing but are actually gathering data on how the Shakri can best wipe out "the human plague."

SHAKRI SERVANTS
The Shakri are served by grate-faced orderlies who kidnap humans for experimentation aboard the Shakri sanctum, and an outlier-droid disguised as a human girl.

The Shakri's spacecraft is in orbit one dimension to the left of our universe. It is connected to Earth through seven portals and seven minutes.

DATA FILE
HOMEWORLD:
UNKNOWN

SPECIAL ABILITIES:
HOLOGRAPHIC PROJECTION, LASER-FIRING

DOCTORS:
11TH

SHARAZ JEK
MASKED ANDROID CREATOR

Sharaz Jek was a doctor before the study of androids took over his life. A brilliant, but slightly mad scientist, he and his business partner, Morgus, settle on planet Androzani Minor, a barren world that contains a highly prized and much fought over substance called spectrox.

MASKED FACE

DATA FILE

HOMEWORLD:
ANDROZANI MINOR

SPECIAL ABILITIES:
BUILDING ANDROIDS

DOCTORS MET:
5TH

PROTECTIVE LEATHERS

A mud burst on Androzani Minor results in Jek being horrifically scalded. He wears a leather suit to protect his damaged body, something that even he cannot bear to see.

ANDROID COPIES
A skilful engineer, Jek makes faultless android copies of the Doctor and Peri. Later, he becomes infatuated with the Doctor's companion, who nearly dies from spectrox toxaemia after falling into a spectrox nest.

DISFIGURED HAND

BENEATH THE MASK
Jek prefers the company of androids because they do not care about his terrible disfigurement. He reveals his face to a shocked Morgus, who later dies.

SIL THE MENTOR
REPTILIAN BUSINESSMAN

Sil is a Mentor from the watery planet Thoros Beta. He looks like a reptilian slug and possesses a vile laugh. Like all Mentors, Sil wants to make lots of money. He is self-obsessed and his favorite food is a local delicacy called marsh minnows.

DATA FILE

HOMEWORLD:
THOROS BETA

INTERESTS:
BUYING AND DEALING

DOCTORS MET:
6TH

SCHEMING SIL
Sil travels to the planet Varos to negotiate a deal for the Galatron Mining Corporation. He tries to exploit the locals, who do not realize the value of the rare mineral on their planet.

BIG BRAINS
Ruler of the Mentors on Thoros Beta, Lord Kiv's brain is too big for his head. He is in considerable pain until his brain is removed and placed inside the head of Peri, the Doctor's companion.

FAULTY TRANSLATOR

An unpleasant creature, Sil likes watching humans suffer. He is particularly interested in the various different tortures shown to people on the planet Varos.

MARSH MINNOWS

THE SILENCE
MEMORY-PROOF HUMANOIDS

These tall, skeletal aliens have the eerie ability to erase themselves from people's memories the instant they look away from them. Worse still, a Silent can easily absorb electricity from their surroundings, which they then unleash from their long fingers, reducing their victims' bodies to burned fragments in the blink of an eye.

The Silence affected humanity's development over thousands of years. They influenced man's decision to go to the moon in 1969. When the Doctor became aware of them, he used the creatures' own powers of post-hypnotic suggestion to turn mankind against them.

MOUTH WIDENS DURING ELECTRICAL DISCHARGE

DATA FILE
HOMEWORLD:
UNKNOWN

SPECIAL ABILITIES:
MEMORY ERASURE, POST-HYPNOTIC SUGGESTION

DOCTORS MET:
11TH

FOUR-FINGERED HANDS

TANK TERROR
In an alternate reality, Earth's military forces believe they have succeeded in capturing dozens of the aliens. However, The Silence are only pretending, and easily break out of their water tanks, before electrocuting everyone in sight.

OVER 6 FEET 5 IN (2 METERS) TALL

SENTINELS OF HISTORY
The creatures are the leaders of The Silence, a religious movement whose sole purpose is to destroy the Doctor before he can provide the answer to the oldest question in the universe... Doctor who?

SILURIANS
HOMO REPTILIA

Silurians are a race of reptilian humanoids that ruled Earth millions of years ago. They went into hibernation deep underground when an apocalypse was predicted, but planned to wake once wthe danger had passed. They believe they are the true owners of Earth and humans are trespassers.

GREEN, SCALY SKIN

LONG WHIP-LIKE TONGUE

COLD-BLOODED

Silurian society is divided into different classes: warriors, scientists and statesmen. Some believe humans are dumb apes that should be wiped out, while others believe that they can live together in harmony.

ARMED WITH HEAT-RAYS

SILURIAN VARIANTS
The Doctor has fought various subspecies of Silurians, including one type with three eyes. Another group have suckers on their fingers, and a third type have tongues laced with venom.

DATA FILE

ORIGIN:
EARTH

SPECIAL ABILITIES:
ADVANCED SCIENCE, POISONOUS TONGUE, HIBERNATION

DOCTORS MET:
3RD, 5TH, 11TH

DRAGGED DOWN
The Silurians awake from hibernation when a powerful drill threatens the safety of their city. They immediately strike back by dragging humans underground for experimentation.

SISTERHOOD OF KARN
GUARDIANS OF THE SACRED FLAME

Along with the High Council of Time Lords on Gallifrey, the Sisterhood of Karn also knows the secret of the Elixir of Life. They are responsible for guarding the Sacred Flame that produces the Elixir. The serious priestesses have many powers, including teleportation.

The Sisterhood has often feared the Doctor is trying to steal the Elixir from them. Yet, during the Time War, priestess Ohila offers the dying Eighth Doctor a draught in the hope that he will then find a way to stop the fighting.

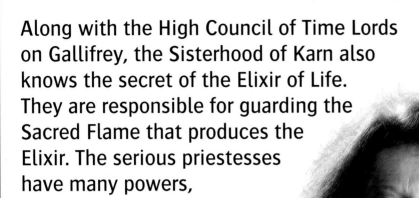

MAREN
High Priestess Maren leads the Sisterhood. She is present at the execution of Morbius on Karn. A strong but old woman, she dies in order to save the Fourth Doctor's life.

···· LONG, GRAY
···· TRESSES

DATA FILE

HOMEWORLD:
KARN

SPECIAL ABILITIES:
TELEKINESIS

DOCTORS MET:
4TH, 8TH

···· FLAME-RED
ROBES OF
SISTERHOOD

TARDIS THEFT
Using teleportation and telekinesis, the Sisterhood is able to transport the Doctor's TARDIS into their shrine so that the Fourth Doctor is not able to escape the planet.

SISTERS OF PLENITUDE
FELINE HUMANOIDS

The Sisters are sinister cat nuns who run the hospital on New Earth in the year 5,000,000,023. They specialize in treating incurable diseases, however the Doctor discovers the Sisters are secretly using humans as lab rats and infecting them with every known disease in the pursuit of developing new cures.

SCULPTED WHITE COWL

FELINE FACE

MATRON'S HABIT

The Matron, Casp, also known as "Whiskers," leads the Sisterhood, which includes Sister Jatt and Sister Corvin. The Catkind nuns worship the goddess Santori.

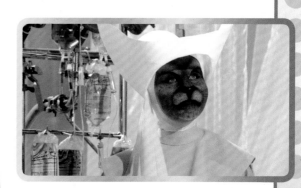

NOVICE HAME
Novice Hame is a young cat nun whose duty it is to look after the dying Face of Boe. When the Sister's secret is exposed, her penance is to care for him for the rest of their lives, a punishment she accepts with humility.

DEADLY DISEASES
When some of the infected humans escape their ward they start passing on diseases to anyone they come into contact with— including Matron Casp, who ends up plummeting to her death!

SLITHEEN
FAMILY OF ALIEN CRIMINALS

Big, green, baby-faced aliens, the Slitheen are notorious criminals from another world. Ruthless and well-organized, they infiltrate the British government by compressing their huge bodies into human skin-suits, enabling them to impersonate politicians. They plan to start a nuclear war and sell off radioactive remnants of Earth as fuel.

EYES BLINK FROM SIDE-TO-SIDE

SLITHEEN REVEALED
After gathering experts on alien life forms in Downing Street, General Asquith unzips his forehead, revealing the Slitheen under the skinsuit. The Slitheen then electrocute their human captives.

COMPRESSION FIELD COLLAR KEEPS SLITHEEN IN HUMAN SKINSUIT

DATA FILE

HOMEWORLD:
RAXACORICOFALLAPATORIUS

SPECIAL ABILITIES:
CAN SHRINK THEMSELVES INTO SKINSUITS

DOCTORS MET:
9TH

STRONG ARMS AND CLAWS

The Slitheen have their weaknesses. They can give themselves away by excessive farting, a side effect of the compression process. As calcium-based creatures, they are vulnerable to acetic acid which causes them to explode!

POISONOUS FINGERTIPS

SMILERS
STARSHIP UK ROBOTS

Smilers are frozen-faced robots who work on the *Starship UK*. Some are teachers, others are guards or information points. They protect a dark secret at the heart of the spaceship and their smiles turn to snarls if anyone tries to discover what it is.

THREE ROTATING MASK-LIKE FACES

COLD AND EMOTIONLESS

PURPLE MONK-LIKE UNIFORM

DATA FILE

HOMEWORLD:
STARSHIP UK

SPECIAL ABILITIES:
ROTATING HEAD, DISPENSING INFORMATION, KEEPING ORDER

DOCTORS MET:
11TH

The Smilers don't want anyone to know that the *Starship UK* is being carried on the back of a tortured star whale. Anyone who finds out this secret is fed to the captured creature.

WINDERS
Winders look human until their heads rotate to reveal a scary Smiler face on the back. They wear keys, which they use to wind up the Smilers like clocks.

FROZEN SMILES
Some Smilers are stationed in glass booths around *Starship UK*. People are terrified of them. They have the ability to walk out of their booths when necessary.

SOLOMON
VICIOUS SPACE TRADER

Violent and ruthless, Solomon is a space trader who only sees people in terms of their monetary value. He searches for opportunities for profit across the nine galaxies. When a Silurian ark crosses his path, Solomon massacres their crew to get his hands on their precious cargo of dinosaurs.

SCARRED FACE

PRECIOUS BOUNTY
Solomon is delighted to learn there is something even more precious than the dinosaurs on board the ark—Queen Nefertiti. He sees her as a bounty that will make him rich.

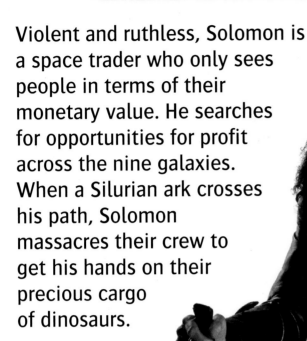

SPACE-FARING TRADER, PIRATE, AND MURDERER

CRIPPLED WHEN RAPTORS CHEWED HIS LEGS

DATA FILE
HOMEWORLD:
UNKNOWN

CHARACTER TRAIT:
RUTHLESS GREED

DOCTORS MET:
11TH

Solomon is motivated by greed. He wants to sell the dinosaurs on the Roxborne Peninsula, but the ark automatically sets a course for Earth instead and Solomon is powerless to stop it.

SOLOMON'S ROBOTS
METAL TANTRUM MACHINES

The space trader Solomon bought these robots at a discount from a concession on Illyria Seven. After two millennia, their bodies are falling apart and rusty. By nature, they are irritable and often snap at each other, but are perfect for Solomon's needs.

The robots follow Solomon's orders without question. They try to repair him when he is attacked by raptors, they murder the Silurians and they shoot Brian. They have no moral code.

TOO SLOW

Acting as Solomon's henchmen, the robots frogmarch the Doctor, Brian, and Rory to their leader. But because of their bulk and age, the robots are not as fast as they used to be. When their captives gallop away on a triceratops, they can't keep up.

DATA FILE
HOMEWORLD:
ILLYRIA SEVEN

SPECIAL ABILITIES:
FIRING LASER-BOLTS

DOCTORS MET:
11TH

SONTARANS
CLONE WARRIORS

Sontarans are a vicious clone race from the planet Sontar. The Eleventh Doctor describes them as "psychotic potato-faced dwarfs." Sontarans live for the honor of battle and have been locked in war with their enemies, the Rutans, for thousands of years.

BATTLE CRY IS "SONTAR-HA!"

SHORT, STOCKY, AND STRONG

Entire legions of Sontaran clones are produced together in factories on Sontar. As a result, they all look similar, though they are assigned different ranks.

NURSE STRAX
Strax suffers the greatest humiliation a Sontaran can endure—he is forced to become a nurse. He aids the Doctor on Demon's Run and also helps him fight the Great Intelligence alongside Madame Vastra and Jenny.

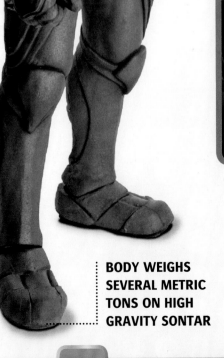

SONTAR-HA!
In the Middle Ages, a Sontaran called Linx tries to claim Earth for his own. Sontarans also attempt to invade Gallifrey and to turn Earth into a clone world.

BODY WEIGHS SEVERAL METRIC TONS ON HIGH GRAVITY SONTAR

STEVEN TAYLOR
PILOT COMPANION

Spaceship pilot Steven is captured by the robotic Mechonoids after crash landing on their planet. The robots keep him prisoner for two years until the Doctor and his friends arrive and help him to escape. Amid a war between Daleks and Mechonoids, Steven barely escapes with his life, and ends up stumbling aboard the TARDIS.

SERIOUS MENTALITY

FITTED SWEATER FOR EASE OF MOVEMENT IN SPACESHIP

THE WILD, WILD WEST
When the TARDIS materializes in the Wild West in 1881, Steven is caught up in events leading to the infamous Gunfight at the OK Corral—and is almost lynched by the outlaw Clanton family!

DATA FILE

ORIGIN:
EARTH

OCCUPATION:
ASTRONAUT

DOCTORS MET:
1ST

Headstrong and courageous, Steven helps the Doctor fight against the Daleks and Drahvins, but eventually leaves to help build a new society on an alien world, uniting the technologically advanced Elders and the planet's savage inhabitants.

SUSAN FOREMAN
THE DOCTOR'S GRANDDAUGHTER

A lively young teenager, Susan is the Doctor's very first traveling companion and also his granddaughter. She is curious about ordinary life on Earth and persuades her grandfather to allow her to attend Coal Hill School in 1960s London. However, her levels of knowledge are so unbalanced that her schoolteachers soon become suspicious of her.

SUSAN AND THE SENSORITES
When the Doctor and his friends encounter a timid race called the Sensorites, Susan discovers she is able to use her powers of telepathy to communicate with the creatures.

DATA FILE

ORIGIN:
GALLIFREY

SPECIAL ABILITIES:
TELEPATHY

DOCTORS MET:
1ST, 2ND, 3RD, 5TH

STRIPED
TUNIC

LOOKS LIKE
A TEENAGER
THOUGH HER
TIME LORD
GENES
MEAN SHE IS
LIKELY TO
BE OLDER

After helping to defeat the Daleks, Susan falls in love with resistance fighter David Campbell. She's upset to leave her grandfather, but the Doctor locks her out of the ship and she remains on Earth to begin a new life.

SUTEKH THE DESTROYER
LAST OF THE OSIRIANS

An ancient and dangerous Osirian, Sutekh the Destroyer longs for the destruction of all living things. Beneath his mask lies the horrific face of a jackal. He is responsible for the destruction of his own planet and is now the very last of his kind.

Trapped beneath an Egyptian pyramid by his brother, Sutekh goes undiscovered for 7,000 years. A British archaeologist eventually opens his tomb and nearly brings about the destruction of all mankind.

PYRAMID POWER

Sutekh uses the strong, silent Osirian robot mummies to aid his escape from imprisonment. He then instructs the building of a rocket designed to destroy the controls that hold him captive, but the Doctor and Sarah Jane manage to stop him.

EYES CAN GLOW GREEN

EGYPTIAN MOTIFS ON MASK

DATA FILE

HOMEWORLD:
PHAESTER OSIRIS

SPECIAL ABILITIES:
SPACE TRAVEL, PATIENCE, MIND CONTROL

DOCTORS MET:
4TH

SYCORAX
HUMANOID SCAVENGERS

The Sycorax are a race of savage, war-like scavengers who roam the universe ransacking planets of their resources and enslaving their inhabitants. On Christmas Day 2006, one of their asteroid spaceships approaches Earth and the Sycorax use blood control to possess a third of its population, ordering the world to surrender.

SKULL-LIKE HELMET

TRIBAL STAFF WITH CLAWS

The Sycorax wear scary bone helmets which both hide and protect an even more terrifying sight beneath. The creatures appear to have no outer skin, their faces made up of only bone and muscle.

FOREARM GUARDS

RED ROBE COMMON AMONG SYCORAX

DUELLING THE DOCTOR
The Doctor challenges the Sycorax leader to a sword fight. He wins the duel and spares the Sycorax's life, on the condition that his people leave the planet and never return.

DATA FILE
HOMEWORLD:
UNKNOWN

SPECIAL ABILITIES:
HYPNOSIS BY BLOOD CONTROL

DOCTORS MET:
10TH

SYLVIA NOBLE
DONNA NOBLE'S MOTHER

Sharp-tongued Sylvia Noble is mother to Donna, wife to Geoff and daughter to Wilfred Mott. She is often critical of her daughter but will snap at anyone else who dares say a word against her. Ever since the Doctor's arrival in Donna's life, Sylvia has been terrified on her behalf.

SPARKLY OUTFIT

MOTHER OF THE BRIDE
When Donna vanishes on her wedding day, Sylvia thinks it is one of her "silly little look-at-me party pieces," then panics that she may be dead. However, all is happily resolved when, a few years later, Donna marries the man of her dreams.

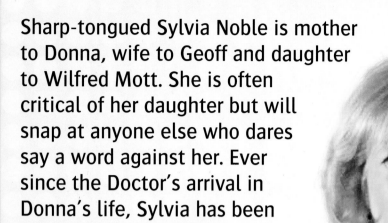

TROUBLE MAKER
In Sylvia's mind, whenever the Doctor appears, disaster follows— such as the time Daleks arrive on her doorstep. She blames the Doctor for ruining Donna's wedding and disapproves of her father Wilfred's friendship with him.

DATA FILE
ORIGIN:
EARTH

SPECIAL ABILITIES:
TELLING PEOPLE OFF

DOCTORS MET:
10TH

Sylvia is amazed to learn her daughter is traveling the stars. And when the Doctor is forced to wipe Donna's mind of their adventures, Sylvia proudly defends her.

TARDIS
THE DOCTOR'S AMAZING BLUE BOX

The TARDIS is a space-time machine used by Time Lords. The Doctor could once change its exterior to match its surroundings, but a fault means its shell is stuck as a 1950s police box. Inside, it has ever-changing console rooms. It is dimensionally transcendental so is far bigger on the inside than it looks.

TARDIS STANDS FOR TIME AND RELATIVE DIMENSION IN SPACE

DATA FILE

HOMEWORLD:
GALLIFREY

SPECIAL ABILITIES:
BEING BIGGER ON THE INSIDE, FLYING THROUGH SPACE AND TIME, TRANSLATING ALIEN LANGUAGES

DOCTORS MET:
ALL

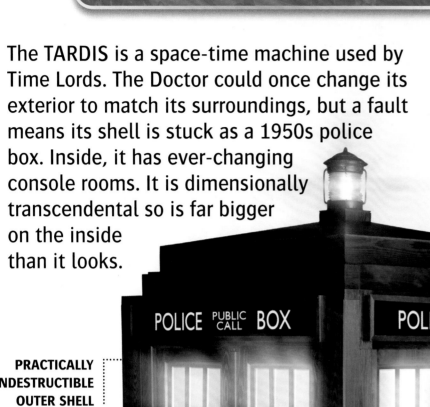

POLICE PUBLIC CALL BOX

POLICE PUBLIC CALL BOX

PRACTICALLY INDESTRUCTIBLE OUTER SHELL

POLICE TELEPHONE
FREE
FOR USE OF
PUBLIC
ADVICE & ASSISTANCE
OBTAINABLE IMMEDIATELY
OFFICERS & CARS
RESPOND TO ALL CALLS
PULL TO OPEN

ST JOHN AMBULANCE BADGE

LOCKED WITH A YALE KEY

GROWN ON GALLIFREY BY TIME LORDS

HUMAN FORM
When the TARDIS took human form, she revealed that she doesn't always take the Doctor where he wants to go, but she always takes him where he needs to be.

The TARDIS is powered by a black hole called the Eye of Harmony. It also refuels using temporal radiation from the Rift. The Doctor can energize it with his life force, too.

TASHA LEM
MOTHER SUPERIOUS

Part-human and part-alien, Tasha Lem is a mystery—and knows a mysteriously large amount about the Doctor. As Mother Superious of the Papal Mainframe, and leader of the Order of the Silence, Tasha brings an air of authority and flirtation to all situations.

CLOTHES MAY BE HOLOGRAPHIC

DATA FILE

HOMEWORLD:
UNKNOWN

SPECIAL ABILITIES:
PSYCHIC POWERS, NEVER SEEMS TO AGE

DOCTORS MET:
11TH

GOBLETS FOR SHARING A DRINK WITH THE DOCTOR

DALEK TAKEOVER

After the Mainframe falls to the Daleks, Tasha becomes a Dalek puppet. The Doctor insults her and calls her a coward—calling Tasha back to herself. She then proceeds to fight off the Dalek inside her, and many more within the Mainframe!

It is Tasha who decrees that the Doctor's name must never be uttered, for fear of the Time War beginning again. She introduces the reign of "Silence" and rules with a stern hand, but has a soft spot for her old friend the Doctor.

A FRIEND IN NEED

When the Doctor is close to dying of old age, it is loyal Tasha who returns to take Clara to him, so that he need not be alone. She also musters his allies to fight alongside him in the Battle of Trenzalore.

TEGAN JOVANKA
ACCIDENTAL COMPANION

A brash and bossy Australian air stewardess, Tegan becomes a traveler in the TARDIS quite by accident, thinking it is a real police box. At first, she is desperate to get back to Heathrow airport, but as time goes by, she comes to accept her new life as the Doctor's companion, even witnessing his regeneration into the Fifth Doctor.

SMART AIR STEWARDESS HAIRCUT

MOUTH ON LEGS
Tegan doesn't suffer fools gladly and her short temper means she often gets into arguments with the Doctor. At one point, she admits her faults, describing herself as "just a mouth on legs!"

PARTYING WITH ALIENS
Aboard one of the Eternal's sailing ships, Tegan gets a rare chance to dress up. However, she doesn't realize one of the creatures intends to plant an explosive device on her!

During her travels, Tegan ends up fighting everything from Sea Devils and Silurians to Terileptils and Tractators. Sadly, during an encounter with the Daleks, Tegan is overcome by all the deaths she has witnessed and decides to leave the Doctor.

BRIGHT 1980S PATTERN

DATA FILE
ORIGIN:
BRISBANE, AUSTRALIA

OCCUPATION:
AIR STEWARDESS

DOCTORS MET:
1ST, 2ND, 3RD, 4TH, 5TH

TERILEPTIL
REPTILIAN CRIMINALS

Terileptils are an intelligent and advanced race of reptile creatures. They love art and beauty, but also love war. They enjoy fighting and believe war is honorable. If convicted, criminal Terileptils are sentenced to life imprisonment, working in the tinclavic mines of the planet Raaga.

SCARRED FACE FROM DANGEROUS MINING WORK

DATA FILE
HOMEWORLD:
UNKNOWN

SPECIAL ABILITIES:
STRENGTH, CREATING ANDROIDS, MIND CONTROL

DOCTORS MET:
5TH

REPTILIAN FEATURES

HUMANOID SHAPE

ANDROIDS
Terileptils use beautifully designed androids to carry out different tasks. On Earth, an android disguises itself as the Grim Reaper to scare the primitive locals it encounters.

In the middle of the 1600s, a group of Terileptil prisoners escape Raaga and become stranded on Earth. Unable to go home, they plan to rid Earth of human life and claim the planet for themselves. However, they die in a fire, which also destroys a large part of London in 1666.

TESELECTA
JUSTICE DEPARTMENT VEHICLE

The Teselecta is a highly advanced, humanoid shape-changing time-space machine from the future. The Teselecta's function is to track down criminals who escaped unpunished during their lives and administer its own justice in the form of torture.

The Teselecta can take the shape of any creature it has scanned. At one point, it even copies a Nazi official in its attempt to bring Adolf Hitler to justice.

INSIDE THE TESELECTA
The *Teselecta* is manned by a crew that has been reduced in size by a compression field.

CHEATING DEATH
In 2011, the Teselecta's Captain agrees to help the Doctor cheat death. Copying his form, the Teselecta is repeatedly shot by a mysterious astronaut, while the real Doctor remains safe inside it.

TESELECTA CAPTAIN CARTER

DATA FILE

HOMEWORLD:
UNKNOWN

SPECIAL ABILITIES:
SHAPE-SHIFTING, INTERNAL COMPRESSION FIELD

DOCTORS MET:
11TH

THALS
PEACEFUL RACE

The Thals come from the planet Skaro, also home of the much-feared Daleks. Thousands of years ago they were at war with the Kaleds—the race that eventually mutated into the Daleks. After a destructive war on their shared home planet, Thals change their ways and become peaceful.

Beautiful humanoids, Thals tend to have blonde hair and fair skin. They take anti-radiation drugs to survive the effects of the nuclear war between them and the Daleks.

ALYDON, LEADER OF THE THALS

FIGHTING DALEKS
In order to survive mass extermination, the Thal people have to learn to fight the Daleks again. It is against all their principles, but without a fight they will become extinct.

UNEVEN MATCH
A group of Thals goes to the planet Spiridon to help stop the Daleks. They discover that the Daleks have a hidden army of 10,000.

DATA FILE
HOMEWORLD:
SKARO

SPECIAL ABILITIES:
LOGIC, FARMING

DOCTORS MET:
1ST, 3RD, 4TH

TOBIAS VAUGHN
CYBERMAN COLLABORATOR

Cold, calm, and incredibly powerful, Tobias Vaughn is the charming managing director of International Electromatics, a large electronics company. His body is part converted by the Cybermen, whom he helps to invade Earth.

POWER TRIP
Vaughn is using the Cybermen as much as they are using him. He wants to rule Earth, but the Doctor persuades him to help defeat the Cybermen. He is killed while helping to stop the invasion.

An almost inhuman character, Vaughn hardly ever blinks. The normal range of human blinking is about once every ten or 15 seconds, but Vaughn blinks far less frequently.

INVASION
Vaughn is unaware that the Cybermen intend to destroy all human life after their invasion of Earth, and turns against them when he discovers this.

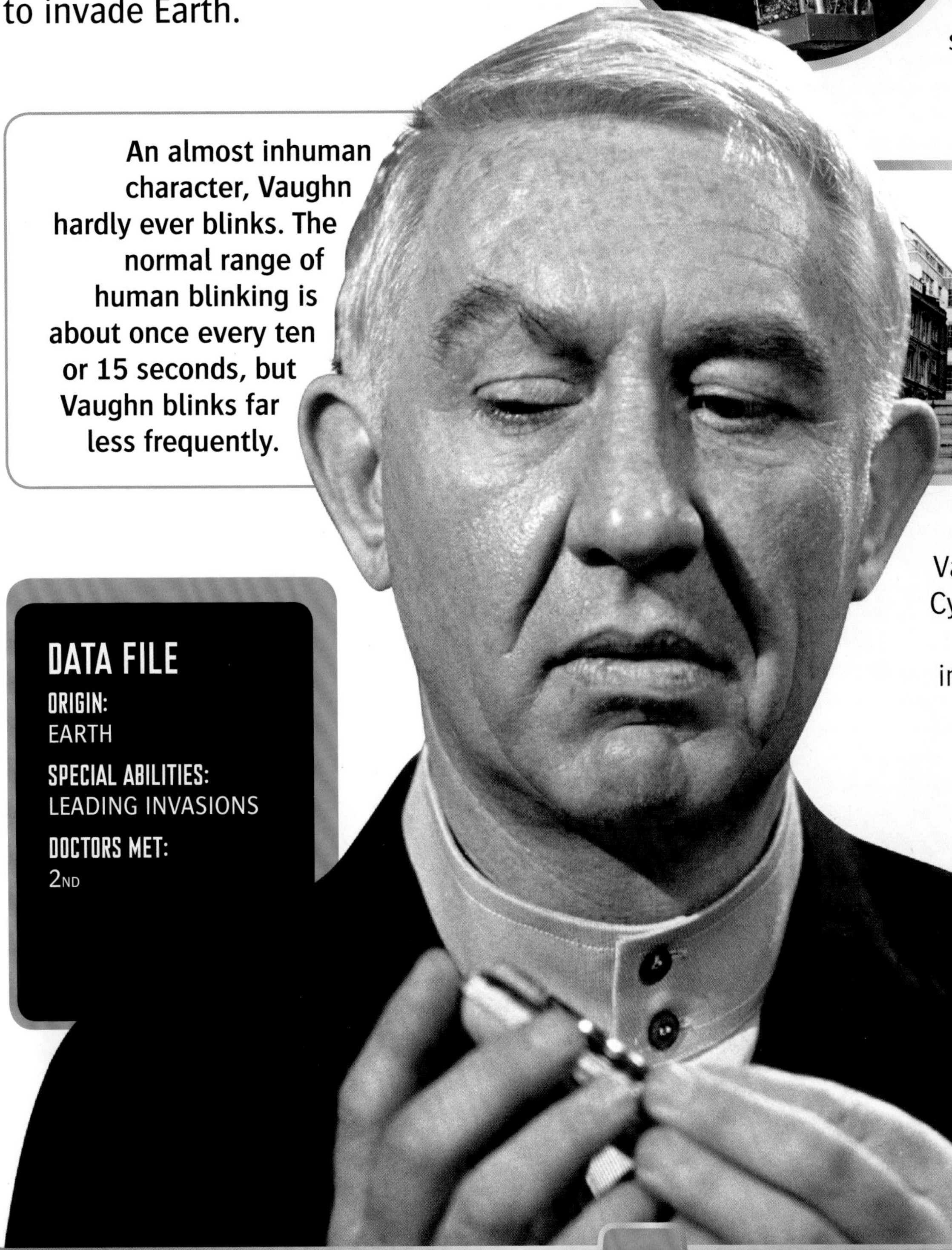

PART-CYBERMAN BODY

DATA FILE

ORIGIN:
EARTH

SPECIAL ABILITIES:
LEADING INVASIONS

DOCTORS MET:
2ND

TOCLAFANE
LAST EVOLUTION OF HUMANITY

At first sight, the Toclafane appear to be hovering robotic spheres, armed with deadly energy beams and razor-sharp knives. Inside each casing, however, is a shriveled, disembodied human head, for the Toclafane are what the human race will become in order to survive trillions of years in the future.

The Master names the Toclafane after a character from a Gallifreyan fairy tale. The creatures speak in childish sing-song voices, share a collective memory, and appear to have regressed to a primitive level, enjoying killing for its own sake.

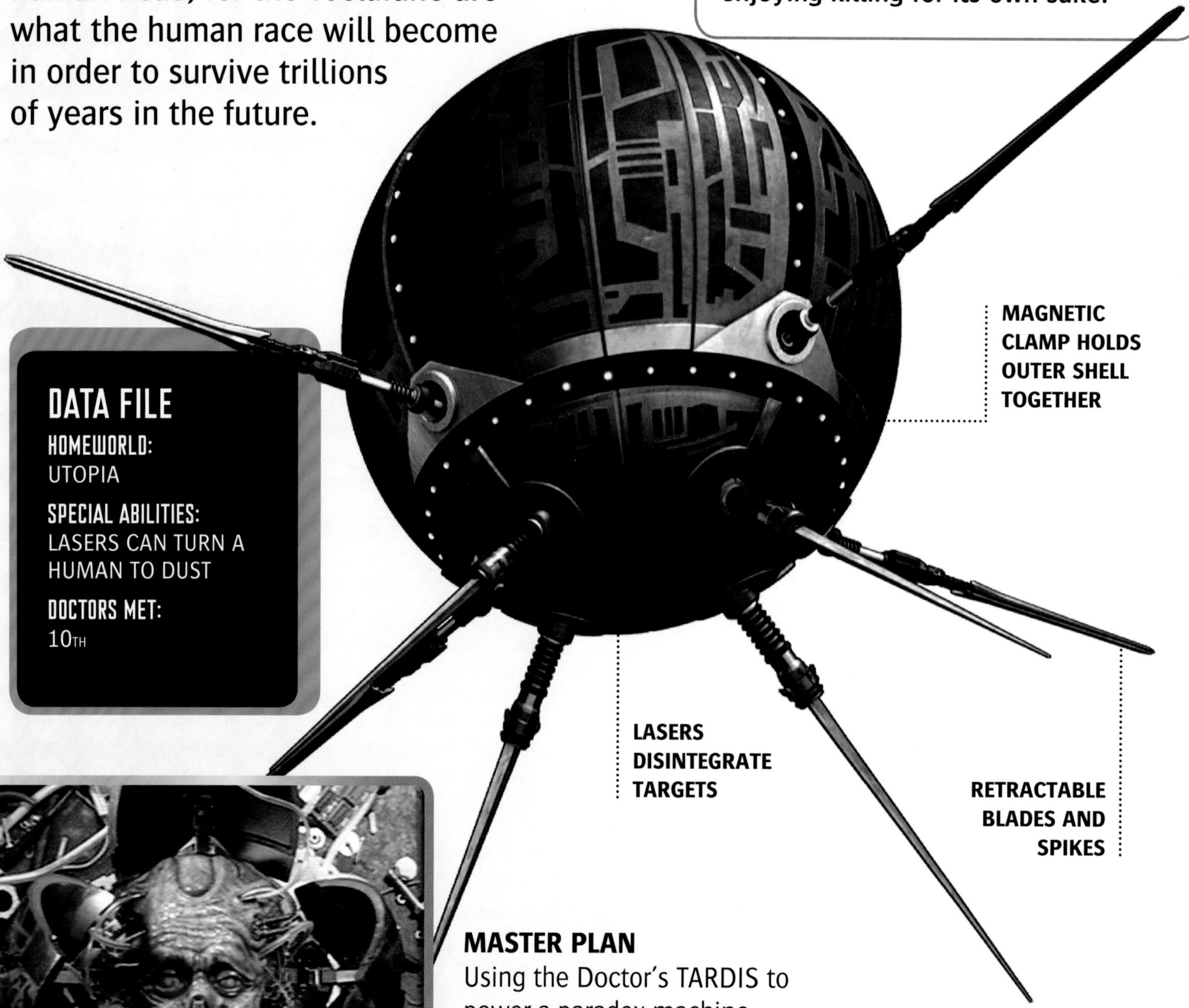

MAGNETIC CLAMP HOLDS OUTER SHELL TOGETHER

DATA FILE

HOMEWORLD:
UTOPIA

SPECIAL ABILITIES:
LASERS CAN TURN A HUMAN TO DUST

DOCTORS MET:
10TH

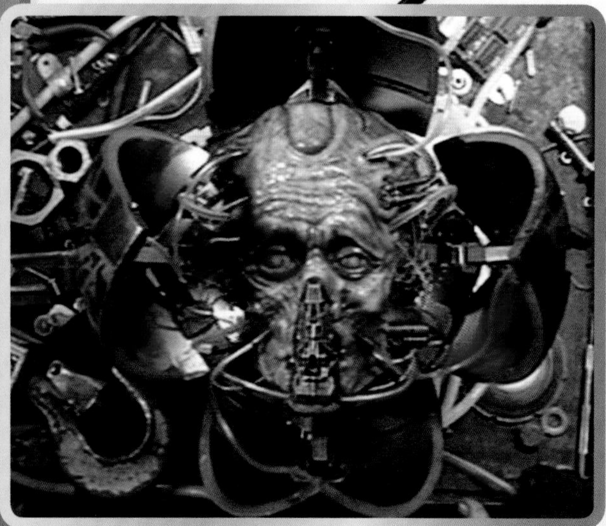

LASERS DISINTEGRATE TARGETS

RETRACTABLE BLADES AND SPIKES

MASTER PLAN
Using the Doctor's TARDIS to power a paradox machine, the Master is able to bring the Toclafane back through time. Billions of them descend to Earth and begin slaughtering their ancestors.

VALEYARD
TIME LORD PROSECUTOR

The word Valeyard means "learned court prosecutor." The Valeyard is an arrogant and angry figure with a dangerous mind, who believes that the Sixth Doctor has broken one of the Laws of Time—and become involved in the affairs of different people and planets.

CUNNING EXPRESSION

The Valeyard puts the Doctor on trial and presents evidence from his past, present, and future. To begin with, he appears to be working for the High Council of Time Lords. However, he is eventually exposed as being an amalgamation of the darker sides of the Doctor's nature.

TIME LORD ON TRIAL
The Valeyard brings his case against the Doctor before the Inquisitor, aboard a massive Time Lord space station. The TARDIS is taken out of time and space as the Doctor fights for his life.

TIME LORD-STYLE CLOTHES

MR. POPPLEWICK
The Valeyard uses a disguise to fool the Doctor inside the Time Lord Matrix. Mr. Popplewick comes across as a helpful, kindly man who works at J. J. Chamber's Fantasy Factory.

DATA FILE
HOMEWORLD:
GALLIFREY

SPECIAL ABILITIES:
MASTER OF DISGUISE, FAKING EVIDENCE

DOCTORS MET:
6TH

VASHTA NERADA
FLESH-EATING MICRO-ORGANISMS

Known as "the shadows that eat the flesh," the Vashta Nerada are swarms of tiny creatures that can live in any patch of darkness. They are found on most inhabited worlds and are normally content to live on road kill, but they can strip a person's flesh from his bones almost instantaneously.

SKELETON ANIMATED BY VASHTA NERADA

NEURAL RELAY COMMUNICATION DEVICE

The Vashta Nerada can hatch from the spores in trees, or even from microspores in paper. When they hunt, they latch on to a food source and keep it fresh, mimicking the shadow cast by their prey.

SPACESUIT

SKELETON ATTACK
The Vashta Nerada start reducing people to skeletal zombies one by one, but even when he's caught, the Doctor somehow manages to avoid being eaten alive!

SWARM IN A SPACESUIT
On a vast library world, the Doctor encounters an infestation of Vashta Nerada who devour the flesh of a man in a spacesuit. The swarm then makes his skeleton pursue yet more victims.

VERVOIDS
DEADLY PLANT LIFE FORMS

The Vervoids are intelligent and deadly. Created by three scientists who planned to sell them on to use as slave labor in farms and factories on Earth, a malfunction in their DNA turned the creatures into dangerous killers wanting to wipe out all of animal-kind.

CAN PRODUCE DEADLY GAS FROM MOUTH

HUMANOID PLANT BODY

CONTAINS STING

DATA FILE

HOMEWORLD:
CREATED ON MOGAR

SPECIAL ABILITIES:
KILLING

DOCTORS MET:
6TH

POD SHOCK
When their large green pods are hit with high intensity light, the Vervoids are unleashed aboard a passenger spaceship where they start to kill the crew and passengers.

Vervoids need only sunlight and water to survive. Although they have a short lifespan, just one leaf placed in soil is able to create another creature. They are completely destroyed by the Doctor before they reach Earth.

VESPIFORM
GIANT ALIEN WASPS

The Vespiform are no ordinary wasps! They are 8 foot tall monsters, armed with lethal stingers and the ability to shape-shift. Their hives are in the Silfrax galaxy, but the Doctor and Donna discover a half-human, half-Vespiform vicar murdering people in the style of a Whodunnit novel in 1920s England.

GIANT WINGS FOR FAST FLYING

Not all Vespiform are bad. One came to Earth and took the form of a man to learn about humankind. He was lost in the Delhi flood in 1885, but left behind him a son. Reverend Golightly has no idea he is part Vespiform until thieves try to steal the church silver and his rage breaks the genetic lock keeping him human.

DATA FILE

HOMEWORLD:
SILFRAX GALAXY

SPECIAL ABILITIES:
SHAPE-CHANGING, FLYING, STINGING

DOCTORS MET:
10TH

VESPIFORM IN NATURAL, RATHER THAN HUMAN, FORM

SUPER-SIZED STINGER

THE FIRESTONE
The Doctor, with the investigative help of Donna and Agatha Christie, discover that the Vespiform's essence is kept in a telepathic recorder called the Firestone—hidden inside a heart-shaped necklace. It beams the Reverend's true identity directly into his brain.

VICKI
ADVENTUROUS COMPANION

Vicki is a young teenager whom the Doctor meets on the planet Dido in the 25th century. She is desperately awaiting rescue after the ship she was traveling in crash-landed on the planet. With her mother already dead, she believes the planet's natives have killed her father and most of the ship's crew.

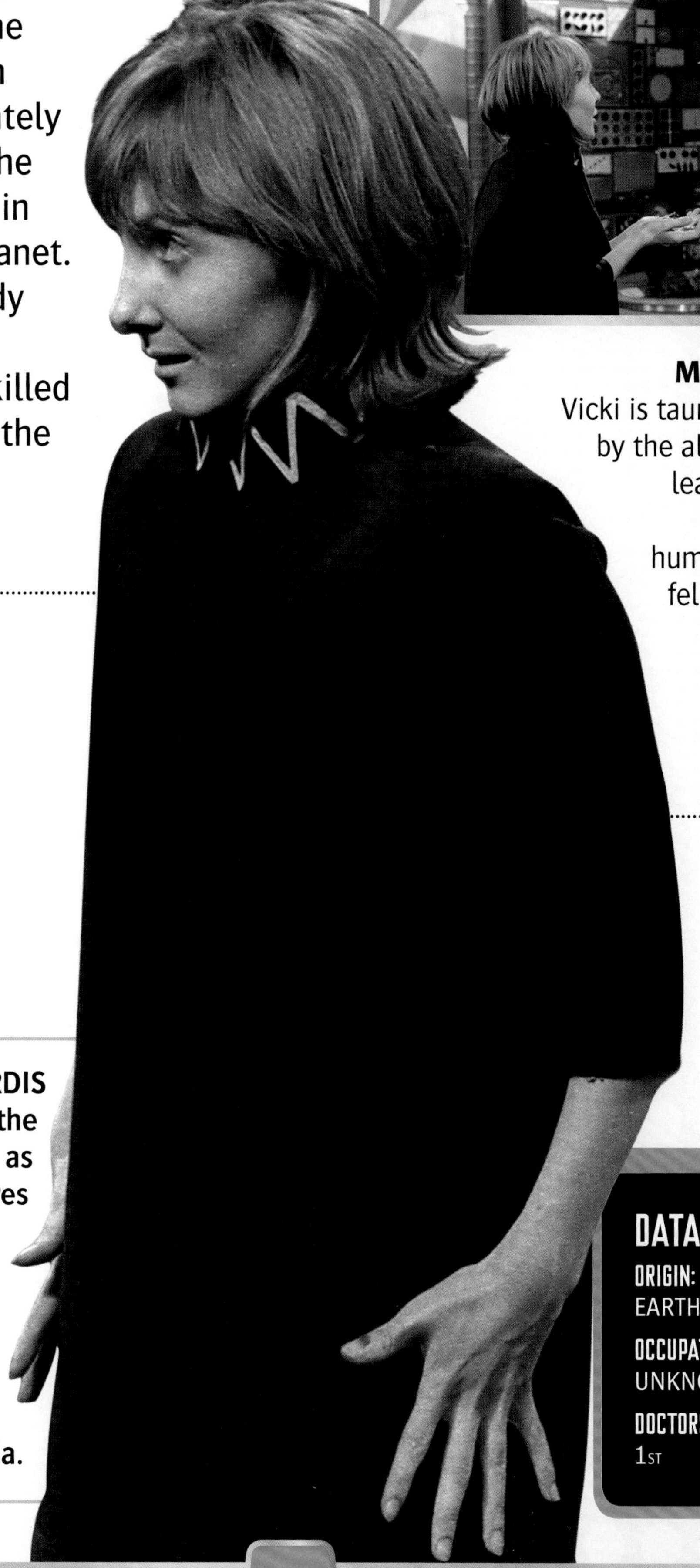

MONSTER MENACE
Vicki is taunted and terrorized by the alien Koquillion, but learns the creature is really Bennett, the human murderer of his fellow crewmembers. He has disguised himself to conceal his guilt.

GOOD ANALYTICAL AND TECHNICAL SKILLS

KEEN FOR ADVENTURE

After joining the TARDIS crew, Vicki encounters the Zarbi and the Drahvins, as well as historical figures such as Emperor Nero and King Richard the Lionheart. She ends up falling in love with Troilus in ancient Troy and adopts a new name: Cressida.

DATA FILE
ORIGIN:
EARTH

OCCUPATION:
UNKNOWN

DOCTORS MET:
1ST

VICTORIA WATERFIELD
BRAVE COMPANION

A modest young girl from the year 1866, Victoria is orphaned when her scientist father Edward Waterfield is killed by the invading Daleks. The Doctor takes her with him in the TARDIS and although Victoria isn't the most willing of adventurers, she overcomes her timidity to stand up to a succession of alien aggressors.

TRADITIONAL VICTORIAN FULL-LENGTH DRESS REPLACED BY MORE PRACTICAL CLOTHES

DALEKS' HOSTAGE
Victoria's father had been experimenting with time travel using mirrors and static electricity. He accidentally linked up with the Daleks and they took Victoria hostage on Skaro.

DATA FILE
ORIGIN:
ENGLAND, EARTH

OCCUPATION:
UNKNOWN

DOCTORS MET:
2ND

STAY CLOSE
The second Doctor's other companion, Jamie McCrimmon, often protects Victoria and rather likes her. Jamie tries in vain to persuade her to stay with him and the Doctor.

During Victoria's travels, she visits the Cyber tombs of Telos and has two terrifying encounters with the Yeti. After destroying a seaweed creature with her amplified screams, she finally tires of being scared and decides to stay on Earth.

VINVOCCI
SPIKY, GREEN HUMANOIDS

Resembling the smaller, red-colored Zocci, the Vinvocci are a technologically advanced species. In December 2009, two of their kind arrive on Earth and pose as human scientists Rossiter and Addams. Their goal is to retrieve the Immortality Gate—a Vinvocci medical device that can be used to heal the population of entire worlds.

As well as possessing teleportation technology, the Vinvocci have advanced devices called "Shimmers" which enable them to appear human, although they are very uncomfortable to use. The Shimmers are worn at the wrist, disguised as wristwatches.

DODGING MISSILES
Rossiter and Addams end up helping the Doctor and Wilfred Mott escape the Master. They fly them back to Earth in their salvaged spaceship, the *Hesperus*, somehow managing to dodge the Master's all-out missile attack.

DATA FILE

ORIGIN:
UNKNOWN

SPECIAL ABILITIES:
SHAPE-CHANGING TECHNOLOGY

DOCTORS MET:
10TH

SPIKY "CACTUS" CRANIUM RESEMBLES ZOCCI COUSINS

LAB COAT ALLOWS VINVOCCI TO POSE AS SCIENTISTS

VISLOR TURLOUGH
ALIEN COMPANION

An alien from Trion, Vislor Turlough is exiled from his home planet in the aftermath of a civil war. He ends up at an English private school on Earth where he is recruited by the Black Guardian to destroy the Doctor. Regarded by some as shifty and untrustworthy, he succeeds in gaining the Doctor's trust.

Turlough finds it harder than he thought he would to kill the Doctor, realizing that the Doctor is a good man. He struggles to live under the shadow of the Black Guardian's promise that he will never be free until his mission is completed.

UNREADABLE EXPRESSION

PRIVATE SCHOOL UNIFORM

TAUNTING TURLOUGH
The Black Guardian is furious with Turlough's continued inability to kill the Doctor. In order to rid himself of his tormentor, Turlough throws an immensely powerful diamond at him and the Black Guardian is instantly consumed by flames.

RETURNING TO TRION
Free from the Black Guardian, Turlough is able to travel with the Doctor without fear. Eventually, though, he learns that there's been a change of regime on Trion, and takes the opportunity to return home as a free man.

DATA FILE
HOMEWORLD:
TRION

OCCUPATION:
PUPIL AT A PRIVATE SCHOOL

DOCTORS MET:
1ST, 2ND, 3RD, 5TH

VOC ROBOTS
ROBOTIC SERVANTS

The Voc Robots are beautiful, elegant creations found onboard the Sandminer. They are programed to carry out the crew's every command from providing refreshments to locating things for them. Usually reliable and unquestioning, the crew are appalled to discover the robots start to disobey and, worse, start to murder crew-members.

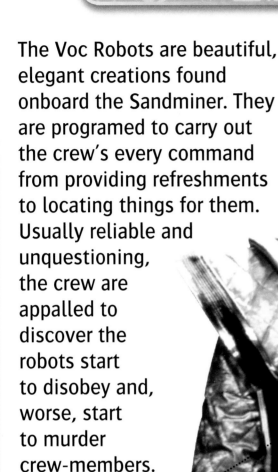

IDENTIFYING NUMBER

TAREN CAPEL
Taren Capel reprograms the robots onboard the Sandminer to kill. He has lived with robots from childhood, and now he wants to free his brothers and let them rule the world.

HUMANOID SHAPE

Incredibly strong, robots like this are programed to obey and never kill. Their design is deliberately humanoid and they have a pleasant, calming, and attractive voice.

DATA FILE
ORIGIN:
KALDOR CITY

SPECIAL ABILITIES:
STRENGTH

DOCTORS MET:
4TH

THE WAR DOCTOR
DOCTOR NO MORE

The Doctor has had many faces, but there is one he chose to forget. During the Time War, he assumes the characteristics of a warrior, and must face the toughest choice he has ever had to make: whether or not to commit genocide of his own people in order to end the Time War.

For hundreds of years, the Doctor assumed he was responsible for wiping out the Time Lords along with the Daleks, thus ending the Time War. It is this incarnation that became known as the "Oncoming Storm," and has tinged later incarnations with darkness and sorrow.

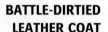

BATTLE-DIRTIED LEATHER COAT

BIG RED BUTTON
To end the Time War, the War Doctor steals The Moment—a galaxy-obliterating weapon locked in Gallifrey's vaults. However, The Moment has a conscience, which takes the form of the Bad Wolf version of Rose Tyler and tries to dissuade him from committing an act he will later regret.

REWRITING TIME
On a mission to find a way to save, rather than destroy, Gallifrey, the War Doctor is joined by the Tenth and the Eleventh Doctors. The trio enjoy mocking one another, but their presence together causes a paradox in time. Despite their success, none of the incarnations of the Doctor will be able to remember what happened.

DATA FILE

INTERESTS:
ENDING THE TIME WAR

REASON FOR REGENERATING:
WORN OUT BY THE EVENTS OF THE TIME WAR

WAR MACHINE
WOTAN'S ARMY

The War Machines are the giant army of tank-like robots created by a super-computer called WOTAN in London's Post Office Tower in 1966. Big, destructive, and powerful, they are used by WOTAN in an attempt to take over the world.

RADAR DISH

GUN

ARMS CAN SWING OUT AND ATTACK

WOTAN

WOTAN stands for Will Operating Thought ANalogue. The computer hypnotizes its creator, Professor Brett, along with several others, in an attempt to conquer Earth, but is eventually destroyed by one of its own War Machines.

DATA FILE

ORIGIN:
EARTH

SPECIAL ABILITIES:
HYPNOSIS

DOCTORS MET:
1ST

Built in a warehouse in London by humans hypnotized by **WOTAN**, each War Machine has a different number on it, deadly weapons attached to its frame, and appears unstoppable.

WEEPING ANGELS
THE LONELY ASSASSINS

One of the deadliest predators in the galaxy, Weeping Angels are an ancient race of stone statues. They are protected by the ultimate defense mechanism—a quantum lock—and can only move when they aren't being observed.

SHARP CLAWS

FEARSOME FANGS

WINGS CAN BREAK WRISTS OR SNAP NECKS

ONE TOUCH CAN SEND A VICTIM BACK IN TIME

CHERUB ANGELS
The Angels have fought the Doctor three times. They have sent him back to 1969 without his TARDIS and formed an army within an Aplan temple. In their third encounter, the Angels took over New York, aided by mean-spirited Cherub Angels.

Weeping Angels feed off temporal energy, zapping their victims back into the past and consuming the energy from the years they would have lived. Without food, they starve and crumble.

DATA FILE
HOMEWORLD:
UNKNOWN

SPECIAL ABILITIES:
QUANTUM LOCKED, LIGHTNING SPEED, EXTREME STRENGTH

DOCTORS:
10TH, 11TH

WENG-CHIANG
TIME TRAVELER'S DISGUISE

Weng-Chiang is the name assumed by a dangerous criminal from the 51st century: Magnus Greel. Greel impersonates the Chinese god Weng-Chiang when he becomes stranded in the 19th century and his body is terribly disfigured by being transported back in time.

DATA FILE

ORIGIN:
EARTH

SPECIAL ABILITIES:
TIME TRAVEL

DOCTORS MET:
4TH

MASK DISGUISING FACE OF MAGNUS GREEL

MR. SIN
Greel travels back in time with a Peking Homunculus cyborg known as Mr. Sin. Mr. Sin looks like a ventriloquist's dummy but underneath he is a lethal, murderous creature, with the brain of a pig.

The extent of the damage to Greel's body is life-threatening, so he drains the energy of young women in Victorian London to keep himself alive. His arrival also has other dangerous side effects—Zygma energy from Greel's machine enlarges creatures. As a result, giant rats are soon roaming the sewers under London.

WEREWOLF
LUPINE-WAVELENGTH HAEMOVARIFORM

In reality, the Werewolf is a ferocious, shape-changing alien that crashed to Earth and landed in Scotland in 1540. The creature survives by infecting a succession of human hosts, and hundreds of years later it attempts to bite and possess Queen Victoria, aiming to establish its own empire on Earth.

ATTACKING THE QUEEN

Upon the arrival of Queen Victoria and the Doctor at Torchwood House, the alien shape-changer switches from human to its true lupine form and goes on a murderous rampage. Luckily, the Doctor manages to destroy the beast with a beam of focused moonlight.

GLAZED EYES REVEAL ALIEN LIFE FORM

SHARP CLAWS

SNARLING, FANGED MOUTH

For all its power, the Werewolf has a weakness— a strange fear of mistletoe. When the Doctor and his friends hide in the library of Torchwood House, the creature refuses to attack, sensing the presence of mistletoe oil in the room's wooden paneling.

POWERFUL LIMBS

DATA FILE

ORIGIN:
UNKNOWN

SPECIAL ABILITIES:
SHAPE-CHANGING, MIGRATION TO NEW HOSTS

DOCTORS MET:
10TH

WHISPER MEN
FACELESS SERVANTS

Speaking almost exclusively in sinister rhyming couplets, the Whisper Men do the bidding of the Great ntelligence. Able to seemingly evaporate into thin air, and unaffected by human weapons, these creatures are as menacing as they are expressionless.

FACE CAN BE MORPHED INTO THAT OF DOCTOR SIMEON

FIERCE TEETH

DOCTOR HUNTING
Instructed to bring the Doctor and his friends to Trenzalore, the Whisper Men kidnap Madame Vastra, Jenny, and Strax, and leave a lyrical message of doom and imminent death for the Doctor.

ARMS CAN REACH THROUGH HUMAN BODIES

Like animals, the Whisper Men often travel in packs, and have an unnerving habit of approaching slowly and silently. Their speech emerges as a threatening hiss and it is rumored that they can kill with a whisper.

TRAPPED IN TIME
The Great Intelligence hopes to destroy the Doctor by stepping into his time line and rewriting his history, but is itself destroyed instead. As the time energy pulses and swirls, the Whisper Men can be seen disintergrating alongside their master.

WILFRED MOTT
GRANDFATHER OF DONNA NOBLE

A wise and gentle old man, Wilf was greatly upset when the Doctor was forced to erase his granddaughter Donna's memories and end her travels. He searched hard to find the Doctor once more, hoping that her condition could be reversed, and ended up joining the Tenth Doctor on his last perilous adventure.

PARACHUTE REGIMENT BADGE FROM DAYS IN NATIONAL SERVICE

DATA FILE

ORIGIN:
LONDON, ENGLAND

OCCUPATION:
RETIRED SOLDIER, NEWSPAPER SELLER

DOCTORS MET:
10TH

AMATEUR ASTRONOMER WITH INTEREST IN ALIEN THEORIES

PRACTICAL OVERCOAT

WARM CLOTHES FOR COLD WINTER WEATHER AND LATE NIGHT STARGAZING

A soldier in his younger days, Wilf's heroic qualities never left him. He bravely helped to defend the Vinvocci ship Hesperus against the Master's missile attack, fearlessly manning the ship's laser cannons until the last missile had been destroyed.

THE DOCTOR'S SACRIFICE
When Wilf becomes trapped in a control booth, the only way for the Doctor to free him was to swap places with him, resulting in him absorbing a massive dose of radiation—enough to force him to regenerate.

WINIFRED GILLYFLOWER
FOUNDER OF SWEETVILLE

Power-hungry Mrs. Winifred Gillyflower establishes the supposedly idyllic town Sweetville, which people enter but never leave. Her sickly sweet public persona masks cruel intentions to wipe out humanity and replace it with a race of genetically "perfect" people. Ultimately her ambition is her downfall.

RUFFLES AND RIBBONS CONCEAL MR. SWEET

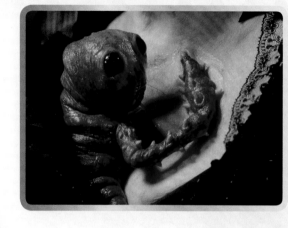

DATA FILE

HOMEWORLD:
EARTH

SPECIAL ABILITIES:
SKILLED IN CHEMISTRY AND ENGINEERING

DOCTORS MET:
11TH

WIDOW'S BLACK MOURNING CLOTHES

Behind her factory walls, with vital assistance from Mr. Sweet, Mrs. Gillyflower develops a deadly leech venom. Her plan is to shower the poison over Earth from a rocket, also built by herself.

MR. SWEET
Mrs. Gillyflower's "silent partner" Mr. Sweet is actually a red leech from the Cretaceous era attached to her chest—and recognized as a past pest to Silurians. Mrs. Gillyflower depends upon his "nectar" and his posions are used in her experiments.

ADA GILLYFLOWER
One of Mrs. Gillyflower's first experiments was on her daugher. Ada was rendered blind by her mother's dabbling with toxins, but led to believe that her father was to blame, and subjected to many further torments. Her mother's death liberates her.

WIRRN
GIANT INSECTOIDS

The Wirrn are large, intelligent, telepathic insect creatures. They live in space, but when they are hungry they will track down a food source on a planet and also find somewhere to breed. They are able to absorb knowledge from creatures and can live for years without fresh oxygen.

DATA FILE
HOMEWORLD:
THE ANDROMEDA GALAXY

SPECIAL ABILITIES:
TELEPATHY

DOCTORS MET:
4TH

INSECT BODY

LAYING EGGS
Like a type of wasp that paralyzes caterpillars and lays eggs, the Wirrn lay their eggs inside creatures and then have a ready-made food supply when the eggs hatch.

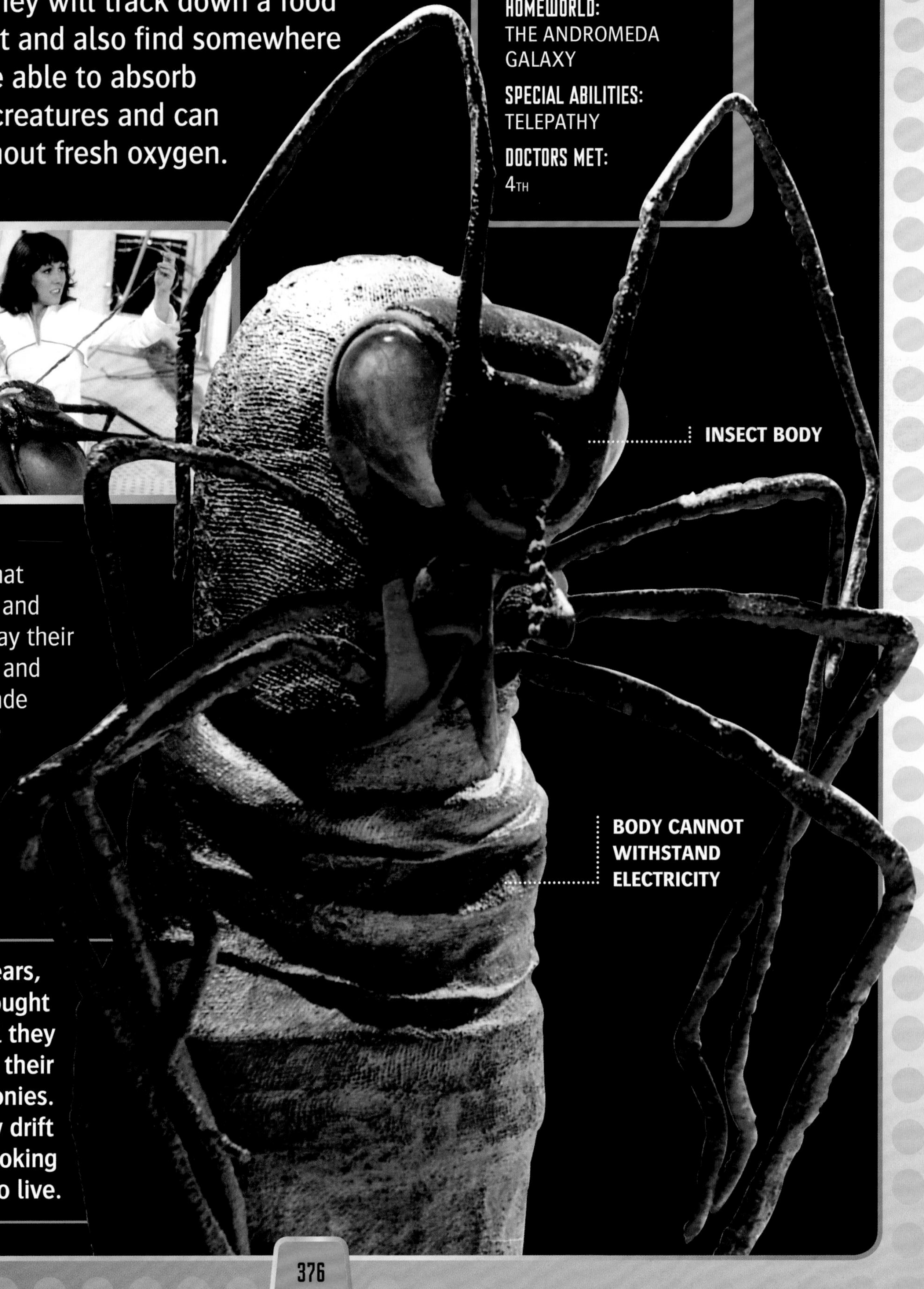

BODY CANNOT WITHSTAND ELECTRICITY

For a thousand years, the Wirrn fought humans until they destroyed their breeding colonies. The Wirrn now drift through space looking for new places to live.

WOODLAND KING AND QUEEN
ANDROZANI TREE ROYALTY

The King and Queen of the Androzani trees are wooden aliens who live on Tree Farm 457 in the year 5345. Their bark is an excellent source of fuel. When harvesters threaten to melt the forest with acid rain for battery fluid, the King and Queen resolve to evacuate their people.

NEURAL RELAY

SKIN OF BARK

PURE LIFE FORCE OF THE FOREST

DATA FILE

HOMEWORLD:
TREE FARM 457

SPECIAL ABILITIES:
FAST GROWING, CAN TRANSMUTE INTO A SUB-ETHERIC WAVEBAND OF LIGHT

DOCTORS MET:
11TH

Although they look scary, the King and Queen are harmless. They believe the Doctor's arrival was foretold and have faith that he will save the forest from the acid rain.

HATCHED!
The Wooden King hatches from a silver tree bauble and grows to full size in less than an hour. But his body is just a vessel for the pure life force inside.

THE MOTHERSHIP
The Queen's crown is a relay. By placing it on Madge Arwell, the souls of all the trees zoom into her head and she flies them through the Vortex to safety.

YETI
MASSIVE ROBOTS

The Yeti are massive furry robots that are first mistaken for the Abominable Snowmen in the Himalayas. They are controlled by the Great Intelligence with silver spheres placed inside their chests. Without the sphere, the Yeti robot is powerless.

CAN PRODUCE HORRIFIC ROAR

DATA FILE

HOMEWORLD:
CREATED ON EARTH

SPECIAL ABILITIES:
STRENGTH

DOCTORS MET:
2ND

CONTAINS A SPHERE THAT POWERS ROBOT

CLAWS

WEB OF FEAR
In one invasion attempt, the Yeti storm into London through the Underground transport system and use a dangerous web to engulf and cripple things.

BULKY BODY

The Great Intelligence —a powerful being from another dimension that can survive without physical form—uses the Yeti in its attempts to take over Earth.

ZARBI
LARGE INSECTOIDS

The Zarbi are large ant-like creatures from the planet Vortis. Normally docile, the Zarbi become menacing when they are taken over by a parasite called the Animus. They are able to control people with a special metal device and also use Vortis Venom Grubs as weapons. Irrationally, they are frightened of spiders.

DATA FILE

HOMEWORLD:
VORTIS

SPECIAL ABILITIES:
STRENGTH, ABLE TO CONTROL OTHERS

DOCTORS: MET
1ST

The Zarbi creatures are not an intelligent life form, but were essential to the life pattern on Vortis. The Animus made them too strong for the other inhabitants on the planet.

MENOPTERA
The Animus parasite causes a war between the Zarbi and the Menoptera, a race of butterfly aliens from Vortis. When the Animus is destroyed, the two races co-exist in peace again.

TALL INSECT BODY

STRONG LEGS

ZOE HERIOT
SUPER SCIENTIST COMPANION

Zoe is a brilliant astrophysicist who meets the Second Doctor during the Cyberman invasion of the gigantic space-station, the Wheel. After helping him defeat the cyborgs, she decides to stow away in the TARDIS. She soon realizes that there's more to life than logic and mathematics and learns much from her experiences with the Doctor.

LOGICAL MIND

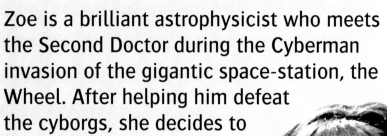

CYBER PLOT
When Zoe intercepts the invading Cybermen's signals, she learns that the silver cyborgs are planning to trap and kill the Doctor. With her new friend, Jamie, she is determined to find a way to warn him of the danger.

SAYING GOODBYE
Zoe travels with the Doctor alongside Jamie McCrimmon. And just like Jamie, when the pair leave the TARDIS, Zoe has her memory wiped of all her travels—excluding her very first encounter with the Time Lord.

DATA FILE
ORIGIN:
EARTH

OCCUPATION:
LIBRARIAN,
ASTROPHYSICIST

DOCTORS MET:
2ND

Among her many adventures, Zoe battles the Cybermen, and encounters the Krotons and Ice Warriors, before she is forced to leave the Doctor by the Time Lords. She returns to the Wheel, while the Doctor is exiled to Earth.

ZYGONS
SHAPE-SHIFTING ALIENS

The powerful Zygons come from a planet that was destroyed centuries ago. A small group of the creatures escape and their ship crashes into Loch Ness, Scotland, where it remains undetected for hundreds of years. Their leader, Broton, wants to make Earth the new Zygon homeworld.

The Zygons possess a massive cyborg creature called the Skarasen, which is often mistaken for the Loch Ness Monster. The Zygons use this "pet" to destroy oil rigs off the coast of Scotland.

BODY DOUBLES
Zygon technology allows them to take on the appearance of other beings. By keeping the original alive, this horrifying alien shape can change into any creature it captures.

VENOM SACS IN TONGUE

SUCKERED BODY

DEADLY TOUCH CAN STUN OR KILL

ROYAL TAKEOVER ATTEMPT
In 1562, the Zygons attempt an elaborate plot. Using historical portraits, they position themselves to attack in a future time, when the planet is more interesting and worth invading. By assuming the appearance of Queen Elizabeth I, they even fool the Tenth Doctor!

SLIMY ORANGE SKIN

DATA FILE

HOMEWORLD:
ZYGOR

SPECIAL ABILITIES:
SHAPE-CHANGING, BODY COPYING

DOCTORS MET:
4TH, WAR DOCTOR, 10TH, 11TH

INDEX

Numbers in **bold** indicate main entries

Penguin
Random
House

SENIOR EDITORS Victoria Taylor, Garima Sharma
EDITORS Emma Grange, Kath Hill, Rahul Ganguly
SENIOR DESIGNERS Clive Savage, Neha Ahuja
DESIGNERS Rhys Thomas, Anne Sharples, Mark Richards, Era Chawla,
Suzena Sengupta, David McDonald
ADDITIONAL EDITORIAL AND DESIGN Matt Jones, Arushi Vats,
Dimple Vohra, Pallavi Kapur
PRE-PRODUCTION PRODUCER Marc Staples, Siu Chan
SENIOR PRODUCERS Shabana Shakir and Kathleen McNally
MANAGING EDITOR Simon Hugo
DESIGN MANAGER Guy Harvey
CREATIVE MANAGER Sarah Harland
ART DIRECTOR Lisa Lanzarini
PUBLISHER Julie Ferris
PUBLISHING DIRECTOR Simon Beecroft

First published in the United States in 2015
by Dorling Kindersley Limited,
345 Hudson Street, New York, New York 10014

Contains content previously published in *Doctor Who: Character Encyclopedia
Updated Edition* (2015) and *Doctor Who: The Visual Dictionary
Updated and Expanded* (2014)

001-289207-Aug/15

Artworks: The TARDIS (pages 6–7) by Lee Binding; Sonic Screwdrivers
(pages 22–23) by Peter McKinstry; Leadworth Map (pages 38–39) by James
Southall; Dalek Flagship by John Maloney (pages 54–55); The Satan Pit by Richard
Bonson (page 105); Pandorica Panel (page 146) by Peter McKinstry.

ACKNOWLEDGMENTS

DK would like to thank Annabel Gibson, and Moray Laing; Jason Loborik for his
writing; Sam Bartlett, Pamela Shiels, Rhys Thomas, and Lynne Moulding for design
assistance; Julia March, Shari Last, Tori Kosara, Cécile Landau, Jo Casey, Pamela
Afram, and Alan Cowsill for editorial help; Lisa Eyre for the index, and Neha Ahuja,
Chitra Subramanyam, Umesh Singh Rawat, and Anant Sagar from the Delhi team.

www.bbc.co.uk/doctorwho
www.dk.com

A WORLD OF IDEAS:
SEE ALL THERE IS TO KNOW